TRAUMA AND THE
VIETNAM WAR
GENERATION

BRUNNER/MAZEL PSYCHOSOCIAL STRESS SERIES
Charles R. Figley, Ph.D., Series Editor

1. *Stress Disorders Among Vietnam Veterans*, Edited by Charles R. Figley, Ph.D.
2. *Stress and the Family Vol. 1: Coping with Normative Transitions*, Edited by Hamilton I. McCubbin, Ph.D., and Charles R. Figley, Ph.D.
3. *Stress and the Family Vol. 2: Coping with Catastrophe*, Edited by Charles R. Figley, Ph.D., and Hamilton I. McCubbin, Ph.D.
4. *Trauma and Its Wake: The Study and Treatment of Post-Traumatic Stress Disorder*, Edited by Charles R. Figley, Ph.D.
5. *Post-Traumatic Stress Disorder and the War Veteran Patient*, Edited by William E. Kelly, M.D.
6. *The Crime Victim's Book, Second Edition*, By Morton Bard, Ph.D., and Dawn Sangrey
7. *Stress and Coping in Time of War: Generalizations from the Israeli Experience*, Edited by Norman A. Milgram, Ph.D.
8. *Trauma and Its Wake Vol. 2: Traumatic Stress Theory, Research, and Intervention*, Edited by Charles R. Figley, Ph.D.
9. *Stress and Addiction*, Edited by Edward Gottheil, M.D., Ph.D., Keith A. Druley, Ph.D., Steven Pashko, Ph.D., and Stephen P. Weinstein, Ph.D.
10. *Vietnam: A Casebook*, By Jacob D. Lindy, M.D., in collaboration with Bonnie L. Green, Ph.D., Mary C. Grace, M.Ed., M.S., John A. MacLeod, M.D., and Louis Spitz, M.D.
11. *Post-Traumatic Therapy and Victims of Violence*, Edited by Frank M. Ochberg, M.D.
12. *Mental Health Response to Mass Emergencies: Theory and Practice*, Edited by Mary Lystad, Ph.D.
13. *Treating Stress in Families*, Edited by Charles R. Figley, Ph.D.
14. *Trauma, Transformation, and Healing: An Integrative Approach to Theory, Research, and Post-Traumatic Therapy*, By John P. Wilson, Ph.D.
15. *Systemic Treatment of Incest: A Therapeutic Handbook*, By Terry Trepper, Ph.D., and Mary Jo Barrett, M.S.W.
16. *The Crisis of Competence: Transitional Stress and the Displaced Worker*, Edited by Carl A. Maida, Ph.D., Norma S. Gordon, M.A., and Norman L. Farberow, Ph.D.
17. *Stress Management: An Integrated Approach to Therapy*, By Dorothy H.G. Cotton, Ph.D.
18. *Trauma and the Vietnam War Generation: Report of Findings from the National Vietnam Veterans Readjustment Study*, By Richard A. Kulka, Ph.D., William E. Schlenger, Ph.D., John A. Fairbank, Ph.D., Richard L. Hough, Ph.D., B. Kathleen Jordan, Ph.D., Charles R. Marmar, M.D., and Daniel S. Weiss, Ph.D., and David A. Grady, Psy.D.
19. *Strangers at Home: Vietnam Veterans Since the War*, Edited by Charles R. Figley, Ph.D., and Seymour Leventman, Ph.D.
20. *The National Vietnam Veterans Readjustment Study: Tables of Findings and Technical Appendices*, By Richard A. Kulka, Ph.D., William E. Schlenger, Ph.D., John A. Fairbank, Ph.D., Richard L. Hough, Ph.D., B. Kathleen Jordan, Ph.D., Charles R. Marmar, M.D., and Daniel S. Weiss, Ph.D.

BRUNNER/MAZEL PSYCHOSOCIAL STRESS SERIES No. 18

TRAUMA AND THE VIETNAM WAR GENERATION

REPORT OF FINDINGS FROM THE NATIONAL VIETNAM VETERANS READJUSTMENT STUDY

Richard A. Kulka, Ph.D. /William E. Schlenger, Ph.D.
John A. Fairbank, Ph.D. /Richard L. Hough, Ph.D.
B. Kathleen Jordan, Ph.D. /Charles R. Marmar, M.D.
Daniel S. Weiss, Ph.D.

With a Chapter by
David A. Grady, Psy.D.

FOREWORD BY SENATOR ALAN CRANSTON

Routledge
Taylor & Francis Group
New York   London

This report is dedicated to the Vietnam veterans who participated in the study. These veterans both represent and symbolize all of the men and women who served during the Vietnam era. Their willingness to invest the time and emotional energy required to tell their stories in the interest of increased understanding of the consequences of war demonstrates their courage, maturity, and concern for their brothers and sisters. We are deeply grateful for their participation.

First published 1990 by BRUNNER/MAZEL, INC.

This edition published 2013 by Routledge

Routledge
Taylor & Francis Group
711 Third Avenue
New York, NY 10017

Routledge
Taylor & Francis Group
2 Park Square, Milton Park
Abingdon, Oxfordshire OX14 4RN

First issued in paperback 2014

Routledge is an imprint of the Taylor and Francis Group, an informa business

Library of Congress Cataloging-in-Publication Data

Trauma and the Vietnam War generation : report of findings from
the National Vietnam Veterans Readjustment Study / Richard A. Kulka
. . . [et al.] ; foreword by Alan Cranston.
    p.   cm. — (Brunner/Mazel psychosocial stress series ; no. 18)
    Includes bibliographical references.
    ISBN 0-87630-573-7
    1. Post-traumatic stress disorder.   2. Veterans—Mental health—
United States.   3. Vietnamese Conflict, 1961–1975—Psychological
aspects.   I. Kulka, Richard A.   II. Series.
    [DNLM: n-us / a-vt]
    RC552.P67T747   1990   89-71185
    616.85'21—dc20   CIP

This Report of the findings from the National Vietnam Veterans Readjustment Study was prepared for the Veterans Administration under Contract Number V101(93)P-1040 by a private research team with public funds and thus is part of the public domain. The version presented in this volume has been altered for readability and material has been added. Some of the material in this version is copyright protected. Royalties from this book will be donated to the Vietnam Veterans Aid Foundation.

Published by Brunner/Mazel, Inc., 19 Union Square West, New York, New York 10003. Distributed to the trade by Publishers Group West, 4065 Hollis St., Emeryville, CA 94608. (800) 982-8319; in CA call collect 415-658-3453.

ISBN 13: 978-0-87630-573-7 (hbk)
ISBN 13: 978-1-138-00470-2 (pbk)

Foreword

Twenty years after "peace with honor" was declared in Vietnam, a significant number of veterans continue to wage their own battle with post-traumatic stress disorder (PTSD). While postwar psychological problems have long been known to occur among war veterans—under such labels as "shell shock," "war neurosis," and "combat fatigue"—the impact of the Vietnam War on its generation of warriors has been and continues to be extraordinary.

As this book, and the study on which it is based, reveals, 829,000 of the 3.14 million—over one-fourth—of the veterans who served in Vietnam are *currently* suffering from some degree of PTSD.

In 1980, the American Psychiatric Association officially adopted the term PTSD to denote a psychological disorder that stems from exposure to an extraordinary traumatic event. PTSD is known among clinicians as a spectrum disorder, and the effect on a person's life can vary greatly—from dampening an individual's ability to participate in life to the fullest degree to total incapacitation when suicide appears to be the only hope of escape.

The National Vietnam Veterans Readjustment Study (NVVRS) of the postwar psychological problems of Vietnam veterans, which was mandated by legislation I authored as section 102 of Public Law 98-160, indicates an alarming prevalence of PTSD among Vietnam theater veterans. According to the NVVRS data, 15.2 percent of the male Vietnam theater veterans (479,000) and 8.5 percent of the female theater veterans (610) are currently suffering from full-blown cases of PTSD. Another 11.1 percent of male and 7.8 percent of female theater veterans, or a total of 350,000 theater veterans, suffer from PTSD symptoms that adversely affect their lives but are not of the intensity or breadth required for a diagnosis of PTSD. These data indicate that, over 20 years later, psychological problems associated with service in our nation's most divisive war since the Civil War continue to take a terrible toll on the lives of those who served in Vietnam.

The reasons for the dramatic psychological impact of fighting the Vietnam War on those who fought it remain a matter of controversy, as, indeed, does the war itself. Certainly the unrest at home played a part. Whereas veterans from other wars returned to heroes' welcomes and were allowed, if not encouraged, to discuss their war experiences, Vietnam veterans received no such welcome and little encouragement or understanding. Another factor may have been the lack of time to decompress after the war experience. Within a 24-hour period, a soldier could be transported from the jungle to the streets of San Francisco. Another factor may have been the relatively short-term, one-year experience in-country, which inhibited both the willingness of the soldiers to form cohesive bonds within their units and the natural development of those bonds.

What can no longer be in controversy is our need to respond to these problems. I have been deeply committed to finding ways to raise the public's awareness of these problems so that solutions can be found and treatment opportunities increased. This book will be another vital part of the ongoing effort to educate the public about PTSD.

SENATOR ALAN CRANSTON
Chairman
United States Senate
Committee on Veterans' Affairs

Contents

Key Acronyms and Abbreviations

ASP	Antisocial personality disorder
BLK	Blacks
CDC	Centers for Disease Control
CIV	Civilian counterparts
DIS	Diagnostic Interview Schedule
DMDC	Defense Manpower Data Center
DSM-III	*Diagnostic and Statistical Manual of Mental Disorders,* third edition
ECA	Epidemiologic Catchment Area Project
ERA	Veteran of Vietnam era who did not serve in Vietnam (except in Chapter II)
ERA	Veteran who served during the Vietnam Era (in Chapter II)
ESG	Environmental Support Group (Department of Defense)
FI	Family interview
GAD	Generalized anxiety disorder
HISP	Hispanics
HWZ	High war-zone-stress exposure
LAM	Living as though married
LWZ	Low/moderate war-zone-stress exposure
MOS	Military Occupational Specialty
M-PTSD	Mississippi Scale for Combat-Related Post-Traumatic Stress Disorder
NIOSH	National Institute of Occupational Safety and Health
NPRC	National Personnel Records Center
NS	Not (statistically) signficant
NSVG	National Survey of the Vietnam Generation
NT	Not tested for statistical significance

NVVRS   National Vietnam Veterans Readjustment Study
P   (Statistical) probability
PERI   Psychiatric Epidemiology Research Interview
POW   Prisoner of war
PTSD   Post-traumatic stress disorder
PWPP   Postwar psychological problems
RTI   Research Triangle Institute
SCPD   Service-connected physical disability
SEI   Socioeconomic Index
SMSA   Standard Metropolitan Statistical Area
S/P   Spouse or partner with whom veteran is living as though married
SUBABUSE   (Those with) substance abuse
THR   Vietnam theater veteran
VA   Veterans Administration (now Department of Veterans Affairs)
VES   Vietnam Experience Study
W/O   White/others

Acknowledgments

Reflecting on the more than four-year life of the National Vietnam Veterans Readjustment Study evokes in us a kaleidoscope of memories and their associated emotions. Conduct of the Readjustment Study has in some way recapitulated the Vietnam era, in that it has at various times been vexingly difficult, frighteningly chaotic, overwhelmingly sad, and powerfully gratifying.

From the beginning, we were firmly committed to the premise that to achieve the objectives set forth in the Congressional mandate, decisions concerning the many important technical aspects of the study would have to be made on the basis of broad consensus among experts working in the many relevant technical fields. The need for broad-based input into the design and operation of the study resulted from the confluence of several factors: the scientific complexity of the study's subject matter; the potential political and programmatic implications of the findings; and the intense and genuine emotional investment in some of our beliefs about Vietnam veterans, despite the sometimes nonsystematic basis of those beliefs.

The research team's insistence on broad input and full discussion of issues prior to the formulation of decisions reflected our commitment to the principle that the well-being of the study was more important than the narrow self-interest of any of the participating parties. Adherence to this principle made the research team shameless in the pursuit of advice and counsel from experts in the many areas in which expertise was required for the design and conduct of the study. As a result, we are indebted to the large number of consultants, collaborators, and colleagues from whose advice both the study and the research team have benefitted greatly. Also as a result of this pursuit, we believe that the credibility of the entire enterprise has been substantially enhanced.

Consequently, we want to acknowledge the important roles played by many persons and organizations in the conduct of the Readjustment Study. Our acknowledgments must begin with recognition of the wisdom and courage of the U.S. Congress in enacting the legislation mandating the study. Also, we appreciate the patience of Congress in tolerating the delays that have accompanied the evolutionary development of the research design.

The study was conducted under contract number V101(93)P-1040 from the Veterans Administration (VA). We are very grateful to the VA for providing the substantial resources required to conduct a national epidemiologic study. We are also grateful to the VA for establishing the mechanisms needed to assure that primacy was given to scientific considerations when decisions were made about major design features of the study.

Although responsibility for the scientific aspects of the study rested with the coprincipal investigators, the work was carried out by staff from a consortium of organizations. These included the Research Triangle Institute (RTI); Louis Harris and Associates, Inc. (LHA); the Graduate Center of the City University of New York (CUNY); the Langley Porter Psychiatric Institute at the University of California, San Francisco; the Hispanic Research Center at San Diego State University; and Equifax, Inc. We also want to acknowledge the participation of a number of persons in leadership roles at these organizations: Dr. James Chromy of RTI for providing overall leadership and management participation; Donald King and Michael Weeks of RTI for managing the survey data collection effort; James Batts of RTI for managing the data processing component; Frank Potter of RTI for managing the sampling component; Dr. Lisa LaVange of RTI for managing much of the statistical data processing; Dr. John Boyle, Esther Fleischman, and Alice Stackpole for managing the survey operation at LHA; and Prof. Charles Kadushin for managing the participation of CUNY.

Because the work was carried out under a federal contract, its conduct was overseen administratively on behalf of the government by a number of federal officials, including Drs. Nathan Denny, Arthur Blank, Thomas Murtaugh, and Terence Keane. Each of these individuals was a collaborator in the research, and each made important contributions to the study in his own unique way.

The study was also formally overseen on behalf of the government on an ongoing basis by two groups. From its inception, the scientific aspects of the study were overseen by an independent Scientific Advisory Committee, chaired by Dr. Stanislav Kasl of the Yale University Medical School. The charge of this committee was to review study plans and progress, and to make recommendations to the government concerning the study's scientific aspects. The committee met regularly with the research team over the course of the study, and worked with us on the difficult design, operational, and analytical challenges that the study presented. The collegial nature of the interactions between the research team and the committee, which is a tribute to Dr. Kasl's leadership style, served as an effective catalyst toward the ultimate improvement of the research. We are indebted to the committee for providing a forum in which ideas and their consequences could be thoroughly and dispassionately considered, and for the many creative suggestions and sound decisions that the committee made.

The second group that provided ongoing oversight was the VA's Technical Advisory Group (TAG), chaired by Dr. Terence Keane. The TAG comprised administrators of some of the federal programs to whose missions the Readjustment Study mandate was most relevant. The TAG's charge was to oversee the administrative aspects of the research and to receive and act on the scientific advice provided by the Scientific Advisory Committee. As such, the TAG had the treacherous task of trying to implement the committee's scientific advice while simultaneously negotiating the fiscal and political realities under which the study was conducted. The research team is grateful to the TAG for its efforts to shield the study from much of the political and bureaucratic furor, and for having the wisdom to recognize those points on which compromise would have worked to the detriment of the scientific quality (and therefore the ultimate credibility) of the research.

A third federal group that provided advice, though on a more limited basis, was the Congressional Office of Technology Assessment (OTA). Acting in response to a request from the Senate and House Veterans' Affairs Committees, OTA convened a panel of experts over the summer of 1986 to review the progress of the study to date. The research team appreciated the opportunity to discuss many of the important scientific issues involved in the study with the OTA panel, and the study benefitted from the recommendations made in the subsequent staff report.

Other federal officials also contributed to the study. Invaluable assistance in developing veteran sampling frames and/or gaining access to military record information was provided by Richard Christian and the staff of the Department of Defense's (DoD) Environmental Support Group; Michael Dove and Deborah Eitelberg and other staff of the DoD Defense Manpower Data Center; Diane Rademacher and other staff of the DoD National Personnel Records Center; Major Robert Elliott and other staff of the U.S. Army Reserve Components Personnel and Administration Center; and

Drs. Patricia Breslin and Han Kang of the VA. Additionally, David Brown of the National Institute of Occupational Safety and Health provided valuable assistance in obtaining current address information for sampled veterans from the Internal Revenue Service. Also, Stephen Dienstfrey, Lynne Heltman, and Dr. Victor Tsou of the VA provided data from official VA files concerning current veteran population counts and official records of service-connected disability.

In addition to external review groups, the research team made liberal use of consultants and other collaborators in the conduct of the study. One person on whom we repeatedly called for help, and who repeatedly answered the call, was Dr. David Grady. A highly decorated Vietnam veteran who is now a practicing clinical psychologist, Dr. Grady provided both personal and professional insight into many of the important issues in the study, particularly those concerning the phenomenology of post-traumatic stress disorder (PTSD) and the conceptualization of war-zone stress. His willingness to take on difficult tasks and his ability to carry them out successfully have been a tremendous contribution to the study. We are both personally and professionally indebted to Dr. Grady for his efforts in the service of the study.

Another person to whom the research team is particularly indebted is Dr. John Boyle. Dr. Boyle participated in the study initially as part of his duties as a vice-president of Louis Harris and Associates and project director for the LHA subcontract, and later as a consultant to the research team. Dr. Boyle's extensive knowledge and experience in conducting survey research were a vital resource in the planning and execution of the National Survey of the Vietnam Generation.

Continuing advice and support were also received from our colleagues at the Traumatic Stress Study Center at the University of Cincinnati: Drs. Bonnie Green and Jacob Lindy, and Mary Grace. We consulted with them on many of the study's most difficult issues, and always received insightful advice delivered in a thoughtful and supportive way. The research team is grateful for having had the benefit of their extensive experience in traumatic stress research, and for their continuing support.

Over the course of the study, the research team relied heavily on groups of professionals to help us with specific tasks. Early in the study, we convened an ad hoc panel on the Definition and Measurement of PTSD, in cooperation with the American Psychiatric Association's Work Group to Revise DSM-III [the third edition of the *Diagnostic and Statistical Manual of Mental Disorders*]. This panel made recommendations on revisions to the definition of PTSD that were subsequently incorporated into the revision of the official nomenclature, and advised the research team on issues of PTSD assessment. The advice of this panel was a great contribution to this study and an advance in the state of the art in diagnosis and assessment of stress disorders.

Along this line, the research team is indebted to Drs. Robert Spitzer and Janet Williams and to Miriam Gibbon of the New York State Psychiatric Institute. Dr. Spitzer, in his role as chair of the Work Group to Revise DSM-III, was very helpful in providing for coordination between the study team and the work group, helping to assure that the Readjustment Study estimates of PTSD prevalence represented the disorder as officially defined at the time results became available. Also, Drs. Spitzer and Williams and Ms. Gibbon provided valuable training in the administration of the Structured Clinical Interview for DSM-III-R for several groups of clinicians who participated in the clinical interview components of the study.

A second instance in which professionals provided invaluable assistance was in the conduct of the study's preliminary validation component. This component was conducted as a cooperative effort of the study team and teams of mental health professionals at eight sites located across the country. The preliminary validation study, which was a critically important part of the Readjustment Study, could not have been carried out without the participation of this large group of expert clinicians, site coordinators, and site activators.

A third group of professionals who made a substantial contribution to the study was the team, led by Dr. David Grady, that trained the study's survey interviewers in veterans' issues and in dealing with sensitive material, and supported them throughout the survey interviewing period. The team included Dr. George Carnevale, Joan Craigwell, and Forest Farley, Jr., and was assisted in its planning by Rose Sandecki. The low incidence of "problems" during NSVG survey interviews is a tribute to the success of this team.

A fourth group who made an invaluable contribution to the study is the over 140 professional survey interviewers who participated. Readjustment Study interviews were long and sometimes difficult to conduct. The high response rates and the low problem rates are an indication of the professionalism and care with which these interviewers took on the task.

A fifth group of professionals who made an important contribution to the study was the mental health clinicians who conducted follow-up clinical interviews with a subsample of veterans from the national survey. These clinicians, working at 28 locations across the country, made possible the Readjustment Study's multiple-indicators approach to PTSD assessment. Their sensitivity and professionalism in conducting the interviews, and their tenacity and flexibility in making themselves available to respondents so that the interviews could be completed, assured the success of this critical component of the study. The clinicians involved were: Drs. Stephen Bailey, Roland Brauer, Raymond Costello, Yael Danieli, Kathryn DeWitt, Phil Ellis, Johanna Gallers, William Gordon, David Hansen, Carol Hartman, Ronald Kidd, Walter Knake, Charles Lawrence, Bert Levine, Richard McNally, Bruce Marcus, Mary Merwin, Phillip Ninan, Frank Ochberg, Erwin Parson, Patricia Resick, Ralph Robinowitz, Sherry Roth, Philip Saigh, Thomas Scarano, Robert Ursano, Charles VanValkenburg, Nicholas Winter, and John Zajecka.

Important contributions also were made by the Vietnam theater veteran refusal conversion team. This was a group of Vietnam veterans who made calls to those Vietnam veterans who were selected in the national survey sample but had refused to participate in the interview when contacted by the interviewer. The purpose of these calls was to make sure that the potential respondent understood the nature of the study and the importance of his or her participation. The team included Daniel Cummings, William Gordy, Sr., Laurence Kolman, William Miller, Jerome Odorizzi, Linda Schwartz, and Philip Smith. Their efforts made a significant contribution to the high participation rate of theater veterans.

Another consultant who was generous with his time and expertise was Dr. W. Grant Dahlstrom of the University of North Carolina at Chapel Hill. Professor Dahlstrom arranged for us to have access to Form AX of the Minnesota Multiphasic Personality Inventory (MMPI) for use in the Clinical Interview component of the study. This allowed the study to be coordinated with the ongoing research that will result in a revised version of the MMPI. Also, the work of the National Computer Systems in scoring the completed MMPIs is greatly appreciated.

We are indebted as well to a number of experts who advised us on issues of instrumentation. These include Drs. Richard Berrego, Dan Blazer, Ghislaine Boulanger, Lois Johns, Robert Laufer, Erwin Parson, and Frank Putnam. Similarly, we greatly appreciate the invaluable assistance provided by Paul Truseck and the staff and clients of the Greensboro (N.C.) Vet Center in the development of instrumentation and of materials for use in the training of interviewers.

Additionally, we want to express our gratitude to the superb survey operations, data processing, analytic, and other support staff who have done the study's work and participated in the preparation of the various reports and other documents. They include Maggie Allison, Wendy Foran, and Susan Westneat of RTI, who participated in a variety of tasks over the course of the study; Lisa Packer and Pat Kristiansen of RTI, who were diligent in keeping track of the study's budget and schedule; Dr. Ralph Folsom and Frank Potter of RTI, who created the study's multicomponent sampling design; and Michael Johnson, Ms. Packer, and Mr. Potter of RTI, who constructed the sampling frames, selected the samples, and computed the sampling weights; James Andrews, Anne Crusan, Michael Davis, Dan Roentsch, Kathy Rourke, Cathy Rowley, Susan Siegrist, David Wilson, and Carrotte of LHA, who participated in survey interviewer training and oversaw the interviewing for LHA; Richard Boytos, James Devore, Janice Kelly, and Ellen Stutts of RTI, who participated in the training of survey interviewers; Jerry Durham, Donald Jackson, Ms. Stutts, and Harvey Zelon of RTI, who oversaw the day-to-day survey data collection for RTI; Viviane Cobb, Susan Freeman, Tim Gabel, Mr. Johnson, Ms. Packer, and Angela Perez-Michael of RTI, who provided excellent analytical and data processing support; Pat Kerr and Karla Colegrove of RTI, who managed the field operation of the clinical subsample; Ms. Colegrove, Ms. Kristiansen, Liz Stewart, and the editing teams of LHA and RTI, who were persistent in ensuring the quality of the survey data; Judy Weir of San Diego State University, who provided analytic support and participated in the writing of parts of this report; Dr. Louise Gaston of the Langley Porter Psychiatric Institute, who provided support of the clinical interviewing effort; Donna Albrecht, Lil Clark, Linda Miller, and Brenda Smith, who prepared the manuscript for this and the many prior NVVRS documents; and Dr. Robert Kelton and the staff of the Kelton Group, who provided excellent editorial review of this report. The high level of professionalism of these and the many other persons who have worked with us on various aspects of the study has made a substantial contribution to its ultimate outcome.

Finally, we thank the spouses/partners and other family members of the research team for their tolerance, understanding, support, and constructive criticism over the years that it has taken to bring the study to its current state. They have made many sacrifices over this period, during which conduct of the study has consumed the interest and time of the research team. Though their participation was indirect, their influence on the study has been pervasive. We cannot understate the importance of their support, and we hope that they will always understand the value of their contribution to the study and judge that the outcome justified their sacrifice.

Editorial Note

The Brunner/Mazel Psychosocial Stress Book Series is delighted, at long last, to welcome this book as the eighteenth in the Series. This book represents many, many years of work. Its beginnings can be traced to 1982 as the initial idea of Senator Alan Cranston and his U.S. Senate Veterans Affairs Committee to commission a definitive study, which would help the Committee and others develop sound policies and programs to help the Vietnam war generation. The study eventually commissioned by Congress is presented in this important book.

Well before 1982 it had become clear to both the scientific and policymaking communities concerned about Vietnam veterans that a definitive study was needed. Public and private studies of the mental health consequences of military service during the war in Southeast Asia were conclusive: the impact was significant and long-lasting for those who served in extremely stressful roles, such as combat, compared to those who did not. Moreover, one of the most pervasive problems among "theater" veterans (including female nurses who served in the war) was post-traumatic stress disorder (PTSD). This was the latest in a long series of diagnostic terms to describe the state of distress associated with being severely upset or traumatized.

In the late 1970s, President Carter and his VA Administrator, Max Cleland, established the Readjustment Counseling Service within the Veterans Administration in response to growing pressure. The RCS set up a network of "Vet Centers" across the United States. This program was an attempt to address what were seen as the unmet needs of Vietnam veterans. At the time it was created, the hope was that a Vet Center system could be put into place quickly, do its job, and then be dismantled. Over its first years of operation, however, veterans began coming into Vet Centers—

and kept coming in. As a result, Congress renewed the program in 1981 and 1983, and included the mandate for a national study in the 1983 renewal legislation.

It is important to remember that the actions by Congress did not occur in a vacuum. During the period following the war's official end in 1975, Vietnam veteran organizations became increasingly vocal in expressing their views about the needs of Vietnam veterans and their families, and their disappointment in government efforts to meet those needs. Early in 1981 the hostages in Iran were freed and the nation responded in a collective sigh of relief. Their highly publicized release and heartwarming welcome home stood in stark contrast to the "welcome home" that Vietnam veterans had received, and it served to reinforce profound questions for the Vietnam veteran. Veterans' organizations, nearly unanimously now, were moved to call for a continuation of the Vet Centers, citing the growing evidence of the lasting problems of Vietnam veterans and their families. Of special concern were the problems associated with war-related PTSD.

The decision in 1983 to mandate a definitive study of Vietnam veterans was the result of a compromise between two factions in Congress: those who held the view that the readjustment problems of Vietnam veterans were behind them, and those who believed that the effects of exposure to traumatic stress might result in chronic problems requiring long-term solutions. The former group had begun to apply pressure for the dismantling of the Vet Center program, asserting that it had done its job and should be closed. The latter group, however, saw it differently, sensing that there remained a substantial unmet need. The compromise, then, was to continue the Vet Center program until definitive information about Vietnam veterans' mental health could be developed. Thus, the fate of the Vet Center program was closely tied to the findings of the NVVRS.

For the first time we now have an understanding of the immediate and long-term psychosocial consequences of military service in a war for all races and both genders compared to those who never served in war or who never served in the military. This is the first comprehensive, published report of this study. Many less inclusive reports have already been published in scholarly journals. More will follow.

This book is a joint venture between truly outstanding groups of professionals with very different competencies: the authors and the publishers. The authors, who were forced to structure their lives around this study for over four years, spent hundreds of hours writing the final report to Congress. Then, for a little compensation, they further revised and tailored it for a more general readership.

An equally outstanding group of professionals at Brunner/Mazel Publishers (especially President, Mark Tracten, Editorial Vice President, Natalie Gilman, and Managing Editor Suzi Tucker) worked to transform an extremely technical document into a more readable and "friendly" book.

It is especially important, finally, to note that the royalties for this book will be donated to charity. The authors named the *Vietnam Veterans Aid Foundation* as the recipient. The VVAF is the only nonpolitical, nonprofit group dedicated to helping Vietnam veterans. They have raised hundreds of thousands of dollars over the last several years to help many thousands of needy Vietnam veterans. Readers are welcome to send donations to the VVAF by writing to the Vietnam Veterans Aid Foundation, PO Box 998-237, El Segundo, California 90245, USA.

It has been far too long a wait for a definitive study of the long-term effects of the Vietnam war. It is hoped that one byproduct of this study will be that additional services will emerge to help Vietnam veterans and others who continue to suffer as a result of being traumatized in service to their country. Most important, perhaps when next confronted with the prospect of sending citizens to fight a war—the purpose of which is questionable—policymakers will consider these findings. Perhaps they will be moved to acknowledge the vast and enduring costs of such a war to an entire generation of this country's children. Perhaps.

CHARLES R. FIGLEY, PH.D.
Florida State University

Preface

A STUDY OVER A DECADE IN THE MAKING

This book presents findings from the National Vietnam Veterans Readjustment Study (NVVRS). The United States Congress mandated this study in 1983 as part of Public Law 98–160 and directed that it establish "the prevalence and incidence of post-traumatic stress disorder (PTSD) and other psychological problems in readjusting to civilian life" among Vietnam veterans. With the evacuation of Saigon on March 25, 1973, America's direct involvement in over a decade of war in the Republic of Vietnam and its environs came to an end. Yet more than 10 years after the evacuation, the Congress was still faced with broadly conflicting testimony from experts and little "hard evidence" regarding the effects of the war on its veterans, especially the potential emotional or psychological toll that it took. In response to conflicting opinion, and lack of concrete evidence, Congress directed that a specific and comprehensive study be conducted of the mental health status and general life adjustment of Vietnam veterans, a study of sufficient size and scope to resolve this issue once and for all.

At the very least it was essential to know precisely how many Vietnam veterans continue to suffer from emotional turmoil 15–20 years or more after the end of their military service and return to civilian life? In turn, how many such veterans are seeking assistance for their problems, and how many who are not receiving help would benefit from it? These and other questions are fundamental both to understanding and to meeting the needs of the veterans who served in Vietnam and who are the principal focus of the research described in this book.

The contract to conduct this study was awarded to the Research Triangle Institute and its collaborators on September 12, 1984, and, by the time of its completion in November 1988, over four years and $9 million had been expended. However, though the official contract period spanned over four years, the evolution or incubation period for this study was far longer. On May 7, 1975, President Gerald R. Ford officially proclaimed an end to the "Vietnam era." In the years immediately following that proclamation, the nation hotly debated the nature and extent of the problems faced by veterans in readjusting to civilian life. Since then, hundreds of articles and dozens of books on the subject have been published, and the plight of these veterans has been a popular theme in the news media, television, and motion pictures. In part, the resurgence of public interest in the Vietnam war and its veterans reflects some dramatic and precedent-setting changes in our country's socioemotional climate in recent years, changes that have gradually defused somewhat our debate over the mental health of Vietnam veterans. This gradual transformation of our nation's psyche regarding the war and its veterans may well have been a necessary, though not sufficient, condition for conducting a study of the scope, complexity, and depth of the Readjustment Study.

At the same time, it is important to note that neither the people nor research tools required to conduct such a study were fully in place much before 1983–84. In conception, spirit, and method the research team—all members of which were working independently of one another, at widely scattered sites, and using quite different approaches—was, in effect, preparing for such a study over a decade ago. For example, one of us (Kulka) had the "good fortune" both to serve in Vietnam in 1970–71 and to subsequently join a research team at the Survey Research Center at the University of Michigan in 1976 to repeat a survey originally conducted in 1957, a nationwide survey of how Americans themselves viewed their mental health—their worries and problems, the extent to which they felt anxious, depressed, or otherwise psychologically distressed, and their feelings of general happiness, satisfaction, and well-being.

In 1979, when the National Institute of Mental Health (NIMH), the principal federal agency charged with stimulating research and disseminating research knowledge on mental health and illness in the United States, issued a special request for proposals to conduct research on the mental health and illness of Vietnam veterans, no one was especially surprised that a proposal surfaced from Michigan to conduct a national survey of how "Vietnam Veterans View Their Mental Health." This study would be modeled on the one of the general public still under way, once again focusing on worries, unhappiness, and reports of problems in work, marriage, and family, as well as feelings of anxiety, depression, and psychological distress or well-being. Although a team of experts reviewing the proposal strongly suggested that the study would be of little value unless it was redesigned to assess the prevalence of specific mental disorders among Vietnam veterans, the investigators balked, for two basic reasons.

First, the "diagnosis" of specific psychiatric disorders (such as panic or major depressive disorders) requires the application of very specific rules or "criteria," as defined by the American Psychiatric Association. Since, at that time, no appropriate survey interview or questionnaire existed with which one might carry out such an assessment, it was impossible to conduct a nationwide survey of any population (either veterans or the general public) that would tell us the numbers or proportions of persons suffering from specific psychiatric disorders. Second, it was assumed that the majority of Vietnam veterans would not (at least at the time of our survey) have any specific diagnosable mental disorder. Yet it was thought that a study focusing on perceived problems, worries, and inadequacies, and feelings of anxiety, depression, and psychological distress among this group (and in comparison with other veterans and nonveterans) would still have considerable merit in its own right—though not quite enough merit apparently to be approved and proceed at that time.

However, during this same period (1979–1980) a questionnaire explicitly designed to detect specific mental disorders gleaned from interviews conducted by survey research interviewers, rather than by mental health professionals, was under development and testing at Washington University in St. Louis. The Diagnostic Interview Schedule (DIS), a standardized questionnaire designed for use by survey research interviewers to gather information on symptoms of a broad range of major mental disorders, was first used in the NIMH-sponsored Epidemiologic Catchment Area (ECA) program, which surveyed the mental health status of people living in five specific geographic areas (New Haven, Baltimore, St. Louis, the Piedmont area of North Carolina, and Los Angeles). Members of the Readjustment Study research team were active directly in the ECA studies in North Carolina (Jordan) and at UCLA (Hough), as well as in other studies using the DIS, including a study of the prevalence of mental disorders among men in prison (Schlenger and Jordan) and the development and testing of a new set of questions to detect symptoms of post-traumatic stress disorder (Hough).

Parallel to the development and use of these innovative survey research methods to detect the presence of mental illness in the general population were the intensive efforts of others to better understand one specific psychiatric disorder—post-traumatic stress disorder (PTSD). Of special note were a series of clinical studies at the Langley Porter Psychiatric

Institute of the University of California, San Francisco (Marmar and Weiss) which examined the nature and causes of "stress response syndromes," responses to extremely stressful experiences or circumstances, and clinical research with Vietnam veterans suffering from PTSD at the Veterans Administration Medical Center in Jackson, Mississippi (Fairbank). Moreover, it is important to realize that the official nomenclature and diagnostic criteria ("rules") which are used to define PTSD as it is known today were first published only in 1980, as part of the third edition of the *Diagnostic and Statistical Manual of Mental Disorders* (DSM-III) of the American Psychiatric Association.

Thus, by 1984 several key elements had come together that made it possible for the first time to seriously *think* about doing a nationwide survey of Vietnam veterans capable of providing valid estimates of the prevalence of PTSD and other mental disorders among them, a study that was essentially not even conceivable just five years earlier. These elements included: (1) the formation of a team of social and clinical psychologists, sociologists, and a psychiatrist, all bringing different perspectives to the study; (2) the availability of specific published criteria or rules for the diagnosis of PTSD; (3) new survey and clinical research methods; and (4) a rapidly accumulating knowledge of the nature of extreme stressors and PTSD. Thinking about such a study and actually doing it are entirely different matters, of course, and this book basically describes the results of our efforts to translate this potential—this concept—into reality, while also revealing some of the problems encountered along the way.

Overall, we have often described the National Vietnam Veterans Readjustment Study as perhaps the most far-reaching and ambitious national mental health epidemiological study ever attempted with any population. We believe that this study has "pushed the outside of the envelope" in survey, clinical, and epidemiological research, in much the same way that America's early astronauts probed the outer limits of their craft in flight-test and in the exploration of outer space. We have learned a great deal in the process about how *not* to do things, and some about how to do things better. We are pleased to provide in this forum both the fruits and "other by-products" of our efforts. We also understand that the Veterans Administration is currently making arrangements for the production and distribution of a public-use data tape from this study for use by others in the research community who seek to better understand the current circumstances of Vietnam veterans and the nature, distribution, and causes of PTSD. We welcome that initiative and we are pleased to have participated in this very important enterprise.

HIGHLIGHTS OF FINDINGS

- Conducted in response to Public Law 98–160, the National Vietnam Veterans Readjustment Study (NVVRS) is the most rigorous and comprehensive study to date of the prevalence of post-traumatic stress disorder (PTSD) and other psychological problems in readjusting to civilian life among Vietnam veterans.

- The sample of veterans examined in the NVVRS was broader and more inclusive than those of past studies. As a result, the descriptions of Vietnam theater and era veterans found in this report are in some ways different from, but more representative than, descriptions provided in previous research.

- The majority of Vietnam theater veterans have made a successful reentry into civilian life and currently experience few symptoms of PTSD or other readjustment problems.

- Although, in general, male Vietnam theater veterans do not differ greatly in their current life adjustment from their era veteran counterparts, there is some evidence that female theater veterans currently experience more readjustment problems than Vietnam era veteran women of similar age and military occupation.

- NVVRS findings indicate that 15.2 percent of all male Vietnam theater veterans are current cases of PTSD. This represents about 479,000 of the estimated 3.14 million men who served in the Vietnam theater. Among Vietnam theater veteran women, current PTSD prevalence is estimated to be 8.5 percent of the approximately 7,200 women who served, or about 610 current cases. For both males and females, these rates of current PTSD for theater veterans are consistently and dramatically higher than rates for comparable Vietnam era veterans (2.5 percent male, 1.1 percent female) or civilian counterparts (1.2 percent male, 0.3 percent female).

- An additional 11.1 percent of male theater veterans and 7.8 percent of female theater veterans—350,000 additional men and women—currently suffer from "partial PTSD." That is, they have clinically significant stress reaction symptoms of insufficient intensity or breadth to qualify as full PTSD, but may still warrant professional attention.

- NVVRS analyses of the *lifetime* prevalence of PTSD indicate that over one-third (30.6 percent) of male Vietnam theater veterans (over 960,000 men) and over one-fourth (26.9 percent) of women serving in the Vietnam theater (over 1,900 women) had the full-blown disorder at some time during their lives. Thus, about one-half of the men and one-third of the women who have ever had PTSD *still* have it today. These findings are consistent with the conceptualization of PTSD as a chronic, rather than acute, disorder.

- NVVRS findings also indicate a strong relationship between PTSD and other postwar readjustment problems: having PTSD increases the likelihood of having other specific psychiatric disorders and a wide variety of other postwar readjustment problems. These findings confirm that, in addition to the painful symptoms of PTSD itself, the lives of Vietnam veterans with PTSD are profoundly disrupted, in that they experience problems in virtually every domain of their lives.

- The prevalence of PTSD and other postwar psychological problems is significantly, and often dramatically, higher among those with high levels of exposure to combat and other war-zone stressors in Vietnam, by comparison either with their Vietnam era veteran and civilian peers or with other veterans who served in the Vietnam theater and were exposed to low or moderate levels of war-zone stress. This suggests a prominent role for exposure to war stress in the development of subsequent psychological problems, and confirms that those who were most heavily involved in the war are those for whom readjustment was, and continues to be, most difficult.

- Among men who served in the Vietnam theater, substantial differences in current PTSD prevalence rates were also found by minority status. The current prevalence of PTSD is estimated to be 27.9 percent among Hispanics, 20.6 percent among Blacks, and 13.7 percent among Whites/others. Analyses of several factors that may account for these differences suggested that differences between Blacks and Whites/others may be attributed to their differing levels of exposure to war-zone stress, but differences between Hispanic men and the other two groups could not be explained by this factor. More generally, the evidence suggests that Black and Hispanic Vietnam theater veteran men have experienced more mental health and life-adjustment problems subsequent to their service in Vietnam than White/other veterans.

- Interviews conducted with the spouses or partners of Vietnam theater veterans with and without PTSD revealed that PTSD has a substantial negative impact not only on the veterans' own lives, but also on the lives of spouses, children, and others living with such veterans.

- Vietnam veterans with postwar psychological problems are more likely to have sought mental health care provided by the VA than those without such problems. Such veterans have also made greater use of mental health services in general, both from the VA and from other sources (e.g., private physicians or clinics), with non-VA sources accounting for the majority of their total mental health service use. Nevertheless, very substantial proportions of Vietnam veterans with readjustment problems have *never* used the VA or any other source for their mental problems, especially during the previous 12 months.

CHAPTER I

The Challenge: Finding and Studying the Vietnam War Generation

COMMENTARY

In the years that followed termination of U.S. military involvement in Vietnam, Congress found itself faced with conflicting testimony about the fate of the men and women who had served in the war. Though the military had maintained an accurate record of the numbers who had died fighting the war, no one was keeping track of what happened to those who had survived it. Each time that Congress held hearings concerning programs for veterans, witnesses presented contradictory accounts of veterans' problems and needs. On the one hand, some testified that Vietnam veterans were "doing just fine": they had responded to their country's call, had done their duty, and had returned smoothly to civilian life. However, others testified that for at least a significant minority of the men and women who served during the Vietnam war, "the war was not yet over"; in other words, they continued to suffer from emotional turmoil long after the end of their military service and reentry into civilian life. But estimates of the numbers of veterans suffering readjustment problems varied widely, from as few as 250,000 (a not insignificant number), to over two million. The fundamental problem was that all of these estimates were based on expert opinion rather than on sound epidemiologic research.

Recognizing this lack of reliable, research-based information and the critical importance of such information for the planning of service programs to meet the needs of veterans, Congress took action in 1983 to resolve this apparent conflict. In Public Law 98–160, Congress mandated that a comprehensive study be conducted of the mental health status and general life adjustment of Vietnam veterans. The study was to be of sufficient size and scope to provide accurate national

1

estimates of the extent of Vietnam veterans' mental health and other health needs and to permit sophisticated analyses of the nature, extent, and causes of their readjustment difficulties.

To assure that the study was conducted impartially and according to the highest scientific standards, a competitive bid process was established through which a research team would be selected to conduct the study. The government issued a Request for Proposals, which invited scientific organizations to submit proposals describing their ideas about how best to accomplish the objectives that Congress had specified. A group of distinguished scientists representing the many fields in which expertise would be needed was established to review the proposals. On the basis of this competitive process, in September 1984 the Veterans Administration awarded a contract to the Research Triangle Institute and its collaborators to conduct this mandated study, which subsequently became known as the "National Vietnam Veterans Readjustment Study" (NVVRS).

By the time it was over, the study had taken more than four years and $9 million to complete. Major collaborating organizations included Louis Harris and Associates, the Langley Porter Psychiatric Institute at the University of California, San Francisco, and San Diego State University, and the Hispanic Research Center at San Diego State University. The scientists who had reviewed the proposals formed the nucleus of what became the Scientific Advisory Committee that advised the VA on scientific issues relating to the study and made a substantial contribution to the process through which the study's design and implementation evolved.

Thus the NVVRS was born out of a need to know — the need to know the effects of Vietnam service on the subsequent lives of those who had participated in it. This knowledge was necessary to enable Congress to make informed policy decisions concerning veterans' programs.

In this introductory chapter, we describe briefly the background, objectives, and design of the study.

CHAPTER OVERVIEW

This report presents findings from the National Vietnam Veterans Readjustment Study (NVVRS). Congress mandated this study in Public Law

98-160 and directed that it address "the prevalence and incidence of post-traumatic stress disorder (PTSD) and other psychological problems in readjusting to civilian life" among Vietnam veterans. Our report concentrates on the issues specified in the Congressional mandate.

The NVVRS had three broad goals, as mandated by the Congress and evolved by the Veterans Administration (VA), its consultants, and the research team:

1. To provide information about the incidence, prevalence, and effects of PTSD and related postwar psychological problems among Vietnam veterans.

2. To describe comprehensively the total life adjustment of Vietnam theater veterans and to compare their adjustment with the adjustment of era veterans (persons who served in the Armed Forces during the Vietnam era but did not serve in the Vietnam theater) and nonveterans.

3. To provide detailed scientific information about PTSD in particular.

To meet the Readjustment Study's ambitious informational and methodological objectives, the NVVRS research design contained a number of components. The component designed to meet the study's major informational objectives was the National Survey of the Vietnam Generation (NSVG). The NSVG research design involved in-depth face-to-face interviews averaging three to five hours in length with samples of respondents drawn to represent the study's three major groups of interest. These are:

1. *Vietnam theater veterans.* Persons who served on active duty in the U.S. Armed Forces during the Vietnam era (August 5, 1964, through May 7, 1975) in Vietnam, Laos, or Cambodia, or in the surrounding waters or airspace of these three countries.

2. *Vietnam era veterans.* Persons who served on active duty in the U.S. Armed Forces during the Vietnam era but did not serve in the Vietnam theater.

3. *Nonveterans* or *civilian counterparts.* Persons who did not serve in the military during the Vietnam era. We matched members of this group to the theater veterans on the basis of age, sex, race/ethnicity (for men only), and occupation (for women only).

WHY ANOTHER STUDY?

In preparing this report, we have made a conscious effort to focus the text on the study's findings and their implications, and have discussed the study's methods and other technical details primarily in appendices and in separately bound volumes. Because tabular presentation of NVVRS findings and technical aspects of the study (Appendices A through G) are extensive, the basic tables and appendices have been bound separately as Volume II of the report.* By binding these separately, we have tried to make it easier for the reader to reference the information while reading the text. As an aid to interpretation, we have also included exhibits in Volume I that summarize important findings.

The following chart summarizes the organization of Volume I.

Chapter I	• A brief description of the background of the NVVRS. • An overview of its design. • The standard format for the presentation of findings and statistical tests of the differences among study groups.
Chapter II	• Definitions of the study groups. • Description of the characteristics of those groups.
Chapter III	Findings about the prevalence of the component symptoms of PTSD.
Chapter IV	Findings about the prevalence of PTSD.
Chapter V	Contribution of differences in premilitary characteristics and Vietnam experience to group differences in current PTSD prevalence.
Chapter VI	Findings on the prevalence of other psychiatric disorders.
Chapter VII	Findings on the prevalence of other readjustment problems.
Chapter VIII	Findings on the prevalence of physical health problems.
Chapter IX	Findings about the use of health and mental health services.
Chapter X	Impact of PTSD in theater veterans on their spouses or partners and their children.
Chapter XI	Directions for the future analysis of the NVVRS data in light of what we have learned from the primarily descriptive analyses presented in this report.
Chapter XII	General overview of findings
Chapter XIII	• Clarification of presented topics. • Comprehensive list of veterans' services nationwide.

---

*The National Vietnam Veterans Readjustment Study: Tables of Findings and Technical Appendices, is available through Brunner/Mazel Publishers.

WHAT WE ALREADY KNOW

With the evacuation of Saigon on March 25, 1973, the role of overt American intervention in the Republic of Vietnam ended. On May 7, 1975, President Gerald R. Ford proclaimed an end to the "Vietnam era." The Vietnam era had officially begun on August 5, 1964.

By September 30, 1983, an estimated 8,238,000 men and women who served in the U.S. Armed Forces (both in the Vietnam theater and elsewhere) during the Vietnam era had returned to civilian life (U.S. Veterans Administration, 1984). During the years since the Ford proclamation, the nation has hotly debated the nature and extent of the problems faced by these Vietnam era veterans in readjusting to civilian life. Hundreds of articles and dozens of books concerning Vietnam veterans' readjustment to civilian life have been published, and the plight of these veterans has been a popular theme in the news media, television, and motion pictures. In part, the resurgence of public interest in the Vietnam war and its veterans reflects some dramatic and precedent-setting changes in the country's socioemotional climate in recent years, changes that gradually have depoliticized somewhat the debate over the mental health of Vietnam veterans.

During the years following the termination of U.S. military involvement, evidence began to mount suggesting that (1) a substantial number of Vietnam veterans continued to experience problems of readjustment, and (2) many Vietnam veterans either could not or would not avail themselves of services within the traditional VA system. For a significant minority of the men and women who served during the Vietnam war, "the war is not yet over," because they continue to suffer from emotional turmoil 15–20 years or more after the end of their military service and return to civilian life. However, previous estimates of the actual numbers of veterans suffering from readjustment problems have varied widely, from as few as 250,000 (for example, Wilson, 1978) to over two million (Egendorf, 1982). Although the consensus today is that some Vietnam veterans suffer from PTSD and other psychological problems in readjusting to civilian life, precise national estimates of the number of Vietnam veterans experiencing such problems simply have not been available.

In response to the mounting evidence and public concern, Congress enacted legislation in 1979 (Public Law 96-22) directing the VA to establish a readjustment counseling program, frequently referred to as the "Vet Center" program, separate from the existing VA medical center system. At the time of its enactment, the Vet Center program was expected to be a short-term program to deal with what was believed to be a temporary quirk in the demand for services. However, demand for Vet Center services continued to exceed expectations. Consequently, Congress renewed the program in 1981 (Public Law 97-72), and again in 1983 (Public Law 98-160).

At the time of the 1981 renewal, Congress mandated that the VA evaluate the readjustment counseling program and formulate plans for meeting Vietnam veterans' future mental health needs through the regular VA system. To comply with these mandates, the VA created a Readjustment Counseling Planning Task Force and contracted for a study to evaluate the effectiveness of the Vet Centers in meeting the needs of the clients served. These efforts helped keep the program's attention focused on meeting the needs of those veterans who came to it seeking service.

By the time of the 1983 renewal, the Vet Center program had been in operation for four years and had provided services to a substantial number of Vietnam veterans. Although it seemed to serve the needs of those veterans who used it, the program prompted an additional question: How many more Vietnam veterans are experiencing significant readjustment problems but have not yet sought help? To address this question, the 1983 legislation mandated a study of the prevalence, incidence, and effects of PTSD and related postwar psychological problems in Vietnam veterans. The study was to be of sufficient size, scope, complexity, and design to provide national estimates of the extent of Vietnam veterans' mental health and other health needs. The study also needed to permit sophisticated analyses of the nature, scope, covariation, and etiology of Vietnam veterans' readjustment difficulties.

On September 12, 1984, the VA awarded a contract to the Research Triangle Institute (RTI) to conduct the mandated study, which became known as the National Vietnam Veterans Readjustment Study (NVVRS).

WHAT WE HOPED TO FIND

The NVVRS had three broad goals, as mandated by the Congress and evolved by the VA, its consultants, and the research team (see Exhibit I-1). The first major goal of the study was to provide information about the incidence, prevalence, and effects of PTSD and related postwar psychological problems among Vietnam veterans.

A second major goal of the study was to provide a comprehensive description of the total life adjustment of Vietnam theater veterans and to compare their adjustment with that of era veterans (i.e., persons who served in the Armed Forces during the Vietnam era but did not serve in the Vietnam theater) and nonveterans. It was intended that this description

EXHIBIT I-1
NVVRS Objectives
Conduct a Comprehensive Study in the Population
of Vietnam Veterans (VVs) of:

I.   Prevalence and incidence of:
       A. Post-traumatic stress disorder (PTSD)
       B. Other psychological problems of readjusting to civilian life—other
          "postwar psychological problems" (PWPPs)
          1. Other DSM-III psychiatric disorders
          2. Malfunctions in:
             A. Marital roles
             B. Familial roles
             C. Vocational roles and careers
             D. Educational roles and careers
          3. More general and subjective disturbances
             A. Life satisfaction, dissatisfaction, quality of life
             B. Demoralization or nonspecific distress

II.   Effects of PWPPs on such veterans, especially:
       A. Those with service-connected disabilities
       B. Women veterans

III.   Assess correlations between PTSD and other PWPPs:
       A. Physical disabilities (by type)
       B. Alcohol and drug abuse
       C. Minority group membership
       D. Incarceration in penal institutions

IV.   Evaluation of long-term effects of PWPPs on:
       A. Families
       B. Others in primary social relationships

V.   Extent to which VVs with PWPPs use VA and other resources

---

document in the aggregate the course of the lives of these three groups: the problems they have faced, the ways in which they have coped, and the quality of their lives. The description was to cover many dimensions of life—education, work, family, interpersonal relations, emotional stability, etc. The aim was to look at the broad spectrum of adjustment, and to identify factors that have made both positive and negative contributions to these citizens' lives.

A third major goal of the study was to provide detailed scientific information about one specific type of postwar psychological problem: PTSD. Of particular interest are its antecedents, its course, its consequences, and its relationship to other physical and emotional disorders. Relationships between PTSD and other postwar psychological problems, physical disabilities, substance abuse, minority group membership, and criminal justice involvement were all to be examined. Additionally, information describing the impact of postwar psychological problems on veterans' families and on their use of VA facilities was to be developed.

In short, the Congressional mandate was both detailed and far-reaching. Fulfillment of that mandate required perhaps the most ambitious national mental health epidemiologic study ever attempted on *any population*.

HOW WE PLANNED TO FIND IT

Overview of Major Components

Clearly, to achieve these broad and very ambitious objectives, we needed a rather extraordinary research design. This design required careful attention to sampling and location procedures, instrument development and validation, data collection, and numerous other special methodological issues. In addition, the controversial nature of some of the study's subject matter (for example, PTSD), the intense interest in the study on the part of groups across the political spectrum, and the programmatic implications of the study's findings have all intensified the importance of the design to the ultimate utility of the study's findings. If the findings are to be useful to policy makers, they must be credible to the scientific community, to various political interest groups, and ultimately to the Congress. As with all research projects, the credibility of the findings from the Readjustment Study is predicated on the rigor of its research design.

To ensure that critical statistical comparisons could be made reliably, certain subgroups were oversampled, including females, Black and Hispanic males, and theater veterans with service-connected physical disabilities.

The survey interview was designed to cover the broad spectrum of adjustment, including such topics as:

- marriage and family
- education and occupation
- military service and Vietnam experience
- stressful and traumatic life experiences
- substance use
- psychiatric disorder
- physical health
- use of health and mental health services

A summary outline of the topics covered and the average number of minutes of interview time allocated to each is shown in Exhibit I-2.

EXHIBIT I-2
National Survey of the Vietnam Generation
Average Interview Times by Section
for the Household Interview

	Time in Minutes		
Section/Title	Vietnam Theater Veterans	Vietnam Era Veterans	Civilian Counterparts
Section A: Preamble and Eligibility	2	2	2
Section C: Marital History and Adjustment	10	10	10
Section D: Parenting History and Adjustment	10	10	10
Section E: Educational History	6	6	6
Section F: Occupational History and Work Role Adjustment	9	9	9
Section G: Childhood and Family History	12	12	12
Section H: Military Service History	16	16	12
Section J: Vietnam Experience	60	—	—
Section K: Postservice	22	22	—
Section M: Stressful and Traumatic Life Events	22	18	10
Section N: Self-Perceptions, Attitudes, and Nonspecific Distress	18	18	24
Section P: Physical Health Status	9	9	9
Section R: Diagnostic Interview Schedule (DIS)	79	73	72
Section S: Use of Health and Mental Health Services	16	15	13
Section T: Social Support	6	6	5
Section U: Demographics	11	11	11
Total	308	237	195
	(5 hours, 8 minutes)	(3 hours, 57 minutes)	(3 hours, 15 minutes)

Three additional components of the NVVRS that are closely related to the NSVG were also of key importance in meeting the study's objectives:

1. Preliminary Validation Study component, conducted and analyzed in preparation for the NSVG.
2. Clinical Interview component conducted after the NSVG interview.
3. Family Interview component, also conducted after the NSVG interview.

Because at the time this study was initiated none of the measures currently available for a survey-based assessment of PTSD had yet been validated, an integral part of the study design was the completion of an elaborate Preliminary Validation Study component. We administered candidate PTSD measures to 225 Vietnam theater veterans whose mental health status with regard to PTSD and other psychiatric disorders was already known. The validation study determined how well diagnostic decisions about PTSD made on the basis of information from a survey interview would correspond with diagnostic decisions made by trained clinicians with extensive experience in diagnosing and treating PTSD. By providing information about the ability of the candidate survey interview instruments to identify true cases of PTSD, this validation component provided a scientific basis for selecting the actual PTSD instruments to be used in the NSVG.

For the Clinical Interview component, we selected a subset of more than 300 theater veterans and 100 era veterans to undergo a follow-up Clinical Interview with an expert mental health professional. This semistructured diagnostic interview was designed to provide additional information about the validity of diagnoses made on the basis of information collected in the survey interview, particularly the diagnosis of PTSD. The clinical interviews were conducted by mental health professionals located in 28 specific geographic areas around the country who were experienced in diagnosing and treating stress disorders. The Clinical Interview sample was drawn from among NSVG theater and era veteran respondents who lived within "reasonable commuting distance" of these 28 areas; the sample included all those who appeared on the basis of their survey interview to be PTSD positive and a sample of those who appeared to be PTSD negative.

The Family Interview component involved one-hour follow-up interviews with the spouses or other coresident partners (that is, someone with whom the veteran was living as though married) of over 450 theater veterans. The purpose of these interviews was to collect information about the veteran from someone close to him or her, and to assess the impact of postwar psychological problems of Vietnam theater veterans on persons sharing their lives. The Family Interview subsample was selected from the entire theater veteran sample. The subsample was designed to include adequate numbers of both spouses or partners of veterans whose survey interviews suggested substantial levels of postwar psychological problems and spouses/partners of those without such problems.

Sample Design of the NSVG

Two important requirements in the design of the NSVG were (1) that the sample of persons interviewed be nationally representative of the corresponding populations, and (2) that the survey include adequate comparison groups to provide a context for understanding the current adjustment problems of Vietnam veterans. To meet these requirements, the NSVG design specified the selection of national probability samples of Vietnam (theater and era) veterans and their civilian counterparts of sufficient size to support estimates for and contrasts among the groups of interest. For example, the study design contrasts Vietnam theater veterans with other Vietnam era veterans (male and female) and theater veterans with nonveterans (male and female). The study also contrasts racial/ethnic subgroups of male theater veterans (Black, Hispanic, and White/other) and subgroups exposed to different levels of combat or war-zone stress.

Operationally, the NSVG sample design combined (1) a military-records-based sample designed to yield 1,500 Vietnam theater veterans and 730 era veterans, (2) a household sample of 450 male and 50 (nonnurse) female civilian counterparts, and (3) a list sample of 150 female civilian registered nurses. The Vietnam theater veteran sample was augmented with 100 theater veterans with service-connected disabilities, for a total of 1,600 theater veterans.

The veteran respondent universe was defined as all persons who served on active duty in the military forces of the United States during the Vietnam era (August 5, 1964, through May 7, 1975), except those currently on active duty. Under this definition, career retirees, enlistment terminations, and persons who served on active duty during the Vietnam era and are now reservists or National Guard personnel are all included. By this definition, the study population contained an estimated 93 to 94 percent of all living persons who served on active duty during the Vietnam era, the most comprehensive coverage of the Vietnam veteran population of any study conducted to date.

The task of selecting the veteran samples was complicated by the fact that no master list existed of the over eight million veterans who served in the military during the Vietnam era. As a consequence, one of the study's initial tasks was to create such a list (or sampling frame), from which the samples of veterans could be selected. The most common means for creating such a list in past studies had been to screen households either by telephone or in person to identify Vietnam era veterans. However, this approach necessarily relies on self- or proxy reports to identify veterans, and the screening rates obtained by the most rigorous surveys employing this method (Fischer, Boyle, Bucuvalas, & Schulman, 1980; Rothbart, Fine, & Sudman, 1982) suggest significant underreporting of Vietnam theater and era veteran status, resulting in undercoverage of the order of 32 to 38 percent relative to 1980 Census findings. To avoid this problem of undercoverage, the NVVRS sampling frame for veterans was compiled directly from military personnel records, using three sources:

- The National Personnel Records Center (NPRC)
- The Defense Manpower Data Center (DMDC)
- A special list compiled for the VA by the Department of Defense's Environmental Support Group (ESG), purported to contain the names of all female theater veterans

From a sample of 34,000 accession numbers selected from the NPRC Chronological Model (which includes accession numbers assigned to personnel records received between January 1966 and June 1977), 25,000 personnel records were fully abstracted. From the DMDC master files, we selected a total of 966 cases. These two sources served as the basis for the male theater and era veteran samples. These abstraction samples were designed to include sufficient numbers of minority members to produce the required oversamples of Blacks and Hispanics. Although the number of Black veterans available was enough to produce the Black oversample, the number of Hispanics was insufficient to provide an adequate yield. As a result, we had to include a supplemental sample of 6,800 accession numbers from NPRC to obtain sufficient numbers of Hispanic male theater veterans to meet the statistical requirements of the study.

The NPRC and DMDC files were also the basis for the female era veteran sample. However, because more than 80 percent of female veterans serving in the Vietnam theater were nurses, we modified the sample design for these female veterans to produce a similar proportion of nurses in that subsample to ensure more valid comparisons between these two groups. To obtain adequate numbers of era veteran nurses for that purpose, we screened a sample of 205,000 accession numbers from the NPRC Chronological Model to identify all of those with potentially female names. We then retrieved the military records for all those with potentially female names and examined the records to determine the veteran's gender. All records verified as identifying female veterans were abstracted to identify nurses on the basis of the recorded military occupational specialty (MOS). This procedure resulted in a pool large enough to provide sufficient numbers of era veteran nurses.

We also used the ESG list of female theater veterans to select the female theater veteran sample.

Implementation

Implementing this complex, multiple-component research proved to be especially challenging—indeed, it proved to be a formidable test of some of the hypothetical limits of survey research. For example, although identification of the veteran samples from military records provided the advantage of a more representative sample than could have been achieved through identification via household screening, it had the distinct disadvantage of requiring the research team to track down all sampled veterans wherever they were currently living to interview them. The resulting sample literally was scattered throughout the world, and address information in their military records was often up to 20 years old. However, through an interagency agreement with the National Institute of Occupational Safety and Health (NIOSH), it was possible to obtain current addresses for most veterans from the Internal Revenue Service (IRS). Those for whom the IRS-supplied address was inaccurate, or for whom the IRS could not supply a current address, were located by specialized tracing procedures.

Even when located, the sample was very widely scattered, and interviews were conducted in virtually every part of the 50 states and Puerto Rico. This resulted in an unusually high level of interviewer travel (averaging 200 miles and seven hours per case for theater veterans) in conjunction with the administration of a highly sensitive interview averaging three to five hours in length. In turn, the complexity and sensitivity of the latter required ten full days of training and a special certification procedure for over 140 interviewers.

In spite of these and some other formidable challenges, the NVVRS achieved virtually all of its performance objectives. In the NSVG, over 95 percent of the veterans sampled were located (over 96 percent of the theater and 93 percent of the era veterans). The 3,016 total interviews conducted exceeded the targeted number of 2,980. For Vietnam theater veterans, over 83 percent of those sampled and eligible (87 percent of those located and eligible) were interviewed, ranging from 81 percent among Hispanic male theater veterans to 86 percent for female theater veterans. Response rates for Vietnam era veterans and nonveterans were 76 and 70 percent respectively, reflecting, in part, the lower salience of the survey to these groups in relation to the level of burden required for their participation.

Similarly, 344 of the 403 Vietnam theater veterans selected for the Clinical Interview component (85 percent) were successfully interviewed. Response rates for demographic subgroups ranged from 80 percent among Hispanic males to 97 percent among women. Among era veterans, 96 of the 116 era veterans selected for the Clinical Interview subsample (83 percent) were interviewed.

Finally, of the 557 spouses or partners of theater veterans who were selected for the spouse/partner interview, 474 were interviewed, for an overall response rate of 85 percent. Response rates for the demographic subgroups ranged from 83 percent for Black and Hispanic males to 91 percent for female theater veterans.

A WORD ABOUT VOLUME II

The basic NVVRS findings described in this volume that are presented in tabular form in Volume II are always referred to as "Tables." Summary findings presented in *this* volume are always referred to as "Exhibits." And the appendices presented in Volume II are referred to by letter — Appendix A, B, and so on. (Also see p. 4 for other information about Volume II.)

Most of the findings in Volume II are presented in a standard tabular format that consists of two parts. The first part of each table presents the NVVRS *estimates* (that is, the findings) for each of the study's groups and subgroups; the second part presents the results of *statistical contrasts* between selected study groups or subgroups.

Each table presents the NVVRS findings for one characteristic, or "outcome," that was included in the study. Examples of the outcomes include current PTSD diagnosis, educational attainment, and use of mental health services. Tabulations are provided for the outcomes for each study group and subgroup, and are always presented separately for men and women. For example, the table of findings about current PTSD diagnosis shows separate prevalence rates for male and female theater veterans, era veterans, and civilian counterparts.

The tables provide estimates for the study's major groups: theater veterans, era veterans, and civilian counterparts. For men, estimates are also provided for racial/ethnic subsets of the major study groups: Hispanic, (non-Hispanic) Black, and White/other. Additionally, within the theater veteran group, estimates are provided for some specific subgroups, selected because of their relevance to the Congressional mandate. These include subgroups based on level of exposure to war-zone stress (high and low/moderate; see Appendix C in Volume II for details); current PTSD diagnosis (positive and negative; see Appendix D in Volume II for details); level of service-connected physical disability (SCPD) as indicated in official VA records (none, 0–20 percent, and 30–100 percent); and lifetime substance abuse diagnosis (ever met the criteria for alcohol or drug abuse or dependence, positive and negative).

In addition to estimates, the tables also present the results for a standard set of "contrasts." These contrasts are statistical tests of the differences in the outcome between specific pairs study groups or subgroups (for example, male theater veterans versus male era veterans) in terms of the outcome being tabulated. Each table shows, for example, the contrast between theater and era veterans, separately for men and women. Results of these statistical tests tell whether the findings indicate that the groups being contrasted are or are not different in terms of the outcome being examined.

The Introduction to Volume II provides a more detailed explanation of the table structure and of the statistical tests used to evaluate the contrasts.

CHAPTER II
Those Who Served in the Vietnam War Era

This book is decidedly about Vietnam veterans and the effects of their service in Vietnam, Laos, or Cambodia on the subsequent course of their lives. Yet we really know very little about who these veterans are and how they might differ from those who served elsewhere in the military during the Vietnam era. Perhaps the most common image of the "Vietnam veteran" is one of young men recently out of school, drafted into the Army, quickly trained in the art of combat and sent to the jungles in Southeast Asia for a year, soon thereafter discharged to return to the streets of Chicago or New York or to the countryside and main streets of Nebraska or Alabama. The descriptions provided in this chapter afford a unique opportunity to test this conception of Vietnam veterans and others that each of us may harbor against the reality of a comprehensive statistical portrait of those who served in the military and in Southeast Asia during this period.

This is the case because a not insignificant "by-product" of the Congressionally mandated National Vietnam Veterans Readjustment Study was the opportunity to gain a better understanding of characteristics of the men and women who served in the U.S. Armed Forces during the Vietnam era—both those who served in Southeast Asia and its surrounding environs and those who served elsewhere. Up until the time of this study, certain fairly rigid preconceptions, or "stereotypes," had emerged concerning what Vietnam veterans "were like" and how they differed from both those not serving in the Vietnam theater of operations and those of the same generation who avoided serving in the military at all. With regard to possible differences in the subsequent course of their lives—their hopes and fears, successes and failures, happiness and worries—the Readjustment Study was explicitly designed to test

16

assumptions based on expert opinion and previous research conducted with more limited samples of veterans and their peers.

To meet that objective, it was imperative that the sample for this study include all *veterans who served during the Vietnam era—men and women of all ages, from all branches of service, draftees, retirees from the military, those who enlisted for one or more terms, and those who were on active duty then and who are currently in the Reserves or National Guard. In fact, the only persons excluded for practical reasons were those still on active duty at the time of the study (who were technically not yet veterans) and those veterans living outside of the United States and Puerto Rico. Among veterans serving in Southeast Asia, those represented include infantry "grunts," combat engineers, and cannoneers; pilots and air crews stationed in Thailand; helicopter pilots and door gunners; as well as nurses, medics, and those assigned to the grisly duty of "graves registration"; as well as PX clerks, entertainers, and other REMFs.*

As a result of our careful attention to including all veterans, a goal that consumed an enormous amount of time, effort, and resources, we are highly confident that the group of veterans described in the Readjustment Study is more representative than in any other study to date. From this comprehensive sampling has emerged a more complete and accurate statistical portrait of the men and women who served their country during the Vietnam era than has ever been possible before.

Thus, we were able to specify how many veterans of this period actually served in Southeast Asia, including the small but significant number of women. We were also able to provide information regarding the ages and ethnic and cultural backgrounds of those who served. Were Blacks and Hispanics more likely to serve in Vietnam than Whites? Were those born in the South more likely to serve? Were participants primarily drafted, or did most of them volunteer for the military? How many served in the Air Force or Navy, rather than in the Army or Marines? How many had service in the Korean Conflict as well as service in Vietnam? How many were enlisted, NCOs, and officers? How many were subject to disciplinary action while in the military, and how many had discharges other than honorable? How many now serve in the Reserves or National Guard, are members of veterans organizations, or have service-connected disabilities? How many men and women served more than 12 or 13 months, and how many had multiple tours of duty? How many received combat medals, including the Purple Heart for injuries or wounds? More generally, what are Vietnam veterans like today? What proportion are married or divorced, and how many have children? What levels of education have they achieved, how many are working, and what are their incomes? Where do they live—in the North, South, East, or West; in rural or urban areas—and how long have they lived there?

These are a few of the questions that are answered in this chapter. Therefore, though the descriptive profile provided in this chapter was developed primarily as a backdrop for interpreting information offered in other chapters, the statistical portrait that is revealed also holds considerable interest in its own right as a "reality check" on our basic preconceptions about the characteristics of Vietnam veterans, and, in turn, how we think and feel about them.

CHAPTER OVERVIEW

Because the sample of Vietnam theater and era veterans selected for the NVVRS was designed to be the most representative sample of all Vietnam era veterans studied to date, it differs somewhat from samples for prior studies on a number of major sociodemographic and military characteristics. However, the findings of the NVVRS provide the best available basis for inferences about the entire population of Vietnam veterans. The population of inference for the NSVG was 8,269,881 veterans who served during the Vietnam era, of whom an estimated 3,150,811 (38.1 percent) served in the Vietnam theater of operations. Of those serving in or around Vietnam, an estimated 3,143,645 were men and 7,166 were women.

In this chapter, different terminology was used to refer to the study's groups of veterans than in the rest of the report. This terminology reflects the fact that "Vietnam theater veterans" and "Vietnam era veterans," as the terms are employed throughout the report, are formally *both* "Vietnam era veterans" or "veterans of the Vietnam era." In the descriptive profile in this chapter and summary, the terms "Vietnam theater" and "Vietnam era" or "era" were also used to describe the two major subgroups, while the terms *"all* veterans of the Vietnam era" or *"all* Vietnam era veterans" were used only to describe the *entire* population of veterans serving during the Vietnam era. Because women serving during the Vietnam era were a small proportion of all Vietnam era veterans, overall statistics reflect predominantly distributions for men. In many cases, these distributions are quite different for women, and in selected instances, these are highlighted in this summary.

A majority of veterans serving during the Vietnam era were born between 1940 and 1949, but over one-fourth of the women theater veterans were older. Overall, 87 percent of all Vietnam era veterans were White, 11 percent Black, and 5 percent Hispanic. The majority were born in the southern or north central states.

For all Vietnam era veterans, a near majority entered military service between 1965 and 1969, but over 25 percent entered earlier and over 33 percent of both male and female era veterans entered later. Although 25 percent were drafted, almost 70 percent enlisted. A near majority served only one to three years of active duty, and approximately eight out of ten veterans have had some contact with the VA.

For Vietnam theater veterans, the peak years of entry to the theater of operations for men were 1967–1969 and for women 1968–1970; the peak years for exit were 1968–1970 and 1969–1971 respectively. One man in five served more than one tour, whereas only one woman in 20 did the same. Thirty percent of the men and 20 percent of the women served in Vietnam less than 12 months. About 25 percent of the men and 6 percent of the women received a combat medal, 13 percent and 1 percent, respectively, receiving a Purple Heart. Less than 1 percent of the theater veterans interviewed reported being a prisoner of war.

Three-fourths of all Vietnam era veterans (Vietnam theater and era veterans combined) were currently married, but only half of the women were married. The majority of both men and women had children. One-third of all Vietnam era veterans were high school graduates, and another 40 percent had some college education. Those men who served in the Vietnam theater were not different in education from the Vietnam era veterans who did not, whereas the women who served in the Vietnam theater were better educated and less likely to have had children. Nineteen percent reported family incomes of less than $20,000; 23.1 percent reported an income of $50,000 or more.

Close to 40 percent of all Vietnam era veterans lived in the South. Overall, the majority had lived in their current communities for more than ten years. Theater veteran women were twice as likely as theater veteran men to be living alone. Among all Vietnam era veterans, 58 percent were Protestant, 22 percent Catholic, and 17 percent had no religious preference.

Overall, the characteristics of the veterans who served in Vietnam varied substantially from the characteristics of the veterans who did not, especially for women. In particular, though the majority of Vietnam veterans fit our general stereotype of young "citizen soldiers" (that is, draftees and one-term enlistees who dominated the military numerically throughout the Vietnam era), the NVVRS samples also contained substantial proportions of reenlistees and career military personnel—many now retired—whose attitudes, experiences, and readjustment to civilian life quite plausibly may differ considerably from those of the majority.

WHY IT IS IMPORTANT TO KNOW WHO SERVED

As explained in Chapter I, the sample of Vietnam theater and era veterans selected for the NVVRS was intended to be representative of *all* veterans who served during the Vietnam era, excluding only those currently on active duty residing outside of the 50 United States and Puerto Rico. The population represented by this sample was somewhat different from that examined by previous studies of such veterans, such as the *Legacies of Vietnam* (Egendorf, Kadushin, Laufer, Rothbart, & Sloan, 1981), in which the researchers imposed other restrictions on the sample (for example, age range). In reviewing and interpreting the results of an epidemiological study of veterans of this era, we must consider the extent to which the survey sample represented the entire population of these veterans. In many respects, the Vietnam theater and era veterans selected for the NSVG were quite different from the stereotype that has arisen both from prior research based on nonrepresentative samples and from portrayals in literature and the media. In effect, the only studies that were based on reasonably comprehensive definitions of the Vietnam era veteran population were the *Myths and Realities* study conducted by Louis Harris and Associates (Fischer, Boyle, Bucuvalas, & Schulman, 1980) and the VA's *National Surveys of Veterans* (Hammond, 1980). However, the samples examined in these studies also differed in important ways from the definitions and design employed in the Readjustment Study.

Because of these differences, readers of this report need to gain a general understanding of the characteristics of Vietnam theater and era veterans represented by the NSVG sample. To that end, a "statistical profile" of some major sociodemographic and military characteristics of the Vietnam theater and era veterans is provided in Tables II-1 through II-54 in Volume II. In these tables and in the rest of Chapter II, we have used different terminology to refer to the study's groups of veterans than in the rest of the report. This terminology reflects the fact that "Vietnam theater veterans" and "Vietnam era veterans," as the terms are employed throughout this report, are formally *both* "Vietnam era veterans" or "veterans of the Vietnam era." Thus, in Tables II-1 through II-54, these groups are described as "Vietnam theater veterans," "*other* Vietnam era veterans," and "all veterans of the Vietnam era." In this descriptive profile, the terms "Vietnam theater" and "Vietnam era" or "era" will also be used to describe the two major subgroups, while the terms "all veterans of the Vietnam era" or "all Vietnam era veterans" will be used only to describe the entire population of veterans serving during the Vietnam era.

The data in these tables are based on the self-reports of veterans interviewed in the NSVG, properly weighted to account for different probabilities of selection and further adjusted to compensate for interview-level nonresponse (see Appendix B in Volume II). We have provided separate estimates of characteristics for males and females and, within each group, for veterans who served in the Vietnam theater of operations (Vietnam theater veterans) and for those who served elsewhere during the Vietnam era (other Vietnam era veterans). We have also included overall estimates for all male veterans of this era, all female veterans, and all veterans who served during the Vietnam era—males and females combined. In addition, we have provided tests of statistical significance by sex separately for theater and other era veterans. We have also provided tests for contrasts by theater versus other era veteran status separately for men and women. This profile provides a general picture of the population described by this sample, the population represented by all other estimates provided in this report.

As described in Appendix B, the population of inference for the NSVG component of the Readjustment Study was the 8,269,881 veterans who served during the Vietnam era. An estimated 3,150,811 of these veterans (38.1 percent) served in the Vietnam theater of operations as defined by the study (stationed in Vietnam, Laos, or Cambodia, stationed in the waters in or around these countries, or flew air missions over these areas). The remaining 5,119,070 *other* Vietnam era veterans served in the United States, Europe, Korea, at sea, or elsewhere in the military during the Vietnam era. Of those serving in or around Vietnam, an estimated 3,143,645 were men and 7,166 were women. Of the over five million other Vietnam era veterans, an estimated 4,863,851 were men and 255,219 were women. The proportions presented for these groups in Tables II-1 through II-54 may be applied to these population totals to derive a general idea of the numbers of men and women who have these various characteristics.

BACKGROUND CHARACTERISTICS OF THE VETERANS
(Tables II-1 through II-6)

Gender and Year of Birth

As derivable from the population totals described above, fully 97 percent of these veterans were men—99.8 percent of the theater veterans and 95.0 percent of other era veterans. A majority were born between 1940 and 1949 (current age 39–48), but year of birth varied significantly by group. Over one-fourth of the women who served in the Vietnam theater were born before 1940 (current age 49 and above), and over one-third of the male Vietnam era veterans were born after 1949 (current age 38 and below). Over half of both male theater veterans and female era veterans were born during the second half of the decade of the 1940s (1945–1949).

Race and Ethnicity

Eighty-seven percent of all Vietnam era veterans were White and 11 percent were Black, with the only notable deviation from this pattern observed among Vietnam theater veteran women, 97 percent of whom were White and only 2 percent Black. By comparison, 84.7 percent of the total U.S. population in 1986 was White and 12.2 percent Black (U.S. Bureau of the Census, 1987). Approximately 5 percent of all veterans of the Vietnam era reported that they were of Hispanic origin (compared with 7.5 percent of the total population of the United States in 1986), of whom over half (2.6 percent) were Mexican American and another one-fourth (1.1 percent) of Puerto Rican descent. A higher proportion of Vietnam theater than other era veteran men were of Hispanic origin. In addition, Vietnam theater veteran men were more often Hispanic than were theater veteran women.

Birthplace and Family Size

Approximately one out of three veterans of the Vietnam era was born in the South and another 30 percent in the north central states, with only 12 percent born in the western states.[1] These proportions reflect quite closely the distribution of the total U.S. population living in these areas in 1950 (just after the end of the decade in which most of these veterans were born): 31.2 percent in the South, 29.4 percent in the north central states,

---

[1]The regions and subregions referenced in this report are those established by the U.S. Bureau of the Census (1982; 1987). The *Northeast* includes both New England (Maine, New Hampshire, Vermont, Massachusetts, Rhode Island, and Connecticut) and the middle Atlantic states (New York, New Jersey, and Pennsylvania). The *North Central* (or *Midwest*) includes the east north central states (Ohio, Indiana, Illinois, Michigan, and Wisconsin) and west north central states (Minnesota, Iowa, Missouri, North Dakota, South Dakota, Nebraska, and Kansas). The *South* includes the south Atlantic states (Delaware, Maryland, Virginia, West Virginia, North Carolina, South Carolina, Georgia, and Florida), including the District of Columbia, and the east south central states (Arkansas, Louisiana, Oklahoma, and Texas). The *West* includes the Mountain states (Montana, Idaho, Wyoming, Colorado, New Mexico, Arizona, Utah, and Nevada) and Pacific states (Washington, Oregon, California, Alaska, and Hawaii).

and 13.3 percent in the West (U.S. Bureau of the Census, 1982). The one notable exception was among Vietnam theater veteran women, who were predominantly born in the north central states and the Northeast (rather than the South). Family sizes while growing up were quite similar for all subgroups of Vietnam era veterans, with the majority reporting one to three siblings.

MILITARY SERVICE CHARACTERISTICS
(Tables II-7 through II-29)

Time of Enlistment

A near majority of all Vietnam era veterans entered active duty during the period 1965–1969 (47.9 percent), but over 25 percent entered before the beginning or build-up of the Vietnam war (1940–1964), and over one-third of both male and female Vietnam era veterans entered after 1969. By contrast, over 60 percent of both male and female Vietnam theater veterans entered the military during the critical build up period for the war (1965–1969). Consistent with their places of birth, the majority of all Vietnam era veterans entered the military from the South and the north central states, except for the theater veteran women (north central states and Northeast). The majority was working at the time, but one-third was in school or training. Both theater veteran men and women were more likely to be working than other era veterans, with era veteran men more likely to be in school and era veteran women more likely to be unemployed before entering the service.

Method of Enlistment

Over 25 percent were drafted, but the vast majority (almost 70 percent) enlisted, 56 percent voluntarily and 11 percent to "avoid the draft" (based on their self-reports). Moreover, men who served in the Vietnam theater and those who served elsewhere were equally likely to have enlisted, either voluntarily or otherwise. Reflecting their predominant military occupation as nurses, four of ten women who served in the Vietnam theater received direct commissions. Half of all veterans of this era served in the Army, but the distribution varied considerably by subgroup. A higher proportion of male theater veterans served in the Army and Marines, whereas larger proportions of male era veterans served in the Air Force. Similarly, almost 80 percent of women serving in Vietnam were in the Army, whereas higher proportions of era veteran women were in the Navy and Marine Corps.

Other Military Service

Over 7 percent of all veterans of the Vietnam era served during the Korean conflict as well, and 20 percent between the end of that war and our involvement in Vietnam. Almost 11 percent also served after the Vietnam era, including one-fourth of all women veterans. Over 40 percent of both male and female Vietnam theater veterans had foreign or sea duty other than in Vietnam, as well as two-thirds of the men and one-third of the women not serving in the Vietnam theater. Similarly, 5–10 percent of all groups other than era veteran women had been exposed to combat situations in places other than in Vietnam.

Time of Service and Rank

A large plurality of all groups (42–55 percent), except for female theater veterans, served only one to three years on active duty. Nevertheless, over half of the female theater veterans served more than four years and one-fifth served 20 years or more. Comparable proportions for men serving in Vietnam were 29 and 14 percent respectively. Consistent with this pattern, 54 percent of the women serving in the Vietnam theater reenlisted or extended their period of active duty service, compared with less than one-third of the men serving there and one-fifth of the other Vietnam era veteran women. Overall, 96 percent of all veterans of the Vietnam era served in the enlisted ranks at some time during their period of active duty, over 40 percent became noncommissioned officers, less than 1 percent became warrant officers, and 6 percent became commissioned officers. Over three-fourths of all Vietnam era veterans achieved a highest military rank of noncommissioned officer (grades E4–E9), while approximately 15 percent were below these ranks (grades E1–E3) and 7 percent were commissioned or warrant officers (grades 01–06, W1–W4). Among women, we noted some dramatic differences, however; for example, almost 60 percent of the women era veterans attained only the junior enlisted ranks (E1–E4). In contrast, close to 90 percent of women theater veterans were commissioned officers (01–06), one-fourth in the highest pay grades (e.g., major, lieutenant colonel, or colonel in the Army). Consistent with general promotion trends in the military, men serving in Vietnam also achieved significantly higher rank than those serving elsewhere in the military.

Disciplinary Actions

Over 30 percent of veterans serving during the Vietnam era received some form of disciplinary action (court-martial or nonjudicial punishment) while on active duty—32 percent for all Vietnam era veteran men, compared with less than 2 percent for women serving in Vietnam and 17 percent among other era veteran women. Specifically, 28 percent of all Vietnam era veteran men received an Article 15 or other form of nonjudicial punishment (for example, Captain's Mast, Office Hours) and 13 percent of women (1 percent among theater veterans). Only 4 percent of all veterans of the Vietnam era reported receiving a court-martial (less than 1 percent of the women), and the men serving in Vietnam were more than twice as likely as other era veteran men to have received one.

Discharge

Close to half of all veterans of the Vietnam era were released from active duty between 1970 and 1974, but three-eighths of the men were released *before* 1970 and over one-third of the women left the service *after* 1974. In particular, women serving in the Vietnam theater were twice as likely as men to have left the service in 1975 or later. Reported pay grades at discharge parallel closely the highest ever achieved (described above), but a distinct (though small) trend exists among both theater and era veteran men to have been discharged in lower enlisted pay grades than the highest *ever* achieved while in the service. Almost 96 percent of all Vietnam era veterans received an honorable discharge, including virtually all (99.5 percent) theater veteran women. Six out of ten veterans of the Vietnam era were released from active duty at the end of a normal term of service, and another 19 percent through the "early out program" or mandated reduction in force. Just under 10 percent, however, retired from the military, including 14 percent of the men and 18 percent of the women serving in the Vietnam theater. Over 30 percent of women veterans not serving in Vietnam were released owing to marriage, pregnancy, or children.

Service in the Reserves or National Guard, Participation in Veterans' Organizations, and Service-Connected Disability

One in four veterans serving on active duty during the Vietnam era also served in the Reserves or National Guard (either before or after their active duty service), and theater veteran women were significantly more likely to have done so (32.2 percent versus 22.1 percent) than men serving in or around Vietnam. Among all veterans of this era, three of ten had also been members of a veterans organization since leaving the military, and 19 percent were currently members, though such membership varied a great deal among subgroups. Among those serving in the Vietnam theater, approximately 40 percent of the men had ever been members, and almost one-third of the women, with approximately 25 percent of each group still being members. By contrast, three-fourths of the other era veterans had never been members. Approximately eight of ten veterans in all groups had had some contact with the VA. Among Vietnam theater veterans, 20 percent of the men and closer to one-fourth of the women had applied for—and 13 and 20 percent, respectively, had received—a service-connected disability. Though theater veteran men were more likely to have received such a disability than other male era veterans, their "service-connected" receipt rate was still significantly lower than among women serving in the Vietnam theater.

CHARACTERISTICS OF SERVICE IN THE VIETNAM THEATER
(Tables II-30 through II-40)

Time of Service

Comparisons under this heading are relevant only to Vietnam theater veterans, men and women serving in the Vietnam theater of operations. Overall, the "peak" years in which men began their first Vietnam-related tours of duty were 1967–1969; for women, the peak years were 1968–1970. Overall, a higher proportion of men than women first entered Vietnam in the years preceding 1968, and a lower proportion than women entered in 1968 or later. Correspondingly, men were most likely to have ended their Vietnam tours in 1968–1970 and women in 1969–1971. Overall, just under one-fifth of the men served more than one period of duty in Vietnam, compared with less than one in 20 women. Over three-eighths of the men and close to two-thirds of the women served in Vietnam 12 months, with one-third of the men and 17 percent of the women serving 13 months or more. However, substantial proportions of both men and women—30 and 20 percent, respectively—served less than a 12-month tour. Other than IV Corps, where 7 percent served, men were relatively evenly distributed throughout the four military regions, while over half of the women served in III Corps (the region that included Saigon). Similarly, over 80 percent of the men, and all but 5 percent of the women, were stationed in Vietnam proper, with 17 percent of the men and 4 percent of the women having duty in the waters in or around Vietnam and 6 percent of the men involved in air missions over Vietnam.

Decorations

Over 25 percent of the men and 6 percent of the women reported receiving a combat medal for service in Vietnam, and approximately the same proportions of men and women were wounded or injured in the Vietnam theater, 19 and 1 percent in combat respectively. In turn, 13 percent of the men and 1 percent of the women reported receiving a Purple Heart, and 7 percent and 3 percent, respectively, reported spending time in a military hospital after leaving the Vietnam theater. Less than 1 percent of the theater veterans reported being a prisoner of war (POW).

CURRENT CHARACTERISTICS
(Tables II-41 through II-54)

Family Status

Three-fourths of all veterans of the Vietnam era were married, but only half of both theater and era veteran women were. One-fourth of the era veteran women were divorced and three-tenths of the theater veteran women had never married. By comparison, in the total U.S. population, 78–84 percent of the men and 76 percent of the women aged 35–54 in 1986 were married (U.S. Bureau of the Census, 1987). Four-fifths of the men serving during the Vietnam era and two-thirds of the women had children, with men serving in the Vietnam theater having more children than theater veteran women (predominantly reflecting differences in the numbers "never married"). Over 50 percent of the women serving in Vietnam had no children, compared with less than 20 percent of the men.

Educational Status

One-third of all Vietnam era veterans were high school graduates, and an additional 40 percent had some college education. By comparison, 39 percent of all men and women in the United States aged 35–44 in 1986 were high school graduates, 21 percent had some college, and 26 percent were college graduates or higher (U.S. Bureau of the Census, 1987). Those serving in Vietnam did not differ substantially on education from those who served elsewhere, although women serving in Vietnam (predominantly nurses) were significantly better educated than were theater veteran men.

Occupational Status

Ninety percent of all veterans of the Vietnam era were working, and men serving in Vietnam and those serving elsewhere did not differ in this regard. However, Vietnam theater veteran women were more likely to be retired than men serving in Vietnam and other era veteran women. Among those who worked at a civilian occupation, the distributions of jobs by socioeconomic status did not differ significantly between men who served in Vietnam and other male era veterans, but two-thirds of the theater veteran women fell into one category (that associated with nursing).

Income

The distributions of family income levels for veterans of the Vietnam era were also relatively even, with 18.6 percent reporting incomes of less than $20,000 and 23.1 percent reporting $50,000 or more. Veterans' households were considerably more affluent than U.S. households as a whole in 1986, 40 percent of which had incomes of less than $20,000 and 17 percent reporting $50,000 or more (U.S. Bureau of the Census, 1987). However, women who served in Vietnam reported higher incomes than both theater veteran men and other women veterans of the Vietnam era. That this figure is not entirely a function of their status as professional nurses (or their own salaries per se) is suggested by their significantly lower levels of reported personal income relative to theater veteran males, although their personal incomes were still significantly higher than for era veteran women.

Place of Residence

Partially in contrast to their regions of birth and from where they entered the military, a plurality of all Vietnam era veterans reported currently living in the South (close to 40 percent), with the other three regions being quite similar in their proportions of the remaining population. In part, these shifts reflect general changes in the population distribution of the United States from 1950 to 1986, at which time 34 percent of the population lived in the South, 21 percent in the Northeast, 25 percent in the Midwest (north central states), and 20 percent in the West (U.S. Bureau of the Census, 1987). This distribution was relatively similar within all subgroups, except for era veteran women, who were significantly more likely (than era veteran men) to live in the West. Similarly, over 40 percent of all veterans of the Vietnam era were living in a small town or city (under 50,000 people). Theater veteran women, however, were more likely than men serving in Vietnam to live in a suburb or large city and less likely to live in a small town or city or in open country. Overall, the majority of all Vietnam era veterans had lived in their current communities for more than 10 years, with both the theater and other era veteran men having been less mobile than theater and other era veteran women, respectively. The majority of all veterans of the Vietnam era had also lived at their current residence for more than five years, with other era veteran women being more mobile than era veteran men and theater veteran women. Approximately 30 percent of all these veterans were living in households with four people, although 50 percent lived in households with one to three people (with 14 percent living alone). Theater veteran women were twice as likely as theater veteran men to be living alone (22.2 percent versus 11.3 percent) and had smaller households in general.

Religious Affiliation

Among all Vietnam era veterans, 58 percent were Protestant, 22 percent Catholic, and 17 percent had no religious preference. By comparison, 59 percent of the total U.S. population in 1986 identified themselves as Protestant, 27 percent as Catholic, 6 percent as "other," and 8 percent as "no preference" (U.S. Bureau of the Census, 1987). Theater veteran women were more than twice as likely to be Catholic (36.4 percent) as other era veteran women (15.9 percent), and significantly more likely than theater veteran men to be Catholic, Methodist, or Reformation Era Protestant (for example, Presbyterian, Lutheran, Congregationalist, or Episcopalian). Vietnam theater and other Vietnam era veteran women were also significantly more likely than theater and era veteran men, respectively, to report frequent church attendance.

CONCLUSIONS

In sum, the study shows substantial variation in the characteristics of the four basic subgroups of veterans serving during the Vietnam era, particularly between those serving in the Vietnam theater of operations and elsewhere—especially between theater and era veteran women. In particular, though the majority of these veterans fit our general conception of young "citizen soldiers" (that is, draftees and one-term enlistees who dominated the military numerically throughout the Vietnam era), these samples also contained substantial proportions of reenlistees and career military personnel—many now retired—whose attitudes, experiences, and readjustment to civilian life may quite plausibly differ considerably from the majority. More detail on these and other characteristics of the veterans of the Vietnam era is provided in Tables II-1 through II-54 in Volume II.

CHAPTER III

Evidence of Stress Reactions

COMMENTARY

The standard approach to answering questions about the prevalence of PTSD or any other disorder is to report the number of individuals who meet the full criteria for the diagnosis. In this chapter we complement the standard approach, which is presented in Chapter IV, by providing separate findings on the frequency of traumatic life events, and the cardinal symptoms of reexperiencing, avoidance, and arousal in the various study groups.

This approach provides information about frequency of traumatic life events and levels of stress symptomatology in a way that is not constrained by the formal decision rules of DSM-III-R, the official diagnostic system of the American Psychiatric Association. For a person to receive a diagnosis of PTSD using the DSM-III-R decision rules, he or she must have experienced an event outside the range of usual human experience (criterion A), have at least one of four reexperiencing symptoms (criterion B), at least three of seven avoidance symptoms (criterion C), and at least two of six arousal symptoms (criterion D). This "one from category B, three from Category C, and two from category D" approach has certain advantages in arriving at an overall yes/no diagnostic decision about PTSD. However, it has the disadvantage of not profiling the patterns of the components that make up the syndrome. Chapter III provides this dimensional rather than categorical view of PTSD.

People are often reluctant to remember or discuss traumatic events because of the painful emotions triggered by the recollections. In an effort to overcome the natural reluctance to share such events in a first-time encounter with the interviewer, multiple opportunities were provided during the interview to identify the events. As an alternative strategy to directly asking for a history of traumatic events, when symptoms such as unbidden daytime images or nightmares were reported the respondents were asked if these were based on real experiences.

A broad net was cast to capture the varied dimensions of trauma, including combat exposure, abusive violence, and deprivation. A comprehensive set of civilian traumatic events was surveyed as well. For each traumatic event that was identified, further probes explored the degree of personal participation in the event. For a combat soldier, hearing about an atrocity is very different from witnessing one, which is in turn different from direct participation in it.

In general the results were as expected. Both male and female theater veterans, particularly those with high war-zone-stress exposure, reported more traumatic events and more frequent reexperiencing, avoidance, and arousal symptoms. However, there were some surprise findings as well. For female theater veterans there was a stronger relationship between extent of exposure to war-zone stress and severity of symptoms than was seen for males. For Hispanic males, higher war-zone-stress exposure was associated most strongly with the one particular symptom group, that of avoidance.

CHAPTER OVERVIEW

This chapter examines the prevalence of the component criterion symptoms for diagnosing PTSD as described in the 1987 edition of the *Diagnostic and Statistical Manual of Mental Disorders* (DSM-III-R) of the American Psychiatric Association. The etiological criterion for PTSD requires that the person must have been exposed to one or more traumatic events—events that are psychologically distressing and outside the range of usual human experience. The phenomenological characteristics of PTSD involve three classes of symptoms: reexperiencing of the traumatic event, avoidance of stimuli associated with the event or numbing of general responsiveness, and increased arousal. Examples of reexperiencing phenomena include recurrent, intrusive, and distressing memories or dreams of the event(s). Avoidance and numbing symptoms include deliberate efforts to avoid or escape thoughts or feelings associated with the event(s) and feelings of detachment or estrangement from others that develop after the trauma. Symptoms of increased arousal include difficulty falling or staying asleep, hypervigilance, exaggerated startle response, and physiologic reactivity in the face of events that symbolize or resemble an aspect of the traumatic event.

One of the study's most notable findings was that the lifetime prevalence of experiencing traumatic events was significantly different among the various comparison groups. Vietnam theater veterans were significantly more likely to report having experienced traumatic events than era veterans and civilian counterparts. Particularly striking was the finding that male Vietnam theater veterans who were most involved in the war (i.e., had high levels of exposure to war-zone stress) were 14 times more likely to report having experienced one or more traumatic events than were their civilian counterparts.

THE TRAUMATIC EVENT

As defined by DSM-III-R (American Psychiatric Association, 1987), PTSD is a syndrome characterized by four major criteria: (1) the occurrence of an event that is "outside the range of usual human experience and that would be markedly distressing to almost anyone"; (2) persistent, intrusive, and distressing reexperiencing of that event; (3) persistent avoidance of stimuli associated with the event; and (4) persistent symptoms of increased arousal. DSM-III-R, published by the American Psychiatric Association, serves as the standard for defining mental illness in the United States. The description of PTSD in DSM-III-R provides guidance as to what constitutes an event that is "outside the range . . . and markedly distressing . . .," and also identifies the specific symptoms that provide evidence that the reexperiencing, avoidance, and increased arousal criteria are present. Exhibit III-1 presents the full DSM-III-R definition of PTSD. In the following sections of this chapter, we provide the NSVG findings on the lifetime prevalence of exposure to traumatic events and of the symptoms that constitute the PTSD syndrome.

The NSVG interview contained questions aimed at assessing respondents' lifetime exposure to major stressors (for example, military service in the Vietnam war zone or severe marital difficulties leading to separation and divorce), as well as lifetime exposure to specific military and nonmilitary traumatic events (for example, surviving an enemy rocket attack, a civilian house fire, or an airliner crash in which others were critically injured). The interview was purposely designed to allow respondents *multiple opportunities* to tell the interviewer about traumatic events that had occurred at any time during their lives. The interview provided both direct and indirect opportunities for such expression, on the theory that for at least some respondents, direct questioning might not be the most

EXHIBIT III-1
DSM-III-R Diagnostic Criteria for PTSD

A. The person has experienced an event that is outside the range of usual human experience and that would be markedly distressing to almost anyone (for example, serious threat to one's life or physical integrity; serious threat or harm to one's children, spouse, or other close relatives and friends; sudden destruction of one's home or community; or seeing another person who has recently been, or is being, seriously injured or killed as the result of an accident or physical violence).

B. The traumatic event is persistently reexperienced in at least one of the following ways:

   (1) recurrent and intrusive distressing recollections of the event (in young children, repetitive play in which themes or aspects of the trauma are expressed)
   (2) recurrent distressing dreams of the event
   (3) sudden acting or feeling as if the traumatic event were recurring (includes a sense of reliving the experience, illusions, hallucinations, and dissociative [flashback] episodes, even those that occur upon awakening or when intoxicated)
   (4) intense psychological distress at exposure to events that symbolize or resemble an aspect of the traumatic event, including anniversaries of the trauma

C. Persistent avoidance of stimuli associated with the trauma or numbing of general responsiveness (not present before the trauma), as indicated by at least three of the following:

   (1) efforts to avoid thoughts or feelings associated with the trauma
   (2) efforts to avoid activities or situations that arouse recollections of the trauma
   (3) inability to recall an important aspect of the trauma (psychogenic amnesia)
   (4) markedly diminished interest in significant activities (in young children, loss of recently acquired developmental skills such as toilet training or language skills)
   (5) feeling of detachment or estrangement from others
   (6) restricted range of affect (for example, unable to have loving feelings)
   (7) sense of a foreshortened future (for example, does not expect to have a career, marriage, or children, or a long life)

D. Persistent symptoms of increased arousal (not present before the trauma), as indicated by at least two of the following:

   (1) difficulty falling or staying asleep
   (2) irritability or outbursts of anger
   (3) difficulty concentrating
   (4) hypervigilance
   (5) exaggerated startle response
   (6) physiologic reactivity upon exposure to events that symbolize or resemble an aspect of the traumatic event (for example, a woman who was raped in an elevator breaks out in a sweat when entering any elevator)

productive way of eliciting information about events that were painful to recall and describe.[1]

Interviewers first raised the issue of exposure to major life stressors and potential traumatic events explicitly in NSVG interviews with Vietnam veterans during the interview's second hour, when respondents were asked to describe details of their Vietnam experience. This description included a thorough assessment of the veteran's exposure to combat and to other war-zone stressors. We used information collected in this portion of the interview to develop various indices of exposure to various types of war-zone stress (for example, combat, abusive violence, deprivation), and to create a summary index of exposure (see Appendix C for full details of the NSVG assessment of exposure to war-zone stress).

Somewhat later in the interview, we included sections addressing the lifetime occurrence of specific "stressful" and "traumatic" events. These sections provided respondents with the opportunity to tell the interviewer about other stressful and traumatic experiences that may have occurred during their lives, including those not related to their military service. First, the section on stressful life events inquired about the occurrence during the past year of 12 specific types of stressful experiences (including such things as serious illness, death of a family member, loss of a job, and ending of an important personal relationship). These experiences, although

---

[1]NSVG interviews were conducted by experienced survey research interviewers, trained in administering the NSVG interview in a ten-day training session. In addition to covering the mechanics of the interview process, the training also focused on issues of interviewer sensitivity. During this stage of training, the trainers helped interviewers identify the parts of the interview that were most likely to evoke emotional responses from respondents, to recognize the behavioral cues indicating emotional reactivity, and manage emotionality should it occur. This portion of the training was provided by a team of recognized expert clinicians experienced in diagnosing and treating stress disorders, particularly among combat veterans.

In addition to this training, we established support networks for both respondents and interviewers. Interviewers carried with them to each interview a list of local mental health treatment resources (for example, Vet Centers and mental health centers) in the event that the respondent requested referral information. In addition, we instructed interviewers to report to the clinical training team anything "unusual" that occurred in their contacts with respondents. The clinician would then review the facts of the case with the interviewer, and they would together decide on a course of action (for example, the clinician might call the respondent to make a treatment referral). Finally, each respondent was followed up by phone a week or so after the interview and asked specifically about the interview and its impact. During this phone call, we offered referral assistance to those who requested it.

The number of interviews in which respondents were distressed was quite small, and no reactions were severe. These few cases were resolved by applying the above procedures in a manner that addressed the individual needs and specific circumstances of the respondent.

Interviewers had both professional and peer supports to help them. In addition to their special training, interviewers had access to clinical backup (for advice, support, and other needs) at all times. In addition, we scheduled conference calls for small groups of interviewers with members of the training team to provide peer support and to allow interviewers to benefit from the experiences of their colleagues.

stressful, are the kinds of things that happen to many people at some time in their lives, and are actually not "outside the range of usual human experience." Thus, they do not meet the DSM-III-R defined criteria for traumatic events.

These stressful-life-event questions were followed by a series of questions about potentially traumatic events. The interviewer differentiated these from the stressful life events by noting that: "We've just been talking about events that happen to most people. Now we'd like to talk about *unusual* events that are extraordinarily stressful or disturbing—things that do *not* happen to most people, but when they do, they can be frightening, upsetting, or distressing to almost everyone. By that I mean things like being in a war or heavy combat, being physically assaulted or raped, being in a major earthquake or flood or a very serious accident or fire, seeing other people killed or dead, or experiencing some other type of disastrous event." This transition was intended to help screen out the less serious events (for example, divorces) at this point.

The interviewer then asked specifically whether any of the following ten types of traumatic events had ever happened to the respondent: specific combat or war-related traumatic experiences (included here to give the respondent another opportunity to describe combat-related events); serious accidents or crashes involving a car, boat, or train, or other similar serious accidents or crashes (not war related); large fires or explosions (not war related); serious accidents involving industrial or farm equipment; natural disasters such as tornadoes, hurricanes, floods, or major earthquakes; physical assaults, torture, rape, abuse, or mugging (not war related); seeing someone who was mutilated, seriously injured, or violently killed (not war related); being in serious danger of dying or being seriously injured; receiving news of the mutilation, serious injury, or violent or very unexpected death of someone close; or experiencing any other very stressful event like these.

Finally, the interviewer followed these probes with a question about the existence of "any experiences like these that you feel you can't tell us about." This last question was included on the basis of our field test experience that some persons were willing to acknowledge that such events had taken place but they would or could not describe them.

For each category in which the respondent reported having experienced an event, the interviewer asked a fixed set of probes about each event of the type. These probes were intended to provide information that could serve as the basis for deciding whether the event met the DSM-III-R definitional criteria for a traumatic event, and were aimed at determining the respondent's degree of personal involvement in the event (that is, did he or she experience the event personally, hear about the event, or come upon the aftermath?), the level of personal danger involved, and so on. As a memory aid and to help assure that the list was as complete as possible, the interviewer kept a list of the events visible to the respondent.

In addition, a later section of the interview continued questions about psychiatric symptoms, including the symptoms of PTSD. Questions about symptoms that required linkage to a specific traumatic event for the PTSD diagnosis to be made (for example, recurrent distressing dreams must be referrable to the specific traumatic event or events to be symptoms of PTSD) were asked in such a way as not to force the respondent to link the event and the symptom. For example, when persons responded positively to the question asking whether they had experienced a period of "repeated bad dreams or nightmares," the interviewer asked whether those dreams or nightmares reminded them in some way "of an experience or experiences that [they] had." Those who said Yes were asked whether the experience was one that had been listed earlier (the respondent still had in front of him or her the "traumatic events list" that was created earlier). If so, the interviewer noted which experience it was and moved on; if not, the interviewer added this new event to the list and asked the standard probes about it. In this way, a more complete list of potentially traumatic events was developed.

All "traumatic events" described by respondents were subsequently rated for severity by a trained coder. The rating involved separate judgments about the two factors that criterion A requires of a traumatic event: (1) that an event be "outside the range of usual human experience," and (2) that the event be capable of producing symptoms of distress in nearly anyone. Judgments about the former were made on a four-point scale:

1 = commonplace event (happens frequently to many people)
2 = typical event (happens to many people, but not frequently)
3 = a typical event (not commonplace, but not clearly outside the range of usual human experience)
4 = event clearly outside the range of usual human experience

Judgments about the severity of the stress associated with the event were made using the stressor scale of Axis IV of DSM-III-R. This seven-level scale contains the following values:

1 = not stressful
2 = minimal stress
3 = mild stress
4 = moderate stress
5 = severe stress
6 = extreme stress
7 = catastrophe

Coders were trained in using these scales, and we carefully monitored their ratings. Coding was done conservatively, so that ambiguities were resolved in favor of the lower rating. In addition, coders assigned content codes indicating the nature of the event to each reported event.

A lifetime traumatic-events variable (criterion A) was created by combining the values of the severity and content ratings and categorizing them into a four-level index:

1. no traumatic event
2. possible traumatic event
3. probable traumatic event
4. definite traumatic event

Table III-1 in Volume II shows the NSVG group estimates for the traumatic events index and the results of contrasts among the major study groups and subgroups.

The results of the contrasts among male theater veterans, era veterans, and civilians were striking. Theater veterans were significantly more likely to report ever having experienced traumatic events than era veterans and civilian counterparts. In fact, over four times as many male theater veterans as era veterans reported events that were judged to be definite trauma, while eight times as many male theater veterans as civilians reported clearly traumatic events. The magnitude of these statistically significant differences was even greater when male theater veterans who were exposed to high levels of war-zone stress were compared with male era veterans and civilian counterparts. A remarkable 75.2 percent of male theater veterans who were exposed to high levels of war-zone stress described at least one specific and clearly traumatic event. This is more than eight times greater than the estimate for male era veterans (9.2 percent) and 14 times greater than the rate for civilian counterparts (5.2 percent). Thus, three out of four men who were exposed to high levels of war-zone stress in Vietnam also described one or more discrete events that were judged to be definitely traumatic.[2]

---

[2] In the NVVRS, *war-zone stress* and *traumatic events* are separate variables that are aimed at measuring closely related concepts but are operationalized differently and assessed independently. War-zone-stress exposure is a dimensional measure of the degree of exposure to circumstances and events in Vietnam that were dangerous, threatening, and/or unpleasant. Therefore, it is a risk factor for the occurrence of traumatic events (that is, the higher the level of war-zone-stress exposure, the higher is the probability of the occurrence of a traumatic event in the person's life). Traumatic events are defined as the respondent's report of the lifetime occurrence of one or more specific events that were clearly "outside the range of usual human experience and markedly distressing." Although the NVVRS research team recognizes that exposure to high levels of war-zone stress (for example, frequent long-range patrols in hostile enemy territory) placed theater veterans at increased risk for exposure to specific traumatic events in Vietnam (for example, surviving an ambush in which several comrades were killed or wounded), we also

Nearly a third of Vietnam theater veterans who were exposed to low levels of war-zone stress also reported definite traumatic experiences. Contrasts between low/moderate-exposure theater veterans and male era veterans and male civilian counterparts of the traumatic-events variable were statistically significant, in that low/moderate-exposure theater veterans were more likely to report having experienced specific traumatic events. The finding that 32.9 percent of low/moderate-exposure male theater veterans reported events that were classified as definite trauma indicates that a high proportion of the men who experienced comparatively low level of overall stress in the Vietnam war zone nevertheless were exposed to specific traumatic events.

The contrasts for all male racial/ethnic subgroups followed identical patterns. All Hispanic, Black, and White/other male theater veteran study groups (that is, overall, high war zone, and low war zone) were more likely to report specific traumatic events than their male racial/ethnic counterparts among era veterans and civilians. Contrasts between racial/ethnic subgroups of male theater veterans showed a single statistically significant difference for Hispanics versus White/others. However, comparing the distributions of the two groups on the traumatic events variable revealed a complex relationship with no clear trends.

The results for the female study groups were comparable to the findings for males. Female theater veterans as a group were significantly more likely to report exposure to trauma than female era veteran and civilian counterparts. As expected, the highest proportion (43.7 percent) of female theater veterans who suffered at least one clearly traumatic experience were theater veterans who were exposed to high levels of war-zone stress. Contrasts between female theater veterans in both the high and low war-zone stress subgroups and female era veteran and civilian counterparts were statistically significant, and this finding indicates that women who served in the war zone were much more vulnerable to exposure to traumatic experiences than were their era veteran and civilian counterparts.

Not surprisingly, the theater veteran subgroup contrasts for high war-zone versus low/moderate war-zone stress exposure were statistically significant and in the expected direction for both males and females. Theater veterans with a diagnosis of PTSD were more than twice as likely

---

recognize that the relationship between these two variables is not perfect. For example, some NSVG respondents who were exposed to high levels of war-zone stress (based on their responses to questions about specific experiences in Vietnam) reported to the survey interviewer that they managed to complete their tour of duty in Vietnam without experiencing a specific event that they judged to be "extraordinarily stressful or disturbing, . . . frightening, upsetting, or distressing to almost anyone." Conversely, some theater veterans who were exposed to only low levels of war-zone stress described one or more clearly traumatic experiences that occurred in the Vietnam war zone or elsewhere.

to report exposure to a clearly traumatic event than theater veterans without PTSD. In addition, male and female theater veterans with service-connected physical disabilities (SCPDs) were significantly more likely to report exposure to traumatic events than theater veterans without physical disabilities. Also, both male and female theater veterans with lifetime diagnoses of substance abuse disorder were more likely to report lifetime trauma than theater veterans who never abused alcohol or drugs.

THE FREQUENCY OF TRAUMATIC STRESS TODAY

In addition to assessing exposure to trauma, the NSVG interview also assessed the occurrence of stress-reaction symptoms. One component of the multimeasure approach to the assessment of PTSD in the NVVRS was a set of questions in the NSVG interview concerning the occurrence over the course of the respondent's lifetime of the symptoms of PTSD. These questions were keyed to the specific PTSD symptoms as defined by DSM-III-R, and provided information about both onset (that is, when did the symptom first occur?) and recency (when did the symptom occur most recently?). We created separate subscales representing the number of B, C, and D criterion symptoms the respondent has experienced during his or her life. NSVG findings concerning the three major symptom categories—reexperiencing, avoidance, and arousal—are provided in the following sections.

Reexperiencing the War

This section of the diagnostic criteria for PTSD addresses an often dramatic aspect of the disorder: the intrusion into awareness of painful thoughts and feelings that are associated with or directly related to the traumatic event. These recollections are dreaded by the individual, and their uncontrolled and intrusive nature is central to what makes the disorder so troubling, distressing, and disabling. The often unpredictable and unbidden manner in which painful memories intrude upon awareness is not limited to dreams or nightmares. Reexperiencing frequently occurs in waking states, either arising spontaneously or being triggered by external stimuli that are reminiscent of the traumatic event.

The NSVG findings for the number of reexperiencing symptoms experienced are shown in Table III-2. The findings presented are lifetime occurrences of the following set of specific symptoms:

a. recurrent and intrusive recollections of the event
b. recurrent distressing dreams of the event

c. sudden acting or feeling as if the trauma were recurring (for example, flashbacks)

d. intense psychological distress at exposure to events that symbolize or resemble an aspect of the traumatic event, including anniversaries of the trauma

For the diagnosis of PTSD to be made, according to the DSM-III-R criteria, only one of the four specific intrusive reexperiencing symptoms is required. Consequently, those individuals with two or more of the four symptoms might be considered to have a more severe manifestation of the symptom course. However, we must temper our observations by recognizing the differential routes of expression of the psychological sequelae of the experience of traumatic events.

The major contrasts among theater, era, and civilian males show a clear pattern. Theater males reported significantly more lifetime occurrences of intrusive symptoms than did era males or civilian counterpart males. The magnitude of this difference increased strikingly when theater males exposed to high war-zone stressors were compared with era males and civilian counterparts. The high-war-zone-stressor theater males' average estimate of lifetime "B" symptoms is 1.5 as compared with the average estimate for era males of 0.48 and civilian counterpart males of 0.39. Not surprisingly, the comparison between era males and theater males exposed to only low or moderate stressors was not significant. Neither group produced an estimate, when standardized to theater males, that was more than a mean of 0.50.

The pattern of results for the race/ethnicity breakdowns showed both similarities to and differences from the results for all males. The pattern for White/other was identical to that for all males. Theater veterans have experienced significantly more intrusive symptoms than era males and civilian counterparts, and those exposed to high war-zone stressors showed even more dramatic differences. We noted no significant difference between White/other era males and White/other theater males with low or moderate exposure to war-zone stressors.

The results for the Hispanic males were identical except that the nonsignificant difference between the era and low- or moderate-exposure theater groups in the pooled results was significant for the Hispanic males. That is, Hispanic theater males with low or moderate exposure have a mean lifetime estimate of 0.65 as compared with the Hispanic era males whose standardized estimate is 0.18. The comparable estimate for all males was 0.55 versus 0.48. Thus, for Hispanics, the estimate for those with low or moderate war-zone exposure was only slightly higher than for the total male sample, but the estimate for Hispanic era veterans standardized to theater low/moderate-exposure males was quite a bit lower than for the full male sample.

The picture for Black males was more divergent from the results just presented. Surprisingly, for the Black males, the experience of intrusive symptoms was not different for theater and era males. The mean estimates were 0.81 for theater and 0.66 for era males standardized to theater males. The contrast between those theater vets exposed to low/moderate war-zone stressors as against era vets standardized to that group was not significant, in accord with the dominant pattern of results. Finally, high war-zone theater vets have experienced more intrusive symptoms than either era vets or their civilian counterparts. As well, all theater veterans reported more lifetime intrusive symptoms than did their civilian counterparts, when pooled across race/ethnicity groups.

The results for female veterans did not closely parallel those for the males. Overall, the study did not find a significant difference in lifetime experience of intrusive symptoms between theater and era females, theater and civilian counterpart females, or theater females with low or moderate exposure to war-zone stressors. The only significant differences were those between female theater veterans with high exposure to war-zone stress and comparable era and civilian comparisons. The mean estimates were 1.36 versus 0.59 and 0.59 for the three groups respectively. These data suggested that the effect of exposure to war-zone stressors was more directly connected to the experience of intrusive symptoms for females than it was for males.

When we examined the results for theater veterans only, the comparisons among the male ethnic subgroups showed that Hispanics reported more intrusive symptoms than did either Blacks or White/others; the latter two did not differ. For both males and females, as expected, very strong significant differences were present when we compared those with high war-zone stressor exposure with those with moderate or low, and those with a current diagnosis of PTSD with those without a current diagnosis of PTSD. For the PTSD comparison, the average number of lifetime intrusive symptoms for males was four times higher in those with PTSD and for females it was five times higher. The contrast across the levels of war-zone-stress exposure also revealed significant differences for both males and females.

The effect of service-connected disability on lifetime experience of intrusive symptoms was significant only for male veterans, and only when those with high service-connected disability were compared with those without any service-connected disability. The average number of symptoms for the former group was 1.15, whereas for the latter it was only 0.76.

As would be anticipated, given the knowledge about PTSD and its manifestations, those male and female theater veterans having a positive lifetime diagnosis for substance abuse also more often experienced intrusive symptoms. For the males, those without the diagnosis reported an average level of intrusive symptoms of 0.59 as compared with 1.04 for those with the diagnosis. For females, the comparable figures were 0.73 versus 1.52. Though the effects are not quite as dramatic as for exposure to war-zone stressors, substance abuse does appear to be connected to the increased experience of intrusive symptoms in these theater veterans.

For the most part, the lifetime experience of intrusive symptoms follows the pattern that would be predicted. Theater veterans reported higher levels than era veterans or civilians. Those theater veterans with high exposure to war-zone stressors reported higher levels than those without or comparable nontheater groups. Though some racial/ethnic differences were found within the male sample, for the most part the findings did not change radically within ethnic groups. For females, the effect of exposure to war-zone stressor seemed to have a more pronounced effect than for males. Finally, a lifetime diagnosis of substance abuse for theater veterans, male and female, was associated with more experience of intrusive symptoms.

Avoidance of War Reminders

The C criterion stress-reaction symptoms focus on a phenomenon that is conceptually complementary to the reexperiencing symptoms included under criterion B. These are the symptoms of avoidance—avoidance of circumstances that might lead the sufferer to remember the trauma. The avoidance can be either cognitive or affective, and can be expressed directly (for example, by not talking about the experience) or indirectly (for example, through a generalized numbing of responsiveness). Avoidance symptomatology commonly takes the form of deliberate efforts to avoid thoughts or feelings about the traumatic event. The sufferer also avoids activities or situations that arouse recollections of the trauma. This avoidance of reminders is frequently reflected in psychogenic amnesia for an important aspect of the traumatic event.

Numbing of responsiveness, also described as "emotional anesthesia," is commonly expressed as:

- feelings of detachment or estrangement from other people
- loss of the ability to become interested and vitally involved in previously pleasurable activities
- diminished capacity to experience emotions of any type, particularly those associated with intimacy, tenderness, sexuality, and grief

The NSVG group estimates for the number of symptoms of avoidance and numbing of responsiveness (criterion C) are shown in Table III-3 in Volume II. In examining the contrasts among major study groups for all males, much higher lifetime avoidance symptom reports were found for theater veterans when compared with their civilian counterparts. Theater veterans with high war-zone stress exposure had much higher lifetime counts than both era veterans and civilian counterparts. These findings were consistent with the overall findings of greater stress symptomatology in theater veterans, particularly those with high exposure to war-zone stress. Surprisingly, theater veterans did not report greater avoidance symptomatology as a group when compared with era veteran males. This finding was somewhat perplexing given the highly significant difference in prevalence rates of PTSD in theater veteran males compared with era veteran males. This finding may reflect problems with the sensitivity of the survey interview PTSD symptom instrument.

The subgroup examinations for White/other men revealed that White/other theater men with high exposure the war-zone stress reported significantly greater numbing and avoidance symptomatology when compared with era veteran males or civilian male counterparts. White/other male theater veterans, independent of level of exposure to war-zone stress, showed higher rates of avoidance and numbing symptoms when compared with civilian male counterparts.

Contrasts for Black males on avoidance and numbing symptomatology yielded the following results:

- Black male theater veterans showed significantly greater numbing and avoidance when compared with Black civilian male counterparts.
- Black male theater veterans with high war-zone-stress exposure reported much higher rate of avoidance and numbing symptoms than their civilian male counterparts.
- Black male theater veterans with low/moderate war-zone-stress exposure showed much greater numbing and avoidance symptomatology when compared with Black era veterans.

Contrary to the overall pattern of results, Black era males reported significantly greater avoidance symptoms than Black theater males.

For Hispanic male theater veterans, the contrasts among the major study groups showed the most consistent differences of the three male subgroups. Hispanic male theater veterans reported greater lifetime numbing and avoidance symptoms when compared with Hispanic era veterans. This group also showed a strong trend for greater symptomatology when compared with their civilian counterparts. Further, Hispanic male theater veterans with high war-zone-stress exposure showed much greater avoidance and numbing symptomatology when compared with Hispanic male era veterans and Hispanic male civilian counterparts. Finally, Hispanic male theater veterans who had been exposed to low/moderate war-zone stress also reported greater avoidance and numbing symptoms when compared with Hispanic era veterans. These findings for Hispanic male theater veterans are consistent with the overall high rate of PTSD in this subgroup.

For female theater veterans, the most significant contrasts were found for the subgroup with high exposure to war-zone stress. For that subgroup, higher lifetime avoidance and numbing symptoms were reported when compared with female era veterans and female civilian counterparts. Trends were noted for greater numbing and avoidance symptomatology for female theater veterans when compared with female era veterans and female civilian counterparts. When we contrasted theater veteran subgroups, the race/ethnicity contrasts were strong within male theater veteran groups. Hispanic male theater veterans reported greater avoidance and numbing symptoms when compared with both White/other and Black male theater veterans. This finding was consistent with the overall greater rate of PTSD in Hispanic male theater veterans when compared with White/other and Black male theater veterans.

The study also assessed the role of the level of war-zone-stressor exposure in mediating levels of avoidance and numbing symptomatology in male theater veterans. For both male and female theater veterans, highly significant differences emerged; greater war-zone-stressor exposure was associated with higher rates of numbing and avoidance for both males and females. The strength of these relationships was impressive. For example, for all male theater veterans, 44 percent of those with high war-zone-stress exposure reported two or more avoidance and numbing symptoms compared with only 17 percent of those exposed to low/moderate war-zone stress. Similar distributions were found for female theater veterans. These findings underscore the important mediating role of the level of war-zone-stress exposure in the development of numbing and avoidance symptomatology, a finding consistent with other results for the impact of the level of war-zone-stress exposure on PTSD symptoms.

As was predicted, very marked differences were found in levels of avoidance and numbing symptoms for both male and female theater veterans when we compared those who met current PTSD diagnostic criteria with those who were negative for current PTSD diagnosis. For male theater veterans, 79 percent of those who met current PTSD diagnostic criterian reported one or more lifetime numbing and avoidance symptoms compared with only 22 percent of those who did not meet current PTSD diagnostic criteria. Further, 40 percent of theater male veterans who met current PTSD diagnostic criteria reported four or more lifetime numbing and avoidance symptoms compared with only 4 percent of male theater veterans who did not meet current PTSD diagnostic criteria. Similarly striking findings were found for female theater veterans: 48 percent of those who met current PTSD diagnostic criteria reported four or more lifetime numbing and avoidance symptoms, compared with only 9 percent of female theater veterans in the group that did not meet current PTSD diagnostic criteria.

For both male and female theater veterans, level of service-connected physical disability was not strongly related to the number of lifetime numbing and avoidance symptoms.

When lifetime substance abuse diagnosis was crossed with the number of lifetime avoidance and numbing symptoms, the results were striking. For both male and female theater veterans, those with lifetime substance abuse had much higher avoidance and numbing symptoms. This finding was consistent with the overall results of the study in which a strikingly high comorbidity rate emerged for substance abuse and post-traumatic stress disorder. The use of alcohol and drugs in subjects with PTSD often reflected attempts at self-medication in an effort to increase denial and numbing, damp down nightmares and flashbacks, and diminish bothersome symptoms of chronic hyperarousal, including irritability, hypervigilance, and startle reactions.

Secondary Explosions

The third major cluster of PTSD symptoms are the following six symptoms of increased arousal that, by definition, were not present before the trauma:

1. difficulty falling or staying asleep
2. irritability or outbursts of anger
3. difficulty concentrating
4. hypervigilance
5. exaggerated startle response
6. physiological reactivity to events that symbolize or resemble an aspect of the event

In order to meet DSM-III-R criteria for a diagnosis of PTSD, two or more of these symptoms must be present.

Clinical experience suggests that criterion D arousal symptoms are often linked to criterion B reexperiencing symptoms. For example, a combat veteran who cannot fall asleep because he experiences vivid and distressing visualizations of combat events when he tries to sleep often experiences both arousal and reexperiencing symptoms. Nevertheless, criterion D arousal symptoms also occur at times in which they apparently are not associated with criterion B reexperiencing symptoms, but rather reflect persistent arousal from chronic stress reaction. In addition, some preliminary evidence suggests that the criterion D cluster of autonomic hyperarousal symptoms in chronic PTSD may be related to changes in physiology (for example, central and peripheral adrenergic regulation, Friedman, 1988).

In Volume II, Table III-4 shows the NSVG group estimates for the number of lifetime criterion D symptoms of increased arousal and the results of contrasts among the study groups and subgroups. Contrasts among the three major male study groups revealed that differences in the distribution of lifetime criterion D arousal symptoms were statistically significant, with male Vietnam theater veterans *as a group* reporting more symptoms of negative arousal than both male era veterans and civilian counterparts.

When the subgroup of male Vietnam theater veterans who were exposed to high levels of war-zone stress was compared with male era veterans and civilian counterparts on the number of criterion D arousal symptoms, the contrasts were statistically significant. Among male Vietnam veterans with high levels of exposure to war-zone stress, only 37 percent reported that they had never experienced a PTSD arousal symptom, compared with 63 percent of era veterans and 69 percent of civilians. On the other hand, nearly 19 percent of this highly exposed subset of male Vietnam theater veterans reported four or more lifetime criterion D symptoms, in contrast to only 3 percent of male era veterans and less than 2 percent of male civilians.

Among the NSVG female respondents, 38 percent of theater veterans exposed to high levels of war-zone stress reported never experiencing a criterion D arousal symptom, while another 38 percent reported experiencing two or more symptoms of increased arousal at some time in their lives. Contrasts revealed that the number of lifetime criterion D symptoms reported by female theater veterans who were exposed to high levels of war-zone stress differed significantly from the symptom distribution reported by female era veterans. Sixty percent of female era veterans had never experienced a criterion D symptom in their lives, and over 60 percent of their female civilian counterparts had never suffered any of the PTSD symptoms of criterion D.

For the male racial/ethnic subgroups, the contrasts revealed several statistically significant differences. Specifically, White/other male Vietnam theater veterans reported more lifetime arousal symptoms than either male era veterans or their male civilian counterparts. For Black males, the distribution of arousal symptoms among theater veterans differed significantly from the distribution of arousal symptoms for Black civilians, with theater veterans reporting more criterion D symptoms.

Among Hispanic males, the percent distribution of the number of criterion D symptoms for Vietnam theater veterans differed significantly from that of Vietnam era veterans, with theater veterans reporting a greater number of symptoms of adverse arousal. In contrast, the percent distributions of Hispanic theater veterans and civilians did not differ significantly across levels of criterion D symptomatology. When male Hispanic Vietnam theater veterans who experienced high levels of war-zone stress were compared with Hispanic male Vietnam era veterans and civilians, the differences were strikingly large and statistically significant. Whereas only about 31 percent of high-exposure Hispanic theater symptoms reported never having experienced any PTSD arousal symptoms, 67 percent of era veteran and 58 percent of civilian counterparts reported that they have never had a period in their lives when they were bothered by any criterion D symptoms.

Table III-4 also shows the results of three contrasts for racial/ethnic subgroups of male Vietnam theater veterans: White/other versus Black males; White/other versus Hispanic males; and Black versus Hispanic males. From these contrasts, one significant finding emerged: Hispanic male theater veterans reported more criterion D symptoms than White/other male theater veterans. Specifically, roughly 34 percent of Hispanic male theater veterans reported two or more lifetime PTSD arousal symptoms, compared with about 21 percent of White/other male theater veterans.

For both female and male Vietnam theater veterans, the contrasts on number of criterion D symptoms by level of exposure to war-zone stress were statistically significant. Examination of the subgroup estimates by level of war-zone stress (see Table III-4) clearly shows that theater veterans who reported high levels of exposure to the stresses of war endorsed a greater number of criterion D symptoms than did low-exposure veterans. In addition, contrasts on number of PTSD arousal symptoms by substance abuse were also significant. Consistent with the relationship between substance abuse and the number of criteria B and C symptoms, male and female Vietnam theater veterans with a lifetime diagnosis of substance abuse disorder reported more criterion D arousal symptoms than theater veterans who reported no lifetime problems with substance abuse.

CONCLUSIONS

This chapter has examined the component criteria of the diagnosis of PTSD and discussed several notable findings. First, the prevalence of definite traumatic events derived from the NSVG survey was significantly different among the various comparisons in the directions that were expected. For example, male theater veterans exposed to high war-zone stress were nearly 15 times more likely to report definite traumatic events than their civilian counterparts. For both females and males, theater veterans with a diagnosis of PTSD were more than twice as likely to report at least one definite lifetime traumatic event than were theater veterans without PTSD.

Second, the most part, the lifetime prevalence of symptoms of reexperiencing was greater in theater veterans than in era veterans or civilian counterparts. Theater veterans with high levels of exposure to war-zone stressors have more lifetime intrusive symptoms than other theater, era, or civilian groups. Though some racial/ethnic differences existed for males, the findings, for the most part, did not change radically within racial/ethnic groups. High levels of exposure to war-zone stressors seemed to have a more pronounced effect for female theater veterans than for males.

Third, the lifetime prevalence of symptoms of numbing and avoidance for males was greater for theater veterans than for civilians, but did not differ from era veterans. As expected, the lifetime prevalence of numbing and avoidance symptoms was greater for male theater veterans with high war-zone-stressor exposure than for either era or civilian males. The pattern of results for racial/ethnic groups on numbing and avoidance was consistent for the most part with the overall results for males. However, the impact of serving in the Vietnam theater on the development of avoidance symptoms was most striking for Hispanic males but somewhat less consistent for Black males in that Black era males reported slightly but significantly more symptoms than theater males. For female theater veterans, those with high war-zone-stressor exposure reported much greater lifetime numbing and avoidance symptoms than either era or civilian females.

Fourth, the lifetime prevalence of symptoms of increased arousal were greater in theater veterans than in era veterans or civilian counterparts. Theater veterans, both male and female, with high levels of exposure to war-zone stressors showed more lifetime symptoms of increased arousal than other theater, era, or civilian groups. The results of contrasts between racial/ethnic subgroups of males essentially parallel the findings for the overall male population. Hispanic and White/other theater veterans with exposure to high levels of war-zone stress reported significantly more adverse arousal symptoms than era veteran and civilian counterparts. Although Black male theater veterans reported significantly more PTSD arousal symptoms than Black male civilians, no difference existed between rates reported by Black male theater and era veterans. Finally, the theater veteran contrasts for high war-zone versus low war-zone stress were statistically significant and in the expected direction for both males and females.

CHAPTER IV

Evidence of Post-Traumatic Stress Disorder

COMMENTARY

J.S., a Hispanic male veteran, married for more than 20 years with three children, experienced high sustained war-zone-stress exposure; he walked point, was frequently under fire, and was wounded in combat. He began drinking heavily while in Vietnam, has required treatment for alcohol-related internal medical problems, and alcohol remains a serious problem for him today.

T.L., a 38-year-old Black veteran, described his experience in Vietnam this way: "Every time I turned around someone was getting shot, or had a limb blown off, or their guts hanging out. There was nothing you could do for them." From 1970 to the present he has been troubled by the typical symptoms of post-traumatic stress disorder: "Sometimes my thoughts take me right back to what happened to the guys there. I wish I could have helped them." He has attempted to deal with his searing feelings of guilt over having survived while others died and his nightmares of combat through chronic substance abuse. He has had no medical treatment for almost two years and has never sought help from the Veterans Administration.

These cases are clear indications of the profound and long-lasting disruptions that PTSD can bring to the lives of returning veterans. Their plight raises urgent public policy questions. How many Vietnam veterans have developed PTSD at some time since the war? Of those who developed the disorder, how many still have it today? Did it make a difference if you were White, Black, or Hispanic, male or female, saw heavy or limited combat exposure, were younger or older at the time of entering service, or whether you volunteered or were drafted? These and other fundamental questions are addressed in this chapter.

50

This national survey was designed to make the most accurate possible determination of the percent of Vietnam veterans who have PTSD. Two separate studies were undertaken to arrive at the best set of measures for making this determination, the first conducted before the household survey and the second concurrently with it. Because no single structured interview or scale exists to serve as a gold standard for PTSD diagnosis, multiple diagnostic indicators were used. A subsample of the household survey respondents was reinterviewed by expert clinicians and received a structured diagnostic interview, four scales completed by the clinician, five self-report questionnaires, and spouse/partner scales. A composite diagnosis was arrived at by determining the pattern of agreement across the major indicators. The correspondence of this composite diagnosis in the clinical subsample with PTSD measures in the survey was then determined.

Two types of PTSD prevalence were determined; full PTSD syndrome and partial PTSD, the latter reserved for veterans who suffer from many of the core symptoms of PTSD, whose lives are disrupted, who appear to be in urgent need of treatment, but who do not have all the features necessary to receive the full syndrome diagnosis. We also determined what proportion of those with either the full or partial syndrome have recovered with time versus those more deeply afflicted whose anguish has been unremitting.

The results are striking. A disturbingly large proportion of Vietnam theater veterans have PTSD today. For many who developed the disorder two decades ago, time has not brought relief, and problems compound in work and interpersonal functioning. For those whose nightmares, flashbacks, and startle reactions are as intense today as they were on their return, the war is not over. Only the scene of the battlefield has shifted—from the outer to the inner world.

CHAPTER OVERVIEW

Methods for Estimating PTSD Prevalence

To increase the accuracy of the NVVRS estimates of PTSD prevalence, we included multiple PTSD measures in the study. This approach was taken in acknowledgment of the fact that no single PTSD assessment is completely error-free. Therefore, instead of relying on a single PTSD assessment, current PTSD diagnoses in the NVVRS were made on the basis of information from a number of indicators. The PTSD diagnosis based on information from multiple indicators is called the *composite* diagnosis. It is the convergence of information across PTSD indicators, and the cross-measure confirmation of the diagnosis that results from a multimeasure "triangulation" approach, that provides the foundation for the credibility of the NVVRS PTSD prevalence estimates. This "multimeasure triangulation approach" did not specify a positive diagnosis if only one of the measures suggested the presence of PTSD, a strategy sometimes employed when multiple measures are used. Rather, under the procedure employed by the NVVRS, a conflict among multiple measures might lead to either a "negative" or a "positive" diagnosis, depending on the preponderance of evidence.

By definition, a prevalence rate is the percent of a specified population group or subgroup that has a given disorder during a specified period. To address more completely the "service needs assessment" aspect of the Congressional mandate, we decided to present prevalence estimates for two "types" of PTSD: the full PTSD syndrome (as defined by DSM-III-R) and "partial" PTSD. Estimates of the prevalence of "partial" PTSD are estimates of the percent whose stress-reaction symptoms are of either insufficient intensity or breadth to qualify as the full PTSD syndrome, but may still warrant professional attention. People with partial PTSD today may have had a full syndrome in the past that is currently in partial remission, or they may have never met the full criteria for the disorder. Nevertheless, they do have clinically significant stress-reaction symptoms and might benefit from treatment. Thus, they represent an additional component of the total spectrum of potential "need for treatment."

PTSD Prevalence Estimates

An estimated 15.2 percent of all male theater veterans are current cases of PTSD. This represents about 479,000 of the estimated 3.14 million men who served in the Vietnam theater. Among female Vietnam theater veterans, current prevalence is estimated to be 8.5 percent of the estimated 7,166 women who served, or about 610 current cases.

Also for both sexes, current PTSD prevalence rates for theater veterans are consistently higher than rates for comparable era veterans (2.5 percent male, 1.1 percent female) or civilian counterparts (1.2 percent male, 0.3 percent female). These differences are even more striking when Vietnam era veterans and civilians are compared with the subgroup of Vietnam theater veterans exposed to high levels of war-zone stress. Rates of PTSD among the latter are dramatically higher than those observed among theater veterans exposed to low or moderate levels of war-zone stress.

Among theater veteran males, the current PTSD prevalence rate is 27.9 percent among Hispanics, 20.6 percent among Blacks, and 13.7 percent among White/others. Differences among theater veterans, era veterans, and civilian counterparts are also observed within the three race/ethnicity subgroups: theater veteran rates are consistently higher than rates for era veterans or civilians.

Additionally, NVVRS findings indicate that the *current* prevalence of *partial* PTSD is 11.1 percent among male theater veterans and 7.8 percent among female theater veterans. Together, this represents about 350,000 veterans — in addition to the 480,000 with the full PTSD syndrome today — who have trauma-related symptoms that may benefit from professional treatment.

NVVRS findings indicate that the *lifetime* prevalence of PTSD is 30.9 percent among male theater veterans and 26.9 percent among females. The *lifetime* prevalence of *partial* PTSD among male theater veterans is 22.5 percent, and among female theater veterans 21.2 percent. These findings mean that over the course of their lives, more than half (30.9 + 22.5 = 53.4 percent) of male theater veterans and nearly half (26.9 + 21.2 = 48.1 percent) of female theater veterans have experienced clinically significant stress-reaction symptoms. This represents about 1.7 million veterans of the Vietnam war.

A comparison of the current and lifetime PTSD prevalence rates shows that about one-half (49.2 percent) of the male theater veterans and one-third (31.6 percent) of the female theater veterans who have ever had PTSD still have it today. Also, of those theater veterans who have ever had significant stress-reaction symptoms (full or partial PTSD), about half (49.3 percent) of males and one-third (33.9 percent) of females are experiencing some degree of clinically significant stress-reaction symptoms today. These findings are consistent with the conceptualization of PTSD as a chronic, rather than acute, disorder.

Distribution of PTSD Among Vietnam Theater Veterans

Having established the prevalence of PTSD among the major study groups, we then conducted a series of descriptive analyses designed to identify characteristics associated with higher current PTSD prevalence among theater veterans. These analyses help to clarify who among theater veterans has PTSD today. We present here a general summary of the distribution of PTSD according to a selected group of background characteristics, characteristics of military service and service in Vietnam, and current sociodemographic characteristics. We have summarized the findings separately for men and women.

MALE THEATER VETERANS. Men who served in the Army (16.2 percent) or Marine Corps (24.8 percent) are considerably more likely than those who served in the other branches of the Armed Forces to have PTSD today. Across the services, one in four of those who served in the junior enlisted pay grades (E1–E3) currently have PTSD. By far the lowest rate of PTSD is among those who served on active duty 20 or more years (5.6 percent), while those who served more than four but less than 20 years have the highest rate (24.8 percent).

Somewhat surprisingly, the particular period during which male theater veterans served in Vietnam (for example, during the 1968 Tet offensive) is not strongly related to variation in current rates of PTSD. In contrast, age at entry to Vietnam clearly is. Those who were 17–19 years of age when they first entered Vietnam are much more likely to have current PTSD (25.2 percent) than those who were older at the time of entry. Those who served in Vietnam 13 months (the conventional tour of duty for Marines) or longer are also more likely to meet criteria for current PTSD (19–20 percent) than those who served 12 months or less (12.7–15.3 percent).

In addition to length of service, the nature of Vietnam service also appeared to exert a major influence on the prevalence of current PTSD. For example, among those who served in I Corps (the military region in which the Marine Corps was predominant), the current prevalence of PTSD is 22.5 percent. Similarly, those who were wounded or injured in combat are two to three times as likely to have current PTSD, and the likelihood of having current PTSD is also greater for those who received a Purple Heart (over one-third) or any other combat medal (almost one in four).

In addition, several characteristics of veterans' current lives are related to the prevalence of PTSD today. Its prevalence is higher among theater veteran men who are currently separated or living with someone as though they were married. The rate of disorder is also higher among those who never finished high school (28.7 percent), those who are currently unemployed (34.5 percent), and those who have incomes of less than $20,000 per year (26.2 percent). Conversely, rates of current PTSD are particularly low among those who are currently married, are college graduates, are employed or retired, and have incomes of $30,000 or higher. The prevalence rate is also higher than average for men who reside in the West (23.3) and in very large or medium-sized cities (24.8 and 21.2 percent respectively). Comparisons by current religious preference suggest that men who declare no religious preference are those at highest risk for current PTSD.

FEMALE THEATER VETERANS. Fewer characteristics are associated with an increased prevalence of PTSD among Vietnam theater veteran women than among men. This may reflect the greater homogeneity of this subgroup, in that most were nurses. The small sample size prohibited comparisons by race and ethnicity, but comparisons by year of birth revealed that women born before 1940 have PTSD rates under 5 percent, whereas those born during the 1940s (1940–1949) have essentially twice that rate (approximately 10 percent).

There was also little variation in current PTSD rates among women by type of entry to military service, branch of service, or service in the Reserve or National Guard. However, as with men, those who served on active duty more than 20 years have especially low rates of the disorder, whereas those serving four to 19 years have somewhat elevated rates. Interestingly, women who served in the junior officer pay grades (01–03) have almost twice the rate of current PTSD as the more senior officers (04–06).

As was the case for men, there was little variation for women in PTSD prevalence by year of entry to Vietnam, but also no substantial differences by age at entry or length of service. However, those who served in I Corp and II Corps have higher rates of PTSD today than those who served elsewhere. As was also true for men, women exposed to high levels of war-zone stress, such as exposure to the wounded and dead, have seven times the rate of current PTSD as those with low or moderate levels of exposure.

Women who are divorced, separated, or living as married also have substantially higher rates of PTSD than those who are married, and, unlike the findings for men, the prevalence of current PTSD is higher among female theater veterans with some college (11 percent) or post-graduate training (10 percent) than among high school or college graduates (3.8 and 6.4 percent respectively). The prevalence of current PTSD is also higher among theater veteran women with incomes of less than $20,000 per year (10.4 percent), those who currently reside in the West (14.7 percent) or in medium-sized cities (14.3 percent), and those who state no religious preference (26.8 percent).

WORK TO IDENTIFY CURRENT PTSD CLIENTS

Reflecting the emphasis on PTSD in the Congressional mandate, our research team wanted to create a research design for the Readjustment

Study that would maximize the accuracy of the study's estimate of the prevalence of PTSD among Vietnam theater veterans. This concern was expressed through two important features of the NVVRS design. First, when the NVVRS was being planned, the American Psychiatric Association (APA) was in the process of revising its _Diagnostic and Statistical Manual of Mental Disorders_ (DSM-III), the document that provides the "official" definition of psychiatric disorders in the United States. To assure that the NVVRS assessment of PTSD was consistent with the official definition of PTSD that would be in place when the NVVRS findings became available, the research team coordinated its efforts with the group working on revising the psychiatric taxonomy, APA's Work Group to Revise DSM-III. RTI cosponsored the meeting of the Ad Hoc Panel on the Definition and Measurement of PTSD, whose recommendations for revising the diagnostic criteria for PTSD were incorporated into the revised PTSD definition. As a result of this coordination, the NVVRS clinical estimates of PTSD prevalence are estimates of the prevalence of the disorder _as defined in the current official taxonomy_ (and, therefore, in use by the VA system).

Second, the bedrock of the accuracy of any diagnostic procedure is its _validity_—that is, the extent to which the procedure classifies individuals in whom the disorder is truly present as "cases" and those in whom the disorder is truly absent as "noncases." To achieve the objective of diagnostic accuracy, RTI proposed a double validation design that involved conducting a preliminary validation study before launching the national survey (that is, the NSVG), and then conducting a second validation study to run concurrently with the national survey. In the following sections, we summarize the nature and purposes of these validation components and the methods for integrating validation study findings with those of the national survey to formulate population prevalence estimates. (Full methodological details are provided in Volume II, Appendices D and E.)

Preliminary Efforts

One of the fundamental principles on which RTI's original proposal to conduct the NVVRS was founded was that the national survey component of the study should not go to the field until sufficient evidence existed that cases of PTSD could be validly identified on the basis of survey interview information. This restriction was critical because no published information existed concerning the validity of any of the existing survey instruments used to identify PTSD in earlier research.

Therefore, the NVVRS design called for a preliminary study to examine the ability of several candidate survey measures to discriminate "true" cases of PTSD from "true" noncases. This validation study involved administering a package of candidate PTSD instruments to a group of subjects whose diagnostic status was known. The diagnostic status of subjects, who were mostly veterans undergoing psychiatric treatment, was "known" because their chart diagnosis *and* the diagnosis made by an expert clinician agreed on the presence or absence of PTSD. The expert clinician's diagnosis was made on the basis of an independent diagnostic interview conducted blind to the chart diagnosis.

Results of the study indicated that several instruments in the package could classify people as cases or noncases of PTSD with acceptable accuracy. These findings served as the basis for decisions about the package of instruments to be included in the NSVG (Appendix D details the design and findings of the preliminary validation study).

A Pool of Clients

The preliminary validation study provided information suggesting that we could proceed with the national survey component of the NVVRS. However, it did not (and we did not intend it to) provide *complete* information about every aspect of the validity of the survey-based PTSD measures. For example, the validation study's subjects were (of necessity) people who had sought treatment for their mental health problems, and evidence in the research literature suggests that people who seek mental health treatment are different in many ways from people who meet the diagnostic criteria for a psychiatric disorder but who do not seek treatment for it. Because the national component of the NVVRS involved a community sample rather than a treatment-seeking sample, the relationship between the diagnostic measures and "true" diagnosis (that is, the validity of those measures) could be expected to be at least somewhat attenuated from the estimate made on the basis of a treatment-seeking population.

For this reason the NVVRS design contained a clinical subsample component. The primary purpose of the clinical subsample component was to provide additional information about the correspondence between PTSD measures included in the survey interview and "true" PTSD. The clinical subsample was designed as a multimethod validity study, in which multiple PTSD measures, including a semistructured interview conducted by an experienced mental health professional, could be brought to bear on the diagnostic decision. Thus, we planned a "triangulation" method for PTSD case identification, in which the diagnostic decision process would take into account information collected through a variety of methods and from a variety of sources.

Each clinical subsample respondent underwent a semistructured clinical interview that resulted in a diagnostic decision about PTSD. In addition, the clinician who conducted the interview completed several clinical scales describing his or her clinical impression of the respondent, and the respondent completed several self-report PTSD scales. In addition, the spouse/partner (if the respondent had one) of each clinical subsample respondent was also interviewed. As a result, the research team had at its disposal five self-report scales directly related to PTSD (plus a number of other psychiatric symptom scales related to PTSD but less directly so) and four clinical judgment scales, for clinical subsample respondents. This information base is what we used to make PTSD case determinations.

Identifying in Clients

Although the research team has great confidence in a PTSD diagnosis made by a trained and experienced mental health professional based on a thorough clinical interview, we also recognize that no diagnostic procedure is completely error-free. Therefore, we sought to use information from the full range of PTSD indicators available in the clinical subsample to form a "composite" PTSD diagnosis. The basic idea of the composite diagnosis was to examine the information available from multiple PTSD indicators, including but not limited to the clinical interviewer's diagnosis. In addition, in those cases where some discrepancy among the indicators existed, we used the full array of additional PTSD information to make a diagnostic decision.

Simply stated, composite diagnoses were made on the basis of a detailed review of the PTSD information for each individual clinical subsample subject. Review began by examining the study's three main indicators:

- the Mississippi Combat-Related PTSD (M-PTSD) scale
- the Clinical Interview (SCID) PTSD diagnosis
- the PTSD scale of the Minnesota Multiphasic Personality Inventory (MMPI)

When these three indicators agreed, the diagnosis was considered "settled" (decided). In the event of a discrepancy in PTSD diagnosis among the three indicators, we used information from the study's other PTSD indicators to resolve the discrepancy. We combined information from these other indicators statistically to create two additional main indicators for use in resolving discrepancies. (Details of the logic underlying the composite diagnosis procedure and of its relationship to other potential methods of case determination are discussed in Appendix D.) Application of this procedure resulted in a composite PTSD diagnosis for every subject in the clinical subsample. PTSD prevalence estimates presented in the following sections are based on the composite PTSD diagnosis (details of the procedure by which NVVRS prevalence estimates were formulated are presented in Appendix E).

NATIONAL ESTIMATES OF PTSD

By definition, a prevalence rate is the percent of a specified population group or subgroup that has a given disorder during a specified period. To address more completely the "service needs assessment" aspect of the Congressional mandate, we decided to present prevalence estimates for two "types" of PTSD: the full PTSD syndrome (as defined by DSM-III-R) and "partial" PTSD. Estimates of the prevalence of "partial" PTSD are estimates of the percent whose stress-reaction symptoms are of either insufficient intensity or breadth to qualify as the full PTSD syndrome but still warrant professional attention. People with partial PTSD today may have had a full syndrome in the past that is currently in partial remission, or they may have never met the full criteria. Nevertheless, they do have clinically significant stress-reaction symptoms that could benefit from treatment, and they represent an important component of the total spectrum of "need for treatment."

We have opted to present in this report prevalence rates with respect to two specific reference periods: *current* prevalence and *lifetime* prevalence. Current PTSD prevalence is operationally defined as the percent of the specified population group or subgroup (for example, male Vietnam theater veterans) who met the criteria for the PTSD diagnosis during the six-month period preceding their participation in the NVVRS. The consensus of clinicians involved in the study was that this rate was the most accurate way to identify those who have the disorder today.

The lifetime prevalence rate, on the other hand, represents the percent of the specified population group or subgroup who have met the diagnostic criteria for the PTSD diagnosis at some time during their lives. Thus, the lifetime prevalence rate counts all those who have *ever* had PTSD, whereas the current prevalence counts only those who have PTSD *today*.

Current and lifetime prevalence rates are reported because they provide two different perspectives on the problem. Given that the Readjustment Study was conducted 15 or more years after most veterans' Vietnam service, the lifetime prevalence rate may be thought of as an index of the "total" PTSD problem: what proportion of the men and women who served in Vietnam ever had PTSD? Current prevalence, on the other hand, provides an index of the magnitude of the problem today. Taken together, lifetime and current prevalance of full and partial PTSD provide a relatively complete picture of the stress-reaction sequelae of exposure to trauma.

Additionally, the ratio of current to lifetime prevalence provides some information about the course of the disorder. A finding that only a small portion of those theater veterans who ever had PTSD have it today would be consistent with the notion of PTSD as a relatively acute, or time-limited, disorder. Alternatively, a finding that a substantial proportion of theater veterans who ever had PTSD still have it today would be more consistent with the view of PTSD as a chronic disorder.

Current PTSD

Table IV-1 (in Volume II) shows the estimated current PTSD prevalence rates for the study's major groups and subgroups. An estimated 15.2 percent of all male theater veterans are current cases of PTSD. This represents about 479,000 of the estimated 3.14 million men who served in the Vietnam theater. Among theater veteran females, the prevalence is estimated to be 8.5 percent of the estimated 7,166 women who served, or about 610 current cases.

Among both male and female theater veterans, the current PTSD prevalence is:

- higher for those exposed to high levels of war-zone stress than for those with low/moderate stress exposure (a fourfold difference for men and sevenfold for women);
- higher for men who have a service-connected physical disability than for those without such a disability, but not different for women with and without service-connected disability;
- higher for those with a positive lifetime substance abuse diagnosis than for those without (more than a twofold difference for men and nearly a fivefold difference for women).

Also for both sexes, current PTSD prevalence rates for theater veterans are consistently higher than rates for comparable era veterans (2.5 percent male, 1.1 percent female) or civilian counterparts (1.2 percent male, 0.3 percent female). These rate differences become even wider when era veterans and civilians are compared with theater veterans with high war-zone-stress exposure. The current PTSD prevalence findings for the major study groups are shown graphically in Exhibit IV-1.

Among male theater veterans, the current PTSD prevalence rate is 27.9 percent among Hispanics, 20.6 percent among Blacks, and 13.7 percent

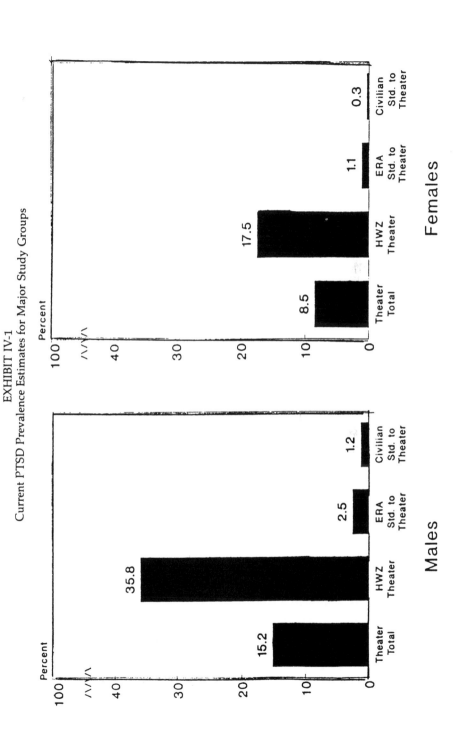

EXHIBIT IV-1
Current PTSD Prevalence Estimates for Major Study Groups

among White/others. The relationship between theater veterans, era veterans, and civilian counterparts also holds within the race/ethnicity subgroups: theater veteran rates are consistently higher than rates for era veterans or civilians. The current PTSD prevalence estimates for the male racial/ethnic subgroups are presented graphically in Exhibit IV-2.

The only group or subgroup contrasts of current PTSD rates that do not indicate significant differences are the service-connected physical disability contrasts for female theater veterans. No significant difference exists in

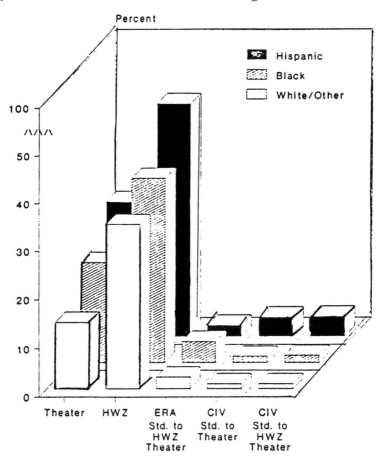

EXHIBIT IV-2
Current PTSD Prevalence Estimates for Racial/Ethnic Subgroups
of Male Theater Veterans

the current PTSD prevalence between female theater veterans with and without service-connected physical disability, or between those with high disability and those with no disability.

Additionally, NVVRS findings indicate that the current prevalence of partial PTSD is 11.1 percent among male theater veterans and 7.8 percent among female theater veterans. Together, this represents about 350,000 veterans—in addition to the 480,000 who have the full PTSD syndrome today—who have trauma-related symptoms that could benefit from professional treatment. The combined findings for the current prevalence of partial PTSD and of the full PTSD syndrome are presented graphically in Exhibit IV-3.

Lifetime PTSD

NVVRS findings indicate that the lifetime prevalence of PTSD is 30.9 percent among male theater veterans and 26.9 percent among females. The lifetime prevalence of partial PTSD among male theater veterans is 22.5 percent, and among female theater veterans 21.2 percent. These findings, also depicted graphically in Exhibit IV-3, mean that over the course of their lives, more than half (30.9 + 22.5 = 53.4 percent) of male theater veterans and nearly half (26.9 + 21.2 = 48.1 percent) of female theater veterans have experienced clinically significant stress-reaction symptoms. This represents about 1.7 million war veterans.

Also presented graphically in Exhibit IV-3 are the findings for the current prevalence of PTSD and partial PTSD. Comparison of the current and lifetime prevalence rates shows that about one-half (49.2 percent) of the male theater veterans and one-third (31.6 percent) of the female theater veterans who have ever had PTSD still have it today. Also, of those theater veterans who have ever had significant stress-reaction symptoms (full or partial PTSD), about half (49.3 percent) of males and about one-third (33.9 percent) of females are experiencing some degree of clinically significant stress-reaction symptoms today. These findings are consistent with the conceptualization of PTSD as a chronic, rather than acute, disorder.

PTSD AMONG VIETNAM WAR VETERANS

Having established the prevalence of PTSD among the major study groups, we conducted a series of descriptive analyses designed to establish potential differences in the distribution of PTSD among Vietnam theater veterans on a broad range of other characteristics. These analyses help to clarify who among theater veterans have PTSD today. These results are

EXHIBIT IV-3

Lifetime and Current Prevalence of PTSD and Partial PTSD
Among Male and Female Vietnam Theater Veterans

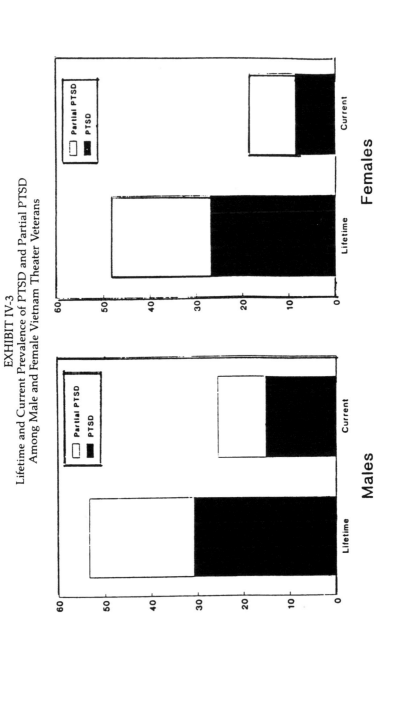

both descriptive and tentative because, although standard errors are provided for all group prevalence estimates, no formal statistical tests of group differences were performed. Nevertheless, as an overall "profile" of the characteristics of Vietnam veterans with PTSD, these analyses are of considerable interest. The full tabulation of these results is presented in Table IV-2 in Volume II. We present here a general summary of the distribution of PTSD according to selected background characteristics, characteristics of military service and service in Vietnam, and some current sociodemographic characteristics. The findings are summarized separately for men and women serving in the Vietnam theater.

Males

BACKGROUND CHARACTERISTICS. As noted earlier in this chapter, PTSD prevalence rates vary considerably by race and ethnicity, with 20.6 percent of Blacks meeting current criteria for PTSD and 27.9 percent of Hispanics, compared with 13.7 percent of White/other men serving in Vietnam. A further breakdown of veterans of Hispanic origin revealed equally high current rates of PTSD among the two primary Hispanic populations in the United States: Mexican Americans and Puerto Ricans.

A notable finding was evident, however, by year of birth, with men born before 1945 having lower current rates of PTSD (4–10 percent) whereas 18–19 percent of those born after 1945 currently have PTSD.

CHARACTERISTICS OF MILITARY SERVICE AND POSTSERVICE. While a substantially lower current PTSD rate was found for those who entered the military other than by induction or enlistment (e.g., direct commission), the sample sizes for these groups were small. Of greater significance, perhaps, was that those who enlisted (either voluntarily or to avoid the draft) have essentially the same rates of current PTSD as draftees and one another. In contrast, men who served in the Army or Marine Corps are considerably more likely than those who served in the other branches of the Armed Forces to have current PTSD (16.2 and 24.8 percent respectively), as were those served in the junior enlisted pay grades (E1–E3), among whom one in four currently has PTSD. By far the lowest rate of PTSD is among those who served on active duty for 20 or more years (5.6 percent), while those who served more than four but less than 20 years have the highest rate (24.8 percent). There were no clear differences in PTSD prevalence among those who had combat duty other than in Vietnam and those who did not, or among those discharged with a "tactical" (e.g.,

Infantry, Armor, Artillery) versus "nontactical" MOS (military occupational specialty).

The prevalence of current PTSD is higher, however, among those male theater veterans who are currently members of veterans' organizations (20.1 percent compared with 12.6 percent for those who have never been members). Similarly, Vietnam veterans who have had at least some contact with the Veterans Administration (VA) after leaving the military have twice the rate of PTSD of those who have not contacted the VA (16.7 versus 8.3 percent respectively).

CHARACTERISTICS OF VIETNAM SERVICE. Somewhat surprisingly, the particular period during which male theater veterans served in Vietnam (for example, during the 1968 Tet offensive) is not related to variation in current rates of PTSD. In contrast, age at entry to Vietnam clearly is. Those who were 17–19 years of age when they first entered Vietnam are much more likely to have current PTSD (25.2 percent) than those who were older at the time of entry. Those who served in Vietnam for 13 months (the conventional tour of duty for Marines) or longer are also more likely to meet the criteria for current PTSD (19–20 percent) than those who served 12 months or less (12.7–15.3 percent).

In addition to length of service, the nature of Vietnam service also appeared to exert a major influence on the prevalence of current PTSD. For example, among those who served in I Corps (the military region in which the Marine Corps was predominant), the current prevalence of PTSD is 22.5 percent. A more obvious example of the importance of the nature of Vietnam experiences—degree of exposure to combat and other war-zone stressors—has already been noted earlier in this chapter. Male theater veterans with high exposure to war-zone stressors are more than four times as likely to suffer from PTSD today as are those with low or moderate exposure. Similarly, those who were wounded or injured in combat are two to three times as likely to have current PTSD, and the likelihood of having current PTSD is also greater for those receiving a Purple Heart (over one-third) or any combat medal (almost one in four).

CURRENT SOCIODEMOGRAPHIC CHARACTERISTICS. There are also several current characteristics of veterans that are related to the current prevalence of PTSD. The prevalence of PTSD is higher among theater veteran men who are separated or living with someone as though they were married. The rate of disorder is also higher among those who never finished high school (28.7 percent), those who are unemployed (34.5

percent), and those who have incomes of less than $20,000 per year (26.2 percent). Conversely, rates of current PTSD are particularly low among those who are married, are college graduates, are employed or retired, and have incomes of $30,000 or higher. The prevalence rate is also higher than average for men who reside in the West (23.3) and in very large or medium-sized cities (24.8 and 21.2 percent respectively). Comparisons by current religious preference suggest that men who declare no religious preference are those at highest risk for current PTSD.

Females

Fewer characteristics are associated with an increased prevalence of PTSD among Vietnam theater veteran women than among men. This may reflect the greater homogeneity of this subgroup, in that most were nurses. The small sample size prohibited comparisons by race and ethnicity, but comparisons by year of birth revealed that, similar to the pattern observed for men, those born before 1940 have PTSD rates under 5 percent, whereas those born during the 1940s (1940–1949) have essentially twice that rate (approximately 10 percent).

There was also little variation in current PTSD rates among women by type of entry to military service, branch of service, or service in the Reserve or National Guard. However, as with men, those who served on active duty for more than 20 years have especially low rates of the disorder, whereas those serving four to 19 years have somewhat elevated rates. Interestingly, women who served in the junior officer pay grades (01–03) have almost twice the rate of current PTSD as the more senior officers (04–06).

Like the men, women also showed little variation in PTSD prevalence by year of entry to Vietnam, but also no substantial differences by age at entry or length of service. However, those who served in I Corp and II Corps have higher rates of PTSD than those who served elsewhere. As noted earlier in this chapter, women exposed to high levels of war-zone stress, such as exposure to the wounded and dead, have seven times the rate of current PTSD as those with low or moderate levels of exposure. Moreover, although the sample sizes are small, those who were wounded (20.3 percent) or received combat medals (15.0 percent) also have higher than average current rates of PTSD. Women who are current or past members of veterans' organizations and those who have had some contact with the VA also have essentially twice the rate of current PTSD of nonmembers and those who have not contacted the VA.

Women who are divorced, separated, or living as married also have substantially higher rates of PTSD than those who are married, and, unlike the findings for men, the prevalence of current PTSD is higher among female theater veterans with some college (11 percent) or postgraduate training (10 percent) than among high school or college graduates (3.8 and 6.4 percent respectively). The prevalence of current PTSD is also higher among theater veteran women with incomes of less than $20,000 per year (10.4 percent), those who currently reside in the West (14.7 percent) or in medium-sized cities (14.3 percent), and those who state no religious preference (26.8 percent).

PTSD CASE EXAMPLES

To illustrate how the PTSD prevalence rates translate into individual human terms, several case examples were drawn from the NSVG theater veteran sample. These cases are ones for which all five of the primary indicators of PTSD were positive; these are clearly current cases of PTSD. The selection of the cases was based on two factors: (1) each was judged by the research team clinicians to embody the hallmark features of PTSD in theater veterans, and (2) each was sufficiently typical that even with changes made for the purposes of disguising individual identities, the essential attributes of the disorder and their impact on work and interpersonal functioning were recognizably retained. Each case description represents a real veteran who participated in the survey and clinical interviews. We have changed a number of specific details and identifying characteristics (including the initials) to preserve the confidentiality and anonymity of each respondent while retaining the richness and vividness of his or her individual human experience.

J.S.'s Story

J.S., a Hispanic male veteran in his late 30s, has been married for almost 20 years, has three children, and works as a semiskilled laborer. He lives in a large metropolitan area in the Northeast. He is the eldest of four children and grew up in a poor but stable and supportive family environment. He was drafted into the U.S. Army in 1966 and served one tour of duty in Vietnam, which ended in 1968.

His primary duty was reconnaissance in an infantry unit. He experienced high and sustained war-zone-stress exposure; he walked at the point of the squad, was frequently under fire, witnessed the death and injury of close buddies, witnessed the mutilation of the bodies of American troops, and was wounded in combat. He received several decorations, including the Purple Heart.

J.S. reports that his experience in Vietnam matured him, but that he had difficulty coping and began to drink heavily for the first time during his tour. On his return to civilian life, his problems with alcohol intensified; he was treated medically for alcohol-related pancreatic disease several years after his return. Alcohol abuse remains a serious problem to the present time.

With respect to the psychological impact of the war, he reported, "I developed a nasty temper, became very nervous, and have bad dreams that take me back into the war, like it's happening all over — then I can't get back to sleep." When reminded of the war, he becomes upset and vividly imagines the sights and smells of the battlefield, including the discovery of bodies that had been left for several days in the jungle heat. He describes himself as frightened by his urges, easily startled, frequently on guard for no reason, emotionally withdrawn, and using alcohol to help forget about his wartime memories. His wife concurs, reporting that he has frequent nightmares, becomes enraged over minor irritations, avoids reminders of the war, and is reluctant to be emotionally close. He says he is fortunate that his wife continues to be supportive, despite his volatility and withdrawal.

He has managed to maintain steady employment and finds satisfaction in his relationship with his children. At present he is most troubled by nightmares, intrusive reliving of painful war memories, alcohol abuse, flashes of temper, difficulty opening up to his wife, and bad nerves, as he is frequently on guard, easily startled, has difficulty concentrating, and sleeps poorly.

He has never been treated for emotional problems. He has intermittently received treatment for alcohol abuse, but his drinking problems have not been addressed in the context of his overall postwar psychological adjustment problems.

T.L.'s Story

T.L. is a 38-year-old Black male living in a primarily blue-collar, working-class suburb of a major city. He has worked for a municipal airport for nearly 15 years and has been married to his second wife for more than ten years. T.L.'s parents separated when he was 12 years old, and he and three siblings were raised by his mother in an inner-city neighborhood, which he described as "rather poor." He indicated that his relationship with his mother was "good," and that there was no known history of mental illness in his family of origin. Soon after graduating from high school in 1967, he enlisted into the U.S. Marine Corps.

From early 1968 to early 1969, T.L. served with the Marine Corps in the Republic of Vietnam, primarily in the vicinity of the DMZ. He reported heavy combat exposure ("daily encounters with booby traps, a lot of fire fights"), as well as the experience of multiple combat trauma. At one point in the NVVRS interview, T.L. described his experience in Vietnam in the following way. "It seemed like every time I turned around, someone was getting shot, or had a limb blown off, or their guts hanging out. There was nothing that you could do for them." He described one of many specific traumatic incidents in these words: "One time on a mission, a land mine exploded. Three guys were killed . . . blown up . . . guys on the ground, screaming." T.L.'s voice faded to a barely audible whisper as he described this event to the NVVRS interviewer.

T.L. reported that severe and persistent problems in his daily functioning began within a few months of his return from Vietnam to the United States. From 1970 to the present, he has been plagued relentlessly by symptoms of post-traumatic stress disorder, the impact of which he has attempted to mollify through chronic substance abuse. He painfully acknowledged the continuing presence of distressing, intrusive memories of death and dying in the combat zone ("Sometimes my thoughts take me right back to what happened to guys there. I wish I could have helped them"). In a voice choked with emotion, he said that he currently attempts to avoid thoughts and reminders of Vietnam, but with little success. "I try (to avoid), but it's hard. In my job I deal with the public and it seems like someone or something is always bringing it up." He also clearly described several discrete episodes during which specific, intrusive, traumatic memories of Vietnam overwhelmed his capacity to cope, precipitating what he described as "nervous breakdowns." These episodes were principally characterized by gut-wrenching pangs of guilt, shame, and despair related to the traumatic memories, persistent agitation and sleep disturbance, and desperate attempts to escape and avoid through social withdrawal and alcohol binges. During these periods of debilitating PTSD symptomatology, T.L. consulted his family physician, asking for pills for his unspecified "nerves." At the time of the NVVRS interviews, T.L. was found to meet diagnostic criteria for severe combat-related PTSD, yet he had not been under any physician's care for almost two years. Moreover, he had never sought help for PTSD and associated symptoms of distress from any mental health professional or from the VA.

B.R.'s Story

This currently unmarried Vietnam veteran who lives in a large metropolitan area was in her late 40s at the time of her participation in the study. She was in the service for more than 15 years and received numerous decorations and commendations. She was one of six children raised by both parents in a happy home. She was trained as a nurse and enlisted in the Air Force because it "sounded interesting."

B.R. volunteered for duty in Vietnam and served one tour in 1966–1967 as a nurse, primarily caring for wounded soldiers in the area of her nursing expertise. Periodically, however, she was assigned to care for patients with injuries or trauma that required expertise outside of her primary area of skills. These episodes were very stressful; sometimes they involved supportive care of obviously terminal patients. She was exposed to mortars infrequently, but when shelling occurred, it was always totally unexpected, and B.R. found it frightening.

She experienced the death of several people with whom she had developed deep attachments—both professionally and personally. Her account of her reactions to these mounting losses was a gnawing lack of time and privacy to mourn because of the exhausting and grinding nursing care she was asked, and willingly agreed, to provide. She described her Vietnam service as the most exciting part of her Air Force career as well as the most distressing, damaging, and traumatic. B.R. recounted that she felt it was especially hard for her to deal with the experiences of what she felt were pointless deaths and injuries and the denial of impending death by those who were terminally injured.

Her return from Vietnam was distressing—she was ostracized, shouted at, and felt ashamed, though she continued her military service. She received commendations for her post-Vietnam service, and reported few psychological signs or symptoms of upset during the span of ten to 15 years before she returned to civilian life. She did report, however, a persistent sense of distance and social withdrawal, though she did not seem to connect these to her service in Vietnam during that period.

Only upon her return to civilian life and her selection of a job that exposed her daily to people dealing with their own traumas, past and present, did her functioning began to deteriorate. B.R. became increasingly withdrawn, irritable, and depressed. She began to have intrusive thoughts about her war experiences and began awakening in early morning from dreams of her time in Vietnam. She could not concentrate, was jumpy and easily startled, felt numb inside, and was prone to angry outbursts.

She felt that no one could understand how she felt and that she could not feel close to anyone. Though she desired closer contact with both men and women, B.R. was unable to reach out or trust enough to get closer. Her episode of PTSD was a clear case of delayed-onset PTSD; most symptoms began well over a decade after the trauma.

Because both her work and interpersonal functioning were impeded, she was encouraged to seek treatment, which she reluctantly did. Though finding the treatment program she selected in the VA system helpful, she is aware that her recovery will be a long process. She now sees that she has buried and avoided a number of powerful and painful feelings for a long time and that she must take time to deal with each one in turn.

CHAPTER V

Why Is It That Some Developed PTSD and Others Did Not?

COMMENTARY

Research projects that have multiple objectives must be designed so that a balance is maintained among the (sometimes conflicting) objectives. Although the single most important objective of the NVVRS was to determine the prevalence of PTSD among Vietnam veterans, from a policy perspective it was also important to determine the relationship between PTSD prevalence and service in Vietnam. The Veterans Administration's primary mandate is to serve the needs of those veterans who have service-connected disabilities. Consequently, from the standpoint of providing information for the planning of VA programs to meet the needs of veterans with service-connected disabilities, it would not be enough for the study simply to show that the prevalence of PTSD is higher among theater veterans than among the comparison groups. Although that would be an important piece of information, such a finding could be explained in a variety of ways. Therefore, it was important that the study be designed in a way that would permit the scientific evaluation of alternative hypotheses that might be offered to explain any differences that were found in PTSD prevalence among the study's cohorts.

The basic problem that we had arose from the fact that although it was possible to include comparison groups in the NVVRS, people had not been assigned to those groups at random. As a result, the possibility of confounding existed—that is, the current prevalence of PTSD might differ among the groups because of differences in their experiences or because of differences in their characteristics that resulted in their becoming theater veterans, era veterans, or civilian counterparts. For example, suppose that mental instability were related to military ser-

vice in such a way that the more unstable a person was, the more likely he or she was to join the military, and once in the military to volunteer for service in Vietnam. If that were the case, the group of theater veterans would have been less stable to begin with, and we would not be surprised if we found them to be less stable now.

Although in principle one can never completely overcome the problem of nonrandom assignment of people to study groups, it is possible to minimize the impact by adjusting statistically for characteristics on which the study groups differ and that are related to the outcome that is being studied. Characteristics on which the groups do not differ, and those that are not related to the outcome being studied, are not of concern, because by definition they cannot confound the analysis.

The major focus of the analyses described in this chapter is the issue of predisposition: Is the prevalence of PTSD higher among theater veterans because of some characteristics that they brought with them to the war? At first blush, if it were to turn out that the current prevalence of PTSD is not higher among theater veterans than among the comparison groups when predisposing characteristics are controlled, then the greater prevalence observed among theater veterans could be attributed to their characteristics, rather than to their wartime experiences. However, the reality is somewhat more complicated. Differences observed today in PTSD prevalence among the study groups might be due to differences in premilitary characteristics; differential military experiences of the groups (service in a war zone, service outside a war zone, and no military service); differential postmilitary experiences, since the study is being conducted 15 years or more after the military service of many veterans had ended; or interactions among these factors. A full analysis of these factors and their interactions would provide detailed answers to some very important scientific questions, but it would be a time-consuming process. However, addressing the important policy questions would not require the complete scientific analysis. The critical policy question is: Do theater veterans have PTSD today because of how they were when they went to Vietnam, and if not, is the current PTSD prevalence related to some aspects of their experiences in Vietnam when their premilitary characteristics are controlled for?

The analyses described in this chapter are aimed at addressing this question. Our analytic strategy was a conservative one: We first exam-

ined the relationship of predisposing factors to current prevalence, and then examined the relationship of exposure to war-zone stress with predisposing factors controlled. This strategy is "conservative" in the sense that it attributes to predisposition the variance in current PTSD prevalence that is due to predisposing factors acting alone (i.e., the "main effect" for predisposition) and the variance due to the interaction of predisposing factors and war-zone-stress exposure. As a result, the effect of predisposing factors may be overestimated by this procedure, relative to what might be found from a more fully specified model. Thus, the findings about the role of predisposing factors may be seen as providing an upper bound for the role of predisposition. However, a finding that exposure to war-zone stress was significantly related to current PTSD prevalence even after the effects of predisposition and the interactive effects of predisposition and stress exposure are taken into account, would be strong evidence that the current PTSD among theater veterans is service-connected.

CHAPTER OVERVIEW

A literal interpretation of the Readjustment Study's Congressional mandate would suggest that the mandate could be fulfilled with respect to PTSD simply by determining the PTSD prevalence rate among Vietnam theater veterans. However, a broader interpretation of the intent of the mandate suggests that more is required. In addition to knowing the current prevalence of PTSD among theater veterans, it is important to the Readjustment Study's "needs assessment" function to determine: (1) whether that rate is different from the PTSD prevalence rate among era veterans and civilian counterparts, and (2) if so, whether the higher prevalence among theater veterans is predominantly due to their experiences in Vietnam, or to characteristics they brought with them to the war (predisposing characteristics).

To examine the extent to which potential predisposing factors might account for observed study group differences, we conducted a series of multivariate statistical analyses. These analyses provided estimates of the difference in current PTSD prevalence for each of the standard study group contrasts, taking into account (or "adjusting for") differences among the groups in the set of potential predisposing variables.

These analyses indicated that among males, controlling for potentially predisposing variables typically reduced the between-group differences in current PTSD prevalence. A generally greater impact of the predisposing variable adjustment was observed in the theater versus civilian contrasts than in the theater versus era veteran contrasts, suggesting larger differences in potentially predisposing characteristics between theater veterans and their civilian counterparts. The variables controlled for in the various contrasts tended to be of two types: those that reflected the socioeconomic circumstances of the person's family while growing up, and those reflecting the presence of psychiatric symptoms prior to service in the military or in Vietnam.

The findings of the adjusted theater versus era veteran and civilian counterpart contrasts indicate that there was a significant "predisposition effect": however, the current prevalence of PTSD among Vietnam theater veterans is much higher than that among era veterans and civilian counterparts even after we take into account differences on a large group of potential predisposing factors. Thus, we cannot explain the high current prevalence of PTSD among Vietnam veterans solely on the basis of characteristics that they brought with them to the war. This finding is consistent with the hypothesis that the experiences to which theater veterans were exposed in Vietnam play a prominent role in determining current PTSD prevalence.

In an effort to obtain a clearer understanding of the role of Vietnam experience in current PTSD prevalence rate among theater veterans, we extended the multivariate analyses that accomplished the adjustment for the potential predisposing factors one additional step. This step involved adding the variable for global war-zone-stress exposure to the predisposition adjustment models for the male theater veteran racial/ethnic subgroup contrasts. Doing so allowed us to determine whether the between-group differences in current PTSD prevalence rates that remained after the predisposition adjustment could be further reduced by taking account of exposure to war-zone stress. Findings indicated that when potential predisposing factors and exposure to war-zone stress are controlled, there is no significant difference between the current PTSD rate for Black and White/other men. However, the current PTSD rate for Hispanics was significantly higher than that for Blacks or White/others even when predisposing and Vietnam experience factors are controlled.

Several conclusions seem warranted from this set of analyses of the role of potential predisposing factors and Vietnam experience factors in current PTSD prevalence. First, the current prevalence of PTSD is much higher among Vietnam theater veterans than among era veterans or civilian counterparts. Second, theater veterans differed from era veterans and civilian counterparts on some background characteristics that are related to current PTSD and that might have rendered theater veterans more vulnerable to the development of PTSD. Nevertheless, the current PTSD prevalence rate is much higher among theater veterans even after these differences in potential predisposing factors are taken into account. Third, exposure to war-zone stress in Vietnam plays a significant role in determining who among theater veterans has PTSD today, even after a broad array of potential predisposing factors have been controlled for.

Taken together, these results are consistent with a model of PTSD that posits a role for individual vulnerability (potentially including biological, psychological, and sociodemographic predisposing factors) *and* a role for exposure to environmental factors (specifically, war-zone stressors) in determining who among theater veterans develops PTSD. However, it is also clear that exposure to war-zone stress makes a substantial contribution to the development of PTSD in war veterans that is independent of a broad range of potential predisposing factors.

CRITICAL FACTORS

A literal interpretation of the Readjustment Study's Congressional mandate would suggest that the mandate could be fulfilled with respect to PTSD simply by determining the PTSD prevalence rate among Vietnam theater veterans. However, a broader interpretation of the intent of the mandate suggests that more is required. In addition to knowing the current prevalence of PTSD among theater veterans, it is important to the Readjustment Study's "needs assessment" function to determine (1) whether that rate is different from the PTSD prevalence rate among era veterans and civilian counterparts, and (2) if so, whether the higher prevalence among theater veterans is due to their experiences in Vietnam. Findings indicating that current PTSD prevalence is significantly higher among theater veterans than among era veterans or civilian counterparts, and that the PTSD prevalence rate is significantly related to war-zone-stressor exposure, would provide powerful evidence that PTSD in theater veterans is indeed a service-connected disability.

Findings presented in Chapter IV demonstrate clearly that the current prevalence of PTSD among theater veterans is much higher than the prevalence among era veterans or civilian counterparts. These findings demonstrate that Vietnam theater veterans as a group are much more "at risk" for having PTSD than are era veterans or civilian counterparts.

These findings lead to an important question: What is it about the characteristics or experiences of Vietnam veterans that puts them "at risk"? The contrasts of PTSD prevalence rates between theater veterans and the era veteran and civilian counterpart comparison groups provide some information in this regard. However, those comparisons are not completely satisfying, because people were not assigned at random to the study's major groups (theater veteran, era veteran, or civilian counterpart status). On the contrary, many powerful social forces operated to determine who served in the military, and, within the military, who served in Vietnam. Because of this nonrandom assignment, differences that we observe today in current PTSD prevalence between the study groups may be attributable to differences in the experiences of the groups (for example, service in Vietnam), but they may also result from differences in some characteristics or experiences that theater veterans *brought with them* to their military service.

Additionally, within the group of Vietnam theater veterans, we know that there was great heterogeneity in their experiences while in Vietnam. Therefore, it is of interest to know whether differences in PTSD prevalence between Vietnam veteran subgroups (for example, Black versus White/other males) reflect differences in premilitary characteristics, differences in their experiences while in Vietnam, or both. A finding that exposure to war-zone stress is significantly related to current PTSD would further increase our confidence that the higher PTSD prevalence among theater veterans results from their war experiences.

For convenience, we refer to the collection of characteristics, experiences, etc., that *predate* military or Vietnam experience and that might conceivably account for differences among the study groups in current PTSD prevalence rates as "potential predisposing factors." To capture variability in experiences while in Vietnam, we will use the measures of exposure to war-zone stress that are described in detail in Volume II, Appendix C.

The problem of nonrandom assignment to study groups is one that is frequently encountered in applied social research. However, by using multivariate statistical techniques, we can partially overcome the problem of nonrandom assignment and thus increase confidence that differences between the groups are attributable to differences in the experiences by which the groups were defined (that is, participation in the military or the war). By examining the study group contrasts in a multivariate analysis framework, we can assess the extent to which potential predisposing factors account for (or explain) the group differences in current PTSD rates that we have observed.

In essence, such analyses allow us to make the group comparisons while *controlling for* the effects of the potential predisposing factors. For example, if the observed differences in current PTSD prevalence rates between theater and era veterans were to be greatly decreased (or even wiped out completely) when the potential predisposing factors are controlled for, then we could see the PTSD rate differences between the two groups as largely a function of the characteristics or experiences that theater veterans had before the war and not as a function of their experiences in Vietnam. On the other hand, if the theater versus era veteran differences in PTSD rate were not greatly reduced (or were increased) by controlling for predisposing factors, then confidence would be increased that the difference we observed are due to group differences in exposure to the Vietnam experience (service in the war zone).

In principle, the list of potential predisposing factors that could be examined is infinite—that is, any number of background characteristics might plausibly be hypothesized to influence the current PTSD prevalence estimates. To address this problem, the NSVG interview included questions about a broad range of potential mental health risk factors and other background characteristics that might predispose a person to develop PTSD. A large group of such variables was selected as candidates for analysis of the effect of predisposing factors on the group prevalence rates. These variables can be divided into those that are appropriate for the specific study group contrasts: childhood and family background factors (characteristics and experiences of the person up to the age of 18) that are relevant to all contrasts; premilitary factors that are relevant to the theater versus era veteran contrast; pre-Vietnam military factors and Vietnam experience factors that are relevant to the within-theater veteran subgroup contrasts. The major categories of variables that we have included, and some illustrative examples of variables from each category, are shown in Exhibit V-1. (The full list of potential predisposing factors that were included in the analysis is shown in Appendix F.)

To examine the extent to which potential predisposing factors might account for observed study group differences, we conducted a series of multivariate statistical analyses. These analyses provided estimates of the difference in current PTSD prevalence for each of the standard study group contrasts, taking into account (or "adjusting for") differences among the groups in the set of potential predisposing variables. Table IV-1 presents the results of these analyses as the "adjusted" contrasts. Appendix F provides details of the statistical procedures involved in making these adjustments.

One way of interpreting the effect of the adjustment for potential predisposing factors is to examine the extent to which the adjustment changes—either reduces or increases—the *difference* in current PTSD prevalence rates among the groups. A hypothetical example may be useful in highlighting the critical aspects of these analyses. Suppose that we were

EXHIBIT V-1
Major Categories of Potential Predisposing Factors for PTSD Contrasts

Category	Example Variables
I. *Childhood and family background factors*	
A. Demographic characteristics	Age, race, family religious background
B. Family socioeconomic status	Parents' education, father's occupation
C. Family social environment	Relationship with parents, health/mental health problems of family/household members, child abuse
D. Biopsychosocial factors	Health/mental health problems among first-degree relatives
E. Childhood behavior problems	"Delinquent" behaviors index
F. Childhood health and mental health status	Health/mental health symptoms during childhood/adolescence
II. *Premilitary factors*	
A. Role status	Age, educational attainment, marital status at time of entry into military
B. Health and mental health status	Health and mental health problems prior to entry into military
III. *Military factors*	
A. General—non-Vietnam	Non-Vietnam combat duty, other overseas military duty
B. Pre-Vietnam role status	Age, educational attainment at beginning of Vietnam service
C. Pre-Vietnam health and mental health status	Health/mental health problems prior to beginning of Vietnam service
D. Vietnam	War-zone-stress-exposure indices

contrasting the current PTSD prevalence rates of groups A and B, and had found the prevalence for group A to be 36 percent and that for group B to be 12 percent. The difference in prevalence between these groups then is $36 - 12 = 24$ points. It is this difference between the groups in current PTSD prevalence that is the focus of these analyses.

Now suppose that after adjusting for potential predisposing factors, we found that the difference in prevalence was only 18 percentage points. We could then say that the adjustment for potential predisposing factors had reduced the prevalence difference from 24 to 18 percentage points, which is a 25 percent reduction [$(24 - 18) \div 24 = 0.25$].

It is important to note that the larger the change in the prevalence difference after adjustment, the greater is the net effect of selection factors in determining who served in the military or who went to Vietnam. Also, a decrease in the PTSD prevalence difference between theater veterans and the comparison groups resulting from the adjustment would suggest adverse selection, in that those who actually went to war had characteristics that made them more likely to develop PTSD. Conversely, an increase in the PTSD prevalence difference would suggest favorable selection, in that those who served had characteristics that made them less likely to develop PTSD.

Those Who Went to War and Those Who Didn't

Exhibit V-2 shows for each of the study's major contrasts the current PTSD prevalence rate difference before and after the adjustment for potential predisposing factors, and expresses the change resulting from the adjustment as a percentage (percent change from the unadjusted difference). Generally, the predisposition adjustment decreased the PTSD prevalence rate difference between theater veterans and the comparison groups. The effect was more pronounced for theater veteran versus civilian counterpart contrasts than for theater versus era veteran contrasts, suggesting that theater and era veterans were more alike in terms of these background characteristics than theater veterans and civilian counterparts.

For total theater males, the percent change in prevalence for both theater versus civilian contrasts (theater versus civilian and theater high war-zone-stress exposure versus civilian) exceeds 20 percent, whereas for theater versus era contrasts the percent change is 4.7 and 12.5 percent for the overall and high war-zone-stress exposure contrasts respectively. This pattern generally holds for the racial/ethnic subgroups as well.

The effect of the predisposition adjustment is generally smaller for women than for men, possibly reflecting the greater occupational (and, therefore, educational and socioeconomic status) homogeneity of the female study groups. In fact, the female theater high war-zone-stress exposure versus era veteran contrast is unchanged by the adjustment, and the PTSD prevalence difference between female theater and era veterans is increased by the adjustment, as are the differences between female service-connected physical disability groups. The prevalence differences for the female disability groups, which were not significant before adjustment, are significantly different after adjustment for predisposing variables.

EXHIBIT V-2
Comparison Group PTSD Prevalence Rate Differences Before and After
Adjustment for Potential Predisposing Factors

		Group PTSD Prevalence Rate Difference:		
Group	Contrast	Before Adjustment	After Adjustment	Percent Change from Adjustment
Males	Theater vs. Era	12.7	12.1	−4.7
(total)	Theater HWZ vs. Era	32.9	28.8	−12.5
	Theater vs. Civilian	14.0	10.4	−25.7
	Theater HWZ vs. Civilian	34.5	26.8	−22.3
White/	Theater vs. Era	11.4	11.3	−0.9
Other	Theater HWZ vs. Era	31.6	27.1	−14.2
Males	Theater vs. Civilian	12.7	9.0	−29.1
	Theater HWZ vs. Civilian	33.1	23.7	−28.4
Black	Theater vs. Era	16.2	14.8	−8.6
Males	Theater HWZ vs. Era	33.2	31.3	−5.7
	Theater vs. Civilian	19.3	18.1	−6.2
	Theater HWZ vs. Civilian	36.8	28.5	−22.6
Hispanic	Theater vs. Era	25.8	24.3	−5.8
Males	Theater HWZ vs. Era	46.2	44.5	−3.7
	Theater vs. Civilian	24.0	19.9	−17.1
	Theater HWZ vs. Civilian	44.4	39.6	−10.8
Females	Theater vs. Era	7.4	7.9	+6.8
	Theater HWZ vs. Era	16.4	16.4	0.0
	Theater vs. Civilian	8.2	8.1	−1.2
	Theater HWZ vs. Civilian	17.2	16.4	−4.7
Theater	White/Other vs. Black	−6.9	−6.2	−10.1
Males	White/Other vs. Hispanic	−14.2	−6.1	−57.0
	Black vs. Hispanic	−7.3	−2.4*	−67.1
	High vs. Low/Moderate WZ	27.3	18.4	−32.6
	SCPD: Yes vs. No	6.9	6.8	−1.4
	SCPD: High vs. No	9.0	9.3	+3.3
	Substance Abuse: Pos vs. Neg	13.9	4.9	−64.7
Theater	High vs. Low/Moderate WZ	14.9	13.2	−11.4
Females	SCPD: Yes vs. No	5.4*	7.1	+31.5
	SCPD: High vs. No	3.7*	7.8*	+110.8
	Substance Abuse: Pos vs. Neg	24.2	21.0	−13.2

*Prevalence rate difference not statistically distinguishable from zero; i.e., there is no difference in current PTSD prevalence between the contrasted groups.

The characteristics that typically contribute significantly to the adjustment models across contrasts include number of problem behaviors in childhood, meeting the criteria for a diagnosis of antisocial personality disorder before age 18, having been a member of a family that had trouble making (economic) ends meet, and having one or more first-degree relatives with a mental disorder. Thus, both socioeconomic factors and mental health factors are important in the adjustment. (Full details of the models and their coefficients for each contrast are provided in Appendix F.)

To summarize, the findings of the adjusted theater versus era veteran and civilian counterpart contrasts indicate that there is a significant predisposition effect. However, the current prevalence of PTSD among Vietnam theater veterans is much higher than among era veterans and civilian counterparts even after we take into account differences in a large group of potential predisposing factors. Thus, we cannot explain the high current prevalence of PTSD among Vietnam veterans solely on the basis of characteristics that they brought with them to the war. This finding is consistent with the hypothesis that the experiences to which theater veterans were exposed in Vietnam play an important role in determining current PTSD prevalence.

Those Who Saw Combat and Those Who Didn't

The greatest impact of the predisposition adjustment was on the contrasts within the theater veteran group. The adjustment reduced the current PTSD prevalence difference between White/other and Hispanic male theater veterans by 57 percent and the difference between Black and Hispanic males by 67 percent. Additionally, the adjustment reduced the difference in current PTSD prevalence between Black and Hispanic males to 2.4 percent, a difference that is not significantly different from zero. In other words, the adjustment for potential predisposing factors greatly reduced the current PTSD prevalence differential between White/others and both Hispanics and Blacks, and wiped out (reduced to zero) the PTSD prevalence difference between Blacks and Hispanics. Also, the difference between high and low/moderate war-zone-stress exposure groups was reduced by 33 percent and the differences between lifetime substance abuse groups by 65 percent.

The variables that consistently contributed to these theater veteran subgroup predisposition adjustment models include four factors: having grown up in a family that had a hard time making ends meet, having had symptoms of drug abuse or dependence before entering the military, having had symptoms of an affective disorder before going to Vietnam, and problem behaviors of childhood. Thus, again the variables being controlled for are a mixture of economic and mental health symptom variables.

THE ROLE OF VIETNAM EXPERIENCE

The fact that current PTSD prevalence rates for theater veterans are consistently and substantially higher than those of era veterans or civilian counterparts, combined with the fact that the prevalence difference between theater veterans exposed to higher levels of war-zone stress and the era veteran and civilian counterpart comparison groups are even higher, even with potential predisposing factors controlled, suggests an important role for Vietnam experience in theater veteran PTSD.

We can gain additional information about the role of Vietnam experience in theater veterans' PTSD by examining the contrasts between subgroups of theater veterans. Exhibit V-2 shows clearly that, even after potential predisposing factors are controlled, the current PTSD prevalence rate among theater veterans exposed to high levels of war-zone stress is much higher than the rate among those exposed to low or moderate levels: 18 percentage points for males, 13 percentage points for females. This suggests a substantial role for war-zone-stress exposure in determining who gets PTSD.

In an effort to obtain a clearer understanding of the role of Vietnam experience in the current PTSD prevalence rate among theater males, we extended the multivariate analyses that accomplished the adjustment for the potential predisposing factors one additional step. This step involved adding the global war-zone-stress exposure variable[1] to the predisposition adjustment models for the male theater veteran racial/ethnic subgroup contrasts. Doing so allowed us to determine whether the between-group differences in current PTSD prevalence rate that remained after the predisposition adjustment could be further reduced by taking into account exposure to war-zone stress.

With the predisposing variables and exposure to war-zone stress controlled, the difference in current PTSD prevalence between White/other and Black theater veterans was reduced to the point where it was not significantly different from zero. Thus, when a set of potential predisposing factors and a global measure of exposure to war-zone stress were controlled, there was no difference in current PTSD prevalence rate between Black and White/other theater veterans.

---

[1]Additional analyses conducted using the specific dimensional measures of war-zone-stress exposure, rather than the single overall index, yielded the same essential results.

Adjusting for significant stress exposure had a different effect on the White/other versus Hispanic contrast and the Black versus Hispanic contrast, however. The difference in current PTSD prevalence between White/other and Hispanic males was reduced slightly, from 6.1 percent (adjusted for predisposition) to 5.4 percent. This difference remains statistically significant. The difference for the Black versus Hispanic contrast, which was reduced to zero by the predisposition adjustment, became 6.3 percent (Hispanic higher than Black) when war-zone-stress exposure was controlled.

Thus, after adjusting for potentially predisposing variables *and* for exposure to war-zone stress, there is no difference in the current PTSD prevalence of White/other and Black theater veterans. However, even after adjusting for a large number of potentially predisposing variables and for exposure to war-zone stress, the current prevalence of PTSD among Hispanics is about 5 percent higher than among Whites and about 6 percent higher than among Blacks. It remains for further analysis to identify the factors that account for these differences.

Several conclusions seem warranted from this set of analyses of the role of potential predisposing factors and Vietnam experience factors in current PTSD prevalence. First, the current prevalence of PTSD is much higher among Vietnam theater veterans than among era veterans or civilian counterparts. Second, theater veterans differed from era veterans and civilian counterparts on some background characteristics that are related to current PTSD and that might have rendered theater veterans more vulnerable to the development of PTSD. Nevertheless the current PTSD prevalence rate is much higher among theater veterans even after these differences in potential predisposing factors are taken into account. Third, exposure to war-zone stress in Vietnam plays a significant role in determining who among theater veterans has PTSD today, even after a broad array of potential predisposing factors have been controlled for.

Taken together, these results are consistent with a model of PTSD that posits a role for individual vulnerability (potentially including biological, psychological, and sociodemographic factors) *and* a role for exposure to environmental factors (specifically, war-zone stressors), in determining who among theater veterans gets PTSD. However, it is clear that exposure to war-zone stress makes a substantial contribution to the development of PTSD in war veterans that is independent of a broad range of potential predisposing factors.

CHAPTER VI

The Prevalence of Other Psychiatric Disorders and Nonspecific Distress

COMMENTARY

Is there a higher rate of mental disorder—aside from post-traumatic stress disorder—among Vietnam theater veterans than among Vietnam era veterans or similar aged civilians? This question provides the focus for Chapter VI, and in addressing it, several related issues must be considered. Do we find similar rates for males and females? Is there a relationship between war-zone stress and mental disorders, aside from that found for PTSD? Do rates vary according to race or ethnicity?

In assessing the prevalence of mental disorders among Vietnam veterans, this study has been more comprehensive than previous studies on the subject. First, it was a national study rather than one conducted at a few select sites in the country, and it estimated rates of disorder for theater veterans and era veterans separately. Second, the study looked at the entire population of Vietnam veterans, that is, men and women from all services, enlisted and officer, career and one term. It is the only study to have developed prevalence rates of mental disorder for female veterans, and it is the first to examine differences in rate by race and ethnicity, and by levels of exposure to war-zone stress. Finally, this study is unique in its use of civilians who were matched (demographically) to theater veterans, and its use of statistical weighting procedures to compensate for (demographic) differences among theater veterans, era veterans, and civilians.

Establishing the relative rates of mental disorders for various veteran and civilian groups can help us to understand better the factors that affect the development of mental disorder. It can also aid in the determining of the level of need for mental health services by Vietnam veterans.

CHAPTER OVERVIEW

This chapter provides information on levels and patterns of general psychiatric symptomatology, as well as lifetime and current prevalence rates of psychiatric disorders other than PTSD.

"Nonspecific distress" refers to symptomatology that may be associated with a variety of psychiatric disorders rather than to the symptoms of a specific diagnostic category. Nonspecific distress was measured in the NSVG using the Demoralization Scale from the Psychiatric Epidemiology Research Interview (PERI).

An examination of patterns of nonspecific distress indicated that the major elevations in levels of nonspecific distress were found among those exposed to high levels of war-zone stress, those with PTSD, those with a lifetime substance abuse disorder, and, for men, those with a high level of service-connected disability. Theater veteran men who were members of a minority group (Black or Hispanic) also had higher rates of distress than White/other men. However, those with the highest rates of nonspecific distress were men and women with PTSD.

This chapter also contains a detailed discussion of prevalence rates, and patterns of prevalence, for nine specific psychiatric disorders (other than PTSD) assessed in the NSVG, as well as a discussion of two summary measures of these disorders. These disorders, which were assessed using the Diagnostic Interview Schedule (DIS), are major depressive episode, manic episode, dysthymia, obsessive compulsive disorder, panic disorder, generalized anxiety disorder, alcohol abuse or dependence, drug abuse or dependence, and antisocial personality disorder.

A *major depressive episode* is an extended period (two weeks or more) during which the person feels pervasively depressed, sad, or blue, and also experiences a variety of other symptoms, such as a profound loss of interest in activities, loss of appetite, and sleep problems. A *manic episode* is a period during which the person experiences an abnormal and persistently euphoric or "high" mood, and also experiences other symptoms, such as hyperactivity, decreased need for sleep, and grandiose ideas. *Dysthymia*, or dysthymic disorder, is a chronic mood disturbance that lasts for at least two years and is characterized by feeling "low" or "blue" most of the time. Dysthymia differs from a major depressive episode in that the depressed mood is less severe but more persistent. *Obsessive compulsive disorder* is characterized by the occurrence of persistent, irrational thoughts and images, or unwanted, recurrent behaviors that the person feels powerless to control. *Panic disorder* is characterized by sudden attacks of severe and disabling irrational fear or terror. *Generalized anxiety disorder* is characterized by anxiety that persists for at least one month, accompanied by an array of cognitive and physiological symptoms, including feeling nervous or jumpy, sweating, heart pounding, and dizziness. Both *alcohol abuse and dependence* and *drug abuse and dependence* are characterized by behavioral changes that result from regular and/or heavy use of psychoactive drugs or alcohol. *Antisocial personality disorder* is characterized by a history of continuous and chronic antisocial behavior in which the rights of others are violated. The category "any NSVG/DIS disorder" is a summary measure for any of the nine psychiatric disorders described above. Except for dysthymia, prevalence rates for all disorders were assessed as "lifetime" (i.e., the individual had the disorder at some time in his/her life) and/or "current," where "current" is defined as within the past six months.

For the nine specific psychiatric disorders other than PTSD assessed in the NSVG, those that occurred most frequently among male Vietnam theater veterans were alcohol abuse or dependence, generalized anxiety disorder (GAD), and antisocial personality disorder (ASP). None of these rates were significantly different from those observed for male Vietnam era veterans, but the theater veteran rates for ASP and alcohol abuse or dependence were higher than those for male civilians. The most prevalent current disorders among male theater veterans are alcohol abuse or dependence and GAD, both of which had rates of above 5 percent. However, for neither disorder were the rates for Vietnam theater veteran males higher than for Vietnam era veteran males or male civilians. Current symptoms of antisocial personality disorder are relatively rare among male theater veterans.

Among Vietnam theater veteran women, the most frequently occurring lifetime disorders were GAD, depression, and alcohol abuse or dependence. The lifetime rates for both depression and alcohol abuse or dependence were significantly higher for women theater veterans than for women era veterans or civilians. This was not true for GAD. The most prevalent current disorders among female Vietnam theater veterans were depression and GAD, both of which were at rates of just over 4 percent. These rates were significantly higher than those for Vietnam era women or civilian women for depression but not for GAD.

In general, the rates for these various psychiatric disorders among Vietnam era veterans, civilians, and Vietnam theater veterans exposed to low levels of war-zone stress were within the ranges reported for community samples in the NIMH-sponsored Epidemiologic Catchment Area (ECA) studies.

Both men and women Vietnam theater veterans had higher levels of current depression than either civilians or Vietnam era veterans. When the era veteran and civilian groups were statistically matched with theater veterans on age and race for men and age and occupation for women, there was *no* disorder for which the rates for Vietnam era veterans and civilians were higher than those of Vietnam theater veterans. However, there were several disorders for which the rates for Vietnam theater veterans, overall, were higher than those for Vietnam era veterans or civilians. In addition to current depression, the disorders for which theater veterans had higher rates differ by gender and comparison group (that is, era veterans or civilians). Based on these results, it appears that having served in Vietnam, in comparison with serving elsewhere in the military during the Vietnam era, did not greatly increase one's risk for most of the NSVG/DIS disorders. However, the number of psychiatric disorders for which theater veterans rates were higher than civilian rates suggests that serving in the military during that time was in and of itself a risk factor for some disorders.

In contrast to the few differences found between theater veterans overall and their Vietnam era veteran counterparts, an examination of data for those most often thought of as "Vietnam veterans," that is, those with high levels of exposure to war-zone stress, produced much more dramatic findings. Male theater veterans who experienced high war-zone stress had higher rates of almost all of these psychiatric disorders than did era veterans and civilians. The rates of virtually all of these disorders were also higher for theater males exposed to high war-zone stress, by comparison with theater males exposed to low/moderate war-zone stress, further validating the finding of higher rates for these disorders among Vietnam theater males most heavily involved in the war.

Among female Vietnam theater veterans, fewer disorders were associated with level of exposure to war-zone stress, although the prevalence rates for some disorders among those exposed to high war-zone stress appear to be quite high. Their rates for lifetime depression and dysthymia were significantly higher than those for era veterans, civilians, and Vietnam theater veteran women exposed to low/moderate levels of war-zone stress. Major depressive episode is the one current disorder for which significantly higher rates were observed among women exposed to high war-zone stress than for all other groups of women: era veterans, civilians, and women exposed to low/moderate levels of war-zone stress.

Having a service-connected physical disability (SCPD) appeared to have very little effect on the prevalence rates of these psychiatric disorders: males with a high level of SCPD had higher rates only for lifetime generalized anxiety disorder, and females with a SCPD did not have higher prevalence rates for any disorder. Being Black also had little effect on rates of disorder, although Blacks did tend to have higher rates of ASP, significantly so for current ASP. Being Hispanic had a somewhat greater impact. When examining data on these various disorders combined, it is seen that Hispanic men had rates 10–15 percent higher than Blacks or White/others, regardless of whether one includes or excludes the alcohol-use disorders. Nevertheless, Hispanic Vietnam theater veterans tended to be particularly troubled by problems with alcohol and drugs.

A very high degree of co-occurence among PTSD, substance abuse, and other psychiatric disorders was perhaps the most striking finding for these specific psychiatric disorders. Male Vietnam theater veterans with PTSD had significantly higher rates for all disorders except manic episode. Female theater veterans with PTSD had significantly higher rates for most of these other disorders as well. Differences between those with and those without PTSD were statistically significant and quite dramatic. Three-fourths of the men with PTSD had a lifetime diagnosis of alcohol abuse or dependence, 44 percent had a lifetime diagnosis of GAD, and more than 20 percent had a lifetime diagnosis of depression, dysthymia, or ASP. Among males with PTSD, three current NSVG/DIS disorders were found to have prevalence rates in the 16–20 percent range: current alcohol disorder, current GAD, and current depression. Forty-two percent of the women with PTSD had lifetime depression, and almost one-fourth had a recent major depressive episode. More than three-eighths of these women had lifetime GAD and one-fifth have it currently. Other lifetime rates above 20 percent for women were for dysthymia, panic disorder, and the alcohol disorders. Other current rates at 10 percent or above for women with PTSD are panic disorder and the alcohol disorders.

This high degree of co-occurence might raise questions concerning the uniqueness of the PTSD diagnosis. However, by noting which disorders have the highest degree of comorbidity—for example, alcohol abuse or dependence, depression, dysthymia, and generalized anxiety—it is clear that these disorders have considerable symptom overlap with PTSD, and are not unlikely to co-occur with the disorder. Also, having almost any psychiatric disorder has been found in previous studies to increase the risk for having another disorder. For example, in the NSVG data, substance abuse also has a high degree of co-occurence with several other disorders. Specifically, males with a history of substance abuse had higher rates for most other disorders than men without such a history, and women with substance abuse also had higher rates for several disorders.

The finding of high rates of ASP among those with PTSD was also discussed. It was hypothesized that the relationship with ASP is probably, at least in part, attributable to a selection bias, since those with ASP were more likely to have experienced high war-zone stress as well. It may also reflect a vulnerability to PTSD among those with ASP.

PATTERNS OF NONSPECIFIC PSYCHOLOGICAL DISTRESS

"Nonspecific distress" refers to symptomatology that may be associated with a variety of different psychiatric disorders, rather than with only one specific diagnostic category, such as post-traumatic stress with disorder or major depressive disorder. Thus, an examination of nonspecific distress entails an assessment of levels of psychological distress experienced by individuals across psychiatric disorders, analogous to the role of body temperature as an indicator of general illness rather than of any specific condition.

To assess nonspecific psychological distress in the NSVG, we included in the interview an index to assess level of "demoralization." This scale was taken from the Psychiatric Epidemiology Research Interview (PERI), which was developed as part of a general research effort to provide measures of multiple dimensions of psychopathology in the general population (Dohrenwend et al., 1980). Items were initially grouped into 25 scales that had been evaluated for clinical meaningfulness, reliability, and empirical distinctiveness. A subset of eight of these scales (dread, anxiety, sadness, helplessness, hopelessness, psychophysiological symptoms, perceived physical health, poor self-esteem, and confused thinking) correlated quite highly with one another (Dohrenwend et al., 1980; Dohrenwend & Shrout, 1981; Dohrenwend, Levav & Shrout, 1986). Together they appeared to reflect a latent construct very similar to "demoralization" as originally described by Frank (1973). The investigators therefore combined these eight scales into a single scale of "demoralization" and subsequently developed a 27-item short form. This version was adapted for the NSVG. A summary of findings related to this Demoralization Scale is found in Exhibit VI-1. (The full data are found in Table VI-1 in Volume II.)

Contrasts Among Vietnam Theater Veterans, Era Veterans, and Civilians

Almost 17 percent of male Vietnam theater veterans reported high levels of nonspecific psychological distress (PERI Demoralization scores of 1.5 or higher), but their scores were not significantly higher than those reported by comparable era veterans (16 percent), either for males overall or within the three racial/ethnic subgroups examined. In contrast, male theater veterans reported significantly higher levels of distress than their

EXHIBIT VI-1
Summary of Contrasts Among Major Study Groups and Vietnam Theater Veteran Subgroups for PERI Demoralization Scores

A. *Males—Total*
1. Thr vs. Era   NS
2. HWZ vs. Era   HWZ > Era***
3. LWZ vs. Era   NS
4. Thr vs. Civ   Thr > Civ*
5. HWC vs. Civ   HWZ > Civ***

B. *Males—White/Other*
1. Thr vs. Era   NS
2. HWZ vs. Era   HWZ > Era***
3. LWZ vs. Era   NS
4. Thr vs. Civ   NS
5. HWZ vs. Civ   HWZ > Civ***

C. *Males—Black*
1. Thr vs. Era   NS
2. HWZ vs. Era   NS
3. LWZ vs. Era   NS
4. Thr vs. Civ   NS
5. HWZ vs. Civ   HWZ > Civ**

D. *Males—Hispanic*
1. Thr vs. Era   NS
2. HWZ vs. Era   HWZ > Era**
3. LWZ vs. Era   NS
4. Thr vs. Civ   Thr > Civ**
5. HWZ vs. Civ   HWZ > Civ***

E. *Females—Total*
1. Thr vs. Era   NS
2. HWZ vs. Era   NS
3. LWZ vs. Era   Era > LWZ***
4. Thr vs. Civ   NS
5. HWZ vs. Civ   NS

F. *Race/Ethnicity*
1. W/O vs. Blk   Blk > W/O**
2. W/O vs. Hisp   Hisp > W/O***
3. Blk vs. Hisp   NS

G. *High vs. Low Warzone Stress*
1. Males   HWZ > LWZ***
2. Females   HWZ > LWZ***

H. *PTSD vs. No PTSD*
1. Males   PTSD > No PTSD***
2. Females   PTSD > No PTSD***

I. *Service-Connected Physical Disability*
1. Males
   a. SCPD vs. None   NS
   b. High SCPD vs. None   High SCPD > None*
2. Females
   a. SCPD vs. None   NS
   b. High SCPD vs. None   NS

J. *Substance Abuse vs. None*
1. Males   SAB > None***
2. Females   SAB > None***

Notes: 1. < = lower than; > = higher than.
2. *p < 0.05; **p < 0.01; ***p < 0.001; NS = not statistically significant; NT = not tested (0 cell).

civilian counterparts. This difference achieved statistical significance among men overall and among Hispanic men, and approached statistical significance among White/other men. Moreover, as one might expect, men most directly involved in the war (those exposed to high levels of war-zone stress) reported significantly higher demoralization scores than both era veterans and civilians. Men exposed to high war stress were almost twice as likely as Vietnam era veterans (32.2 versus 16.9 percent) to score at the highest level on demoralization and over four times as likely as civilians (7.1 percent). We examined these differences within each racial/ethnic subgroup studied, and found that theater veterans who were exposed to high war stress had scores that were significantly higher than those of their civilian counterparts within all groups and that were significantly higher than those of era veterans among both White/others and Hispanics, though not among Blacks. The greatest differences between groups were those involving Hispanic men. For this group, the mean demoralization score for men who were exposed to high war stress was 50 percent higher than the score for either Hispanic male Vietnam era veterans or civilians.

For women, 14 percent of those serving in the Vietnam theater reported high levels of nonspecific distress, a level not significantly higher than those reported by either era veteran or civilian women. Although somewhat larger differences were observed between women who were exposed to high levels of war-zone stress and these two comparison groups, neither of these achieved statistical significance. In fact, among females, the only significant difference was between theater veteran women who were exposed to low to moderate levels of war-zone stress and era veteran women, with the former reporting significantly lower levels of nonspecific psychological distress.

Contrasts Among Vietnam Theater Veterans

MALES. Minority group members, both Blacks and Hispanics, had significantly higher demoralization scores than White/others, but they did not differ significantly from one another. Those with high levels of war-zone stress, with high percentages of service-connected disabilities (SCPD), with PTSD, and with a history of substance abuse (SAB) all had higher levels of nonspecific distress than those with low war-zone stress, with no SCPD or PTSD, and no SAB history, respectively. This difference was particularly striking for those with PTSD. Among men with PTSD, 56 percent scored in the highest category on demoralization, compared with only 10 percent of those without PTSD.

FEMALES. Demoralization scores for women with high war-zone stress exposure were significantly higher than those with low or moderate war-zone stress exposure. As with males, female theater veterans with PTSD and/or a history of substance abuse also reported significantly higher levels of demoralization than those without those conditions. For example, almost two-thirds of women veterans with PTSD scored at the highest level on demoralization, almost eight times higher than those without the disorder.

MEASUREMENT OF SPECIFIC PSYCHIATRIC DISORDERS

The instrument used to assess the prevalence of specific mental disorders in the NSVG was the National Institute of Mental Health (NIMH) Diagnostic Interview Schedule (DIS) (Robins et al., 1981). The DIS is a standardized psychiatric interview designed for use by lay interviewers in community survey settings. The DIS gathers data on symptoms that are germane to the diagnosis of a large range of major mental disorders and can be scored according to the criteria of the American Psychiatric Association's *Diagnostic and Statistical Manual of Mental Disorders*, revised third edition (DSM-III-R). The DIS was first used in the NIMH-sponsored Epidemiologic Catchment Area (ECA) collaborative research program (Eaton & Kessler, 1985; Regier et al., 1984), which surveyed the mental health status of community and institutional populations at five sites (New Haven, Baltimore, St. Louis, the Piedmont area of North Carolina, and Los Angeles). The ECA studies established benchmark community prevalence estimates of psychiatric disorder against which prevalence estimates of psychiatric disorder in other studies could be compared.

The DIS has a number of separate modules, each used for diagnosing a different psychiatric disorder. A subset of these modules was used in the NSVG to assess nine psychiatric disorders (discussed below) that are subsumed under the diagnostic categories of affective disorders, anxiety disorders, substance abuse disorders, and personality disorders.[1]

Affective Disorders

The affective disorders (mood disorders) assessed in the NSVG were major depressive episodes, manic episodes, and dysthymia. A *major*

---

[1]Not all of the diagnostic modules of the DIS were included in the NSVG instrumentation to avoid further lengthening the NSVG interview. The DIS modules omitted were those used to assess disorders that were expected to be rare in the population of Vietnam veterans (e.g., the schizophrenic disorders), and/or less important in understanding the postwar readjustment problems of veterans (e.g., simple phobias).

depressive episode is characterized by a pervasive feeling of being down, sad, or blue as well as by a profound loss of interest in everyday activities. Such a period must last at least two weeks and predominate for virtually the whole two-week period, although a major depressive episode frequently lasts for months at a time. Associated symptoms include sleep disturbances, appetite change, feelings of worthlessness, and hopelessness about the future. A major depressive episode is not the same as the vague or temporary feelings of being sad or blue that individuals often experience in their everyday lives. Rather, it is a major and debilitating psychiatric disorder.

A *manic episode* is usually characterized by an abnormally euphoric mood, although occasionally anger and irritability are present. Thoughts race through the mind and the individual feels endowed with special powers and abilities. Frequently, there is an abnormal increase in ordinary activities such as talking and movement, along with a decreased need for sleep. The irrational beliefs and behaviors associated with a manic episode often have serious negative outcomes for the individual and his or her family.

Dysthymia, or dysthymic disorder, is characterized by a depressive mood and other feelings of being down, blue, sad, or worthless. In contrast to a major depressive episode, dysthymia is longer lasting (at least two years) but less debilitating. There is usually less disruption in ordinary activities than in a major depressive episode, and physiological symptoms, such as changes in appetite and sleep patterns, are less frequent or severe than in major depression. Nonetheless, dysthymia also has a tremendous negative impact on the individual's life for a prolonged period, often several years.

Anxiety Disorders

The anxiety disorders that are assessed in the NSVG and discussed in the presentation to follow are obsessive compulsive disorders, panic disorders, and generalized anxiety disorders. *Obsessive compulsive disorder* is a combination of two distinct phenomena. Obsessions are recurrent thoughts that are irrational and unwanted. These thoughts both interfere with ordinary functioning and come to dominate the person's life. An example of an obsession is an overwhelming fear of contamination by germs or dirt. Compulsions are sets of repetitive behaviors that the individual feels compelled to repeat over and over, and, often, in exactly the same order each time. However, the fears that the behaviors are meant to assuage are not alleviated by the behaviors. An example of a compulsion is the need to check and recheck doors that are known to be locked to deter intruders, and yet the anxiety about intruders is not abated. Obsessive-compulsive disorder is a relatively rare psychiatric disorder.

Panic disorder is uniquely characterized by unexplained, overwhelming, and "out-of-the-blue" experiences of fear or terror that are neither rational nor comprehensible. The attacks occur during distinct, deliminated "spells" and are unpredictable, although they may come to be associated with the settings (for example, shopping centers) in which they initially occurred. There are major physiological symptoms such as dizziness and chest pain, typically accompanied by fearful thoughts such as thoughts that one is going to die or pass out. People with panic disorder often come to the attention of mental health professionals through the emergency room or medical centers to which they come seeking treatment for their symptoms.

Generalized anxiety disorder is marked by chronic feelings of uneasiness, worry, or severe anxiety about future events that are hypothetical and/or unspecified. Symptoms include sweaty palms, tremor, tenseness, restlessness, and vague foreboding of such severity that it impairs the individual's social, occupational, or school functioning.

Substance Abuse Disorders

The substance abuse disorders assessed in the NSVG include *alcohol abuse and dependence* and *drug abuse and dependence*. Substance abuse disorders are characterized by behavioral changes that result from regular and/or heavy use of drugs or alcohol. These behaviors include inability to stop using the substance (that is, feeling dependent); feeling like one needs larger amounts of the substance to get an effect; inability to function normally at work, at school, or among friends or family; withdrawal symptoms when one tries to cut down on the substance; and use of the substance frequently or in large amounts. Although alcohol dependence and abuse and drug dependence and abuse are in fact four separate disorders, dependence and abuse are combined in the analyses presented in this report to provide rates of dependence or abuse, consistent with the ECA studies.

Personality Disorders

The only personality disorder that is assessed by the DIS (and in the NSVG) is *antisocial personality disorder* (ASP). DSM-III states that the essential feature of ASP is "a history of continuous and chronic antisocial behavior in which the rights of others are violated, persistence into adult life of a pattern of antisocial behaviors that began before the age of 15, and failure to sustain good job performance over a period of several years." To meet the diagnostic criteria for ASP, one must have at least three antisocial symptoms before age 15. These "conduct disorder symptoms" include truancy, persistent lying, delinquency, theft, vandalism, and starting fights. After reaching the age of 18, the individual must exhibit at least four more symptoms to receive a diagnosis of ASP. The adult symptoms include the inability to maintain a relationship, recklessness, persistent lying, aggressiveness, and inability to obey rules and/or laws.

Any NSVG/DIS Disorder

This category includes the eight affective, anxiety, and substance abuse disorders described above, as well as ASP. Because of the high level of alcohol abuse and dependence in the male sample, it was felt these disorders might overshadow the other disorders. Therefore, we felt that it was important to examine also a "combined disorders" measure, which excluded the alcohol disorders. Thus, "any NSVG/DIS disorder excluding alcohol abuse and dependence" includes the same disorders as "any NSVG/DIS disorder" except alcohol abuse and dependence.

Lifetime and Current Diagnoses

In the NSVG, data from the DIS were scored by a computer diagnostic algorithm originally written at the St. Louis ECA site. This diagnostic algorithm yields both "lifetime" and "current" diagnoses for each of the specific psychiatric disorders. A "lifetime" diagnosis for a disorder means that the DSM-III criteria for that disorder were met at some point in the respondent's life. It should be noted that while "lifetime" diagnoses are meant to assess the prevalence of psychiatric disorder at any time during a person's life, there is reason to believe that lifetime diagnoses are not as reliable as "current" diagnosis, due to problems such as recall.

Those who meet the criteria for a "lifetime" diagnosis are then assessed for a "current" diagnosis. Those not meeting the lifetime criteria are set to negative for the "current" diagnosis. "Current" diagnoses can be established for several time periods (for example, within the past year, six months, one month). To yield data directly comparable to the community prevalence rates reported by the ECA research program, we elected to report as *current* diagnoses those established within the past six months. To receive a *current* diagnosis, the respondent must have experienced at least one symptom associated with that disorder in the past six months. Because of the way in which the DIS is structured, dysthymic disorder is only assessed *lifetime*. Further, although ASP is usually considered to be a disorder that is present throughout an individual's life, both *lifetime* and *current* ASP are assessed. As with the other disorders, current ASP indicates the presence in the past six months of at least one symptom of the disorder.

Appendix G, Volume II, provides information on validity studies of the various DIS modules. It also presents a table that allows a comparison of the DIS prevalence estimates from the NSVG with those from other relevant studies. Specifically, these are community prevalence estimates from the ECA and Vietnam theater and era veteran prevalence estimates from the Centers for Disease Control's Vietnam Experience Study (VES). Finally, in reading the discussion that follows for contrasts for the various disorders, it is important to remember that the tests of significance were done on era veteran and civilian data that were standardized to theater veterans on age and race/ethnicity for males, and on age and occupation for females. Since statistical contrasts used the standardized data, the rates quoted for theater veterans and civilians were from the relevant standardized data, that is, a discussion of theater/era veteran contrasts would cite era "standardized-to-theater" data, while high war-zone theater/era veteran differences would cite data on era veterans standardized to high war-zone-stress exposed theater veterans. Unstandardized as well as standardized data for era veterans are presented in the tables provided in Volume II. (See the introduction to that volume for a further discussion of standardization.)

Exhibits VI-2 through VI-6 present, in graph form, prevalence estimates of the nine specific psychiatric disorders for the various study groups. For males, these graphs present these disorders in descending order of their prevalence among male theater veterans; for females, they present these disorders in descending order of their prevalence among women theater veterans. These graphs are particularly useful in gaining a general understanding of the magnitude of the differences between groups. Detailed prevalence estimates and contrasts can be found in Volume II, Tables VI-2 through VI-22.

THE AFFECTIVE DISORDERS

Exhibits VI-7 and VI-8 summarize the contrasts among groups for the three affective disorders: depressive episode, manic episode, and dysthymia. Full prevalence estimates and contrasts can be found in Volume II, Tables VI-2 through VI-6.

It is important to note that the prevalence rate estimates for manic episode (lifetime and current) for both era veterans and civilians were zero, so that contrasts with these groups were not tested for this disorder. Even among theater veterans, these rates were low, and zero in some subgroups, so that, for many subgroups, these relationships were also not tested.

(text continued on page 107)

EXHIBIT VI-2

Prevalence of the Specific Psychiatric Disorders: Major Male Study Groups*

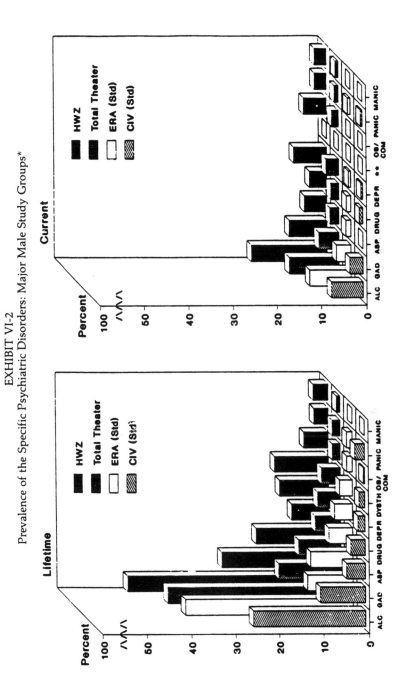

*In order of lifetime prevalence among male theater veterans.
**Current dysthymia is not assessed.

EXHIBIT VI-3

Prevalence of the Specific Psychiatric Disorders: Major Female Study Groups*

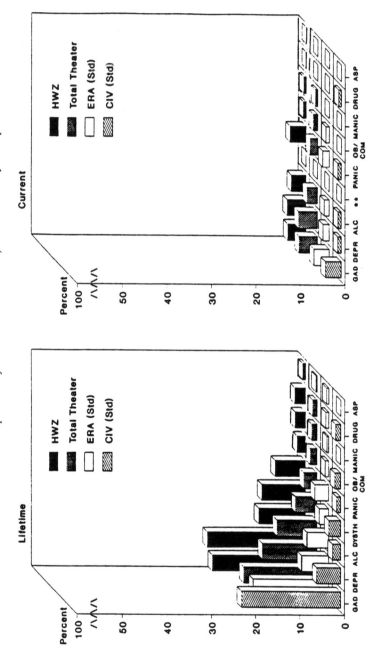

*In order of lifetime prevalence among female theater veterans.
**Current dysthymia is not assessed.

EXHIBIT VI-4

Prevalence of the Specific Psychiatric Disorders: Racial/Ethnic Groups of Male Theater Veterans*

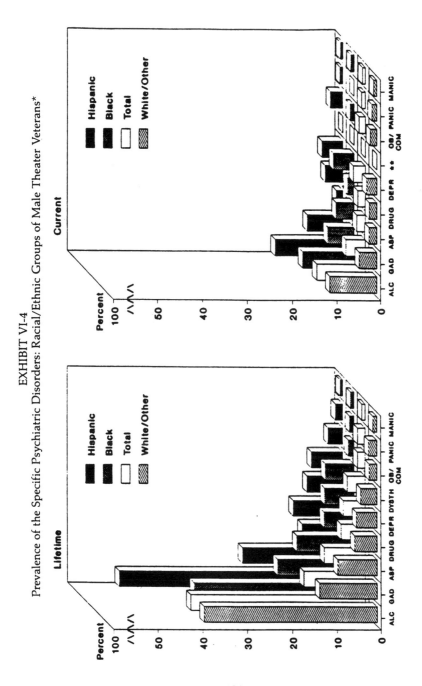

*In order of lifetime prevalence among male theater veterans.
**Current dysthymia is not assessed.

EXHIBIT VI-5

Prevalence of the Specific Psychiatric Disorders: Other Subgroups of Male Theater Veterans*

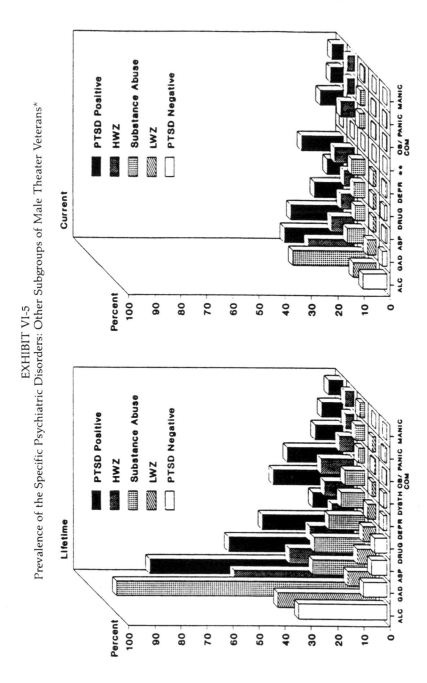

*In order of lifetime prevalence among male theater veterans.
**Current dysthymia is not assessed.

EXHIBIT VI-6

Prevalence of the Specific Psychiatric Disorders: Subgroups of Female Theater Veterans*

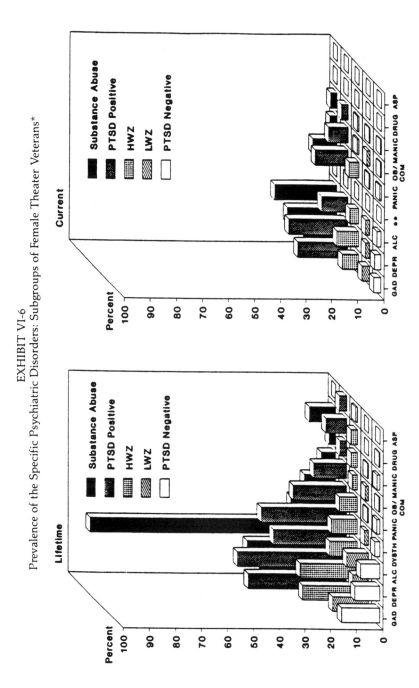

*In order of lifetime prevalence among female theater veterans.
**Current dysthymia is not assessed.

103

EXHIBIT VI-7
Summary of Contrasts for Major Study Groups for the Affective Disorders

| Major Study Groups | Major Depressive Episode | | Manic Episode | | Dysthymia |
	Lifetime	Current	Lifetime	Current	Lifetime
A. *Males—Total*					
1. Thr vs. Era	NS	Thr > Era**	NT	NT	NS
2. HWZ vs. Era	HWZ > Era**	HWZ > Era***	NT	NT	HWZ > Era***
3. LWZ vs. Era	NS	NS	NT	NT	NS
4. Thr vs. Civ	Thr > Civ**	Thr > Civ***	NT	NT	Thr > Era**
5. HWZ vs. Civ	HWZ > Civ***	HWZ > Civ***	NT	NT	HWZ > Civ***
B. *Males—White/Other*					
1. Thr vs. Era	NS	Thr > Era*	NT	NT	NS
2. HWZ vs. Era	NS	HWZ > Era**	NT	NT	HWZ > Era**
3. LWZ vs. Era	NS	NS	NT	NT	NS
4. Thr vs. Civ	Thr > Civ*	Thr > Civ***	NT	NT	NS
5. HWZ vs. Civ	HWZ > Civ**	HWZ > Civ**	NT	NT	HWZ > Civ**

C. *Males—Black*

1. Thr vs. Era	Thr > Era***	Thr > Era**	NT	NT	NS
2. HWZ vs. Era	HWZ > Era***	HWZ > Era**	NT	NT	NS
3. LWZ vs. Era	NS	NS	NT	NT	NS
4. Thr vs. Civ	NT	NT	NT	NT	NT
5. HWZ vs. Civ	NT	NT	NT	NT	NT

D. *Males—Hispanic*

1. Thr vs. Era	Thr > Era**	Thr > Era*	NT	NT	NT
2. HWZ vs. Era	HWZ > Era*	HWZ > Era*	NT	NT	NT
3. LWZ vs. Era	NS	NS	NT	NT	NT
4. Thr vs. Civ	NS	NS	NT	NT	Thr > Civ**
5. HWZ vs. Civ	NS	NS	NT	NT	HWZ > Civ*

E. *Females—Total*

1. Thr vs. Era	Thr > Era**	Thr > Era*	NS	NT	NS
2. HWZ vs. Era	HWZ > Era***	HWZ > Era**	NS	NT	HWZ > Era**
3. LWZ vs. Era	NS	NS	NS	NT	NS
4. Thr vs. Civ	Thr > Civ**	Thr > Civ**	NT	NT	NS
5. HWZ vs. Civ	HWZ > Civ***	HWZ > Civ**	NT	NT	HWZ > Civ**

Notes: 1. $<$ = lower than; $>$ = higher than.
2. $^*p < 0.05$; $^{**}p < 0.01$; $^{***}p < 0.001$; NS = not statistically significant; NT = not tested (0 cell).

EXHIBIT VI-8

Summary of Contrasts Among Vietnam Theater Veteran Subgroups for the Affective Disorders

Contrasts Among Major Study Groups	Major Depressive Episode		Manic Episode		Dysthymia Lifetime
	Lifetime	Current	Lifetime	Current	
A. *Race/Ethnicity*					
1. W/O vs. Blk	NS	NS	NS	NS	NS
2. W/O vs. Hisp	NS	NS	NS	NS	NS
3. Blk vs. Hisp	NS	NS	NS	NS	NS
B. *High vs. Low Warzone Stress*					
1. Males	HWZ > LWZ**	HWZ > LWZ***	NT	NT	HWZ > LWZ***
2. Females	HWZ > LWZ***	HWZ > LWZ**	NS	NS	HWZ > LWZ**
C. *PTSD vs. No PTSD*					
1. Males	PTSD > No PTSD***	PTSD > No PTSD***	NT	NT	PTSD > No PTSD***
2. Females	PTSD > No PTSD***	PTSD > No PTSD**	NS	NS	PTSD > No PTSD***
D. *Service-Connected Physical Disability*					
1. Males					
a. SCPD vs. None	NS	NS	NS	NS	NS
b. High SCPD vs. None	NS	NS	NS	NS	NS
2. Females					
a. SCPD vs. None	NS	NS	NS	NT	NS
b. High SCPD vs. None	NS	NS	NS	NT	NS
E. *Substance Abuse vs. None*					
1. Males	SubAbuse > None**	SubAbuse > None**	SubAbuse >None*	SubAbuse >None*	SubAbuse > None***
2. Females	SubAbuse > None**	SubAbuse > None**	NS	NS	SubAbuse > None*

Notes: 1. $<$ = lower than; $>$ = higher than.
2. *$p < 0.05$; **$p < 0.01$; ***$p < 0.001$; NS = not statistically significant; NT = not tested (0 cell).

106

Contrasts Among Vietnam Theater Veterans, Era Veterans, and Civilians

Prevalence rates among Vietnam theater veterans for the three affective disorders assessed in the NSVG are:

	Lifetime	Current
Major depressive episode		
Males	5.1	2.8
Females	12.4	4.3
Manic episode		
Males	0.8	0.7
Females	1.2	0.5
Dysthymia		
Males	4.2	—
Females	4.9	—

Theater and Era Veterans. When the prevalence of specific NSVG/DIS affective disorders were compared for all male theater and era veterans, the only diagnosis for which there was a statistically significant difference among these two groups was current major depressive episode. A similar pattern was found among all racial/ethnic subgroups. Among White/other men, only current major depression was more common in the Vietnam theater than in the era veterans. In contrast, both Black and Hispanic male theater veterans had significantly higher rates of current and lifetime major depressive episode than did their era veteran counterparts. For female veterans as well, Vietnam theater veterans had a significantly higher prevalence of lifetime and current major depression than era veterans.

Theater Veterans and Civilians. When the rates of affective disorders of male theater veterans were compared with those of their civilian counterparts, more statistically significant differences were found. Theater veteran men had significantly higher rates than their civilian counterparts, not only of lifetime and current major depression, but also of dysthymia. When examined by race/ethnicity, only the lifetime and current major depression differences were significant and only among White/other males. None of these differences were tested among Blacks, because no Black civilian men were diagnosed as either depressed or dysthymic. Among Blacks, however, the differences between the rates for theater veterans (for example, 6.8 percent for lifetime depression and 6.6 percent for dysthymia) and those for civilians (i.e., 0.0 percent for both) were larger than the differences found between theater and civilian males overall. These differences would almost certainly have been found to be statistically significant if they had been tested. In contrast, even though Hispanic theater veterans had the highest rate of lifetime depression among the racial/ethnic subgroups

(8.1 percent), theater veteran Hispanic males had higher rates of dysthymia, but not of depression, than their civilian counterparts. This appeared to result from the fact that Hispanic civilians had the highest rate of depression among the various racial/ethnic subgroups of civilian men (5.7 percent lifetime). The contrast between female theater veterans and their civilian counterparts was essentially the same as that for theater and era veterans: theater veteran women had significantly higher rates of both lifetime and current major depression than did their civilian counterparts.

High War-Zone Stress Theater Veterans. It might be expected that theater veterans exposed to high levels of war-zone stress would report significantly more psychiatric problems than their era veteran and civilian counterparts. This was, in fact, the case. Compared with era veteran and civilian counterpart populations, both male and female veterans with high war-zone-stress exposure had higher rates of all of the affective disorders. While these differences were statistically significant for depression (both lifetime and current) and dysthmia, they were not tested for manic episode because the rates among era veterans and civilians were zero.

Contrasts Among Vietnam Theater Veterans on Race/Ethnicity, War-Zone Stress, and Disability

For male theater veterans, no significant differences in rates of the affective disorders were found across the race/ethnicity of these groups. For either men or women theater veterans, there were no significant differences between those with and without a service-connected physical disability (SCPD) or between those with a high SCPD and none. In contrast, for both men and women, theater veterans exposed to high levels of war-zone stress in Vietnam had significantly higher rates of affective disorder than those exposed to lower levels. Theater veteran males exposed to high war-zone stress had higher rates of prevalence for all affective disorders than those with low/moderate war-zone stress. Again, these differences were significant for both lifetime and current major depression and dysthymia, but were not tested for manic episodes, because of the zero rates among those with low war-zone stress. For female theater veterans, high war-zone stress was also significantly related to elevated rates of lifetime and current major depression and dysthymia. Moreover, these differences were quite large for both men and women. For men and women theater veterans exposed to high levels of war-zone stress, the affective disorder prevalence rates were four or more times greater than those for theater veterans exposed to low or moderate levels.

Co-occurrence With PTSD and Substance Abuse Among Theater Veterans

For males, PTSD appears to be closely linked to all of the affective disorders. The relationships between PTSD and the affective disorders were shown to be statistically significant for lifetime and current major depressive episode and dysthymia. Differences were not tested for manic episode since the prevalence rate among those without PTSD was zero. However, the rate of 5.5 percent for lifetime manic episode among male theater veterans with PTSD was the highest of any study group or subgroup in the NSVG and would appear to be clearly different from the 0 percent observed for those without PTSD. For females, PTSD was also strongly related to lifetime and current depression and dysthymia. For most of the comparisons for depression and dysthymia, the rates for both men and women with PTSD were 10 to 15 times greater than the rates for those without.

A history of substance abuse also appears to be strongly linked to affective disorders, particularly among males. Both male and female theater veterans with a history of substance abuse problems reported higher rates of lifetime and current major depression and dysthymia. For males, a substance abuse disorder was also significantly related to lifetime and current manic episodes. Again, these differences were not only statistically significant but also quite large.

Summary

Among Vietnam era veterans and civilians, the rates of lifetime and current depression and dysthymia, and, for females, lifetime manic episode, appeared to be within the range of the prevalence rates for community samples of the same gender in the ECA program (see Appendix G in Volume II).[2] However, a number of theater veteran subgroups had rates that were higher than those among the era veteran and civilian samples. Virtually all theater veteran subgroups, except those exposed to low war-zone stress, had rates of current depression that were higher than their era veteran and civilian counterparts. The magnitude of the difference

(text continued on page 114)

---

[2]Although there were no cases of manic episode in the male civilian or era veteran samples, because of the relative rarity of manic episode in general community populations, even in randomly drawn community populations one would expect to find no more than one to four individuals with a manic episode in a sample of 400 men or 200 women, the sample sizes for male era veterans and civilians respectively. In samples such as the NSVG, drawn according to specific criteria such as age restrictions, the rates may be even smaller and thereby undetectable in such small samples.

EXHIBIT VI-9
Summary of Contrasts Among Major Study Groups for the Anxiety Disorders

Contrasts Among Major Study Groups	Panic Disorder		Obsessive Compulsive Disorder		Generalized Anxiety Disorder	
	Lifetime	Current	Lifetime	Current	Lifetime	Current
A. *Males—Total*						
1. Thr vs. Era	NS	NS	NS	Thr > Era**	NS	NS
2. HWZ vs. Era	NS	NS	HWZ > Era*	HWZ > Era**	HWZ > Era***	HWZ > Era*
3. LWZ vs. Era	NS	NS	NS	NS	NS	NS
4. Thr vs. Civ	NS	NS	Thr > Civ*	NT	NS	NS
5. HWZ vs. Civ	NS	NS	HWZ > Civ**	NT	HWZ > Civ***	HWZ > Civ*
B. *Males—White/Other*						
1. Thr vs. Era	NS	NT	NS	NT	NS	NS
2. HWZ vs. Era	NS	NT	HWZ > Era*	NT	HWZ > Era**	NS
3. LWZ vs. Era	NS	NT	NS	NT	NS	NS
4. Thr vs. Civ	NS	NS	Thr > Civ*	NT	NS	NS
5. HWZ vs. Civ	NS	NS	HWZ > Civ*	NT	HWZ > Civ**	NS

	1	2	3	4	5	6
C. Males—Black						
1. Thr vs. Era	NS	NT	NS	NS	NS	NS
2. HWZ vs. Era	NS	NT	NS	NS	NS	NS
3. LWZ vs. Era	NS	NT	NS	NT	NS	NS
4. Thr vs. Civ	NT	NT	NT	NT	Thr > Civ**	Thr > Civ***
5. HWZ vs. Civ	NT	NT	NT	NT	HWZ > Civ***	HWZ > Civ***
D. Males—Hispanic						
1. Thr vs. Era	NT	NT	NS	NS	Thr > Era**	Thr > Era*
2. HWZ vs. Era	NT	NT	NS	NS	HWZ > Era***	HWZ > Era*
3. LWZ vs. Era	NT	NT	NS	NS	NS	NS
4. Thr vs. Civ	NS	NS	NT	NT	NS	NS
5. HWZ vs. Civ	NS	NS	NT	NT	NS	HWZ > Civ*
E. Females—Total						
1. Thr vs. Era	NS	NS	NS	NS	NS	NS
2. HWZ vs. Era	NS	NS	NS	NS	NS	NS
3. LWZ vs. Era	NS	NS	NS	NS	NS	NS
4. Thr vs. Civ	NS	NS	NS	NT	NT	NS
5. HWZ vs. Civ	HWZ > Civ**	NS	NS	NS	NS	NS

Notes: 1. < = lower than; > = higher than.
2. *$p < 0.05$; **$p < 0.01$; ***$p < 0.001$; NS = not statistically significant; NT = not tested (0 cell).

111

EXHIBIT VI-10
Summary of Contrasts Among Vietnam Theater Veteran Subgroups for the Anxiety Disorders

Contrasts Among Major Study Groups	Panic Disorder		Obsessive Compulsive Disorder		Generalized Anxiety Disorder	
	Lifetime	Current	Lifetime	Current	Lifetime	Current
A. Race/Ethnicity						
1. W/O vs. Blk	NS	NT	NS	NS	NS	NS
2. W/O vs. Hisp	NS	NS	NS	NS	Hisp > W/O*	NS
3. Blk vs. Hisp	NS	NT	NS	NS	NS	NS
B. High vs. Low Warzone Stress						
1. Males	NS	HWZ > LWZ*	HWZ > LWZ**	HWZ > LWZ**	HWZ > LWZ***	HWZ > LWZ*
2. Females	HWZ > LWZ**	HWZ > LWZ*	NS	NS	NS	NS
C. PTSD vs. No PTSD						
1. Males	PTSD > No PTSD**	PTSD > No PTSD**	PTSD > No PTSD***	PTSD > No PTSD***	PTSD > No PTSD***	PTSD > No PTSD***
2. Females	PTSD > No PTSD**	PTSD > No PTSD*	PTSD > No PTSD*	NS	PTSD > No PTSD**	PTSD > No PTSD*

D. Service-Connected Physical Disability					
1. Males					
a. SCPD vs. None	NS	NS	NS	NS	SCPD > None*
b. High SCPD vs. None	NS	NS	NS	NS	High > None*
2. Females					
a. SCPD vs. None	NS	NS	NS	NS	NS
b. High SCPD vs. None	NS	NS	NS	NT	NS
E. Substance Abuse vs. None					
1. Males	SubAbuse > None**	SubAbuse > None*	NS	SubAbuse > None***	SubAbuse > None*
2. Females	SubAbuse > None*	NS	NS	SubAbuse > None*	NS

Notes: 1. < = lower than; > = higher than.
2. *$p < 0.05$; **$p < 0.01$; ***$p < 0.001$; NS = not statistically significant; NT = not tested (0 cell).

113

was particularly dramatic for those exposed to high war-zone stress, with PTSD, and with a history of substance abuse. In fact, a major finding was that those exposed to high war-zone stress, those with PTSD, and those with substance abuse tended to have substantially higher rates for all of the affective disorders. Among male theater veterans, however, there did not appear to be any racial/ethnic differences in rates of the affective disorders.

THE ANXIETY DISORDERS

Exhibits VI-9 and VI-10 summarize group contrasts for the three anxiety disorders: panic disorder, obsessive compulsive disorder, and generalized anxiety disorder. Full prevalence estimates and contrasts can be found in Volume II, Tables VI-7 through VI-12.

It is important to note that the prevalence rate estimates for panic disorder and obsessive compulsive disorder for both era veterans (current) and civilians (lifetime and current) were zero, so that contrasts with these groups were not tested for these two disorders. These rates were low, even among theater veterans, and zero in some subgroups, so that, for some subgroups, those relationships were also not tested.

Contrasts Among Vietnam Theater Veterans, Era Veterans, and Civilians

Prevalence rates among Vietnam theater veterans for the three anxiety disorders assessed in the NSVG are:

	Lifetime	Current
Panic disorder		
Males	1.8	0.9
Females	3.0	1.7
Obsessive compulsive disorder		
Males	1.8	1.5
Females	1.5	1.0
Generalized anxiety disorder		
Males	14.1	4.5
Females	16.6	4.2

Theater and Era Veterans. Current obsessive compulsive disorder was the only anxiety disorder for which rates among the total male theater veterans group and among era veterans differed significantly. For both Whites/others and Hispanics, this specific contrast was not tested because of a zero value for era veterans. However, the magnitude of the difference for Whites/others and Hispanics was the same or higher than that for the total theater/era veteran contrast. This difference was not found for Blacks. The only other significant contrast within the three racial/ethnic subgroups was a higher rate of lifetime generalized anxiety disorder for Hispanic theater veterans in comparison with era veterans. In all cases, however, male theater veterans had higher rates of anxiety disorder than male era veterans. Among women veterans, there were no statistically significant differences between theater and era veterans for any of the anxiety disorders.

Theater Veterans and Civilians. The major difference between male theater veterans and civilians was, again, between their respective rates of obsessive compulsive disorder. Theater veteran men had significantly higher rates of lifetime obsessive compulsive disorder than their civilian counterparts, and also appeared to have higher rates of current disorder. Although the latter was not tested because of a zero rate for civilians, the magnitude of the difference was about the same as that for the theater/era veteran contrast, which was found to be statistically significant. The difference between rates of lifetime disorder was significant among White/other males, but not among Blacks or Hispanics. Only one other difference was significant within these minority subgroups. Black theater veteran men had higher rates of both lifetime and current generalized anxiety disorder than civilians. Among women, there were no statistically significant differences between Vietnam theater veterans and civilian females.

High-War-Zone-Stress Theater Veterans. Although the difference for current obsessive compulsive disorder between high-war-zone-stress theater veterans and civilians was not tested because of a zero rate for civilians, men exposed to high war-zone stress appeared to have significantly higher rates of obsessive compulsive disorder and generalized anxiety disorder (both current and lifetime) than either era veterans or civilians. In contrast to the zero rate for civilians, theater veterans exposed to high war-zone stress had a 5.2 percent prevalence rate of current obsessive compulsive disorder. The other three contrasts for obsessive compulsive disorder and GAD for males were tested and found to be statistically significant. Differences in rates of panic disorder among men by war-zone stress exposure were not significant. Among the male racial/ethnic subgroups some significant differences between the high war-zone-stress exposure group and other groups were found. The contrasts that were significant varied by subgroup. In contrast, for females, only lifetime panic disorder was higher among women exposed to high war-zone stress than their civilian counterparts, and no disorder was significantly higher among the high-war-stress group than among era veterans.

Contrasts Among Vietnam Theater Veterans on Race/Ethnicity, War-Zone Stress, and Disability

The only difference between rates by race/ethnicity that was observed within the male theater veteran group was a higher rate of lifetime generalized anxiety disorder among Hispanics than among White/other males. The only one of the nine NSVG/DIS disorders for which men with a service-connected disability had higher prevalence rates than those without an SCPD was also lifetime generalized anxiety disorder. Similar differences were found between the high SCPD and "none" groups. In contrast, for the anxiety disorders, the only difference between the high- and low/moderate-war-zone-stress exposed males that was not significant was lifetime panic disorder. For generalized anxiety disorder, for example, rates for those exposed to high war-zone stress were over twice as high as those with low/moderate-war-zone-stress exposure.

For women, the only significant differences between rates for those exposed to high and low war-zone stress were for panic disorder, both lifetime and current, with the high-war-zone-stress group having higher rates. While the rates of GAD among women with high war-zone stress were approximately twice those of women with low to moderate war-zone stress, the contrasts were not statistically significant, although the contrast for lifetime GAD was marginal ($p = 0.051$). There were no significant differences among rates in women by disability status.

Co-occurrence With PTSD and Substance Abuse Among Theater Veterans

The relationship between PTSD and anxiety disorders was once again quite strong. Those with PTSD had rates of disorder up to 20 times higher than those without PTSD. Both men and women with PTSD were significantly more likely to have had each of the anxiety disorders, other than current obsessive compulsive disorder among women, than men and women without PTSD, including panic disorder—both lifetime and current.

Males with a history of substance abuse were also more likely to have had panic disorder and generalized anxiety disorder, both current and lifetime, then men without a history of substance abuse. They were no more likely, however, to have had obsessive compulsive disorder. Females with a lifetime substance abuse diagnosis were more likely to have had both disorders, lifetime generalized anxiety disorder and lifetime panic disorder, than those without.

Summary

No ECA data on generalized anxiety disorder were available to compare with the NSVG data. For panic disorder, among both males and females, prevalence rates not only for Vietnam era veterans and civilians, but also for theater veterans overall, appeared not to be significantly different from those for the ECA community samples. This was also true of males for obsessive compulsive disorder, except for the zero rates observed for Vietnam era veterans and civilians. The latter appeared to reflect the same problem described for manic episode, that is, the rates in community populations were extremely low, so that cases of the disorder may not be found unless one uses very large samples. For obsessive compulsive disorder, the rates for females appeared to be low in comparison with the ECA community samples.[3]

Prevalence rates for the anxiety disorders for some theater veteran subgroups, particularly among male theater veterans, however, appeared to be significantly higher than those for the ECA community samples and for the NSVG era veterans, civilians, and theater veterans overall. Again, a major finding was the significantly elevated rates observed for most or all anxiety disorders among those with high war-zone-stress exposure and those with PTSD or a history of substance abuse. As with the affective disorders, few differences were found between the various racial/ethnic subgroups. Higher rates of lifetime generalized anxiety disorder were also found among those with service-connected physical disabilities than among those without.

SUBSTANCE ABUSE DISORDERS AND ANTISOCIAL PERSONALITY DISORDER

Exhibits VI-11 and VI-12 summarize the group contrasts for alcohol and drug abuse or dependence and antisocial personality disorder (ASP). Full

(text continued on page 122)

---

[3]One may only speculate on the possible reasons for this. One possible reason is that the female samples are primarily nurses, which would imply that these women are more highly educated and perhaps come from more highly educated or successful families than similarly aged women found in the general populations. Many are never-married professional women. These characteristics could well have an effect on mental health outcomes. Differences for current disorder may also result, in part, from the fact that rates of obsessive compulsive disorder are generally higher in the lower age groups. Our female theater veteran group contained few women under 35, and the majority were significantly older. Era veterans and civilians were matched on age with the theater women, and so are also older.

EXHIBIT VI-11
Summary of Contrasts Among Major Study Groups for Substance Abuse
and Antisocial Personality

Contrasts Among Major Study Groups	Alcohol Abuse/Dependence		Drug Abuse/Dependence		Antisocial Personality Disorder	
	Lifetime	Current	Lifetime	Current	Lifetime	Current
A. Males—Total						
1. Thr vs. Era	NS	NS	NS	NS	NS	NS
2. HWZ vs. Era	NS	HWZ > Era*	NS	NS	HWZ > Era*	HWZ > Era*
3. LWZ vs. Era	NS	NS	NS	NS	NS	NS
4. Thr vs. Civ	Thr > Civ***	NS	NS	NS	Thr > Civ**	Thr > Civ***
5. HWZ vs. Civ	HWZ > Civ***	HWZ > Civ*	HWZ > Civ*	NS	HWZ > Civ***	Thr > Civ****
B. Males—White/ Other						
1. Thr vs. Era	NS	NS	NS	NS	NS	NS
2. HWZ vs. Era	NS	NS	NS	NS	NS	NS
3. LWZ vs. Era	NS	NS	NS	NS	NS	NS
4. Thr vs. Civ	Thr > Civ**	NS	NS	NS	Thr > Civ*	NT
5. HWZ vs. Civ	HWZ > Civ**	HWZ > Civ*	NS	NS	HWZ > Civ**	NT

C. Males—Black						
1. Thr vs. Era	NS	Thr > Era*	NS	NT	NS	Thr > Era*
2. HWZ vs. Era	NS	HWZ > Era*	NS	NT	NS	HWZ > Era**
3. LWZ vs. Era	NS	NS	NS	NT	NS	NS
4. Thr vs. Civ	NS	NS	Thr > Civ*	NS	NS	Thr > Civ**
5. HWZ vs. Civ	NS	NS	HWZ > Civ**	NS	HWZ > Civ**	HWZ > Civ**
D. Males—Hispanic						
1. Thr vs. Era	NS	Thr > Era*	NS	NT	NS	NS
2. HWZ vs. Era	NS	HWZ > Era*	NS	NT	NS	NS
3. LWZ vs. Era	NS	NS	NS	NT	NS	NS
4. Thr vs. Civ	Thr > Civ*	NS	NS	Thr > Civ*	Thr > Civ***	Thr > Civ*
5. HWZ vs. Civ	NS	NS	NS	HWZ > Civ*	HWZ > Civ*	NS
E. Females—Total						
1. Thr vs. Era	Thr > Era*	NS	NS	NT	NS	NT
2. HWZ vs. Era	HWZ > Era*	NS	NS	NT	NS	NT
3. LWZ vs. Era	NS	NS	NT	NT	NT	NT
4. Thr vs. Civ	Thr > Civ***	NS	NS	NT	NT	NT
5. HWZ vs. Civ	HWZ > Civ***	NS	NS	NT	NT	NT

Notes: 1. $<$ = lower than; $>$ = higher than.
2. $*p < 0.05$; $**p < 0.01$; $***p < 0.001$; NS = not statistically significant; NT = not tested (0 cell).

119

EXHIBIT VI-12

Summary of Contrasts Among Vietnam Theater Veteran Subgroups for
Substance Abuse and Antisocial Personality

Contrasts Among Major Study Groups	Alcohol Abuse/Dependence		Drug Abuse/Dependence		Antisocial Personality Disorder	
	Lifetime	Current	Lifetime	Current	Lifetime	Current
A. Race/Ethnicity						
1. W/O vs. Blk	NS	NS	NS	NS	NS	NS
2. W/O vs. Hisp	Hisp > W/O*	NS	NS	NS	NS	NS
3. Blk vs. Hisp	Hisp > Blk**	NS	NS	NS	NS	Blk > Hisp*
B. High vs. Low Warzone Stress						
1. Males	HWZ > LWZ*	HWZ > LWZ**	NS	NS	HWZ > LWZ**	HWZ > LWZ*
2. Females	NS	NS	NT	NT	NT	NT
C. PTSD vs. No PTSD						
1. Males	PTSD > No PTSD***	PTSD > No PTSD***	PTSD > No PTSD*	PTSD > No PTSD*	PTSD > No PTSD***	PTSD > No PTSD***
2. Females	PTSD > No PTSD**	NS	NS	NT	NT	NT

120

D. Service-Connected Physical Disability

1. Males					
a. SCPD vs. None	NS	NS	NS	NS	NS
b. High SCPD vs. None	NS	NS	NS	NS	NS
2. Females					
a. SCPD vs. None	NS	NS	NT	NT	NT
b. High SCPD vs. None	NS	NS	NT	NT	NT

E. Substance Abuse vs. None

1. Males	NT	NT	NT	SubAbuse > None***	SubAbuse > None*
2. Females	NT	NT	NT	NT	NT

Notes: 1. < = lower than; > = higher than.
2. *$p < 0.05$; **$p < 0.01$; ***$p < 0.001$; NS = not statistically significant; NT = not tested (0 cell).

prevalence estimates and contrasts may be found in Volume II, Tables VI-13 through VI-18.

Contrasts Among Vietnam Theater Veterans, Era Veterans, and Civilians

Prevalence rates among Vietnam theater veterans for the substance abuse disorders and antisocial personality disorder in the NSVG are:

	Lifetime	Current
Alcohol abuse or dependence		
Males	39.2	11.2
Females	9.1	2.4
Drug abuse or dependence		
Males	5.7	1.8
Females	1.0	0.0
Antisocial personality disorder (ASP)		
Males	9.5	2.0
Females	0.3	0.0

Theater and Era Veterans. Both Vietnam theater and era veteran males had relatively high levels of alcohol abuse or dependence lifetime (approximately 40 percent) compared with civilian males (25 percent). There were no significant differences overall between Vietnam theater and era veteran males for either type of substance abuse or for antisocial personality disorder. This was also true for White/other males. In contrast, Black theater veteran men had higher current rates of ASP than era veteran males, and Hispanic theater veterans had higher rates for both current alcohol disorder and lifetime drug disorder than Hispanic era veteran men. It also appeared that Hispanic theater veterans had significantly higher rates of current drug disorders, although, because of a zero rate for era veteran males, the difference was not tested. The only significant difference between Vietnam theater and era veteran women was for lifetime alcohol abuse, with theater veterans having higher rates than era veterans.

Theater Veterans and Civilians. Overall, male theater veterans had higher rates of lifetime and current ASP and lifetime alcohol abuse or dependence than their civilian counterparts. These differences were evident among both Hispanics and White/other males, although the current ASP comparison was not tested for the latter because of a zero rate among civilian White/other men. Minority theater veteran men were also more likely tô have had a drug problem than civilians: this was true of lifetime drug problems for Blacks and current drug problems for Hispanics. In comparison with civilian Black males, rates for Black theater veterans were also elevated for current ASP. However, it is important to note that the differences observed in all groups for current ASP may result in part from the nature of the civilian sample. Unlike the veteran sample, which was selected from military records, the civilian sample was household-based. A household sample is less likely to include individuals with current ASP because of their transience, the likelihood of their not having a home at all, and their high rates of incarceration. The only difference between Vietnam theater veteran and civilian women was the same as that found between theater and era veteran women: theater women were more likely to have lifetime alcohol abuse or dependence than their civilian counterparts.

High-War-Zone-Stress Theater Veterans. Theater veteran men who were exposed to high levels of war-zone stress had significantly higher rates of ASP (lifetime and current) and current alcohol abuse or dependence, and had marginally elevated rates of current drug abuse, as compared with both male Vietnam era veterans and civilians. Theater veteran men who were exposed to high war stress also had higher rates of both substance abuse disorders than civilian males. The only consistent finding across all racial/ethnic subgroups was a higher rate of lifetime ASP for men exposed to high war stress in comparison with the civilian males. Black theater veteran men who were exposed to high war stress also had higher current rates of antisocial personality disorder than Black civilian males, while White/other men who were exposed to high war stress had higher rates of alcohol abuse or dependence than their civilian counterparts. Hispanic men who were exposed to high war stress had higher current rates of alcohol disorder and higher lifetime rates of drug disorder than Hispanic era veterans, as well as higher current rates of drug abuse or dependence than Hispanic civilian men. The only statistically significant difference found in women who were exposed to high war-zone stress and their era veteran and civilian counterparts was for lifetime alcohol abuse or dependence, with the former having higher rates.

Contrasts Among Vietnam Theater Veterans on Race/Ethnicity, War-Zone Stress, and Disability

No significant differences were observed by levels of service-connected disability. Blacks had higher rates of current ASP than Hispanics, while

Hispanics had higher rates of lifetime alcohol abuse or dependence than either Whites/others or Blacks. Except for lifetime drug dependence or abuse, men exposed to high war-zone stress had significantly higher rates of all these disorders, although the contrast for current drug abuse was marginal ($p = 0.051$). For example, the rate of current alcohol abuse or dependence among those exposed to high war stress was twice that of men exposed to lower levels (17.2 percent vs. 8.8 percent).

There were no statistically significant differences for women by war-zone-stress exposure, although several of these comparisons were not tested because of the zero rates found among those exposed to low/moderate war stress. For example, the rates of lifetime drug abuse were 2.5 percent for theater veterans and 0.0 percent for era veterans, which may be statistically significant, as may the difference observed for lifetime ASP (2.8 percent vs. 0.0 percent).

Co-occurrence With PTSD and Substance Abuse Among Theater Veterans

As has frequently been documented in the literature, substance abuse disorders tend to co-occur with PTSD. It has also been hypothesized that abuse of substances may be a part of the "avoidance syndrome" associated with PTSD. In addition, in the NSVG, prevalence rates for the substance abuse disorders were substantially higher among male theater veterans with PTSD than among male veterans without PTSD. In fact, almost three-fourths of male veterans with PTSD had a lifetime alcohol abuse or dependence disorder, and 22 percent of those with PTSD had these disorders currently. Among women with PTSD, only rates of lifetime alcohol disorders were elevated in comparison with those without the PTSD.

A more unexpected finding was that those with PTSD were also significantly more likely to have antisocial personality disorder. Of those with PTSD, 31 percent had a lifetime ASP diagnosis, and 11 percent had symptoms of ASP in the past six months, all of the latter having also met the criteria for the lifetime disorder. In part, this probably reflected a selection process, since, as noted above, those with ASP were also more likely to have experienced high levels of war-zone stress. It may also reflect, however, a vulnerability among those with ASP to trauma and the subsequent development of PTSD.

Differences between those with and without a history of substance abuse could not be tested for the substance abuse disorders, since, by definition, there are no respondents with an alcohol or drug disorder in the "no substance abuse" group. Since substance abuse is also a symptom of ASP, one might expect that the relationship between ASP and substance abuse disorders would be substantial. However, only 19 percent of men with a history of substance abuse also had ASP, and none of these contrasts were tested for women.

Summary

The rates of alcohol abuse or dependence and ASP found in NSVG civilians appeared to be similar to the rates found in community ECA populations, although the rates of these disorders among veterans, both theater and era, appeared to be somewhat elevated in comparison with the ECA community rates. This could result from a number factors: a selection bias for those who entered the military during the Vietnam era; the sociocultural environment of the military at that time, which may have encouraged drinking; and differences between the NSVG veteran and civilian samples, as described previously (that is, the community household sample would be less likely to pick up those with ASP or chronic homeless alcoholics than would the veteran list sample). In general, rates of drug abuse and dependence for the NSVG civilian sample appeared to be somewhat low in comparison with the ECA community samples. The rates for Vietnam theater and era veterans were similar to those for the ECA community samples. This appeared to indicate an underreporting of drug use among veterans as well, based on the presumption of high levels of drug use in Vietnam.[4]

Because of the relatively high rates of alcohol abuse or dependence found among both Vietnam theater and era veteran males, the only significant difference by veteran status for the alcohol disorders among males overall was that between Vietnam theater veteran males and civilians for the lifetime disorder. The only group with notably high rates for drug abuse or dependence were Hispanic men, particularly those exposed to high war-zone stress (a prevalence of 10.9 percent). As with virtually all of the disorders discussed so far, men exposed to high war stress were more

---

[4]Even among those exposed to high war-zone stress, the rate was only 8.4 percent. Again, we can only hypothesize the reason for these low rates. One factor might be that the ECA data were collected several years ago, before the major antidrug campaigns, drug testing, etc., that we have seen in the past few years. In this new strongly antidrug environment, individuals might be less likely to admit to any drug use. Another factor for the lifetime rates is that data for lifetime disorders are less reliable—individuals may have forgotten (especially if they no longer use drugs) or tend to downplay the amount of drugs they used in the past. With regard to current rates, it appears that the rate of drug use for the population overall is declining, and that individuals in these age categories might be less likely to use drugs now than when they were younger, when the national climate was also more accepting of drug use.

likely to have both an alcohol disorder and ASP than those exposed to lower levels of war-zone stress. The elevated rates of ASP among those experiencing high war-zone stress might be due to a selection factor for those sent into combat.

The most pronounced differences by race/ethnicity were the greater apparent difficulties for Hispanic theater veteran men with alcohol and drug disorders, in comparison with Blacks and Whites/others and/or Hispanic era veterans and civilians, and higher rates of current ASP among Black male theater veterans. There were also very high levels of co-occurrence of PTSD among theater veteran men with both the substance abuse disorders and with ASP. This comorbidity of PTSD with substance abuse has already been well established among treatment-seeking samples of Vietnam veterans. The relationship observed with ASP is probably, at least in part, due to a selection bias, since those with ASP were also more likely to have experienced high war-zone stress. It may also reflect a particular vulnerability to PTSD among those with ASP. ASP may occur in those with low self-esteem, with the manipulative and self-centered behaviors characteristic of ASP reflecting efforts to enhance self-esteem. If this is true, it may be that, when such individuals are confronted with a hostile environment they are not able to control and are instead helpless, they are less able to cope emotionally with the high levels of traumatic stress that they experience.

THE PREVALENCE OF "ANY SPECIFIC NSVG/DIS PSYCHIATRIC DISORDER"

To summarize our examination of specific psychiatric disorders, the rates of experiencing any of these nine specific disorders were also computed. Exhibits VI-13 and VI-14 summarize the group contrasts for the prevalence of any NSVG/DIS diagnosis, with or without alcohol disorder. Exhibits VI-9 and VI-10 present these prevalence estimates for any NSVG/DIS disorder (with and without alcohol abuse or dependence respectively) in graphical form for the various study groups. Full prevalence estimates and contrasts can be found in Volume II, Tables VI-19 through VI-22.

Contrasts Among Vietnam Theater Veterans, Era Veterans, and Civilians

As shown in Exhibit VI-15, 49 percent of male Vietnam theater veterans met the criteria at some point in their lives for at least one of the DIS DSM-III disorders assessed in the NSVG, and 17 percent (over one-third

EXHIBIT VI-13

Summary of Contrasts Among Major Study Groups for Any NSVG/DIS Disorder

Contrasts Among Major Study Groups	Any NSVG/DIS Disorder		Any NSVG/DIS Disorder Excluding Alcohol Disorder	
	Lifetime	Current	Lifetime	Current
A. *Males—Total*				
1. Thr vs. Era	NS	NS	NS	NS
2. HWZ vs. Era	HWZ > Era***	HWZ > Era***	HWZ > Era***	HWZ > Era***
3. LWZ vs. Era	NS	NS	NS	NS
4. Thr vs. Civ	Thr > Civ**	NS	Thr > Civ**	Thr > Civ*
5. HWZ vs. Civ	HWZ > Civ***	HWZ > Civ***	HWZ > Civ***	HWZ > Civ***
B. *Males—White/Other*				
1. Thr vs. Era	NS	NS	NS	NS
2. HWZ vs. Era	HWZ > Era**	HWZ > Era**	HWZ > Era**	HWZ > Era**
3. LWZ vs. Era	NS	NS	NS	NS
4. Thr vs. Civ	Thr > Civ**	NS	Thr > Civ*	NS
5. HWZ vs. Civ	HWZ > Civ***	HWZ > Civ**	HWZ > Civ***	HWZ > Civ**
C. *Males—Black*				
1. Thr vs. Era	NS	NS	NS	NS
2. HWZ vs. Era	NS	HWZ > Era*	NS	HWZ > Era*
3. LWZ vs. Era	NS	NS	NS	NS
4. Thr vs. Civ	NS	NS	Thr > Civ**	Thr > Civ***
5. HWZ vs. Civ	HWZ > Civ**	HWZ > Civ**	HWZ > Civ***	HWZ > Civ***

(continued)

127

EXHIBIT VI-13 (Continued)
Summary of Contrasts Among Major Study Groups for Any NSVG/DIS Disorder

Contrasts Among Major Study Groups	Any NSVG/DIS Disorder		Any NSVG/DIS Disorder Excluding Alcohol Disorder	
	Lifetime	Current	Lifetime	Current
D. Males—Hispanic				
1. Thr vs. Era	Thr > Era*	Thr > Era***	Thr > Era**	Thr > Era**
2. HWZ vs. Era	HWZ > Era**	HWZ > Era***	HWZ > Era***	HWZ > Era***
3. LWZ vs. Era	NS	LWZ > Era*	NS	NS
4. Thr vs. Civ	NS	NS	NS	NS
5. HWZ vs. Civ	HWZ > Civ*	HWZ > Civ**	HWZ > Civ*	HWZ > Civ*
E. Females—Total				
1. Thr vs. Era	NS	Thr > Era*	NS	Thr > Era*
2. HWZ vs. Era	HWZ > Era**	HWZ > Era**	HWZ > Era*	HWZ > Era**
3. LWZ vs. Era	NS	NS	NS	NS
4. Thr vs. Civ	NS	NS	NS	NS
5. HWZ vs. Civ	NS	HWZ > Civ**	NS	HWZ > Civ*

Notes: 1. < = lower than; > = higher than.
2. *$p < 0.05$; **$p < 0.01$; ***$p < 0.001$; NS = not statistically significant; NT = not tested (0 cell).

128

EXHIBIT VI-14
Summary of Contrasts Among Vietnam Theater Veteran Subgroups for Any NSVG/DIS Disorder

Contrasts Among Major Study Groups	Any NSVG/DIS Disorder		Any NSVG/DIS Disorder Excluding Alcohol Disorder	
	Lifetime	Current	Lifetime	Current
A. *Race/Ethnicity*				
1. W/O vs. Blk	NS	NS	NS	NS
2. W/O vs. Hisp	Hisp > W/O***	Hisp > W/O*	Hisp > W/O*	NS
3. Blk vs. Hisp	Hisp > Blk**	NS	NS	NS
B. *High vs. Low Warzone Stress*				
1. Males	HWZ > LWC***	HWZ > LWZ***	HWZ > LWZ***	HWZ > LWZ***
2. Females	HWZ > LWC***	HWZ > LWZ**	HWZ > LWZ***	HWZ > LWZ**
C. *PTSD vs. No PTSD*				
1. Males	PTSD > No PTSD***	PTSD > No PTSD***	PTSD > No PTSD***	PTSD > No PTSD***
2. Females	PTSD > No PTSD***	PTSD > No PTSD***	PTSD > No PTSD***	PTSD > No PTSD***
D. *Service-Connected Physical Disability*				
1. Males				
a. SCPD vs. None	SCPD > None*	NS	NS	NS
b. High SCPD vs. None	NS	NS	NS	NS
2. Females				
a. SCPD vs. None	NS	NS	NS	NS
b. High SCPD vs. None	NS	NS	NS	NS
E. *Substance Abuse vs. None*				
1. Males	NT	SubAbuse > None***	SubAbuse > None***	SubAbuse > None***
2. Females	NT	SubAbuse > None***	SubAbuse > None***	SubAbuse > None***

Notes: 1. $<$ = lower than; $>$ = higher than.
2. $*p < 0.05$; $**p < 0.01$; $***p < 0.001$; NS = not statistically significant; NT = not tested (0 cell).

EXHIBIT VI-15
Proportion of Theater Veterans with Any DIS/DSM-III Disorder

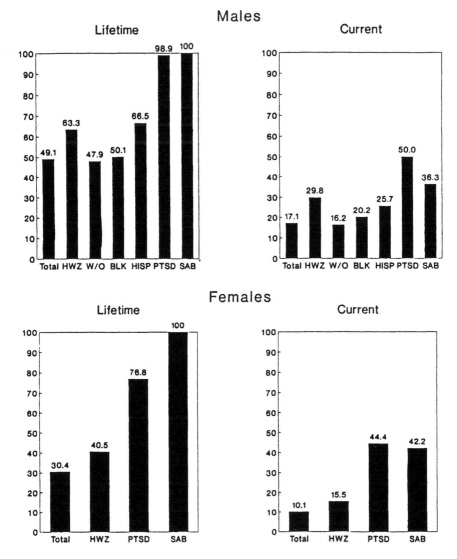

Males

Lifetime

Current

Females

Lifetime

Current

*By definition, those with a substance abuse disorder have a lifetime DIS/DSM-III disorder.

of the former) received a current diagnosis (within the past six months) for one of these disorders. Alcohol abuse or dependence accounts for much of this "any disorder" category among males. As can be seen by an examination of Exhibit VI-16, when the alcohol disorders are excluded from the "total disorders" variable, rates for males decrease from 49.1 percent to 26.5 percent, lifetime, and from 17.1 percent to 8.6 percent, current. A similar effect is evident for females, although of a somewhat smaller magnitude. When the alcohol disorders are excluded from the "total disorder" rates for women, rates decrease from 30.4 percent to 25.6 percent, lifetime, and from 10.1 percent to 8.6 percent, current.

Differences between male Vietnam theater and era veterans for any NSVG/DIS disorder were not significant for either lifetime or current disorder, although the male theater veterans did report significantly higher rates of lifetime disorder than their civilian counterparts. If one excludes the alcohol disorders, the theater versus civilian contrasts were significant for both lifetime and current disorder, and the theater versus era veteran contrast was also marginal ($p = 0.051$) for any current NSVG/DIS disorder. In all cases, significant differences represented higher rates of disorder for male theater veterans than their counterparts. It appears that the relatively high level of alcohol consumption among all male study groups tends to obscure the differences for the other disorders.

Differences between male theater veterans and their era veteran counterparts by race/ethnicity reached statistical significance only among Hispanics, for whom all four contrasts (current/lifetime by with/without alcohol disorder) were significant. As shown in Exhibit VI-9, two-thirds of Hispanic theater veteran men had at least one lifetime disorder and over one-fourth had a current disorder, both significantly higher than the rates observed for Hispanic era veteran men. Although some of the differences observed were marginal, Hispanic theater veteran men did not have significantly higher rates of disorder than their civilian counterparts. In contrast, White/other theater veterans had significantly higher rates of lifetime disorder than their civilian counterparts, either including or excluding alcohol disorders, and, when alcohol disorders were excluded, Black theater veteran men reported higher rates of both lifetime and current disorder than Black civilian men.

Among women, Vietnam theater versus era veteran contrasts for "any current NSVG/DIS disorder" and "any current NSVG/DIS disorder excluding alcohol abuse or dependence" were both statistically significant, although contrasts for lifetime rates were not. In both cases, female Vietnam theater veterans had higher rates of disorder than female era veterans. Although current prevalence rates for the civilian women and

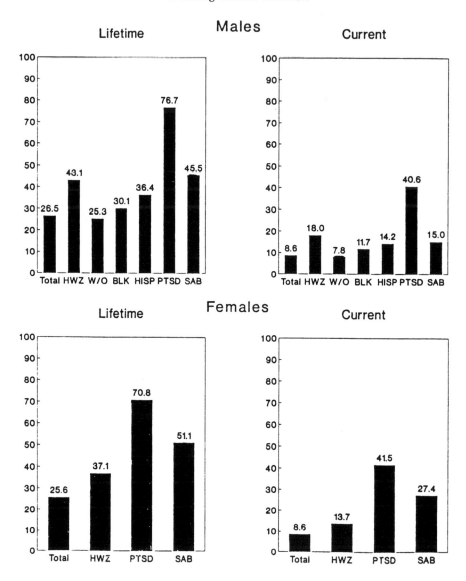

EXHIBIT VI-16
Proportion of Theater Veterans with Any DIS/DSM-III Disorder
Excluding Alcohol Disorders

era veteran women were of a similar magnitude, contrasts with civilians did not quite reach significance for either "any current NSVG/DIS disorder" or for "any current NSVG/DIS disorder excluding alcohol abuse or dependence." The lifetime contrasts were also not significant.

If one contrasts men who were exposed to high levels of war-zone stress with their era veteran and civilian counterparts, *all* of these differences are statistically significant. In fact, in moving from "total theater males" to "total high war zone males," the rates for any NSVG/DIS disorder jump from 49.1 to 63.3 percent lifetime and from 17.1 to 29.8 percent current. Within specific racial/ethnic subgroups, they may go even higher, for example, to 72 percent lifetime and 43 percent current for Hispanic men. Overall, however, the pattern of these differences is quite similar within all racial/ethnic subgroups, repeated exactly among Whites/others and Hispanics and with only two exceptions (lifetime rates in comparison with era veterans) among Black men. For women, those exposed to high war-zone stress also had significantly higher rates of both current and lifetime disorder (with or without alcohol disorders) than era veterans and significantly higher current rates than civilian women.

Contrasts Among Vietnam Theater Veterans on Race/Ethnicity, War-Zone Stress, and Disability

An examination of the effects of minority status on rates of disorder indicates that being an Hispanic male theater veteran significantly increases one's risk of disorder, whereas being Black does not. Exhibit VI-8 shows that the rates for Hispanic theater veteran men are significantly higher than those of both White/other and Black men. Prevalence rates for Hispanics for any NSVG/DIS disorder were 66.5 percent (lifetime) and 25.7 percent (current). For Hispanics who had experienced high levels of war-zone stress, the rates of any NSVG/DIS disorder were 71.8 percent lifetime and 43.2 percent current.

Exposure to war-zone stress in general greatly increased the risk for these NSVG/DIS disorders. Almost two-thirds of male theater veterans exposed to high levels of war-zone stress were classified as having had one of these diagnoses at some point in their lives, and almost three in ten currently had at least one of these disorders. For women, exposure to high war-zone stress had an equally important effect. Prevalence estimates for women exposed to high levels of war-zone stress were 40.5 percent for any lifetime NSVG/DIS disorder, and 15.5 percent for any current NSVG/DIS disorder. All of these contrasts between the high- and low/moderate-war-zone-stress-exposure groups were statistically significant for both men and women. In fact, for both men and women, the current rate of "any NSVG/DIS disorder" among those exposed to high war stress was more than twice as high as that for theater veterans exposed to low/moderate levels of war-zone stress.

Co-occurrence With PTSD and Substance Abuse Among Theater Veterans

Having PTSD also dramatically increases the probability of having another NSVG/DIS disorder. Virtually all male theater veterans with PTSD have met the criteria for another psychiatric disorder at some time in their lives, and half have another disorder currently. Among women, three-fourths of those with PTSD have had another disorder at some time in their lives, and four in ten have another disorder currently. All of these differences between those with and without PTSD were highly significant.

By definition, anyone with a substance abuse disorder has had a lifetime NSVG/DIS disorder. Therefore, all of those with a substance abuse disorder were so classified. However, those with a substance abuse disorder, lifetime, were also more likely than those without to have a current disorder, regardless of whether alcohol disorders are included in the "any NSVG/DIS current disorder" category.

SUMMARY

In examining patterns of nonspecific distress (demoralization), we found that the major elevations in rates of nonspecific distress were among those exposed to high levels of war-zone stress, those with PTSD, those with a lifetime substance abuse disorder, and, for men, those with a high level of service-connected physical disability. Theater veteran men who were members of a minority group (Black or Hispanic) also had higher rates of distress than Whites/others. However, those with PTSD had the highest rates of demoralization, among both men and women.

For the nine specific psychiatric disorders (other than PTSD) assessed in the NSVG, those that occurred most frequently among male Vietnam theater veterans were alcohol abuse or dependence, generalized anxiety disorder (GAD), and antisocial personality disorder (ASP). The lifetime prevalence rates for all three of these disorders was greater than 10 percent, and the rate for alcohol abuse and dependence was 39 percent. Yet none of these rates was significantly different from the rates observed for male Vietnam era veterans, even though the theater veteran rates for ASP and alcohol abuse or dependence were higher than those for male civilians. The most prevalent current disorders among male theater veterans were alcohol abuse or dependence and GAD, both of which were at rates of above 5 percent. However, for neither disorder were the rates for Vietnam theater veteran males higher than those for era veteran males or male civilians. Recent symptoms of antisocial personality disorder are present in only 2 percent of male theater veterans.

Among women Vietnam theater veterans, the most frequently occurring lifetime disorders were GAD, depression, and alcohol abuse or dependence. The lifetime prevalence for all three of these disorders was greater than 9 percent, and the rate for GAD was almost 17 percent. The lifetime rates for both depression and alcohol abuse or dependence were significantly higher for women theater veterans than for women era veterans or civilians. This was not true for GAD. The most prevalent current disorders among female theater veterans were depression and GAD, both of which were at rates of just over 4 percent. These rates were significantly higher than those for era veteran women or civilians for depression but not for GAD.

Overall, the rates for the various psychiatric disorders among Vietnam era veterans, civilians, and low-war-zone-stress theater veterans were within the range for the ECA community samples. Important exceptions were drug abuse or dependence and, for women, obsessive compulsive disorder. NSVG civilians appeared to have lower rates of these disorders than found in the ECA samples. Also, like theater veterans, era veterans had high rates of ASP and alcohol abuse or dependence compared with the ECA community residents.

Both men and women Vietnam theater veterans had higher levels of current depression than either civilians or Vietnam era veterans. When the era veteran and civilian groups were standardized to theater veterans on age and race for men, and age and occupation for women, there was *no* disorder for which the rates of era veterans and civilians were higher than those of theater veterans. In contrast, there were several disorders for which rates for theater veterans, overall, were higher than for era veterans or civilians. Besides current depression, the disorders for which theater veterans had higher rates differ by gender and comparison group (that is, era veterans or civilians). On the basis of these results, it appears that being classified as a "Vietnam theater veteran" did not greatly increase the risk for the NSVG/DIS disorders, as compared with being classified as having served elsewhere in the military during the Vietnam era. However, the number of psychiatric disorders for which theater veterans had elevated rates as compared with civilian rates indicated that serving in the military during that period was in and of itself a risk factor for some disorders.

In contrast to the few differences found between theater veterans overall and their Vietnam era veteran counterparts, an examination of the data for those most commonly thought of as "Vietnam veterans," that is, those exposed to high war-zone stress, produced much more dramatic findings. Male theater veterans who experienced high war-zone stress had higher rates of almost all other psychiatric disorders than Vietnam era veterans and civilians. The rates of virtually all of the same disorders were elevated for theater veteran males exposed to high war-zone stress, in comparison with the rates in low/moderate-war-zone-stress theater males, further validating the finding of elevated rates for these disorders among theater males exposed to high levels of war-zone stress.

Among female Vietnam theater veterans, fewer disorders were associated with war-zone-stress exposure, although the prevalence rates for some disorders in the high-war-stress group appeared to be quite high. Of women exposed to high levels of war-zone stress, 22 percent had a major depressive episode at some time in their lives, 21 percent had lifetime GAD, and 10 percent had dysthymia. The rates for lifetime depression and dysthymia were significantly higher than the rates for era veterans, civilians, and theater veteran women exposed to low/moderate levels of war-zone stress. Major depressive episode was the one current disorder with significantly higher rates among women exposed to high war-zone stress than for all other groups: era veterans, civilians, and low/moderate-war-zone-stress females.

Having a service-connected physical disability (SCPD) appeared to have very little effect on the prevalence rates of psychiatric disorder: males with a high level of SCPD had higher rates only for lifetime generalized anxiety, and females with a SCPD did not have higher rates for any disorder. Being Black also had little effect on rates of disorder, although Blacks did tend to have significantly elevated rates of current ASP. Being Hispanic had a somewhat greater impact. Hispanic men had rates of these various disorders, combined, that were 10 to 15 percent higher than rates for Blacks or Whites/others, regardless of whether the analysis included alcohol disorders. However, Hispanic theater veterans tended to be particularly troubled by problems with alcohol and drugs.

A very high degree of co-occurrence among PTSD, substance abuse, and these other disorders was perhaps the major finding for these specific psychiatric disorders. Male theater veterans with PTSD had significantly higher rates of all disorders except for manic episode, which was not tested. Female theater veterans with PTSD had significantly higher rates of most of the other disorders as well. Differences between those with and without PTSD were statistically significant; they were also quite dramatic. Three-fourths of the men with PTSD had a lifetime diagnosis of alcohol abuse or dependence, 44 percent had lifetime diagnosis of GAD, and more than 20 percent had a lifetime diagnoses of depression, dysthymia, or ASP. Currently, prevalence rates of other NSVG/DIS disorders among males with PTSD are 20 percent with a current alcohol disorder, 20 percent with current GAD, and 16 percent with current depression. Women with PTSD had a 42 percent rate of lifetime depression and a 23 percent rate of current depression. Of these women, 38 percent had lifetime GAD and 20 percent had current GAD. Other disorders for which women with PTSD had lifetime rates of greater than 20 percent were dysthymia (33 percent), panic disorder (21 percent), and alcohol disorders (29 percent). Other disorders with current rates of 10 percent or higher in this group were panic disorder (13 percent) and alcohol disorders (10 percent).

This degree of co-occurrence may raise issues about the uniqueness of the PTSD diagnosis. However, the disorders that have the highest degree of comorbidity (for example, alcohol abuse or dependence, depression, dysthymia, and generalized anxiety) are those that have considerable symptom overlap with PTSD and are likely to co-occur with the disorder. In addition, substance abuse in the NSVG had a high degree of comorbidity with other disorders. Previous studies have found that having almost any psychiatric disorder increases the risk for having another disorder.

Another important finding was that veterans with PTSD were more likely than those without PTSD to have a lifetime diagnosis of antisocial personality disorder (ASP). High rates of ASP among those with PTSD was probably, at least in part, due to a selection bias, since those with ASP were more likely to have experienced high war-zone stress as well. It may also reflect a vulnerability to PTSD among those with ASP.

Those with a lifetime substance abuse disorder also tended to have high rates for other disorders. Males with a history of substance abuse had higher rates for most other disorders than males without such a history, and women with substance abuse also had higher rates for several disorders, although differences for a number of other disorders were not tested because of zero rates for the "no substance abuse" group.

We also compared NSVG findings with prevalence rates of these DIS disorders reported in the Centers for Disease Control's Vietnam Experience Study. As described in Appendix G, some major differences existed between the NSVG and VES in prevalence rates for the various psychiatric disorders. For most of the psychiatric disorders under discussion, lifetime prevalence rates in the VES were much higher than those for the NSVG samples or for the ECA community samples. Among both VES theater and era veterans, lifetime rates of depression, manic episode, generalized anxiety disorder, drug abuse or dependence, and antisocial personality disorder were much higher than in either the ECA community or NSVG veteran samples. For VES theater veterans, lifetime panic disorder and dysthymia also appeared to be higher than in the other samples. Except for depression, current rates for the disorders under discussion tended to be more similar than lifetime rates for the NSVG and the VES. In fact, reports of current drug abuse or dependence were even lower in the VES than in the NSVG.

The reasons for these elevations in lifetime rates in the VES are not clear. Since the prevalence rates in the VES sample appear closer to the NSVG high-war-zone-stress-exposure group than they do the NSVG total theater veteran group, it might be hypothesized that sample differences between the VES and NSVG might account for these results. However, when an NSVG subsample of theater veterans was created that matched the characteristics of VES theater veterans, it was found that the rates for this subsample were not similar to those for the VES, although lifetime rates for antisocial personality disorder and drug abuse or dependence did increase. Our only other hypothesis is that the rate differences may result from modifications made to the DIS during the development of the VES instrument.

CHAPTER VII

The Prevalence of Other Postwar Readjustment Problems

COMMENTARY

When people think about the mental health effects of having served in Vietnam, the central focus of concern is post-traumatic stress disorder. Certainly, mental health practitioners are concerned with the signs and symptoms of this disorder. Planning for mental health services for Vietnam veterans also tends to focus on the prevalence of the disorder. Nonetheless, there are other important issues about the legacy of having served in Vietnam that may not involve mental health at all. A major focus of the NVVRS, and a major question that Congress and the Veterans Administration wanted answered, was: What other problems of readjustment do Vietnam veterans have and how serious are they?

This chapter presents answers to the questions. The participants in the NVVRS responded to a series of questions regarding financial and vocational issues, educational goals, career paths, marital and family functioning, and overall feelings of life satisfaction or dissatisfaction. In sum, the NVVRS attempted to get a fix on the quality of life each study participant was enjoying.

Other specific adjustment problems that were studied — the results of which are presented in this chapter — are the more poignant, upsetting, and gnawing issues sometimes associated with very troubled Vietnam veterans: homelessness, isolation and loneliness, violence and belligerence, and involvement with the criminal justice system in terms of arrest, conviction, and incarceration.

Very important for understanding the results for Vietnam theater veterans are the comparable results for the two main study control groups — era veterans and civilian counterparts. Even though there

*may be serious readjustment problems within some subgroups of the-
ater veterans, the overall comparison of theater veterans with era
veterans and civilian counterparts is a better gauge of the impact of
service in the Vietnam theater on readjustment to civilian life.*

CHAPTER OVERVIEW

Readjustment Problems in General

A substantial minority of both men and women who served in the
Vietnam theater of operations reported experiencing at least one serious
readjustment problem after returning to civilian life, and the majority of
these continue to experience at least one such problem. Although male
Vietnam theater veterans in general do not differ significantly from Vietnam era veterans in their reported levels of readjustment problems, those
who most literally fought the war—theater veterans exposed to high levels
of war-zone stress—were significantly more likely than era veterans to
report such problems. Analyses by race and ethnicity revealed that this
pattern was evident among both White/other and Hispanic males. These
differences were not observed among Blacks, primarily because the levels
of readjustment problems reported by Black era veterans were particularly high. However, comparisons between male theater veterans by
race/ethnicity indicate that both Black and Hispanic men serving in
Vietnam reported significantly more readjustment problems than White/
other males. Among women, those serving in Vietnam—and especially
those exposed to higher levels of war-zone stress—reported significantly
higher levels of readjustment problems than Vietnam era veterans serving
elsewhere. In addition, some evidence exists that Vietnam theater veteran
women experiencing lower levels of war stress have experienced *fewer*
such problems than Vietnam era veterans. Among both men and women
serving in Vietnam, the prevalence of readjustment problems is strongly
and positively related to war-zone-stress exposure, PTSD, a history of
substance abuse, and having a service-connected physical disability.

Education and Occupation

The major significant differences between Vietnam theater and era
veterans were found on educational attainment, with the differences

essentially reversed between male and female veterans. Among men, theater veterans in general and the subgroup exposed to high war stress were *less* well educated today than era veterans, whereas the opposite was observed for women, reflecting the fact that theater veteran women were predominantly nurses. Moreover, the observed education difference in favor of male era veterans was observed only among White/other males. Significant differences between theater veterans and civilians also varied by sex and race/ethnicity. Hispanic and Black Vietnam theater veteran males and, especially, female theater veterans were better educated than their civilian counterparts, whereas White/other theater veteran males tended toward the middle of the educational distribution, with civilians being both better and less well educated. A work history characterized by instability was also more common among theater veteran men than among civilians. This difference was not found among Blacks, however, owing to a high rate of occupational instability among Black civilian males.

Among theater veterans, Blacks were significantly less educated than Hispanics, and somewhat less educated than Whites/others. In contrast, Hispanics serving in Vietnam were somewhat better educated than White/ other males. Both White/other and Hispanic males were more likely to be working than Blacks. While men exposed to high levels of war-zone stress were less educated than those exposed to lower levels, the opposite was true for women (who were primarily nurses). Though better educated, women experiencing high stress were also more likely to be working and reported higher levels of instability in their work histories. Among both men and women, those with PTSD reported significantly higher levels of occupational instability, and men with PTSD were both less educated and more likely to be unemployed (though seven in ten were currently working).

Marital/Relationship and Family Adjustment

Vietnam theater veteran males, including those most highly exposed to war-zone stress, were significantly more likely to be living as though married than Vietnam era veterans and civilians, a pattern generally observed among all subgroups except Hispanic men. Vietnam theater veteran women and those exposed to high war stress were less likely to be married and more likely never to have been married than era veterans or civilian women. More generally, in virtually every subgroup, male and female veterans exposed to high war-zone stress reported poorer levels of adjustment than era veterans and/or civilians on at least one (and fre-quently several) indicator(s) of marital/relationship or family adjustment, including more divorces, marital or relationship problems, parental problems, and/or poor family functioning.

Among Vietnam theater veterans, Black men were significantly less likely to be currently married than Hispanic and White/other men, and the last reported fewer marital/relationship problems than either of the two minority subgroups. For men, level of war-zone-stress exposure was positively correlated with number of divorces, marital or relationship problems, and parental problems, with the divorce relationship also evident for women. Both men and women with PTSD were less likely than those without the disorder to be married, have had more divorces, and to have experienced more marital/relationship problems. Men with PTSD also reported more problems related to parenting and substantially poorer family adjustment. Men and women who had experienced substance abuse problems were less likely married, more often divorced, and experienced higher levels of marital and parental problems.

Subjective Well-Being and Adult Behavior Problems

Although contrasts vary somewhat from indicator to indicator, and by race/ethnicity, in general, Vietnam theater veterans exposed to high levels of war-zone stress were significantly more likely than their civilian counterparts, and to a lesser extent than their era veteran counterparts, to report problems in this area. With one exception (social isolation), however, relationships observed for women do *not* follow this pattern. Nevertheless, this relative disadvantage of those exposed to high war stress in comparison with civilians was evident in (1) lower levels of life happiness and satisfaction among White/other and Hispanic men; (2) higher levels of social isolation among *all* Vietnam theater veteran subgroups (including women); (3) a higher prevalence of homelessness or vagrancy among White/other males; (4) higher levels of active hostility and actual violent behavior among *all* male theater veteran subgroups; and (5) higher levels of arrests and incarceration. Moreover, a similar disadvantage relative to Vietnam *era* veterans was observed among White/other men for subjective well-being, social isolation, homelessness or vagrancy, and violent behavior, and among Black and Hispanic men for active expression of hostility. Theater veteran women in general and those exposed to high war-zone stress reported significantly *less* violent behavior than era veteran women.

Among Vietnam theater veteran males, White/other men reported higher levels of general well-being and fewer violent acts during the past year than both Black and Hispanic men, who did not differ significantly from each other. Black men also reported significantly higher levels of involvement with the criminal justice system (arrests, incarceration, felony convictions) than either White/other or Hispanic men.

Differences observed by level of war-zone-stress exposure, PTSD diagnosis, and substance abuse were quite consistent and striking. Although women serving in the Vietnam theater did not differ significantly on *any* of these measures by level of exposure to war-zone stress, men exposed to high war stress reported significantly poorer adjustment *on every one* of these feelings/behaviors. Similarly, men suffering from PTSD and those with a history of alcohol or drug abuse reported dramatically poorer adjustment on *all* of these feelings/behaviors, as did women for two of these: subjective well-being and social isolation. Among men and women with PTSD, for example, one in four reported extreme unhappiness, and 24 percent of these women and 47 percent of the men reported extreme levels of social isolation. Similarly, fully 35 percent of men with PTSD had been homeless or vagrant, over four in ten scored at the highest level on hostility, one in four had committed 13 or more acts of violence during the past year, and almost half had been arrested or jailed more than once in their lives. Although the relationships differed in strength, essentially the same pattern was observed for those with a history of substance abuse as for those currently suffering from PTSD.

Although the primary focus of the Readjustment Study was to establish the prevalence of post-traumatic stress disorder and its correlates among Vietnam veterans, a parallel focus on "other psychological problems in readjusting to civilian life" has also been of considerable importance to this study since its inception. The range of such "other" problems that might be examined is extremely broad, and several have already been examined in the preceding chapter; namely, other forms of psychiatric disorder as defined in DSM-III, as well as more general, nonspecific forms of psychological distress.

In addition to these categories of "postwar psychological problems," the study's basic objectives specified an examination of "malfunctions in marital, familial, vocational, and educational roles and careers," as well as more general "feelings of life satisfaction, dissatisfaction, and feelings about quality of life." To round out this general picture of the relative postwar adjustment of Vietnam veterans, several other indicators of problem behaviors or circumstances often speculated to be especially common among Vietnam veterans were selected from among the multitude of other possible measures under the rubric of "postwar psychological problems." These included measures of social isolation, homelessness or vagrancy, hostility and violent behavior, and involvement with the criminal justice system.

READJUSTMENT PROBLEMS IN GENERAL: THE READJUSTMENT INDICES

Measures

In order ultimately to facilitate comparing NVVRS findings with those of previous research, the NSVG survey interview included 12 items on various "problems of returning to civilian life" originally used in the *Myths and Realities* study of veterans of the Vietnam era conducted by Louis Harris and Associates in 1980 (Fisher, Boyle, Bucuvalas, & Schulman, 1980) and later (in a slightly different form) in the CBS News–*New York Times* Poll of Vietnam veterans conducted on the tenth anniversary of the end of the Vietnam war. These items asked whether the veteran had problems with finding and holding jobs, not having enough money to live on, using drugs or drinking too much, maintaining mental and physical health, finding meaning in life, being in trouble with the law, finishing school, being discriminated against because of being in the military, and having a relationship with family. All items were coded into four-level ordinal variables in ascending order according to current "seriousness":

1. never had the problem
2. had problem only in the past and it was not serious
3. had a serious problem in the past but not currently
4. currently has a serious problem in this area

Consistent with the previous studies from which these items were derived, whether or not each problem was regarded as "serious" was left to the discretion of the responding veteran.

Index of Readjustment Problems. To derive an overall picture of the level of readjustment problems experienced by veterans in the NVVRS, three separate measures were developed from these items. The first, designated the "Index of Readjustment Problems," was based on a principal components analysis of these items, and was conducted separately for males and for females. For men, all 12 items loaded on a single general factor, suggesting that, in combination, they tapped a general dimension of "readjustment problems" and could be combined into a single measure. For women, this was not the case for three of the items: problems with drugs, with the law, and with discrimination based on military service (primarily due to low occurrence). The index was thus created as the mean of all 12 items for men and (the remaining) nine items for women. Respondents with high scores on this index (that is 1.5+) endorsed more readjustment problems and/or more current or serious readjustment problems than those with low scores (1.0, indicating never having had any readjustment problems).

Number of Serious Readjustment Problems. Two other indices focused specifically on reports of serious postmilitary readjustment problems (as defined by the veteran)—past or present. The first index represented a count of the number of such problems *ever* experienced after leaving the military and regarded by the veteran as serious, that is, the number of problems coded 3 or 4, as described above. The second was an index of current problems and was represented by a count of the number of serious readjustment problems still being experienced, that is, the number of problems coded 4, as described above.

The results of comparisons between Vietnam theater veterans and era veterans on these three indices, as well as comparisons among various subgroups of Vietnam theater veterans, are presented in Tables VII-1 through VII-3 of Volume II respectively.

Contrasts Among Vietnam Theater and Era Veterans

Before examining contrasts among groups, we must mention the overall prevalence of readjustment problems among Vietnam theater veterans. A substantial minority of both men and women serving in the Vietnam theater reported having at least one serious postwar readjustment problem, 44.5 and 37.1 percent respectively. Moreover, approximately 60 percent of these veterans reported that they have continued to experience at least one such problem, 26.0 and 23.6 percent respectively. Overall, then, approximately one in four Vietnam theater veterans currently has at least one serious readjustment problem.

A summary of all comparisons among Vietnam theater veterans and the comparison sample of era veterans is presented in Exhibit VII-1 for all three measures of readjustment problems. The results of comparing these theater veterans with era veterans for all three measures are, on the whole, quite consistent. For males, no significant differences between Vietnam theater and era veterans existed on *any* of these measures. However, for each measure, those who actually fought the war—theater veterans exposed to high levels of war-zone stress—were substantially more likely than era veterans to have experienced readjustment problems. Theater veterans

EXHIBIT VII-1
Summary of Contrasts Among Major Study Groups for Readjustment Problems

Contrasts Among Major Study Groups	Index of Readjustment Problems	No. of Serious Readj. Problems Postmilitary	No. of Current Serious Readjustment Problems
A. Males—Total			
1. Thr vs. Era	NS	NS	NS
2. HWZ vs. Era	HWZ > Era***	HWZ > Era***	HWZ > Era***
3. LWZ vs. Era	NS	NS	NS
4. Thr vs. Civ	—	—	—
5. HWZ vs. Civ	—	—	—
B. Males—White/Other			
1. Thr vs. Era	NS	NS	NS
2. HWZ vs. Era	HWZ > Era***	HWZ > Era***	HWZ > Era***
3. LWZ vs. Era	NS	NS	NS
4. Thr vs. Civ	—	—	—
5. HWZ vs. Civ	—	—	—
C. Males—Black			
1. Thr vs. Era	NS	NS	Thr < Era*
2. HWZ vs. Era	NS	NS	NS
3. LWZ vs. Era	LWZ < Era*	LWZ < Era*	LWZ < Era*
4. Thr vs. Civ	—	—	—
5. HWZ vs. Civ	—	—	—
D. Males—Hispanic			
1. Thr vs. Era	NS	NS	NS
2. HWZ vs. Era	HWZ > Era***	HWZ > Era**	HWZ > Era**
3. LWZ vs. Era	NS	NS	NS
4. Thr vs. Civ	—	—	—
5. HWZ vs. Civ	—	—	—
E. Females—Total			
1. Thr vs. Era	Thr > Era*	Thr > Era*	Thr > Era***
2. HWZ vs. Era	HWZ > Era***	HWZ > Era***	HWZ > Era***
3. LWZ vs. Era	LWZ < Era**	NS	NS
4. Thr vs. Civ	—	—	—
5. HWZ vs. Civ	—	—	—

Notes: 1. $<$ = lower than; $>$ = higher than; $<>$ = both lower than *and* higher than (relationship not ordinal); — = not applicable to this variable.
2. *$p < 0.05$; **$p < 0.01$; ***$p < 0.001$; NS = not statistically significant.

Key: Thr = Vietnam theater veterans.
Era = Vietnam era veterans
Civ = Civilian counterparts
HWZ = Theater veterans exposed to high levels of war zone stress
LWZ = Theater veterans exposed to low-to-moderate levels of war zone stress.

exposed to high war-zone stress were almost twice as likely as comparable era veterans to score at the highest level on the Index of Readjustment Problems (42.3 vs. 21.8 percent) and to report four or more serious readjustment problems since leaving the military (23.6 vs. 11.2 percent). Moreover, over four in ten (42.1 percent) theater veterans exposed to high war-zone stress reported having at least one current serious readjustment problem, and almost one-third of these reported four or more (13.6 percent). By comparison, only one in four era veterans reported currently experiencing any serious readjustment problems, and only 5.3 percent reported four or more. None of the comparisons between era veterans and theater veterans exposed to low or moderate levels of war-zone stress was statistically significant.

A further examination of these comparisons by race/ethnicity indicates that the pattern observed for all males is repeated exactly among both Hispanic and White/other males. In each group, theater veterans in general and those exposed to moderate or low levels of war stress did not differ significantly from era veterans, whereas theater veterans exposed to high levels of war stress reported substantially more readjustment problems. By contrast, this heretofore consistent pattern is essentially *reversed* for Black theater veterans, among whom differences between veterans exposed to high war-zone stress and era veterans were not statistically significant. The predominant relationship consistently observed for this group was a significantly lower level of readjustment problems reported by Black theater veterans exposed to lower levels of war-zone stress in comparison with Black era veterans. In fact, for the number of current serious problems, Black theater veterans in general reported *fewer* readjustment problems than comparable era veterans. These figures appear to result from a high level of readjustment problems among Black era veterans. On all three indices, the means for Black era veterans were higher than those for the total high-war-zone-stress-exposure group.

Women veterans, not only those exposed to high war-zone stress, but also those serving in the Vietnam theater in general, reported significantly higher levels of readjustment problems than their era veteran counterparts on all three measures. Moreover, consistent with the result observed among Black males, those exposed to low or moderate levels of war stress scored significantly lower than comparable era veterans on the Index of Readjustment Problems. Female theater veterans exposed to high war-zone stress were almost three times more likely than comparable era veterans to score at the highest level on the Index of Readjustment Problems (28.6 vs. 9.9 percent) and even more so to report four or more serious readjustment problems since leaving the military (12.0 vs. 3.4 percent).

Almost one-third of women veterans exposed to high war stress reported experiencing at least one readjustment problem that remains a serious problem today, and almost one-third of these (10.6 percent) reported four or more such problems. By comparison, only 4 percent of era veterans reported currently experiencing any serious readjustment problems, and virtually none (0.3 percent) reported four or more.

Contrasts Among Vietnam Theater Veterans

A summary of contrasts between various subgroups of Vietnam theater veterans on these readjustment problem indices is presented in Exhibit VII-2. Regardless of which of the three indices is examined, the pattern of relationships observed is virtually identical. Among male theater veterans, White/other males reported significantly lower levels of readjustment problems than either Blacks or Hispanics, while the latter two did not differ significantly from each other. For example, the proportions reporting at least one serious current readjustment problem were 22.8, 43.2, and 38.8 percent among White/other males, Blacks, and Hispanic, respectively, and 5.1, 11.0, and 8.3 percent, respectively, reported experiencing four or more serious problems at the time of interview. Thus, although Black theater veterans reported significantly fewer current readjustment problems than Black male era veterans, the former still reported significantly more current readjustment problems than White/other male theater veterans.

Among both male and female veterans serving in the Vietnam theater, those exposed to high levels of war-zone stress reported significantly higher levels of readjustment problems than those experiencing lower levels of exposure. Those suffering from post-traumatic stress disorder also reported significantly more readjustment problems than those who are not. Among men, those experiencing high war-zone stress were twice as likely to report at least one current readjustment problem as those exposed to low or moderate levels (42.1 percent vs. 20.7 percent), and almost four times more likely to report four or more serious readjustment problems at the time of interview (13.6 percent vs. 3.5 percent). Although the absolute levels are somewhat lower for women, the ratios are essentially the same—two to one (32.1 percent vs. 18.0 percent) and four to one (4.1 percent vs. 1.3 percent) respectively. The contrasts between those meeting the criteria for PTSD and those who do not are even more striking, with men having PTSD being close to four times more likely (68.7 percent vs. 17.9 percent) to report at least one serious problem and ten times more likely (22.1 percent vs. 2.9 percent) to report four or more

EXHIBIT VII-2
Summary of Contrasts Among Vietnam Theater Veteran
Subgroups for Readjustment Problems

Contrasts Among Theater Veteran Subgroups	Index of Readjustment Problems	No. of Serious Readj. Problems Postmilitary	No. of Current Serious Readjustment Problems
A. Race/Ethnicity			
1. W/O vs. Blk	W/O < Blk***	W/O < Blk***	W/O < Blk***
2. W/O vs. Hisp	W/O < Hisp***	W/O < Hisp**	W/O < Hisp***
3. Blk vs. Hisp	NS	NS	NS
B. High vs. Low War Stress			
1. Males	HWZ > LWZ***	HWZ > LWZ***	HWZ > LWZ***
2. Females	HWZ > LWZ***	HWZ > LWZ***	HWZ > LWZ***
C. PTSD vs. No PTSD			
1. Males	PTSD > No PTSD***	PTSD > No PTSD***	PTSD > No PTSD***
2. Females	PTSD > No PTSD***	PTSD > No PTSD***	PTSD > No PTSD***
D. Service-Connected Physical Disability			
1. Males:			
a. SCPD vs. None	SCPD > None**	SCPD > None***	SCPD > None***
b. High SCPD vs. None	High > None***	High > None***	High > None***
2. Females:			
a. SCPD vs. None	SCPD > None*	NS	SCPD > None**
b. High SCPD vs. None	High > None*	NS	High > None**
E. Substance Abuse vs. None			
1. Males	Sub Abuse > None***	Sub Abuse > None***	Sub Abuse > None***
2. Females	Sub Abuse > None***	Sub Abuse > None***	Sub Abuse > None***

Notes: 1. < = lower than; > = higher than; <> = both lower than *and* higher than (relationship not ordinal).

2. *$p < 0.05$; **$p < 0.01$; ***$p < 0.001$; NS = not statistically significant.

such problems. Comparable proportions for women were 66.7 versus 18.6 and 12.8 versus 1.3 percent for at least one and four or more current serious problems respectively.

Also observed among both male and female theater veterans were consistent relationships between readjustment problems and both lifetime substance abuse and service-connected disabilities. Those having service-connected disabilities for physical problems were significantly more likely than those without such disability to report readjustment problems, and these differences were even stronger when those with higher percentages of disability were compared with those with none. The only nonsignificant contrasts in these comparisons were those for the number of serious readjustment problems ever experienced by women after leaving the military. Similarly, those who had ever met the criteria for alcohol or drug dependence or abuse reported higher levels of readjustment problems than those who had no such history. Since physical health problems and problems with alcohol and drugs are embedded in the list of readjustment problems, at least a modest relationship with each of these variables would be expected.

Summary

A substantial minority of both men and women who served in the Vietnam theater of operations have experienced at least one serious readjustment problem after returning to civilian life, and a majority of these continue to experience at least one such problem. While among men, theater veterans in general do not differ significantly from era veterans *not* serving in Vietnam in their reported levels of readjustment problems, those who most literally fought the war—theater veterans exposed to high levels of war-zone stress—were significantly more likely than era veterans to report such problems. Analyses by race and ethnicity revealed that this pattern was evident among both White/other and Hispanic males. While these significant differences were not observed among Blacks, Black theater veterans with high war-zone stress had levels of readjustment problems comparable to those of Hispanics; but levels of readjustment problems reported by Black era veterans were so high as to wipe out such differences among Blacks. In fact, comparisons between male theater veterans by race/ethnicity indicate that both Black and Hispanic men serving in Vietnam reported significantly more readjustment problems than White/other males. Among women, those serving in Vietnam—and especially those exposed to higher levels of war-zone stress—report significantly higher levels of readjustment problems than Vietnam era veterans serving elsewhere. Some evidence exists that those veterans experiencing lower levels of war stress have experienced fewer such problems than era veterans. Among both men and women serving in Vietnam, the prevalence of readjustment problems was strongly and positively related to high war-zone stress, PTSD, a history of substance abuse, and a service-connected physical disability.

EDUCATION AND OCCUPATION

Measures

Although a thorough examination of "malfunctions in vocational and educational roles and careers" among Vietnam veterans would constitute a major study in its own right, this study examined six general indicators to describe the experiences of Vietnam theater veterans in these areas and to compare these experiences with those of Vietnam era veterans and civilians. These indicators were:

1. a measure indicating current (at time of interview) level of educational attainment;
2. a measure indicating changes in educational attainment from that achieved at entry into the military to the present time;
3. a measure of current employment status;
4. a measure of current occupational status controlled for *current* educational attainment;
5. a parallel measure of current occupational status controlled for premilitary educational attainment;
6. a composite measure of occupational or career instability.

Both the educational attainment measures and the employment status measures were derived from standard demographic items. Current educational attainment was assessed as the highest level achieved at the time of interview. The extent to which current level of educational attainment represented a change (increase) in educational level from that at entry to military service was summarized in a variable coded as follows:

(a) some high school at (military) entry—no change
(b) some high school at entry—additional education (after entry or postmilitary)
(c) high school graduate at entry—no change
(d) high school graduate at entry—additional education

(e) some college at entry—no change
(f) some college at entry—additional education
(g) college graduate (or higher) at entry (no change possible)

The "other" category under employment status included going to school or training, keeping house, disabled and unable to work, or not working —institutionalized.

The occupational status measures were based on an index of socioeconomic status first developed by Duncan (1961) and calibrated to the 1980 Census occupational classificatory scheme by Stevens and Cho (1985). This socioeconomic index (SEI) is based on "predicted" prestige scores for occupations obtained in the regression of prestige (people's evaluations of the relative merits of the occupation) on levels of income and education. Scores on the SEI have a theoretical range of 0 to 100. However, because differences among groups on the SEI may merely reflect differences in education or income, some type of "adjusted" measure was desired. Therefore, two "occupational status relative to education" variables were constructed, one based on current education and the other on premilitary educational attainment.[1] Those high on these measures are working jobs with an SEI rating significantly above what would be predicted from their current or premilitary levels of education, whereas those scoring very low are working at jobs whose status is substantially below what one might expect from their current or premilitary education. The "current" measure highlights potential inconsistencies between current education and occupation, and the "premilitary" measure indicates possible differences in postmilitary "occupational mobility" relative to education at service entry. The occupation for which the SEI is coded is either the current main job or the kind of work done for the majority of one's working life (nonmilitary). Because of the nature of the female sample—the majority of women in all groups were nurses—we could not derive these measures in a sensible way for women.

We derived rates of occupational instability from four different summary measures of each respondent's work history:

1. number of different employers
2. number of different kinds of jobs
3. longest period held a job with the same employer
4. number of periods of unemployment

---

[1] To obtain these measures, the SEI scores were regressed on educational attainment and the residuals of actual from predicted values retained and standardized. The resulting variables were then categorized according to the number of standard deviations above or below the mean a particular respondent fell.

These items were intercorrelated — separately for men and women — and subjected to a principal components analysis. Since all but item 3 loaded on a single general factor for both men and women, item 3 was dropped and factor scores computed to created a measure reflecting low to high levels of occupational instability based on these components.

The results of comparisons among Vietnam theater veterans, era veterans, and civilian counterparts on these six measures, as well as comparisons among various subgroups of Vietnam theater veterans, are presented in Tables VII-4 through VII-7 respectively.

Contrasts Among Vietnam Theater Veterans, Era Veterans, and Civilians

Exhibit VII-3 presents a summary of all comparisons among Vietnam theater veterans and the comparison samples of era veterans and civilians. The results of these comparisons are considerably less consistent than those observed for the readjustment indices in general. Overall, significant differences between Vietnam theater veterans and Vietnam era veterans (with two minor exceptions) were found only on educational attainment, and these vary considerably in direction by sex and race/ethnicity. For example, while, on the whole, male theater veterans and those exposed to high levels of war-zone stress were less educated than era veterans, among women this relationship was reversed. Even when their distributions are standardized by age and nursing status to theater veterans, era veteran women were significantly less educated than theater veteran women overall and those exposed to high war stress. Moreover, the finding that theater veteran males and those exposed to higher war stress tended to be less educated than era veterans was apparent only among White/other males. Differences between era and theater veterans among Black men showed no clear trend, and the significant contrasts among Hispanic men suggest that theater veterans were somewhat *better* educated than era veterans.

Significant differences observed between theater veteran males as a whole and White/other males exposed to high war stress on changes in educational attainment (from that at military entry) reflect primarily differences in current educational attainment per se. However, similar differences observed among Black men and women appear to reflect real differences in "educational mobility" among groups. For example, that Black theater veteran men (notably those exposed to low or moderate levels of war-zone stress) were significantly more likely than Black era veterans to have remained high school graduates reflects the fact that 70

(text continued on page 158)

EXHIBIT VII-3
Summary of Contrasts Among Major Study Groups for Education and Occupation

Contrasts Among Major Study Groups	Current Educational Attainment	Current Educational Attainment Relative to Premilitary Education	Current Work Status
A. Males—Total			
1. Thr vs. Era	Thr < Era*	NS	NS
2. HWZ vs. Era	HWZ < Era*	HWZ < Era (Coll Grad— No Chg)*	NS
3. LWZ vs. Era	NS	NS	NS
4. Thr vs. Civ	Civ <> Thr***	—	Thr > Civ (Wrk)/Thr < Civ (Ret)***
5. HWZ vs. Civ	HWZ < Civ**/Civ <> HWZ***	—	HWZ < Civ (Retired)**
B. Males—White/Other			
1. Thr vs. Era	Thr < Era*	NS	NS
2. HWZ vs. Era	HWZ < Era**	HWZ > Era (Some HS+ Addl)*	NS
3. LWZ vs. Era	NS	NS	NS
4. Thr vs. Civ	Thr < Civ*/Civ <> Thr***	—	Thr > Civ (Unemp)/Thr < Civ (Ret)***
5. HWZ vs. Civ	HWZ < Civ***	—	HWZ < Civ (Retired)**

C. Males—Black			
1. Thr vs. Era	NS	Thr > Era (HS Grad—No Chg)*	NS
2. HWZ vs. Era	NS	NS	NS
3. LWZ vs. Era	LWZ > Era (HS Grad)*	LWZ > Era (HS Grad—No Chg)*	NS
4. Thr vs. Civ	Thr > Civ (HS Grad/S Coll)***	—	NS
5. HWZ vs. Civ	HWZ > Civ (HS Grad/S Coll)***	—	NS
D. Males—Hispanic			
1. Thr vs. Era	Thr > Era (Grad/Prof)*	NS	NS
2. HWZ vs. Era	NS	NS	NS
3. LWZ vs. Era	LWZ > Era (Grade/Prof)*	NS	LWZ > Era (Working)*
4. Thr vs. Civ	Thr > Civ (Some Coll)***	—	NS
5. HWZ vs. Civ	HWZ > Civ (Some Coll)***	—	NS
E. Females—Total			
1. Thr vs. Era	Thr > Era*	Thr > Era (HS Grad + Addl)*	NS
2. HWZ vs. Era	HWZ > Era**	HWZ < Era (HS Grad—NC)*/ HWZ > Era (HS Grad+)**	NS
3. LWZ vs. Era	NS	NS	NS
4. Thr vs. Civ	Thr > Civ***	—	NS
5. HWZ vs. Civ	HWZ > Civ***	—	NS

Notes: 1. $<$ = lower than; $>$ = higher than; $<>$ = both lower than *and* higher than (relationship not ordinal); — = not applicable to this variable.
2. *$p < 0.05$; **$p < 0.01$; ***$p < 0.001$; NS = not statistically significant.

(continued)

EXHIBIT VII-3 (Continued)

	Occupational Status Relative to Current Education	Occupational Status Relative to Premilitary Education	Occupational Instability Index
A. *Males—Total*			
1. Thr vs. Era	NS	NS	NS
2. HWZ vs. Era	NS	NS	NS
3. LWZ vs. Era	NS	NS	NS
4. Thr vs. Civ	NS	—	Thr > Civ***
5. HWZ vs. Civ	NS	—	HWZ > Civ***
B. *Males—White/Other*			
1. Thr vs. Era	NS	NS	NS
2. HWZ vs. Era	NS	NS	NS
3. LWZ vs. Era	NS	NS	NS
4. Thr vs. Civ	NS	—	Thr > Civ***
5. HWZ vs. Civ	NS	—	HWZ > Civ**

C. Males—Black

1. Thr vs. Era	NS	NS	NS
2. HWZ vs. Era	NS	NS	NS
3. LWZ vs. Era	NS	NS	NS
4. Thr vs. Civ	NS	—	NS
5. HWZ vs. Civ	NS	—	NS

D. Males—Hispanic

1. Thr vs. Era	NS	NS	NS
2. HWZ vs. Era	NS	NS	NS
3. LWZ vs. Era	NS	NS	NS
4. Thr vs. Civ	NS	—	Thr > Civ*
5. HWZ vs. Civ	NS	—	HWZ > Civ**

E. Females—Total

1. Thr vs. Era	—	—	NS
2. HWZ vs. Era	—	—	NS
3. LWZ vs. Era	—	—	LWZ < Era***
4. Thr vs. Civ	—	—	NS
5. HWZ vs. Civ	—	—	NS

Notes: 1. $<$ = lower than; $>$ = higher than; $<>$ = both lower than *and* higher than (relationship not ordinal); — = not applicable to this variable; NS = not statistically significant.
2. $*p < 0.05$; $**p < 0.01$; $***p < 0.001$; NS = not statistically significant.

157

percent of era veterans who were high school graduates when they entered the service subsequently obtained more education, compared with only 47 percent of the theater veterans. In contrast, theater veteran women (especially those exposed to high levels of war-zone stress) who were high school graduates when they entered the service were significantly more likely than female era veterans to have received additional education (72.7 vs. 43.9 percent for those exposed to high war stress and era veterans respectively). Since the vast majority of the former were nurses, much of this additional education was likely obtained while these women were *in* the military.

Significant contrasts between Vietnam theater veterans and civilians abound, not only on education, but also on employment status and occupational instability. Once again, however, these contrasts are not entirely consistent. For example, among males overall, theater veterans were marginally less educated than civilians, and those veterans exposed to high war stress were significantly less educated. However, this overall assessment masks considerable complexity, because civilians were both less *and* more educated than male theater veterans. While theater veterans were more likely to be high school graduates or to have attended some college, civilians were more likely both not to have graduated from high school and to be college graduates or higher. Once again, this overall pattern for theater males was predominantly characteristic of White/other men, while among both Black and Hispanic men, significant differences were primarily in the direction of *higher* levels of education among theater veterans in general, and those exposed to high war stress, than among their civilian counterparts. Among women, this education advantage in favor of a veterans overall and those experiencing high war stress was even more substantial.

Significant differences between Vietnam theater veterans and civilians on current employment status do not appear to reflect any consistent or important trend. No such differences were found for women, and, among men, theater veterans were slightly more likely to be currently working, while civilians were somewhat more likely than theater and high-war-zone-stress-exposed males to be retired, a not too exciting trend once again found only among White/other males. In contrast, male theater veterans and veterans exposed to high war stress tended to have a work history characterized by occupational instability more often than civilians. For example, theater veteran men experiencing high war stress were almost twice as likely as their civilian counterparts to score at the highest level on occupational instability (25.3 vs. 14.2 percent). Although no such differences were found among Black men or among women, these distinctions were evident among both White/other and Hispanic men. Again, the lack of differences observed among Blacks was caused in part by the elevated rates of problems among Black civilians.

Finally, none of the contrasts between Vietnam theater veterans and either era veterans or civilians on occupational status (adjusted for either current or premilitary education) achieved statistical significance. These data offered no support for the hypothesis that theater veterans are either less or more likely to achieve an occupational status commensurate with their education than are other Vietnam era veterans or civilians.

Contrasts Among Vietnam Theater Veterans

Exhibit VII-4 presents a summary of contrasts between various subgroups of Vietnam theater veterans on these same education and occupation variables. Among male theater veterans, significant differences by race/ethnicity were found on both education and employment status. On educational attainment, although Black theater veterans were significantly less educated than Hispanics, no clearcut "high–low" difference was evident in contrasts between these two groups and White/other men. Blacks were somewhat less represented at the highest education levels than White/other men (a difference also reflected in the educational change variable), but, if anything, Hispanic male theater veterans were somewhat better educated than White/other theater veterans. In fact, the significant differences observed between Hispanic men and both Black and White/other males on changes in education from premilitary levels reflect the fact that Hispanic male theater veterans who entered the service as high school graduates were substantially more likely to have received additional education than men in these other two subgroups with the same levels of premilitary education (75 percent for Hispanics vs. 47 and 52 percent for White/others and Blacks respectively). Similarly, White/other and Hispanic males did not differ significantly on employment status, but both groups were more likely than Blacks to be working, whereas the last were more likely to be unemployed. No significant differences by race/ethnicity were found for either occupational status (adjusted for either current or premilitary education) or instability.

Significant differences *were* found, however, by levels of exposure to war-zone stress and PTSD for all measures except the occupational status indicators. Among men, the only significant contrasts by war-zone stress indicated that those exposed to high stress were less educated than those

(text continued on page 164)

EXHIBIT VII-4

Summary of Contrasts Among Vietnam Theater Veteran Subgroups
for Education and Occupation

Contrast Among Theater Veteran Subgroups	Current Educational Attainment	Current Educational Attainment Relative to Premilitary Education
A. *Race/Ethnicity*		
1. W/O vs. Blk	W/O > Blk (Coll Grad/Grad-Prof)*	W/O > Blk (Some Coll+/Coll Grad—NC)**
2. W/O vs. Hisp	W/O > Hisp (HSG)/W/O < Hisp (S Coll)**	W/O > Hisp (HS Grad—NC)/W/O < Hisp (HS Grad+)***
3. Blk vs. Hisp	Blk < Hisp*	Blk > Hisp (HS Grad—No Chg)**
B. *High vs. Low War Stress*		
1. Males	HWZ < LWZ*	HWZ > LWZ (Some HS+)/HWZ < LWZ (Coll Grad—NC)**
2. Females	HWZ > LWZ***	HWZ < LWZ (HS Grad—No Chg)**
C. *PTSD vs. No PTSD*		
1. Males	PTSD < No PTSD**	PTSD > No PTSD (Some HS/HS Grad+)/ PTSD < No PTSD (Some Coll)*
2. Females	NS	PTSD < No PTSD (HS Grad—No Chg)*

D. *Service-Connected Physical Disability*		
1. Males:		
a. SCPD vs. None	NS	SCPD > None (Some HS+)/SCPD < None (Some Coll—NC)**
b. High SCPD vs. None	NS	High < None (Some Coll—No Chg)**
2. Females:		
a. SCPD vs. None	NS	NS
b. High SCPD vs. None	NS	NS
E. *Substance Abuse vs. None*		
1. Males	SAB > (LTHS/S Coll)/SAB < (HSG/GPS)***	SAB > None (Some HS/HS Grad+)/SAB < None (HSG—NC/Coll Grad—NC)***
2. Females	NS	NS

(continued)

Notes: 1. $<$ = lower than; $>$ = higher than; $<>$ = both lower than *and* higher than (relationship not ordinal); — = not applicable to this variable.
  2. *p < 0.05; **p < 0.01; ***p < 0.001; NS = not statistically significant.

EXHIBIT VII-4 *(Continued)*

Theater Veteran Subgroups	Current Work Status	Occupational Status Relative to Current Education	Occupational Status Relative to Premilitary Education	Occupational Instability Index
A. Race/Ethnicity				
1. W/O vs. Blk	W/O > Blk (Wrk)/W/O < Blk (Unemp)*	NS	NS	NS
2. W/O vs. Hisp	NS	NS	NS	NS
3. Blk vs. Hisp	Blk < Hisp (Wrk)**/Blk > Hisp (Unemp)*	NS	NS	NS
B. High vs. Low War Stress				
1. Males	NS	NS	NS	NS
2. Females	HWZ > LWZ (Wrk)/HWZ < LWZ (Ret)*	—	—	HWZ > LWZ***
C. PTSD vs. No PTSD				
1. Males	PTSD < No (Wrk)/PTSD > No (Unemp)***	NS	NS	PTSD > No PTSD***
2. Females	PTSD < No PTSD (Ret)**	—	—	PTSD > No PTSD*

D. Service-Connected Physical Disability				
1. Males:				
a. SCPD vs. None	SCPD < None (Wrk)/ SCPD > None (Othr)**	NS	NS	SCPD < None*
b. High SCPD vs. None	High < None (Wrk)/High > None (Othr)***	NS	NS	NS
2. Females:				
a. SCPD vs. None	SCPD < None (Wrk)/ SCPD > None (Ret)***	—	—	SCPD < None*
b. High SCPD vs. None	High < None (Wrk)/High > None (Ret)***	—	—	High < None*
E. Substance Abuse vs. None				
1. Males	SAB < None (Wrk)/SAB > None (Othr)*	NS	NS	Sub Abuse > None***
2. Females	NS	—	NS	NS

Notes: 1. $<$ = lower than; $>$ = higher than; $<>$ = both lower than *and* higher than (relationship not ordinal); — = not applicable to this variable.
2. *$p < 0.05$; **$p < 0.01$; ***$p < 0.001$; NS = not statistically significant.

163

exposed to lower levels (a finding consistent with common assumptions regarding selection biases with respect to who saw combat in Vietnam). The reverse was true for women (higher stress was associated with *more* education). In addition, those women exposed to high levels of war stress were more likely to be currently working, but they also had higher occupational instability than those exposed to lower levels of stress. Consistent with the difference observed between theater veteran women exposed to high war-zone stress and female era veterans, theater veteran women exposed to high war stress who entered the service as high school graduates were significantly more likely to have obtained additional education than those exposed to lower levels of such stress.

Among both males and females, those with PTSD were more likely to report work histories characterized by instability than those without the disorder. Among males, those with PTSD had acquired less education and were more likely to be unemployed than those not suffering from the disorder. Males with PTSD were also more than twice as likely (42.2 percent vs. 19.1 percent) and females more than four times as likely (21.8 percent vs. 5.6 percent) as those without the disorder to report high levels of occupational instability. In addition, male theater veterans with PTSD were more than five times more likely to be unemployed (13.3 percent vs. 2.5 percent). However, almost 70 percent of theater veterans with PTSD were currently working. Interestingly, among both male and female theater veterans entering the military with a high school education or (for males) less, those with PTSD were significantly more likely to have continued their education than those without PTSD.

Not surprisingly, those with service-connected disabilities were less likely than those with none to report being currently working, with the disabled men more likely to report the status that includes "disabled—not able to work" (other), and disabled women more likely to be retired. Also not surprisingly, those so disabled were less likely to report unstable work histories (that is, multiple employers, periods of unemployment). Among men entering the military with some high school or some college, those with service-connected physical disabilities were also more likely to have sought additional schooling than those without such disabilities. In contrast, male theater veterans with a history of substance abuse were significantly more likely than those without such a history to report less stable work histories. This trend was also reflected in their being less likely to be working at the time of interview. Among those entering the military as high school graduates, men with a history of substance abuse were also more likely to have obtained additional education than those with no such histories.

Summary

None of the contrasts involving occupational status adjusted for education (either current or premilitary) were statistically significant. Significant differences between Vietnam theater and era veterans were found predominantly on current educational attainment, with the differences essentially reversed between male and female veterans. Among men, theater veterans in general and the subgroup exposed to high war stress were *less* educated than era veterans, whereas for women the opposite trend was observed. Moreover, the observed education difference in favor of male era veterans was observed only among White/other males, while Hispanic theater veterans in particular were somewhat better educated. Among those entering the military as high school graduates, Black male theater veterans were less likely than era veterans to have subsequently obtained additional education. The reverse was true among women entering the military as high school graduates. Significant differences between theater veterans and civilians also varied by sex and race/ethnicity. Hispanic and Black theater veteran males and, especially, female theater veterans were currently better educated than their civilian counterparts. But White/other males tended toward the middle of the educational distribution, with their civilian counterparts both better educated and less well educated. While significant differences between theater veterans and civilians on current employment status appeared to reflect no consistent tend, a work history characterized by instability was more common among theater veteran men (notably Whites/others and Hispanics) than among civilians.

Among theater veterans, Blacks were significantly less educated at the time of interview than Hispanics, and somewhat less educated than Whites/others. In contrast, Hispanics serving in Vietnam were somewhat better educated than White/other males. In fact, Hispanic male theater veterans who entered the military as high school graduates were significantly more likely than Black or White/other men entering as high school graduates to have continued their education. Both White/other and Hispanic males were more likely to be working than Blacks. While men exposed to high levels of war-zone stress were currently less educated than those exposed to lower levels, the opposite was true for women. Among those entering the service as high school graduates, theater veteran women exposed to high levels of war-zone stress were significantly more likely than those exposed to lower levels to have continued their education, and, overall, those exposed to high war stress were currently better educated. Though better educated, women having experienced high war stress were also more likely to report higher levels of instability in their work histories. This group of women was also more likely to be working.

Among both men and women, those with PTSD reported significantly higher levels of occupational instability, and men with PTSD were both less educated and more likely to be unemployed (though seven in ten were currently working). Among those entering the military with a high school education or less, men and women with PTSD were more likely than those without to have obtained more education. Among both men and women, service-connected-disability status was positively related to not working and negatively related to occupational instability. For men entering the military with some high school or some college, having a service-connected disability was also positively related to educational mobility. For males, those with a history of substance abuse were less likely to be employed and had more unstable work histories. However, for those veterans entering the service as high school graduates, a history of substance abuse was also positively related to continuing their education.

MARITAL/RELATIONSHIP AND FAMILY ROLES

Measures

To assess potential "malfunctions in marital and familial roles," we included a number of different measures related to marital, relationship, and family roles and potential problems of adjustment within those roles, in the NSVG interview. These included conventional measures of marital status and history, marital and relationship problems, parental role dissatisfaction or problems, and family adaptability and cohesion. From these, five separate indicators were derived. The first, a measure of current marital status, was based on a standard demographic item on which people reported themselves as married, separated, divorced, widowed, or never married, augmented by an item used to reclassify those not formally married, but living with some *as though married*, into a separate category. A second, more direct measure of marital problems was a history of divorce, represented by the number of divorces reported among those who had ever been married.

The third indicator was a marital or relationship problems index derived for those currently married or living as married. Measures of malfunctions in marital and relationship roles were drawn from several different sources, including a few from Veroff, Douvan, and Kulka (1981) and Campbell, Converse, and Rodgers (1976), as well as subsets of items from the Dyadic Adjustment Scale (Spanier, 1976) and the PERI Marital Dissatisfaction Scale (Dohrenwend, 1982). These included the following items:

- separations (not leading to divorce)
- marital or relationship happiness

- problems with getting along
- feelings of inadequacy as a spouse/partner
- the amount of companionship
- the number of quarrels
- the amount of satisfaction felt during the past year with the marriage/relationship

To derive an overall index or composite measure, we ran intercorrelations among these items for all veterans and for males and females separately. We also conducted a principal components analysis. All but two items loaded on a single principal factor. These two items—separations and feelings of inadequacy as a spouse—were dropped, the remaining items recorded as necessary from 1 (low) to 5 (high), and a Marital Problems Index created by taking the mean of these 16 items (range 1-5).

A similar (fourth) index of parental problems was created from a set of items also adapted from Campbell et al. (1976) and Dohrenwend (1982). These items characterized:

- the extent to which respondents felt their children presented problems for them
- the extent to which they found being a parent enjoyable
- feelings of inadequacy as a parent
- their degree of satisfaction in getting along with their children
- their satisfaction as a parent with how their children were turning out

Intercorrelations among these five items were examined for all veterans, and for males and females separately. Based on this examination, the measure of feelings of inadequacy as a parent was dropped (due to low correlations with others), and the Parental Problems Index was derived by taking the mean of the other four items, ranging from 1 (low) to 5 (high).

Finally, to derive an overall measure of "family" as opposed to marital or relationship adjustment, the Family Adaptability and Cohesion Evaluation Scales (FACES II)—developed by Olson and his colleagues (Olson, Bell, & Portner, 1978; Olson et al., 1983) based on a "Circumplex Model" —were included in the interview to allow veterans to describe how they perceived their families. The Circumplex Model is based on two primary dimensions— adaptability and cohesion—each represented by a series of items in FACES II. The family *adaptability* index provides ratings of the extent to which the family system is flexible and able to change (in power structure, role relationships, and relationship rules) in response to situational or developmental stresses. The four levels of adaptability derivable from this index range from rigid (very low) to structured (low to moderate) to flexible (moderate to high) to chaotic (very high). The family *cohesion* index measures the degree to which family members are perceived to be separated or connected, addressing component issues including emotional bonding, shared use of time and space, and decision making. The four levels of cohesion range from disengaged (very low) to separated (low to moderate) to connected (moderate to high) to enmeshed (very high).

It is hypothesized that central levels of adaptability (structured and flexible) or cohesion (separated and connected) are most viable or conducive to family functioning, whereas extremes on either (rigid or chaotic; disengaged or enmeshed) are generally seen as problematic. From the 16 distinct types of marital and family systems derivable from this model, three basic groups were identified:

    1. *Balanced* (based on the four groups having scores at the two central levels on both dimensions)

    2. *Mid-range* (based on the eight groups that are extreme only on one dimension)

    3. *Extreme* (based on the four groups that are extreme on *both* dimensions)

In general, balanced family types tend to function more adequately than extreme types, and the Family Adjustment Index used in this report is based on these three levels (reflecting two forms of FACES II), one for couples with children and the other for couples without children. Because of restrictions in sample sizes, analyses of this measure were conducted separately for all couples and for couples with children only.

The results of comparisons among Vietnam theater veterans, era veterans, and civilians on these three indices, as well as comparisons among various subgroups of Vietnam theater veterans, are presented in Tables VII-10 through VII-15.

Contrasts Among Vietnam Theater Veterans, Era Veterans, and Civilians

Exhibit VII-5 presents a summary of all comparisons among Vietnam theater veterans and the comparison samples of era veterans and civilians on marital/relationship and family adjustment. Among males, contrasts between theater veterans and these comparison groups on marital status are relatively consistent, except for Hispanic men, for whom none of these contrasts are statistically significant. Though in absolute terms these differences are slight, both Vietnam theater veteran males in general and the subset exposed to high levels of war stress were significantly more likely to be living with someone as though married (though not formally

EXHIBIT VII-5

Summary of Contrasts Among Major Study Groups for Marital/Relationship and Family Roles

Contrasts Among Major Study Groups	Current Marital Status	Number of Times Divorced	Marital Relationship Problems Index	Parental Problems Index	Family Adjustment (All Couples)	Family Adjustment (Couples W/Children)
A. Males — Total						
1. Thr vs. Era	Thr > Era (LivasMrd)*	NS	NS	NS	NS	Thr < Era*
2. HWZ vs. Era	HWZ > Era (LivasMrd)**	HWZ > Era*	NS	HWZ > Era*	NS	HWZ < Era*
3. LWZ vs. Era	NS	NS	NS	NS	NS	NS
4. Thr vs. Civ	Thr > Civ (LivasMrd)*	Thr > Civ*	Thr > Civ**	Thr > Civ**	NS	NS
5. HWZ vs. Civ	HWZ < (Mar)/ HWZ > (LAM)*	HWZ > Civ***	HWZ > Civ***	HWZ > Civ***	NS	NS
B. Males — White/ Other						
1. Thr vs. Era	NS	NS	NS	NS	NS	NS
2. HWZ vs. Era	HWZ > Era (LivasMrd)*	HWZ > Era*	NS	HWZ > Era*	NS	HWZ <> Era*
3. LWZ vs. Era	NS	NS	NS	NS	NS	NS
4. Thr vs. Civ	Thr > Civ (LivasMrd)*	NS >	Thr > Civ*	Thr > Civ*	NS	NS
5. HWZ vs. Civ	HWZ > Civ (LivasMrd)**	HWZ > Civ**	HWZ > Civ**	HWZ > Civ**	NS	NS

(continued)

EXHIBIT VII-5 (Continued)

Contrasts Among Major Study Groups	Current Marital Status	Number of Times Divorced	Marital Relationship Problems Index	Parental Problems Index	Family Adjustment (All Couples)	Family Adjustment (Couples W/Children)
C. Males— Black						
1. Thr vs. Era	Thr > (LAM)** /Thr < (Nvr)*	NS	NS	NS	NS	NS
2. HWZ vs. Era	HWZ > (LAM)**/ HWZ < (Nvr)*	NS	NS	NS	NS	NS
3. LWZ vs. Era	LWZ > (LAM)*/ LWZ < (Nvr)*	NS	NS	NS	NS	NS
4. Thr vs. Civ	Thr > (LAM/ Div)/Thr < (Wdw)**	NS	NS	NS	NS	NS
5. HWZ vs. Civ	HWZ > Civ (LivasMrd)**	HWZ > Civ*	NS	NS	NS	NS

D. *Males—*
   Hispanic

1. Thr vs. Era	NS	NS	Thr > Era**	Thr > Era*	NS	NS
2. HWZ vs. Era	NS	NS	HWZ > Era***	HWZ > Era*	NS	NS
3. LWZ vs. Era	NS	NS	LWZ > Era*	NS	NS	NS
4. Thr vs. Civ	NS	NS	NS	Thr > Civ*	Thr > Civ**	Thr > Civ*
5. HWZ vs. Civ	NS	NS	NS	HWZ > Civ*	HWZ > Civ*	NS

E. *Females — Total*

1. Thr vs. Era	Thr < (Mar)/Thr > (Nvr)***	NS	Thr > Era*	Thr > Era*	NS	NS
2. HWZ vs. Era	HWZ < (Mar)/HWZ > (Nvr)***	NS	HWZ > Era*	NS	HWZ < Era*	HWZ < Era*
3. LWZ vs. Era	LWZ < Era (Divorced)*	LWZ < Era***	NS	NS	NS	NS
4. Thr vs. Civ	Thr < (Mar/Wdw)/Thr > (LAM/Nvr)***	Thr > Civ*	NS	NS	NS	NS
5. HWZ vs. Civ	HWZ < (Mar/Wdw)/Thr > (LAM/Nvr)***	HWZ > Civ**	HWZ > Civ*	NS	NS	NS

Notes: 1. < = lower than; > = higher than; <> = both lower than *and* higher than (relationship not ordinal); — = not applicable to this variable.
2. *$p < 0.05$; **$p < 0.01$; ***$p < 0.001$; NS = not statistically significant.

married) than era veterans and civilians (approximately 11 percent vs. 3 percent for those exposed to high war stress). In one form or another, these relationships were observed among both White/other and Black men, elaborated in each case by some other significant contrasts. Men exposed to high war-zone stress as a group were also significantly less likely to be married than civilian males. Black theater veteran men (including those at both high and low levels of war stress) were also less likely than era veterans to be never married, less likely than civilians to be widowed, and more likely than civilians to be divorced. Among women, theater veterans and their high-war-zone-stress subgroup were both less likely currently — and more likely never — married than female era veterans. In comparison with civilian women, theater veterans and their high-war-zone-stress subgroup were less likely to be married and widowed and more likely never to have been married or to be living with someone as though married.

With regard to the more direct indicators of marital/relationship and family adjustment, among men, theater veterans exposed to high levels of war stress were significantly more likely than era veterans to have been divorced. If these same veterans had children, they reported having more problems in parenting and poorer family adjustment (the latter contrast also being significant for theater veterans in general). Similarly, both male theater veterans as a whole and those among them exposed to high levels of war stress were more likely to be divorced and reported higher levels of both marital and parental problems than civilian males. In each case, these relationships were primarily characteristic of White/other males. While Black theater veteran males exposed to high war stress were more likely to have been divorced than their civilian counterparts (49.1 percent vs. 31.0 percent), none of the other contrasts for the subgroup achieved statistical significance. Among Hispanic men, theater veterans reported significantly higher levels of marital and parental problems than era veterans, as well as greater marital and family adjustment problems than Hispanic male civilians. Among women, theater veterans exposed to high levels of war stress were significantly more likely than era veterans to report marital or relationship problems and exhibited more problematic levels of family adaptability and cohesion. In contrast, those women experiencing lower levels of war-zone stress were substantially less likely than era veterans to have been divorced. Women with high-war-zone-stress exposure were also significantly more likely than civilian women to have been divorced and reported marital/relationship problems. In summary, among those exposed to high war-zone stress, virtually every subgroup reported somewhat poorer adjustment than era veterans and/or civilians on at least one indicator of marital/relationship or family adjustment.

Contrasts Among Vietnam Theater Veterans

Exhibit VII-6 summarizes the contrasts between various subgroups of Vietnam theater veterans on these measures of marital/relationship and family adjustment. Although significant differences among male theater veterans by race/ethnicity are few, they are relatively consistent. Black men were significantly less likely than both Hispanic and White/other males to currently married and, if not currently married, more likely to be living as though married or to be separated. In turn, White/other and Hispanic males were quite similar on marital status, but the former were significantly less likely than both Blacks and Hispanics to report marital problems. As implied by the comparisons cited above by veteran status, both the level of war-zone-stress exposure and a PTSD diagnosis were significantly related to adjustment in this area. Theater veteran males and females exposed to high war stress were significantly more likely than those exposed to lower levels to have been divorced, and the former were also more likely to have marital and parental problems.

Men with PTSD were less likely than those without to be currently married or divorced. They were also more likely to be currently separated or living as though married. Women with PTSD were also currently less likely to be married but more often never married. Both men and women with PTSD were also significantly more likely to have been divorced at some time and to report marital/relationship problems. For example. 69.9 percent of men with PTSD had been divorced, 22.4 percent two or more times, compared with only 34.9 percent and 8.1 percent, respectively, among those not suffering from this disorder. For women, the comparable proportions (though based on a small sample size) were 79.1 versus 26.7 percent and 10.6 versus 3.3 percent respectively. In addition, men with PTSD also reported higher levels of parenting problems and significantly poorer family adjustment (even without children). Among theater veterans with children, over half (54.8 percent) of those with PTSD described their families as extreme (that is, more poorly functioning) on both adaptability and cohesion, compared with only 19.3 percent of those without PTSD. Comparable proportions for all couples were 49.2 and 21.9 percent respectively.

While males with service-connected disabilities were less likely than those without such disability to have been "never married," female theater veterans with such disabilities were more frequently never to have married and less likely to be currently married. Among those in a relationship, the latter were also *less* likely than women without disability to report marital/relationship problems and poorer family functioning. Men and women serving in Vietnam with a history of alcohol or drug dependence

EXHIBIT VII-6
Significant Contrasts Among Vietnam Theater Veteran Subgroups for Marital/Relationship and Family Roles

Contrasts Among Theater Veteran Subgroups	Current Marital Status	Number of Times Divorced	Marital Relationship Problems Index	Parental Problems Index	Family Adjustment (All Couples)	Family Adjustment (Couples W/Children)
A. Race/Ethnicity						
1. W/O vs. Blk	W/O > (Mar)/ W/O < (LAM/ Sep)**	NS	W/O < Blk***	NS	NS	NS
2. W/O vs. Hisp	NS	NS	W/O < Hisp*	NS	NS	NS
3. Blk vs. Hisp	Blk < (Mar)*/ Blk > (LAM)*	NS	NS	NS	NS	NS
B. High vs. Low War Stress						
1. Males	HWZ > (LAM/ Sep)*	HWZ > LWZ*	HWZ > LWZ*	HWZ > LWZ***	NS	NS
2. Females	NS	HWZ > LWZ*	NS	NS	NS	NS
C. PTSD vs. No PTSD						
1. Males	PTSD < (Mar/ Div)**/ PTSD > (LAM/ Sep)***	PTSD > No PTSD***	PTSD > No PTSD***	PTSD > No PTSD***	PTSD < No PTSD***	PTSD < No PTSD***
2. Females	PTSD < (Mar)*/ PTSD > (Nvr Mar)*	PTSD > No PTSD***	PTSD > No PTSD*	NS	NS	NS

D. Service-Connected Physical Disability					
1. Males:					
a. SCPD vs. None	SCPD < None (Nvr Married)***	NS	NS	NS	NS	NS
b. High SCPD vs. None	High < None (Nvr Married)***	NS	NS	NS	NS	NS
2. Females:					
a. SCPD vs. None	SCPD < (Mar)***/SCPD > (Nvr)***	NS	SCPD < None*	NS	SCPD < None*	SCPD < None*
b. High SCPD vs. None	High < (Mar)***/SCPD > (Nvr)***	NS	High < None*	NS	High < None***	High < None*
E. Substance Abuse vs. None					
1. Males	SAB < (Mar)*/SAB > (LAM)*	SubAbuse > None***	SubAbuse > None***	SubAbuse > None***	NS	NS
2. Females	SAB < (Mar)**/SAB > (Div)*	SubAbuse > None***	SubAbuse > None***	SubAbuse > None*	NS	NS

Notes: 1. < = lower than; > = higher than; <> = both lower than *and* higher than (relationship not ordinal); — = not applicable to this variable.
2. *p < 0.05; **p < 0.01; ***p < 0.001; NS = not statistically significant.

or abuse were also less likely to be married than those with no such history. This group of men and women also experienced more divorces, marital problems, and parental problems as well.

Summary

Vietnam theater veteran males, including those most highly exposed to war-zone stress, were significantly more likely to be living as though married than era veterans and civilians, a pattern generally observed among all subgroups except Hispanic men. Theater veteran women and those exposed to high war stress were less likely to be currently married and more likely never to have been married than era veterans or civilians. More generally, in virtually every subgroup, male and female veterans exposed to high war-zone stress reported poorer levels of adjustment than era veterans or civilians on at least one indicator of marital/relationship or family adjustment. These veterans had more divorces, more marital or relationship problems, more parental problems, and poorer family functioning.

Among Vietnam theater veterans, Black men were significantly less often currently married than Hispanic and White/other men. In addition, the White/other group reported fewer marital/relationship problems than either of the two minority subgroups. For men, the level of war-zone-stress exposure was positively correlated with the number of divorces, the frequency of marital or relationship problems, and the number of parental problems. For women, the relationship between war-stress exposure and the number of divorces was also evident. Both men and women with PTSD were less likely than those without the disorder to be married, to have had more divorces, and to have experienced more marital/relationship problems. Men with PTSD also reported more problems related to parenting and substantially poorer family adjustment. Men with service-connected disabilities less often had never married and disabled women more often had never married than theater veterans with no such disabilities. Men and women who had experienced substance abuse problems were less likely to be married, more often to be divorced, and more likely to have experienced higher levels of marital and parental problems.

SUBJECTIVE WELL-BEING AND ADULT BEHAVIORS

Measures

To gain a somewhat more comprehensive view of the prevalence of "other psychological problems in readjusting to civilian life" among Vietnam veterans, we selected a specific set of other indicators from the NSVG interview that tapped various domains of adult life in which it has been widely speculated that Vietnam veterans may experience particular problems. These indicators gave us a broader understanding of veterans' psychological problems than we could gain by examining the general items that composed the readjustment problems indices or by studying the indicators of adjustment relating to education, work, marriage, and family. The first such area was explicitly addressed in the study's basic objectives, which called for an examination of "more general feelings of life satisfaction" and "feelings about quality of life."

Although no comprehensive assessment of overall quality of life — analogous to those conducted by Campbell et al. (1976) and Andrews and Withey (1976) — was attempted in the NSVG, the interview did contain questions about both the respondents' overall perceived life happiness and life satisfaction. The first item, adopted from Gurin, Veroff, and Feld (1960), asked whether "taking things all together," the respondent was very happy, pretty happy, or not too happy "these days." The second [a life satisfaction measure taken from Veroff et al (1981)], asked, "In general, how satisfying do you find the way you're spending your life these days?" Respondents answered: "completely satisfying," "pretty satisfying," or "not at all satisfying." The variables for these questions were recorded so that 1 = low and 3 = high. Then we summed the variables to create an overall Index of Subjective Well-Being, ranging from 2 (not too happy/not at all satisfying) to 6 (very happy/completely satisfying).

Keane, Scott, Chavoya, Lamparski, and Fairbank (1985) found that Vietnam veterans with PTSD symptoms retrospectively reported gradual reductions over time in their social support networks (cf. Green & Berlin, 1987), and Smith (1985) has emphasized that "lack of social support" in its most extreme form — isolation — is a major factor in evaluating the need for and course of treatment of Vietnam veterans suffering from PTSD. In an effort to capture this more extreme form of social isolation (as opposed to low levels of social support), we created an index using the measures of social support included in the NSVG, adapted from Donald and Ware (1984), Card (1983), Veroff et al (1981), Cohen, Mermelstein, Kamarck, and Hoberman (1985), and others. In all, we used 22 items, and we created the Social Isolation Index as the number of these items on which the most extreme response was endorsed (for example, the respondent knew *no* families in the neighborhood well enough to visit; the respondent had *no* close friends; the respondent had *not* talked on the telephone with a close friend or relative during the past month; the respondent felt he or she had *no one* to turn to in times of need). This variable has a theoretical range of

0–22, but a cutoff of 7 or more was established for the highest level of social isolation.

With increasing national concern about the nation's homeless (for example, Bassuk, 1984) has come speculation that Vietnam veterans may account for a disproportionate share of the homeless population. To address this question, we extracted two questions from the antisocial personality disorder section of the Diagnostic Interview Schedule (DIS) to create a measure of "vagrancy" or "homelessness":

1. Did the respondent travel around for a month or more with no arrangements ahead of time and without knowing how long he or she would stay or where he or she would work?

2. Was there a period when the respondent had no regular place to live for at least one month?

From these items, respondents were coded as:

1. never having been homeless or vagrant
2. having been vagrant at some time
3. having been homeless at some time
4. having both homeless and vagrant at some time

Researchers have also speculated, with some evidence, that Vietnam combat veterans may experience more feelings of anger and hostility (for example, Laufer, Yager, Frey-Wouters, & Donnellan, 1981; Strayer & Ellenhorn, 1975) and have a greater capacity for violence (Buchbinder, 1979; Petrik, Rosenberg, & Watson, 1983; Boulanger & Kadushin, 1986). Levels of hostility were assessed in the NSVG using the Active Expression of Hostility Scale from the Psychiatric Epidemiology Research Interview (PERI) (Dohrenwend, 1982). The hostility items asked how frequently in the past year the respondent had expressed his or her anger:

- by cursing
- by getting into an argument
- by trying to hide anger
- by shouting
- by trying to explain his or her feelings calmly
- by avoiding an argument and doing something else
- by making a fist and facially expressing anger
- by exhibiting violence toward inanimate objects

Respondents chose one of five responses for each way of expressing anger, ranging from "never" to "very often." The items were scored in the standard manner for this instrument, yielding a mean score ranging from 0 (low) to 4 (high).

Violence was assessed with a set of measures adapted from the family violence research and "Conflict Tactics Scales" developed by Straus and his colleagues (e.g., Straus, Gelles, & Steinmetz, 1980). For use in the NSVG, we revised these items to include both family and nonfamily violence (excluding war or other occupationally required behaviors). Nine types of violent acts were included in the index:

- threatening to hit or throw something at someone
- actually throwing something at someone
- pushing, grabbing, shoving someone
- slapping another person
- kicking, biting, or hitting someone with fist
- hitting someone with an object
- beating up someone
- threatening someone with a gun or knife
- actually using a gun or knife on someone

The original codes assigned to this scale were: (0) never, (1) once, (2) twice, (3) three to five times, (4) six to ten times, (5) 11 to 20 times, and (6) more than 20 times. The midpoints of categories (3) through (6) were assigned (21 to the highest category) and the items summed to yield an index of the "Number of Violent Acts in the Past Year."

Another popular stereotype with some empirical support holds that Vietnam veterans have a significant chance of being arrested, convicted, and put up in jail or prison (for example, Yager, Laufer, & Gallops, 1984; Pentland & Dwyer, 1985; Shaw, Churchill, Noyes, & Loeffelholz, 1987). We assessed criminal justice involvement in the NSVG by four items:

- whether the respondent was currently in jail or prison
- the number of times ever arrested since age 18 for anything other than traffic violations
- the number of nights ever spent in jail or prison (since age 18)
- the number of lifetime convictions for a felony offense

Current incarceration was kept as a separate item, and a composite measure of "Degree of Criminal Justice Involvement" created from the other three as follows: (1) no involvement, (2) arrested or jailed once, (3) arrested or jailed more than once, and (4) convicted of a felony.

The results of comparisons among Vietnam theater veterans, era veterans, and civilians on these measures, as well as comparisons among various subgroups of Vietnam theaters, are presented in Tables VII-16 through VII-21 in Volume II.

Contrasts Among Vietnam Theater Veterans, Era Veterans, and Civilians

Exhibit VII-7 summarizes the comparisons among Vietnam theater veterans and the comparison samples of era veterans and civilians on subjective well-being and these adult problem behaviors. Among females, *none* of the comparisons on subjective well-being were statistically significant. But for White/other and Hispanic males exposed to high levels of war stress in Vietnam, the ratings of subjective well-being were significantly lower than for civilians and (for the White/other group) era veterans. Similarly, among both White/other and Black males, those with lower levels of exposure to war stress reported higher levels of happiness and satisfaction than Vietnam era veterans, a difference also significant among theater veterans in general. In combination, then, male theater veterans exposed to high war stress expressed lower levels of subjective well-being than their civilian comparisons, while their low- to moderate-war-stress counterparts reported *higher* levels of satisfaction than era veterans.

Comparisons among the groups on social isolation and homelessness or vagrancy are somewhat more consistent. For women, and within every race/ethnicity subgroup for men, theater veterans exposed to high levels of significant stress reported significantly higher levels of social isolation than their civilian counterparts. Among White/other men and males overall, this difference was also apparent for theater veterans as a whole in comparison with era veterans. Similarly, theater veteran men exposed to high war stress were significantly more likely than era veterans and civilians to report having been homeless or vagrant at some time in their lives. However, analyses by race/ethnicity indicate that the comparison with era veterans is significant only among White/other males, and the civilian comparison only among Blacks.

Among all male subgroups, theater veterans overall, as well as the subset exposed to high war stress, reported committing significantly more violent acts during the past year than their civilian comparisons, and, except for Hispanics, this same pattern was observed for active expression of hostility. For men overall, those exposed to high war stress also reported higher levels of hostility and violent behavior than era veterans, a finding consistent with Boulanger and Kadushin (1986). In turn, these findings are reflected among minority males in higher levels of expressed hostility by those exposed to high war stress in comparison with era veterans, and

EXHIBIT VII-7

Contrasts Among Major Study Groups for Subjective Well-Being and Adult Problem Behaviors

Contrasts Among Major Study Groups	Subjective Well-Being	Social Isolation Index	Ever Homeless or Vagrant	Active Expression of Hostility	No. of Violent Acts in Last Year	Criminal Justice Involvement
A. Males—Total						
1. Thr vs. Era	NS	Thr > Era*	NS	NS	NS	NS
2. HWZ vs. Era	NS	HWZ > Era***	HWZ > Era*	HWZ > Era*	HWZ > Era*	NS
3. LWZ vs. Era	LWZ > Era*	NS	NS	NS	NS	NS
4. Thr vs. Civ	NS	Thr > Civ***	NS	Thr > Civ***	Thr > Civ***	Thr > Civ*
5. HWZ vs. Civ	HWZ < Civ***	HWZ > Civ***	HWZ > Civ*	HWZ > Civ***	HWZ > Civ***	HWZ > Civ**
B. Males—White/ Other						
1. Thr vs. Era	NS	Thr > Era*	NS	NS	NS	NS
2. HWZ vs. Era	HWZ < Era*	HWZ > Era***	HWZ > Era*	NS	HWZ > Era*	NS
3. LWZ vs. Era	LWZ > Era*	NS	NS	NS	NS	NS
4. Thr vs. Civ	NS	Thr > Civ**	NS	Thr > Civ**	Thr > Civ***	Thr > Civ (Arrest >1)*
5. HWZ vs. Civ	HWZ < Civ***	HWZ > Civ***	NS	HWZ > Civ**	HWZ > Civ***	HWZ > Civ*
C. Males—Black						
1. Thr vs. Era	Thr > Era**	NS	Thr > Era (Homeless)*	NS	NS	Thr < Era*
2. HWZ vs. Era	NS	NS	NS	HWZ > Era*	NS	HWZ <> Era*
3. LWZ vs. Era	LWZ > Era**	NS	NS	NS	NS	LWZ < Era*
4. Thr vs. Civ	NS	NS	Thr > Civ (Vagrant)***	Thr > Civ*	Thr > Civ*	Thr > Civ*
5. HWZ vs. Civ	NS	HWZ > Civ**	HWZ > Civ (Vagrant)**	HWZ > Civ**	HWZ > Civ*	HWZ > Civ**

(continued)

EXHIBIT VII-7 (Continued)

Contrasts Among Major Study Groups	Subjective Well-Being	Social Isolation Index	Ever Homeless or Vagrant	Active Expression of Hostility	No. of Violent Acts in Last Year	Criminal Justice Involvement
D. Males—						
Hispanic						
1. Thr vs. Era	NS	NS	NS	Thr > Era*	NS	NS
2. HWZ vs. Era	NS	NS	NS	HWZ > Era**	NS	NS
3. LWZ vs. Era	NS	NS	LWZ > Era (Vagrant)*	LWZ > Era*	NS	LWZ < Era*
4. Thr vs. Civ	NS	NS	NS	NS	Thr > Civ**	Thr > Civ (Arrest >1)*
5. HWZ vs. Civ	HWZ < Civ*	HWZ > Civ*	NS	NS	HWZ > Civ**	HWZ > Civ (Arrest >1)*
E. Females— Total						
1. Thr vs. Era	NS	NS	NS	NS	Thr < Era*	NS
2. HWZ vs. Era	NS	NS	NS	NS	HWZ < Era**	NS
3. LWZ vs. Era	NS	LWZ < Era***	NS	NS	NS	NS
4. Thr vs. Civ	NS	NS	NS	NS	NS	NS
5. HWZ vs. Civ	NS	HWZ > Civ*	NS	NS	NS	NS

Notes: 1. < = lower than; > = higher than; <> = both lower than *and* higher than (relationship not ordinal); — = not applicable to this variable.
2. *p < 0.05; **p < 0.01; ***p < 0.001; NS = not statistically significant.

higher levels of violent behavior among similarly exposed White/other males. In contrast, theater veteran women, including those exposed to high war-zone stress, committed significantly *fewer* violent acts during the past year than era veteran women.

Results of comparisons for current incarceration are not summarized in Exhibit VII-7 (or in Volume II) because so few respondents were currently in prison—0.5 percent of Vietnam theater veteran men, 0.6 percent of male era veterans, and none of the women veterans. Although significant contrasts between theater veterans and civilians were observed, these contrasts were artifacts of the civilian sample being household-based. Moreover, these estimates for male veterans are quite likely to be somewhat too low, because some of those who could not be located for the NSVG undoubtedly were in jail or prison, although others were in fact interviewed in such institutions. Nevertheless, independent of current incarceration, in every race/ethnicity subgroup, theater veteran men, including those most highly exposed to combat and other war stress, reported significantly higher levels of criminal justice involvement than their civilian counterparts. Among both Blacks and Hispanics, men exposed to lower levels of war stress reported lower levels of criminal justice involvement than era veterans, and among Black men this comparison with era veterans was also significant for all theater veterans. For women, veteran status did not make a significant difference in degree of criminal justice involvement.

Contrasts Among Vietnam Theater Veterans

Exhibit VII-8 summarizes the contrasts among various subgroups of Vietnam theater veterans on these measures of subjective well-being and adult problem behaviors. While Vietnam theater veteran men did not have a significantly different degree of social isolation or expression of hostility by race/ethnicity, White/other men did report higher levels of happiness and life satisfaction and fewer violent acts than both Black and Hispanic men. Black and Hispanic men, in turn, did not differ significantly from each other on these measures. Black theater veteran men also reported significantly higher levels of criminal justice system involvement than White/other and Hispanic males, who, in turn, were not significantly different from one another. Although Black men who served in Vietnam were also more likely to report a period of vagrancy than Whites/others and Hispanics, these differences are not of particular interest, because they are mostly balanced by higher levels of *combined* homelessness and vagrancy in the latter two subgroups.

EXHIBIT VII-8

Contrasts Among Vietnam Theater Veteran Subgroups for Subjective Well-Being and Adult Problem Behaviors

Contrasts Among Theater Veteran Subgroups	Subjective Well-Being	Social Isolation Index	Ever Homeless or Vagrant	Expression of Hostility	Active Violent Acts in Last Year	Criminal Justice Involvement
A. Race/Ethnicity						
1. W/O vs. Blk	W/O > Blk***	NS	W/O < Blk (Vagrant)*	NS	W/O < Blk***	W/O < Blk***
2. W/O vs. Hisp	W/O > Hisp***	NS	NS	NS	W/O < Hisp***	NS
3. Blk vs. Hisp	NS	NS	Blk > Hisp (Vagrant)*	NS	NS	Blk > Hisp (Felony)*
B. High vs. Low War Stress						
1. Males	HWZ < LWZ***	HWZ > LWZ**	HWZ > LWZ**	HWZ > LWZ*	HWZ > LWZ***	HWZ > LWZ**
2. Females	NS	NS	NS	NS	NS	NS
C. PTSD vs. No PTSD						
1. Males	PTSD < No PTSD***	PTSD > No PTSD***	PTSD > No PTSD**	PTSD > No PTSD***	PTSD > No PTSD*	PTSD > No PTSD***
2. Females	PTSD < No PTSD***	PTSD > No PTSD***	NS	NS	NS	NS

D. Service-Connected Physical Disability						
1. Males:						
a. SCPD vs. None	NS	NS	NS	NS	NS	SCPD < None*
b. High SCPD vs. None	High SCPD < None*	NS	NS	NS	NS	NS
2. Females:						
a. SCPD vs. None	NS	NS	NS	NS	SCPD < None***	NS
b. High SCPD vs. None	NS	High SCPD < None**	High SCPD < None***	NS	High SCPD < None**	NS
E. Substance Abuse vs. None						
1. Males	SubAbuse < None***	SubAbuse > None***	SubAbuse > None***	SubAbuse > None***	SubAbuse > None***	NS
2. Females	SubAbuse < None**	SubAbuse > None*	NS	NS	NS	NS

Notes: 1. < = lower than; > = higher than; <> = both lower than *and* higher than (relationship not ordinal); — = not applicable to this variable.
2. *$p < 0.05$; **$p < 0.01$; ***$p < 0.001$; NS = not statistically significant.

Differences by level of war-zone stress and PTSD are both more consistent and of considerable importance. Although, perhaps surprisingly, *none* of the comparisons by level of war-zone stress among female theater veterans were statistically significant, *all* of these differences were for men serving in the Vietnam theater. Men exposed to high levels of war stress reported lower levels of life satisfaction and happiness, were more socially isolated, had more often been homeless or vagrant, expressed higher levels of hostility, had committed more violent acts, and more often had been arrested or jailed and convicted of a felony than those exposed to lower levels of stress in Vietnam. In addition, these differences were substantial. Those exposed to high war stress were:

- five times more likely (24.7 percent vs. 4.8 percent) to report being unhappy or unsatisfied with their lives;
- six times more likely (46.5 percent vs. 7.6 percent) to be highly isolated;
- twice as likely to have been homeless or vagrant (16.8 percent vs. 8.8 percent);
- twice as likely to have committed 13 or more violent acts in the past year (14.4 percent vs. 7.6 percent);
- one and one-half times more likely (39.1 percent vs. 27.7 percent) to have been arrested or jailed; and
- three times more likely (8.8 percent vs. 2.8 percent) to have been convicted of a felony

than those experiencing moderate low levels of war stress.

Comparisons between those with and without PTSD were also quite consistent and, if anything, more striking. Women with PTSD were ten times more likely than those without (26.2 percent vs. 2.6 percent) to report being very unhappy or dissatisfied with their lives and eight times more likely (24.3 percent vs. 3.1 percent) to report being extremely isolated. Comparable ratios for men with and without PTSD were five to one (24.7 percent vs. 4.8 percent) and six to one (46.5 vs. 7.6 percent) respectively. Fully 35 percent of men with PTSD had also been homeless or vagrant (23.8 percent homeless) at least once in their lives, compared with 6.3 percent of male theater veterans who do not suffer from this disorder, a finding that lends some credence to current concerns about the plight of homeless Vietnam veterans. Men with PTSD were also especially prone to active forms of expressing their hostility (over 40 percent scoring in the highest category) and to violent behavior (averaging 13.31 violent acts in the past year compared with only 3.54 among those without PTSD). Almost half of these (45.7 percent) had been arrested or jailed more than once—one-fourth of these (11.5 percent) convicted of a felony—compared with only 11.6 percent of those without a stress disorder.

Differences in violent behavior for those veterans with a service-connected disability were relatively predictable. Men and women with service-connected disabilities reported fewer violent acts than those without such disabilities, and men with disabilities were also less happy or satisfied with their lives. Disabled women were less likely to have been homeless or vagrant. The pattern observed for substance abuse was virtually identical to that observed for PTSD, although the strength of certain relationships varies somewhat. Theater veteran women with a history of substance abuse reported lower levels of subjective well-being and higher levels of social isolation than those with no history of alcohol or drug dependence or abuse. Male substance abusers reported poorer levels of adjustment not only on these but also on every other indicator of adult problem behavior.

Summary

The overall pattern observed in comparisons by veteran status and war-zone-stress exposure is relatively clear. Although contrasts vary somewhat from indicator to indicator and by race/ethnicity, in general, theater veterans exposed to high levels of war-zone stress were significantly more likely than their civilian counterparts, and to a lesser extent their era veteran counterparts, to report problems in this area. With one exception (social isolation), however, relationships observed for women do *not* follow this pattern. Nevertheless, this relative disadvantage of those exposed to high war stress in comparison with civilians was evident in:

    1. lower levels of life happiness and satisfaction among White/other and Hispanic men

    2. higher levels of social isolation among *all* theater veteran subgroups (including women)

    3. a higher prevalence of homelessness or vagrancy among White/other males

    4. higher levels of active hostility and actual violent behavior among *all* male theater veteran subgroups

    5. higher levels of arrests and incarceration

Moreover, a similar disadvantage relative to Vietnam *era* veterans was observed among White/other men for subjective well-being, social isolation, homelessness or vagrancy, and violent behavior, and among Black and Hispanic men for active expression of hostility. Theater veteran women in general and those exposed to high war-zone stress reported significantly less violent behavior than era veteran women.

Among theater veteran males, White/other men reported higher levels of general well-being and fewer violent acts during the past year than both Black and Hispanic men, who did not differ significantly from each other. Black men also reported significantly higher levels of involvement with the criminal justice system (arrests, incarceration, felony convictions) than either White/other or Hispanic men.

Differences observed by level of war-zone-stress exposure, PTSD, and substance abuse were quite consistent and striking. Although women serving in the Vietnam theater did not differ significantly on *any* of these measures by level of exposure to war-zone stress, men exposed to high war stress reported significantly poorer adjustment *on every one* of these behaviors. Similarly, men suffering from PTSD and those with a history of alcohol or drug abuse reported dramatically poorer adjustment on all of these feelings/behaviors, as did women for two of these: subjective well-being and social isolation. Among men and women with PTSD, for example, one in four reported extreme unhappiness, and nearly one-fourth of these women and one-half of the men reported extreme levels of isolation. Similarly, fully 35 percent of men with PTSD had been homeless or vagrant, over 40 percent scored at the highest level on hostility, 25 percent had committed 13 or more acts of violence during the past year, and almost 50 percent had been arrested or jailed more than once since age 18. Although the relationships differed in strength, essentially the same pattern was observed for those with a history of substance abuse as for those currently suffering from PTSD.

CHAPTER VIII

The Prevalence of Physical Health Problems

COMMENTARY

In this chapter, we examine what Vietnam veterans say about their physical health. How do they perceive their current physical health compared with other veterans and civilians of the same age? Do Vietnam veterans see themselves as suffering from chronic physical health problems to a greater or lesser degree than others? Are physical health problems associated with exposure to high levels of stress in Vietnam, as is the case with psychological readjustment problems? Are veterans with PTSD in worse physical health than veterans who do not have PTSD? How many Vietnam veterans are recognized by the Veterans Administration as physically disabled in connection with their service in the military?

In our effort to answer more fully the questions posed by Congress regarding the overall impact of the Vietnam war on the current well-being of Vietnam veterans, we asked our respondents to provide us with information on their physical health. One might wonder why we would choose to investigate physical health problems in a study that focuses on psychological and social readjustment. The answer is really quite simple. Given the complexity of human behavior, there is good reason to believe that psychological and social difficulties are not the only problems that can potentially result from exposure to extreme stress in Vietnam. In point of fact, health-care providers have quite frequently observed a relationship between the occurrence of all kinds of stressful life events and the onset of a range of physical illnesses. For this reason, the NVVRS research team concluded that a comprehensive study of the postwar readjustment of America's Vietnam veterans should examine the relationship between current physical health and

189

important aspects of veterans' experience in the military, such as amount of exposure to stress in Vietnam.

CHAPTER OVERVIEW

This chapter provides information on the prevalence of physical health problems among Vietnam theater veterans, era veterans, and civilian counterparts. Self-ratings of current health status and the number of active chronic physical health problems were contrasted among the major study groups and subgroups. Rates of service-connected physical disabilities were obtained from official VA records and contrasted for the subgroups of Vietnam theater veterans. Eleven percent of male Vietnam theater veterans were listed as having a service-connected physical disability, 4 percent at 30 percent or higher. Comparable disability rates for Vietnam theater veteran women were 16 and 10 percent respectively.

For both male and female Vietnam theater veterans overall, few comparisons with era veteran and civilian counterparts showed significant differences on physical health measures. However, a key finding was that men and women who were exposed to high levels of war-zone stress in Vietnam consistently reported higher rates of physical health problems than other theater veterans, era veterans, and civilians. Specifically, male Vietnam veterans who experienced high levels of war-zone stress have a significantly more negative perception of their current physical health status, and report more chronic health problems, than the era veteran and civilian comparison groups. In general, the prevalence of active chronic health problems reported by male racial/ethnic subgroups parallel the findings for the main male study groups: Hispanic, Black, and White/other theater veterans with high levels of exposure to war-zone stress report significantly higher rates of persistent health problems than era veteran and civilian counterparts. In addition, these men who were most exposed to the stressors of war in Vietnam have higher rates of service-connected physical disabilities than those with less exposure to stress in the war zone.

Vietnam theater veteran women exposed to high levels of war-zone stress also reported a significantly greater number of active chronic physical health problems than other female theater veterans and civilian counterparts. Both female and male theater veterans with current diagnoses of PTSD and/or lifetime problems with substance abuse reported significantly more active physical health problems, and poorer perceptions of their current physical health, than theater veterans without either of these disorders.

This chapter presents, contrasts, and summarizes information on the prevalence of physical health problems among Vietnam theater veterans and their era veteran and civilian counterparts. Specifically, we examined self-ratings of current health status and the active number of chronic physical health problems for all NSVG study groups and subgroups. In addition, rates of VA-recognized service-connected physical disabilities were tabulated and contrasted for the subgroups of Vietnam theater veterans. Finally, we compared the NSVG findings and the perceived physical health status of Vietnam veterans with the results of another national study of Vietnam veterans' health status, the Vietnam Experience Study, conducted by the Centers for Disease Control.

PERCEIVED PHYSICAL HEALTH STATUS

Respondents' evaluation of their current physical health status was assessed with two questions: (1) "Now I'd like to ask you some questions about your physical health. First, would you say your health in general is excellent, very good, good, fair, or poor?," (2) "Compared with other people your age, would you say that your health is much better than others, better, about the same, worse, or much worse than others?" We coded item responses from 1 ("poor"/"much worse") to 5 ("excellent"/"much better"), and created an index of respondents' perceptions of their general and comparative physical health by multiplying the two values and categorizing them from high (scores of 20 or 25) to low (scores of 8 or lower). The distribution of responses of study groups and subgroups on this index, as well as the results of tests of statistical significance, appear in Volume II, Table VIII-1. Exhibits VIII-1 and VIII-2 summarize the results of these contrasts.

Among male Vietnam theater veterans who were exposed to high levels of war-zone stress, nearly 25 percent scored in the lowest category of the index, and slightly less than 22 percent scored in the highest. In comparison, 12 percent of the male era veterans and 11 percent of civilian counterparts scored in the lowest category of the health index, while 24 percent of male era veterans and 29 percent of civilians scored in the highest. Contrasts performed on the distribution of index scores among these groups revealed that the differences were statistically significant. Specifically, male Vietnam theater veterans who were exposed to high levels of war-zone stress rated

EXHIBIT VIII-1
Summary of Contrasts Among Major Study Groups for Physical Health Problems

Contrasts Among Major Study Groups	Index of Perceived Current Health Status[a]	No. of Chronic Health Problems	Service-Connected Physical Disabilities
A. Males—Total			
1. Thr vs. Era	NS	NS	—
2. HWZ vs. Era	HWZ < Era**	HWZ > Era**	—
3. LWZ vs. Era	NS	NS	—
4. Thr vs. Civ	Thr < Civ*	NS	—
5. HWZ vs. Civ	HWZ < Civ***	HWZ > Civ**	—
B. Males—White/ Other			
1. Thr vs. Era	NS	NS	—
2. HWZ vs. Era	HWZ < Era*	HWZ > Era*	—
3. LWZ vs. Era	NS	NS	—
4. Thr vs. Civ	NS	NS	—
5. HWZ vs. Civ	HWZ < Civ***	HWZ > Civ*	—
C. Males—Black			
1. Thr vs. Era	Thr < Era*	Thr > Era*	—
2. HWZ vs. Era	HWZ < Era*	HWZ > Era**	—
3. LWZ vs. Era	NS	LWZ > Era*	—
4. Thr vs. Civ	NS	NS	—
5. HWZ vs. Civ	NS	NS	—
D. Males— Hispanic			
1. Thr vs. Era	NS	Thr > Era**	—
2. HWZ vs. Era	NS	HWZ > Era***	—
3. LWZ vs. Era	NS	NS	—
4. Thr vs. Civ	NS	NS	—
5. HWZ vs. Civ	NS	HWZ > Civ**	—
E. Females—Total			
1. Thr vs. Era	NS	NS	—
2. HWZ vs. Era	NS	NS	—
3. LWZ vs. Era	NS	LWZ < Era*	—
4. Thr vs. Civ	NS	NS	—
5. HWZ vs. Civ	NS	HWZ > Civ*	—

[a]High scores on this index indicate a positive perception of current physical health status.

Notes: 1. < = lower than; > = higher than; <> = both lower than *and* higher than (relationship not ordinal); — = not applicable to this variable.

2. *$p < 0.05$; **$p < 0.01$; ***$p < 0.001$; NS = not statistically significant.

EXHIBIT VIII-2

Summary of Contrasts Among Major Study Groups for Physical Health Problems

Contrasts Among Theater Veteran Subgroups	Index of Perceived Current Health Status[a]	No. of Chronic Health Problems	Service-Connected Physical Disability (SCPD)
A. *Race/Ethnicity*			
1. W/O vs. Blk	W/O Blk***	NS	W/O < Blk**
2. W/O vs. Hisp	NS	NS	NS
3. Blk vs. Hisp	NS	NS	Blk > Hisp**
B. *High vs. Low War Stress*			
1. Males	HWZ < LWZ***	HWZ > LWZ*	HWZ > LWZ**
2. Females	NS	HWZ > LWZ*	NS
C. *PTSD vs. No PTSD*			
1. Males	PTSD < No PTSD***	PTSD > No PTSD***	NS
2. Females	PTSD < No PTSD***	PTSD > No PTSD***	NS
D. *Service- Connected Physical Disability*			
1. Males:			
a. SCPD vs. None	SCPD < None***	SCPD > None***	—
b. High SCPD vs. None	High < None***	High > None***	—
1. Females:			
a. SCPD vs. None	SCPD < None***	SCPD > None***	—
b. High SCPD vs. None	High < None***	High > None***	—
E. *Substance Abuse vs. None*			
1. Males	SubAbuse < None*	NS	NS
2. Females	NS	SubAbuse > None**	NS

[a]High scores on this index indicate a positive perception of current physical health status.
Notes: 1. < = lower than; > = higher than.
2. *p < 0.05; **p < 0.01; ***p < 0.001; NS = not statistically significant.

the current status of their physical health much more negatively than both male era veterans and civilian counterparts.

When male Vietnam theater veterans as a group (that is, independent of level of exposure to war-zone stress) were contrasted with male era veteran and civilian counterparts, the findings were less consistent. We found a statistically significant difference in the distributions of health index scores between male theater veterans as a group and civilian counterparts, with proportionately more theater veterans assessing their current physical health negatively. Another finding, however, was that male theater veterans as a group did not differ from male era veterans in their overall perception of their current health status.

Examination of the contrasts for male racial/ethnic subgroups in the NVVRS revealed a number of statistically significant results. First, White/other male Vietnam theater veterans exposed to significant war-zone stress provided a less favorable rating of the current status of their physical health than did either their era veteran or civilian White/other male counterparts. Second, Black male theater veterans, both as a group and those exposed to high war-zone stress, evaluated their physical health as poorer than Black male era veterans. However, Black male theater veterans did not differ from Black male civilians in their perception of their current physical health status. One-fifth to one-quarter of each group scored in the lowest category of this index, while roughly equivalent proportions gave ratings that fell within the highest category. Third, the subgroup contrasts for Hispanic male theater veterans, era veterans, and civilians showed no statistically significant differences in the pattern of ratings on the index of physical health. Clearly, we need additional analyses to begin to specify the factors that account for the differential evaluations of physical health status among veterans and nonveterans within the male racial and ethnic subgroups of the NVVRS.

Among women, higher percentages of Vietnam theater veterans scored in the lowest category of the physical health index—nearly 13 percent of female theater veterans as a group and 17 percent of the subset of female theater veterans who were exposed to high levels of war-zone stress—compared with an estimated 6 percent of female era veterans and civilians. However, despite these numerically large differences at the lower end of the index, the distributions converged at higher levels, and contrasts among the female study groups revealed that the overall distributions of scores did not differ significantly. Convergence of the female distributions was especially evident at the highest level of the index, where the largest estimated between-group difference was roughly only 6 percentage points.

As Exhibit VIII-2 shows, contrasts among the subgroups of male Vietnam theater veterans revealed a significant finding for race/ethnicity. Specifically, the index scores for Black male theater veterans indicated that they reported poorer current physical health than White/other male theater veterans.

When we contrasted groups according to their level of exposure to war-zone stress, we found statistically significantly differences for men, but not for women. Male theater veterans exposed to high levels of war-zone stress reported poorer current physical health when compared with male compatriots who experienced a lower level of exposure to stressors in the war zone. This finding is clearly consistent with the outcome of numerous other NVVRS analyses that have crossed level of war-zone stress with a host of postwar readjustment variables. Female theater veterans exposed to high levels of war-zone stress did not differ significantly from female theater veterans counterparts exposed to lower levels. Although many more high-exposure female theater veterans obtained scores in the lowest health category of the index (17 percent vs. 10 percent), the percentages of high- and low-war-zone-stress respondents scoring at higher levels of the index were essentially equivalent.

As expected, contrasts revealed that both male and female Vietnam theater veterans with service-connected physical disabilities (SCPDs) gave a significantly lower rating to the current status of their physical health than theater veterans without SCPDs. Also predictably, male and female Vietnam veterans with current diagnoses of PTSD rated their physical health much more negatively than theater veteran counterparts without this disorder. Crossing lifetime-substance-abuse diagnosis with the physical health index revealed that male and female theater veterans who were positive for lifetime substance abuse had much lower self-ratings of physical health. Thus, this set of contrasts indicates that both SCPDs and major psychological disorders such as current PTSD and lifetime-substance-abuse disorder are associated with negative appraisal of current physical health status among male and female theater veterans.

NUMBER OF CHRONIC HEALTH PROBLEMS

We assessed the number of chronic health problems by reading to respondents a comprehensive list of physical health problems after instructing them to "tell me if you have ever had any of these conditions, even if you have mentioned them before." This list of health problems tended to emphasize diseases, syndromes, conditions, and injuries that are permanent or tend to occur repetitively. The lifetime presence or absence of each physical health problem on the list was assessed individually by asking, "Have you ever had [name of health problem]?" Respondents also were asked to identify any chronic conditions that had been active within the past 12 months. In Volume II, Table VIII-2 shows the percent distribution of the number of active (that is, current) chronic health problems for study groups and subgroups and the results of testing for the significance of differences. Exhibits VIII-1 and VIII-2 summarize the results of these contrasts.

Examination of the contrasts among the major male study groups revealed that theater veterans who were exposed to high levels of war-zone stress reported a greater number of active chronic health problems than male era veterans and civilian counterparts. However, when male theater veterans as a group (that is, independent of the level of war-zone stress) were compared with male era veterans and civilians, none of the contrasts were statistically significant. These findings suggest that a strong relationship exists between the level of exposure to war-zone stress and the number of current chronic physical health problems reported by Vietnam theater veterans.

For the male subgroups, the contrasts for White/other males were similar to the contrasts for the overall male study groups. Specifically, White/other Vietnam veterans who were exposed to high levels of war-zone stress reported a significantly greater number of active chronic health problems than both White/other era veterans and civilian counterparts. However, White/other male theater veterans as a group did not differ significantly from the White/other comparison groups.

Examination of the contrasts for Black male Vietnam theater veterans showed a pattern of chronic health complaints that was somewhat similar to that of White/other males. Black male theater veterans overall, as well as Black male theater veterans exposed to both high and low levels of war-zone stress, reported significantly more current chronic health problems than Black male era veterans. However, none of the contrasts between Black male theater veterans and Black male civilians were statistically significant.

The contrasts for Hispanic male Vietnam theater veterans on current chronic health problems also produced findings similar to the results for white/other and black male theater veterans. Overall, Hispanic male theater veterans reported suffering a greater number of active chronic health problems than their era veteran counterparts. As expected, Hispanic male theater veterans with high exposure to war-zone stress reported a significantly greater number of persistent health problems than Hispanic era veterans and civilians.

Female theater veterans who were exposed to high levels of war-zone stress reported a significantly greater number of chronic physical health problems than their female civilian counterparts. Conversely, female theater veterans who were exposed to low levels of war-zone stress reported fewer active chronic physical health problems than female era veterans.

The following variables had a strong effect on the number of active chronic health problems for both male and female theater veterans (see Exhibit VIII-2):

- level of exposure to war-zone stress
- level of SCPD
- current PTSD diagnosis
- lifetime-substance-abuse disorder

Specifically, both male and female theater veterans exposed to high levels of war-zone stress reported more active chronic physical health problems than theater veteran counterparts exposed to lower stress levels. Theater veterans with SCPDs also reported more current physical health problems than their counterparts without SCPDs. In addition, male and female theater veterans with a current diagnosis of PTSD had more active chronic health problems than theater veterans without PTSD. Similarly, theater veterans who ever met criteria for diagnosis of substance abuse reported a higher prevalence of current chronic physical conditions than theater veterans who never abused alcohol or drugs.

VIETNAM EXPERIENCE STUDY COMPARISON

The Centers for Disease Control (CDC) (1988) recently completed a national study of the physical health status of male U.S. Army Vietnam theater and era veterans. The CDC project, known as the Vietnam Experience Study (VES), employed a two-stage design, with the first stage consisting of a telephone health survey of 7,924 male U.S. Army theater veterans and 7,364 era veterans. In the second stage, a random subsample of 2,490 theater and 1,972 era veteran respondents to the telephone survey underwent a comprehensive physical examination (Centers for Disease Control Vietnam Experience Study, 1988).

When asked to rate the current status of their "health in general" at the beginning of the VES telephone survey, 19.1 percent of the theater veteran respondents described their general health as "fair" or "poor," whereas

11.1 percent of the VES era veterans appraised their health equivalently — a nearly twofold difference. However, the CDC reported that subsequent comprehensive physical examinations found few significant differences in the physical health status of Vietnam theater and era veterans. Thus, the CDC VES research team concluded that "during the telephone interview, Vietnam veterans reported current and past health problems more frequently than did non-Vietnam veterans, although results of medical examinations showed few current objective differences in *physical* [emphasis added] health between the two groups (p. 2708)."

One plausible explanation of the apparently discrepant findings of the survey and medical examination components of the VES is that the survey item assessing "health in general" confounded respondents' appraisal of the overall status of their physical *and* mental health, whereas the validating medical examination focused only on specific physical health problems, not mental health problems (in spite of the availability of considerable data on the psychological status of veterans also collected as part of the total clinical protocol).

When interviewers asked NSVG respondents about their current physical health in face-to-face interviews, 13.8 percent of male theater veterans rated their current physical health as either "fair" or "poor," compared with 11.1 percent of male era veterans, a difference that was not statistically significant (see Table VIII-4 for more details). As Table VIII-5 shows, analysis of physical health ratings from our VES-equivalent subsample of 616 male Army veteran respondents (taken from the total NSVG sample) produced quite similar results: 11.9 percent of theater veterans and 9.3 percent of era veterans reported "fair" or "poor" physical health, a difference that also was not statistically significant.

These analyses clearly show that Vietnam theater veterans as a group do not perceive their physical health status in ways that are meaningfully different from the self-appraisal of their era veteran counterparts. In point of fact, the self-report data from the NSVG survey and the objective medical data from the VES physical examinations converge upon the same finding: Vietnam theater veterans in general and Vietnam era veterans do not differ markedly with respect to their current physical health status. Thus, it appears that the "high" rates of health problems found in the VES telephone survey do not reflect how Vietnam theater veterans perceive their physical health today, but are an artifact of the nonspecific and confounding nature of the VES health survey question.

Finally, an important finding of the NSVG is that perceptions of current physical health *do* vary by theater veteran subgroups. For example, Table VIII-4 shows that male veterans exposed to high levels of war-zone stress perceived their physical health much more negatively than did their male era veteran and civilian counterparts. Similarly, both male and female theater veterans with a current diagnosis of PTSD and/or a lifetime diagnosis of substance abuse or dependence rated their current physical health as substantially worse than did their theater veteran cohorts without these disorders. In conclusion, although theater veterans as a whole did not differ from era veterans in their perception of their health status, the subgroup of theater veterans who were most exposed to war-zone stress and the subgroup that suffers from PTSD perceived themselves to be in significantly poorer health than did era veterans.

SUMMARY

In this chapter, we reported on the prevalence of physical health problems among Vietnam theater veterans and their era veterans and civilian counterparts. The overarching finding that emerged from contrasts among these groups was that the men and women who experienced the highest levels of war-zone stress in Vietnam tended to report higher prevalences of physical health problems than did a variety of comparison groups. Highly exposed male Vietnam theater veterans had a more negative perception of their current physical health, and reported a greater number of chronic health problems, than male era veterans and civilian counterparts (except for Black theater veterans and their civilian counterparts). Elucidation of the factors that account for differential appraisal of current health status among racial and ethnic subgroups of veterans and nonveterans will require further analysis beyond the scope of the present report. In addition, male theater veterans who were most involved in the war in Vietnam had higher rates of SCPDs than did men with less exposure to war-zone stress. For women, theater veterans exposed to high levels of war-zone stress reported a greater number of current chronic physical disorders than both theater veterans who experienced lesser amounts of war-zone stress and female civilian counterparts.

Contrasts among Vietnam theater veterans revealed a strong relationship between two major psychological disorders and negative perceptions of current physical health. Specifically, both female and male theater veterans with a current diagnosis of PTSD or a lifetime diagnosis of substance abuse reported a poorer view of their current physical health and more chronic physical health problems than did theater veterans without either of these disorders.

CHAPTER IX

Use of Physical and Mental Health Services[1]

COMMENTARY

Are veterans who have serious mental health problems seeking out and finding appropriate help? This seemingly straightforward question is at the heart of this chapter—and our data reflect the complexity of the answer.

The image often portrayed in the mass media is that Vietnam theater veterans, particularly those afflicted with PTSD or other forms of psychological readjustment problems, do not receive the care they need. However, the research literature has not always supported this popular notion. In terms of physical health care, for example, some studies have found no differences in the use of physical health care services between veteran and non-veteran populations of the same age. Further, these studies suggested that there may be little need for special planning or efforts to provide physical health care for Vietnam or other veterans because they were receiving care in about the same proportions as non-veterans.

In terms of mental health care, the story is different. It has been estimated that approximately 10 percent of all veterans use the VA health care system for mental health reasons and that as much as 25 percent of veterans' mental health care is provided through the VA. However, there have been no solid data on how many veterans use non-VA mental health care and what proportion of veterans with mental health problems receive care.

Chapter IX brings new and more complete data to bear on these

---

[1]Judy Weir of San Diego State University was a coauthor of this chapter.

issues. Overall, the findings do not suggest that Vietnam theater veterans are less likely to use mental health services than non-veterans.
The data suggest that male Vietnam theater veterans are as likely as
non-theater veterans and civilians to have used mental health services
at some point in their lives, as well as in the last six months to a year.
The male theater veterans were more likely to have used a VA service
for mental health problems than were non-theater veterans. For females,
the pattern was slightly different. Female theater veterans tend to use
VA and non-VA services more currently and VA services more on a
lifetime basis than female era veterans, but not more than their civilian
counterparts.

In examining those with PTSD, it was revealed that this group was
more likely to report use of VA and non-VA services for mental health
problems on both the current and lifetime basis than were theater
veterans without PTSD. For example, 62 percent of the males and 73
percent of the females with PTSD reported post-military use of some
VA or non-VA health care service for mental health problems. Among
theater veterans without PTSD, only 25 percent of the males and 39
percent of the females reported any kind of mental health care use.

Though these figures suggest that a significant proportion of Vietnam
theater veterans with PTSD have found their way at least to some
mental health care resource, they do not justify complacency on the
part of the health care delivery system. First, it should be kept in mind
that these data only reflect those persons who have made at least one
visit about a mental health problem to a health care provider. More
than one half of those visits were made to general health care personnel
and not to mental health specialists. Further, the data from the study
analyzed to date reports no information on the amount, quality, or
effectiveness of services received.

When the data were analyzed in terms of whether theater veterans
with PTSD were receiving current help, the results were more discouraging.
Some three quarters of the male and almost half of the female Vietnam
theater veterans with current PTSD do not receive any mental health
care. It is noted in this chapter that among some subgroups of theater
veterans, particularly Hispanics, significantly larger proportions of
those with PTSD are currently receiving no mental health care. Some
22 percent of the males and 55 percent of the females who currently
have PTSD report receiving some mental health care in the last six

months. Approximately one half of those receiving any care report having used a VA resource in the last year.

CHAPTER OVERVIEW

Chapter IX presents findings on the patterns of use of services for physical and mental health problems. Separate analyses are provided for a number of subtypes of mental and physical health services. First, because the mental health status of Vietnam veterans was a particular focus of the NVVRS, findings for the use of mental and physical health services are presented separately. Because Public Law 98–160, which mandated the Readjustment Study, expressly stipulated that data be presented on use of services provided by the Veterans Administration (VA), data on VA services (VA medical centers, VA outpatient clinics, and Vet Centers) are presented separately from those for other services, although the total use of services, VA and non-VA combined, is also examined. To determine whether Vietnam theater veterans have sought more care overall than comparison groups—and whether they have sought more or less care recently—lifetime use of services is also distinguished from more recent use. Finally, because use of inpatient care often reflects the presence of more serious problems than outpatient care, but yet typically represents only a small proportion of total care, separate information is also provided for the use of inpatient and outpatient physical health care. However, because inpatient mental health care is a particularly rare event, use of inpatient mental health care is not separated for either analysis or discussion.

Utilization of Services for Physical Health Problems

DIFFERENCES IN VA UTILIZATION. Only one significant difference was found between male Vietnam theater and era veterans in their use of VA facilities for physical health care. Since leaving the military, Vietnam theater veterans were approximately 35 percent more likely than era veterans to have used VA outpatient services. Overall, 26 percent of male Vietnam theater veterans have used VA outpatient services since leaving the military, and 3 percent had used these services within the past six months. Twelve percent of male theater veterans reported using VA inpatient services since leaving the military and 1 percent reported having used such services in the past 12 months.

Among women, more differences were found between Vietnam theater and era veterans. Since their separation from the military, women theater veterans were approximately three times more likely than era veteran women to have used VA services (both inpatient and outpatient). Vietnam theater veteran women had used VA facilities in the following proportions: 27 percent, lifetime outpatient; 3 percent, current outpatient; 6 percent, lifetime inpatient; and 1 percent, current inpatient.

Within the male Vietnam theater veteran subgroups, a number of differences were found in the rates of use of VA services. Overall, Black Vietnam theater veteran men were significantly more likely to have used VA services for physical health problems than Whites/others or Hispanics. Use of inpatient VA services (both lifetime and current) by Black theater veterans was more than double the rate of Whites/others, while their relative postmilitary use of VA outpatient services was almost double and current use three times the rate of White/other theater veteran men. In contrast, we found no significant differences between White/other and Hispanic theater veterans.

Overall, theater veterans with PTSD, a service-connected physical disability (SCPD), or a lifetime diagnosis of substance dependence or abuse were more likely to have used VA services for physical health problems than their counterparts without these conditions. Not surprisingly, the largest difference observed was for those with a SCPD. The rate of postmilitary use of VA outpatient services for both male and female Vietnam theater veterans with a SCPD was more than triple that of theater veterans without a SCPD. For men with a SCPD, there was also an almost threefold elevation in the postmilitary use of inpatient VA services. Although current rates of use for VA services are predictably much lower than overall or lifetime rates, among men the magnitude of the difference between those with and without a SCPD did not diminish for use of inpatient care, and actually increased to a sevenfold difference for use of outpatient care. This difference for current VA outpatient service use was also found for female theater veterans with a SCPD, but no significant difference was found for current inpatient use by women Vietnam theater veterans.

Differences in rates of VA use for physical health problems between those with and without PTSD or a history of substance abuse were not quite as extreme, but still quite large. Men with one of these conditions had rates of postmilitary VA physical health service use ranging from 30 to 140 percent higher than their counterparts without the disorder, and differences for current service use were even higher. For women with PTSD or substance abuse problems, lifetime rates of VA inpatient and outpatient use for physical health problems were three to five times higher than those of their counterparts without this disorder. Current utilization rates for women theater veterans showed fewer statistically significant differences between those with and without these disorders.

Overall, male Vietnam theater veterans who were exposed to high levels of war-zone stress used the VA for physical health care at approximately twice the rate of male theater veterans exposed to low or moderate levels of war-zone stress, although these rate differentials were not reflected in current use. Differences in recent use between the two groups were much smaller. Female Vietnam theater veterans with high-war-zone-stress exposure had rates of lifetime VA outpatient physical-health-care use more than 50 percent higher than female theater veterans with low to moderate exposure to war-zone stress, but this difference was not evident for use of VA inpatient care for physical health problems. No differences in current VA use were found among female Vietnam theater veterans by level of exposure to war-zone stress.

DIFFERENCES IN THE USE OF "ANY PHYSICAL HEALTH SERVICE." We found no statistically significant differences between Vietnam theater veterans (male or female) and era veterans in their rates of any current physical-health-care-service use (that is, VA and non-VA combined), inpatient or outpatient. In addition, we found only one difference among subgroups of male theater veterans for current use of any type of service for physical health problems. This finding indicated that male theater veterans with PTSD were more likely to have used outpatient physical health services in the past six months than male theater veterans without PTSD. Among female theater veterans, we found several differences in the current use of "any physical-health-care services." Elevated rates in the use of "any physical-health-care service" were found for female theater veterans exposed to high war-zone stress (both inpatient and outpatient), those with a SCPD (outpatient), and those with a history of substance abuse (outpatient).

Utilization of Services for Mental Health Problems

Vietnam theater veterans as a group (both men and women) were more likely to have used the VA for mental health services than their era veteran counterparts (7.5 percent vs. 3.3 percent for men and 8.2 percent vs. 1.0 percent for women). Among women, theater veterans were also more likely than comparable era veterans to have ever sought assessment or treatment specifically for mental health problems at Vet Centers in particular (4.6 percent vs. 0.5 percent), while the rates of utilization of Vet Centers for such problems by Vietnam theater and era veteran men were quite similar (2.3 percent vs. 1.2 percent). Lifetime utilization of *any* mental health facility (that is, non-VA and VA combined) was essentially the same for theater and era veterans, among men and women. Comparisons of Vietnam era veterans with theater veterans most directly exposed to the adverse aspects of war were even more telling and consistent. Theater veteran men and women exposed to high levels of war-zone stress were significantly more likely than comparable era veterans to have ever received mental health services from a Vet Center, any VA mental health service (including VA Medical Centers and outpatient clinics), and (for men) any type of mental health facility (including private, state, and federal facilities). For example, male theater veterans who were exposed to high war-zone stress were more than four times (and women theater veterans more than 20 times) as likely as comparable era veterans to have ever sought treatment for mental health problems from an agency affiliated with the VA (15.9 percent vs. 3.8 percent for men and 15.8 percent vs. 0.7 percent for women). In addition, male theater veterans who were exposed to high levels of war-zone stress were more than three times as likely, and women eight times as likely, as comparable era veterans to have sought mental health services from the VA within the past 12 months (6.1 percent vs. 1.9 percent for men and 8.1 percent vs. 0.1 percent for women).

The NSVG data thus suggest that Vietnam theater veterans—especially those exposed to high levels of war-zone stress—have made greater use of mental-health-care resources than their era veteran and civilian counterparts. In fact, there was not a single contrast on which theater veterans were significantly lower than comparable era veterans and civilians, and there were a great many on which they were more likely to have used services for mental health problems. Although further analyses are clearly needed to identify factors that explain the greater use of these services among Vietnam theater veterans, one plausible hypothesis is that this higher rate of use reflects their greater need for such services.

We also examined variations in mental health care use within White/other, Black, and Hispanic subsamples of Vietnam theater veteran men. Overall, we found that the White/other and Hispanic subgroups used all mental health resources in much the same way as the total population of theater veterans. Among Blacks, however, the picture was somewhat different. For example, in contrast to the other two racial/ethnic subgroups, the proportions of Black theater and Black era veterans who had ever used VA mental health facilities did not differ significantly on any contrast. An examination of the lifetime VA usage rates for these groups revealed a similar propensity among both Black theater and Black era veterans to have used VA mental health services, thereby minimizing differences between these groups.

Another issue of considerable importance to both Congress and the VA is the use of mental health services by Vietnam veterans with PTSD. We found that both male and female theater veterans with PTSD were significantly more likely than theater veterans without this disorder to have ever used any type of formal mental health service. For example, male theater veterans with PTSD were nearly four times more likely than theater veterans without PTSD to have ever been treated for a mental health problem at a VA facility (20.0 percent vs. 5.2 percent), while the usage ratio for female theater veterans with and without PTSD was nearly nine to one (41.4 percent vs. 4.7 percent). Similarly, we found that 62 percent of male and 73 percent of female theater veterans with current PTSD had made at least one visit to a mental health care provider for treatment of mental health problems at some point in their lives. Vietnam veterans with PTSD were also significantly more likely than their counterparts without this disorder to have used mental health services within the past 12 months. Some 22 percent of male and 55 percent of female theater veterans with a current diagnosis of PTSD had visited a health-care professional for treatment of a mental health problem within the past year, and approximately half of the facilities used for such treatment, in each case, were VA facilities.

These data on use of mental health services by Vietnam veterans with PTSD beget the age-old question, "Is the glass half empty or half full?" As is usually the case, the answer depends on one's perspective. Clearly, the NSVG data on utilization suggest that many veterans with PTSD are seeking and receiving mental health services through the auspices of federal, state, and private health-care providers. Yet, the findings also indicate that three-eighths of male and one-quarter of female Vietnam theater veterans with current PTSD have never seen a health professional about a mental health problem, and that roughly 78 percent of current PTSD cases among male theater veterans and 45 percent among female theater veterans have not done so within the past year. Since PTSD is a major and debilitating psychiatric disorder, a considerable unmet need for mental health services probably remains.

We also looked for significant variations in the use of mental health resources by level of SCPD and presence or absence of a lifetime diagnosis of substance abuse or dependence. Among male Vietnam theater veterans, those with SCPDs were significantly more likely than theater veterans without SCPDs to have reported seeking treatment for mental health problems at Vet Centers, any VA facility, or any mental health facility. Female veterans with SCPD's did not differ from their theater veteran counterparts on lifetime and current use of any mental health services.

However, both male and female theater veterans with a lifetime diagnosis of substance abuse or dependence were more likely than their nonabusing and nonaddicted theater veteran counterparts to have used mental health services of all types, both since their separation from the military and within the past year.

PHYSICAL-HEALTH-CARE UTILIZATION INDICES

Any Utilization of VA Physical-Health-Care System

Interviewers asked veterans if they had used any VA inpatient facilities for physical health care since they had left active military duty. Then, to determine whether VA outpatient facilities were used for physical health care, interviewers also asked: "Have you ever been treated or examined on an outpatient basis at a VA clinic or VA hospital outpatient department since you were last released from active duty?" (We did not assess premilitary use of VA facilities, inpatient or outpatient, and we assessed the use of facilities other than the VA only for current physical health care.)

Current Utilization of Any Health-Care System

We assessed current physical health inpatient utilization by asking respondents if, during the past 12 months, they had stayed "at least one night in a hospital, nursing home, or other medical-care facility because of their physical health." We assessed current outpatient care for physical health problems by asking if, during the past six months, they had received any care or treatment for a physical health problem from a doctor or other medical person in an office, clinic, or emergency room. For both inpatient and outpatient care, we then asked supplemental questions to determine the source of the care received. The "any service" category (for both inpatient and outpatient) included current utilization of any physical-health-care facility, either VA or non-VA. Because this study is particularly interested in the use of VA resources, we examined care from a VA facility separately from care received at other facilities. The VA and "any service" utilization categories were, therefore, not mutually exclusive, and VA use was a subset of the "any service" utilization.

In sum, the following measures of physical-health-care utilization were used in the analysis:

Any VA physical-health-care utilization (that is, postmilitary)

- Ever used VA inpatient facility
- Ever used VA outpatient facility

Current inpatient physical-health-care utilization

- Used VA inpatient physical-health-care services in past 12 months
- Used any inpatient physical-health-care services (VA or non-VA) past 12 months

Current outpatient physical-health-care utilization

- Used VA outpatient physical-health-care services in past *six* months
- Used any outpatient physical-health-care services (VA or non-VA) in past *six* months

PHYSICAL HEALTH CARE: PATTERNS OF UTILIZATION

Differences Among Veterans and Civilians (Exhibit IX-1)

The patterns of physical-health-care use by Vietnam theater and era veterans and civilian counterparts discussed below are summarized in Exhibit IX-1. For complete data, see Volume II of this report. Table IX-1 of Volume II gives prevalence rates and Tables IX-1-1 to IX-1-6 provide statistical contrasts.

Postmilitary VA Physical-Health-Care Utilization. We found no statistically significant difference between the proportion of male theater and era veterans who had ever used VA *inpatient* facilities. Reported usage ranged from approximately 9 to 12 percent. However, reported use of VA *outpatient* facilities since leaving the military was significantly higher for theater veterans than for era veterans (26 percent vs. 20 percent).

When comparing male theater and era veterans within racial/ethnic subgroups, we found few significant differences. Utilization rates were not significantly different between White/other theater veterans (10 percent) and era veterans (7 percent) for VA inpatient physical health care. Once again, however, outpatient rates were significantly higher for White/other theater veterans (24 percent) than for era veterans (17 percent). Among Black and Hispanic veterans, we found no significant differences between theater and era veterans in the postmilitary use of inpatient or outpatient VA physical-health-care facilities. Inpatient utilization rates ranged from 9 percent (era) to 12 percent (theater) for Hispanics and from 18 to 24 percent (era and theater respectively) for Blacks. Outpatient rates for era and theater veterans were 17 and 25 percent for Hispanics and 38 and 43 percent for Blacks.

Overall, male theater veterans with high war-zone stress had utilization rates for outpatient VA physical-health-care services (both inpatient and

EXHIBIT IX-1

Contrasts Among Major Study Groups for Physical Health Care

Major Study Group Contrasts	Ever Used Any VA		Current† Inpatient Care		Current‡ Outpatient Care	
	Inpatient	Outpatient	VA	Any	VA	Any
A. Males—Total						
1. Thr vs. Era	NS	Thr > Era*	NS	NS	NS	NS
2. HWZ vs. Era	HWZ < Era**	HWZ > Era***	NS	NS	NS	NS
3. LWZ vs. Era	NS	NS	NS	NS	NS	NS
4. Thr vs. Civ	NT	NT	NT	NS	NT	NS
5. HWZ vs. Civ	NT	NT	NT	NS	NT	NS
B. Males—White/ Other						
1. Thr vs. Era	NS	Thr > Era*	NS	NS	NS	NS
2. HWZ vs. Era	HWZ < Era**	HWZ > Era***	NS	NS	NS	NS
3. LWZ vs. Era	NS	NS	NS	NS	NS	NS
4. Thr vs. Civ	NT	NT	NT	NS	NT	NS
5. HWZ vs. Civ	NT	NT	NT	NS	NT	NS

(continued)

EXHIBIT IX-1 (Continued)

Major Study Group Contrasts	Ever Used Any VA		Current† Inpatient Care		Current‡ Outpatient Care	
	Inpatient	Outpatient	VA	Any	VA	Any
C. Males—Male						
1. Thr vs. Era	NS	NS	NS	NS	NS	NS
2. HWZ vs. Era	NS	NS	NS	NS	NS	NS
3. LWZ vs. Era	NS	NS	NS	NS	NS	NS
4. Thr vs. Civ	NT	NT	NT	NS	NT	NS
5. HWZ vs. Civ	NT	NT	NT	HWZ > Civ*	NT	NS
D. Males— Hispanic						
1. Thr vs. Era	NS	NS	NS	NS	NS	NS
2. HWZ vs. Era	HWZ < Era*	HWZ > Era*	NS	NS	NS	NS
3. LWZ vs. Era	NS	NS	NS	NS	NS	NS
4. Thr vs. Civ	NT	NT	NT	NS	NT	NS
5. HWZ vs. Civ	NT	NT	NT	HWZ > Civ*	NT	NS
E. Females—Total						
1. Thr vs. Era	Thr > Era**	Thr > Era*	NS	NS	Thr > Era*	NS
2. HWZ vs. Era	HWZ < Era**	HWZ > Era***	NT	NS	HWZ > Era*	NS
3. LWZ vs. Era	NS	NS	NS	NS	NS	NS
4. Thr vs. Civ	NT	NT	NT	NS	NT	Thr > Civ*
5. HWZ vs. Civ	NT	NT	NT	NS	NT	HWZ > Civ***

†Current Inpatient Care is for the past 12 months; ‡Current Outpatient Care is for the past 6 months.
Notes: 1. $<$ = lower than; $>$ = higher than.
2. $*p < 0.05$; $**p < 0.01$; $***p < 0.001$; NS = not statistically significant; NT = not tested (0 cell).

outpatient) that were almost twice that of male era veterans. This twofold increase in rates for theater veterans with high war-zone stress over era veterans was also found for White/other and Hispanic male theater veterans, both inpatient and outpatient. Although Black theater veterans with high war-zone stress had the highest lifetime VA utilization rates with an inpatient rate of 28 percent and an outpatient rate of 51 percent, theater veterans did not differ significantly from era veterans in this group. Male theater veterans who experienced low war-zone stress did not differ from era veterans in use of either inpatient or outpatient VA physical-health-care facilities within any subgroup comparison.

We also found threefold or greater differences between the proportion of female theater veterans overall and era veterans who had ever used VA inpatient facilities (6 percent and 2 percent respectively) and the proportion who had ever used VA outpatient facilities (2 percent and 10 percent respectively). Female theater veterans with high war-zone stress had rates four to nine times higher than female era veterans for inpatient (9 percent vs. 1 percent) and outpatient (35 percent vs. 8 percent) VA health-care use since leaving the military.

Current Inpatient Physical-Health-Care Utilization (VA and non-VA). Male theater and era veterans did not differ significantly in the proportion using VA inpatient care in the past 12 months (1 percent theater and 3 percent era). We also found no significant difference between theater and era males for "any" inpatient care (VA and non-VA combined) in the past 12 months, with 9 percent reporting such usage in both groups. Among racial/ethnic subgroups, we also did not find significant differences between theater and era veterans in current inpatient use of physical-health-care resources.

Male theater veterans with high war-zone stress had neither significantly higher VA inpatient utilization rates nor higher rates for "any" inpatient service than veterans with low to moderate war-zone stress (in the past 12 months). This finding was also true within racial/ethnic comparison subgroups. Nor did we find the contrasts significant between theater veterans with low war-zone stress and era veterans on current inpatient physical-health-care use (overall or within racial/ethnic subgroups).

In examining the data for female veterans, we found that the rate of recent inpatient health care use did not differ significantly between female theater and era veterans. Approximately 1 percent of female theater veterans reported using VA inpatient care and 11 percent reported using "any" (VA or non-VA) inpatient care services within the past year. The female theater veterans with high war-zone stress reported no recent VA inpatient use, although 15 percent reported current use of some type of inpatient physical health services (that is, "any service"). This rate was not different from that of women era veterans. In addition, the utilization rates between female theater veterans with low war-zone stress and their era comparison group did not differ significantly.

When comparing theater veterans with their civilian counterparts, we found no significant difference in the rate of "any" recent inpatient physical-health-care use. Nine percent of the male theater veterans used these health-care services, and 8 percent of their civilian counterparts did also. In addition, male theater veterans with high war-zone stress did not have higher utilization rates for "any service" than their civilian counterparts. However, both Black and Hispanic current inpatient utilization rates for "any service" were significantly greater for high-war-zone-stress theater veterans (16 percent) than for their civilian counterparts (7 percent Black and 4 percent Hispanic). Contrasts between female theater veterans and their civilian counterparts for any inpatient care did not yield statistically significant results.

As a group, male theater veterans did not differ significantly from their era veteran counterparts in recent outpatient services utilization. Two to 3 percent of male veterans reported recent use of VA outpatient physical-health-care facilities, while some 33 percent (era) to 40 percent (theater) of male veterans had used any (VA or non-VA) outpatient facilities within the past six months. When we examined male theater and era veterans within racial/ethnic subgroups, none of the theater/era contrasts were statistically significant.

When comparing theater veterans with high war-zone stress with their era counterparts, were found no significant differences in either VA or "any" (VA or non-VA) current outpatient care use. In addition, within racial/ethnic subgroups, theater veterans with high war-zone stress had no higher rates. Finally, rates for theater veterans with low war-zone stress were not significantly different from their era counterparts for VA or "any" (VA or non-VA) recent outpatient physical-health-care utilization.

Even though female veterans' current VA outpatient care use was not high, the rates for female theater veterans (just over 3 percent) were significantly different from those for female era veterans (approximately 1 percent). Current outpatient utilization of "any service" (VA or non-VA) for both female theater and female era veterans was 53–54 percent. Female theater veterans with high war-zone stress had used VA physical-health-care facilities significantly more often in the past six months than their era counterparts (5 percent vs. 1 percent). "Any" current outpatient use (VA or non-VA) was much higher than VA use, but theater veterans with high war-zone stress reported no higher rates than era veterans. Exposure to low war-zone stress also did not significantly affect utilization rates for female theater veterans.

Overall and within the racial/ethnic subgroups, male theater veterans did not have statistically different utilization rates for any recent outpatient services than their civilian counterparts. Neither did male theater veterans with war-zone stress have higher rates than civilians overall or within racial/ethnic subgroups. However, for both female theater veterans overall (54 percent) and female theater veterans with high war-zone stress (60 percent), utilization rates were significantly higher than for the female civilian comparison groups (39 percent and 38 percent).

Differences Among Racial/Ethnic War Veterans (Exhibit IX-2)

Black theater veterans were significantly more likely to have ever used VA inpatient (24 percent) and VA outpatient (43 percent) facilities for physical health care than were Whites/others (10 percent inpatient and 24 percent outpatient) or Hispanics (12 percent inpatient and 25 percent outpatient). They were also more likely than Whites/others to have used VA inpatient or outpatient facilities recently (3 percent vs. 1 percent inpatient; 9 percent vs. 3 percent outpatient) and more likely than Hispanics to have used VA outpatient services recently (Hispanics, 3 percent). No significant racial/ethnic differences were observed in VA use between Hispanics and Whites/others. In addition, we found no significant differences between racial/ethnic subgroups of male theater veterans in their use of "any service" (VA or non-VA) for current outpatient physical-health-care facilities.

Differences Among Theater Veterans

The proportions of male theater veterans with high war-zone stress reporting ever having used postmilitary VA inpatient (20 percent) or VA outpatient (39 percent) physical health care were significantly higher than the proportion reporting such use among those with low war-zone stress (9 percent inpatient and 23 percent outpatient). However, we found no differences in recent physical-health-care use patterns (either VA or "any") between male veterans who experienced high war-zone stress and veterans with low/moderate war-zone stress.

Female theater veterans with high war-zone stress were significantly more likely than those with low/moderate war-zone stress to have used VA outpatient services since their release from active duty (35 percent vs.

EXHIBIT IX-2
Contrasts Among Vietnam Theater Veteran Subgroups for Physical Health Care

Major Study Group Contrasts	Ever Used Any VA		Current† Inpatient Care		Current‡ Outpatient Care	
	Inpatient	Outpatient	VA	Any	VA	Any
A. Race/Ethnicity						
1. W/O vs. Blk	Blk > W/O***	Blk > W/O***	Blk > W/O*	NS	Blk > W/O**	NS
2. W/O vs. Hisp	NS	NS	NS	NS	NS	NS
3. Blk vs. Hisp	Blk > Hisp**	Blk > Hisp***	NS	NS	Blk > Hisp**	NS
B. High vs. Low Warzone Stress						
1. Males	HWZ > LWZ***	HWZ > LWZ***	NS	NS	NS	NS
2. Females	NS	HWZ > LWZ**	NT	HWZ > LWZ*	NS	LWZ > LWZ*
C. PTSD vs. No PTSD						
1. Males	PTSD > No PTSD***	PTSD > No PTSD**	NS	NS	PTSD > No PTSD*	PTSD > No PTSD**
2. Females	PTSD > No PTSD**	PTSD > No PTSD***	NS	NS	NS	NS

D. Service-Connected Physical Disability					
1. Males					
a. SCPD vs. None	SCPD > None***	SCPD > None***	SCPD > None**	NS	SCPD > None***	NS
b. High SCPD vs. None	High > None***	High > None***	High > None**	High > None*	SCPD > None**	NS
2. Females					
a. SCPD vs. None	NS	SCPD > None***	NS	NS	SCPD > None**	SCPD > None*
b. High SCPD vs. None	NS	High > None***	NS	NS	High > None**	NS
E. Substance Abuse vs. None					
1. Males	SubAbuse > None*	SubAbuse > None*	SubAbuse > None*	NS	NS	NS
2. Females	SubAbuse > None*	NS	NS	NS	NS	SubAbuse > None*

†Current Inpatient Care is for the past 12 months; ‡Current Outpatient Care is for the past 6 months.

Notes: 1. $\leq$ = lower than; > = higher than.

2. *$p < 0.05$; **$p < 0.01$; ***$p < 0.001$; NS = not statistically significant; NT = not tested (0 cell).

22 percent). However, for inpatient services, the difference was not as significant—9 percent with high war-zone stress sought inpatient treatment compared with only 5 percent with low/moderate war-zone stress. Female theater veterans with high war-zone stress were also significantly more likely to report recent use of "any" (VA or non-VA) inpatient (15 percent) and outpatient physical-health-care facilities (60 percent) than those with low war-zone stress (8 percent inpatient and 50 percent outpatient). Rates did not differ for recent inpatient or outpatient VA use between women theater veterans with high war-zone stress and those with low/moderate stress.

Differences Between Those With and Without PTSD

Male theater veterans and female theater veterans with PTSD reported significantly more use of VA inpatient services for physical health care since leaving the military (23–24 percent) than did male and female theater veterans without PTSD (10 percent and 5 percent respectively). This finding was also true for postmilitary use of outpatient VA physical health services. (PTSD: males, 37 percent; females, 57 percent. No PTSD: males and females, 14 percent.) For recent outpatient VA physical health care, rates for males with PTSD (8 percent) were higher than for males without PTSD (3 percent), but the differences were not statistically significant for females (10 percent vs. 2 percent). Higher rates for male theater veterans with PTSD as compared with male theater veterans without PTSD were also found for "any" (VA/non-VA) recent use of services for physical health problems (52 percent and 38 percent). Again, the difference was not found to be statistically significant for women (65 percent vs. 52 percent). In addition, no statistically significant differences were found by PTSD diagnosis for recent inpatient care.

Differences Between Theater Veterans With and Without Service-Connected Physical Disabilities (SCPDs)

Men with SCPDs had higher rates than those without SCPDs for all VA service use: inpatient, outpatient, lifetime, and current. Since separating from the military, 70 percent of those with an SCPD have received some outpatient VA care and 27 percent have received some inpatient VA care. Fifteen percent reported receiving outpatient care from the VA in the past six months and 4 percent reported having received VA inpatient care in the past 12 months. Even higher lifetime rates of VA use were reported by those with an SCPD of 30 percent or greater: 78 percent reported receiving

VA outpatient care and 42 percent reported receiving VA inpatient care since the military. We did not find any differences between those with and without an SCPD for current inpatient or outpatient use of "any" (VA or non-VA) services for physical health care.

For women theater veterans, we found differences between those with and without an SCPD for lifetime VA inpatient use (11 percent vs. 5 percent), lifetime VA outpatient use (67 percent vs. 20 percent), current outpatient VA use (13 percent vs. 1 percent), and current use of "any" outpatient services (65 percent vs. 52 percent). Current inpatient utilization rates did not differ across the female SCPD groups for either VA or "any" use.

Relationship Between Health-Care Use and Lifetime Substance Abuse

Male theater veterans with lifetime substance abuse were more likely to have received physical health care from the VA at some time since leaving the military than those without lifetime substance abuse. This finding was consistent for both inpatient (15 percent vs. 9 percent) and outpatient use (31 percent vs. 23 percent). Male theater veterans with lifetime substance abuse were also more likely to have received inpatient care from the VA for physical health problems in the past 12 months than other theater veterans (2 percent vs. less than 1 percent). For women theater veterans, we found two differences between those with and without substance abuse: lifetime inpatient VA use (18 percent vs. 5 percent) and current outpatient use of "any" services (68 percent vs. 52 percent).

Summary

DIFFERENCES IN VA UTILIZATION. Only one significant difference was found between male Vietnam theater and era veterans in their use of VA facilities for physical health care. Since leaving the military, Vietnam theater veterans were approximately 35 percent more likely than era veterans to have used VA outpatient services. Overall, 26 percent of male Vietnam theater veterans have used VA outpatient services since leaving the military, and 3 percent had used these services within the past six months. Twelve percent of male theater veterans reported using VA inpatient services since leaving the military, and 1 percent reported having used such services in the past 12 months.

Among women, more differences were found between Vietnam theater and era veterans. Since their separation from the military, women theater veterans were approximately three times more likely than era veteran women to have used VA services (both inpatient and outpatient). Vietnam theater veteran women had used VA facilities in the following proportions: 27 percent, lifetime outpatient; 3 percent, current outpatient; 6 percent, lifetime inpatient; and 1 percent, current inpatient.

Within the male Vietnam theater veteran subgroups, a number of differences were found in the rates of use of VA services. Overall, Black Vietnam theater veteran men were significantly more likely to have used VA services for physical health problems than Whites/others or Hispanics. Use of inpatient VA services (both lifetime and current) by Black theater veterans was more than double the rate of whites/others, while their relative postmilitary use of VA outpatient services was almost double and current use three times the rate of White/other theater veteran men. In contrast, we found no significant differences between White/other and Hispanic theater veterans.

Overall, theater veterans with PTSD, a service-connected physical disability (SCPD), or a lifetime diagnosis of substance dependence or abuse were more likely to have used VA services for physical health problems than their counterparts without these conditions. Not surprisingly, the largest difference observed was for those with a SCPD. The rate of postmilitary use of VA outpatient services for both male and female Vietnam theater veterans with an SCPD was more than triple that of theater veterans without an SCPD. For men with an SCPD, there was also an almost threefold elevation in the postmilitary use of inpatient VA services. Although current rates of use for VA services are predictably much lower than overall or lifetime rates, among men the magnitude of the difference between those with and without an SCPD did not diminish for use of inpatient care, and actually increased to a sevenfold difference for use of outpatient care. This difference for current VA outpatient service use was also found for female theater veterans with an SCPD, but no significant difference was found for current inpatient use by women Vietnam theater veterans.

Differences in rates of VA use for physical health problems between those with and without PTSD or a history of substance abuse were not quite as extreme, but still quite large. Men with one of these conditions had rates of postmilitary VA physical health service use ranging from 30 to 140 percent higher than their counterparts without the disorder, and differences for current service use were even higher. For women with PTSD or substance abuse problems, lifetime rates of VA inpatient and outpatient use for physical health problems were three to five times higher than those of their counterparts without this disorder. Current utilization rates for women theater veterans showed fewer statistically significant differences between those with and without these disorders.

Overall, male Vietnam theater veterans who were exposed to high levels of war-zone stress used the VA for physical health care at approximately twice the rate of male theater veterans exposed to low or moderate levels of war-zone stress, although these rate differentials were not reflected in current use. Differences in recent use between the two groups were much smaller. Female Vietnam theater veterans with high war-zone stress exposure had rates of lifetime VA outpatient physical-health-care use more than 50 percent higher than female theater veterans with low to moderate exposure to war-zone stress, but this difference was not evident for use of VA inpatient care for physical health problems. No differences in current VA use were found among female Vietnam theater veterans by level of exposure to war-zone stress.

DIFFERENCES IN THE USE OF "ANY PHYSICAL HEALTH SERVICE." We found no statistically significant differences between Vietnam theater veterans (male or female) and era veterans in their rates of any current physical-health-care service use (that is, VA and non-VA combined), inpatient or outpatient. In addition, we found only one difference among subgroups of male theater veterans for current use of any type of service for physical health problems. This finding indicated that male theater veterans with PTSD were more likely to have used outpatient physical health services in the past six months than male theater veterans without PTSD. Among female theater veterans, we found several differences in the current use of "any physical-health-care services." Elevated rates in the use of "any physical-health-care service" were found for female theater veterans exposed to high war-zone stress (both inpatient and outpatient), those with a SCPD (outpatient), and those with a history of substance abuse (outpatient).

MENTAL HEALTH CARE: MEASURES OF LIFETIME AND CURRENT USE

Lifetime Use

In the NSVG, we provided respondents several opportunities to report lifetime use of health-care resources for mental health problems. First, we asked the following open-ended question:

Problems often come up in life. Sometimes they're personal problems— people are very unhappy, or nervous and irritable all the time. Sometimes they're problems in a marriage. . . . Or, sometimes, it's a personal problem with a child or a job. Sometimes, when people have problems like that, they go someplace for help. Sometimes they go to a special place for handling personal problems—like a psychiatrist or a marriage counselor or social agency or clinic. How about you—have you ever gone anywhere like that for advice or help with any personal problems?

Responses to the open-ended question were coded by type of care provider. If the respondent had received treatment in a physical-health-care setting in the past six months, the individual was asked if he or she had used the occasion to discuss with the physician any problem with emotions, "nerves," mental health, or any drug or alcohol problem. If so, this visit was also treated as mental-health-care use. Following the open-ended question, the interviewer read the respondent a checklist of specific places and people from whom "someone might get help with his or her emotions, nerves, drugs, alcohol, or mental health." For each place or person mentioned, the respondent was asked if he or she had gone to that place or talked with that person. Finally, the interviewer asked the respondent if he or she had ever stayed at or been admitted to a hospital or other treatment program because of family or personal problems, a mental or emotional problem, trouble with "nerves," or a problem with drugs or alcohol.

We performed separate analyses on the following variables:

- Ever used any formal mental-health-care facility or service provider, inpatient and outpatient combined, including VA and non-VA use.
- Ever used any VA mental health facilities, inpatient and outpatient combined, including VA Medical Centers, VA outpatient clinics, and Vet Centers (postmilitary use).
- Ever used Vet Centers for outpatient mental health services.[2]

Respondents' use of "informal" mental-health-care resources (that is, friends or relatives, ministers, priests, rabbis, teachers, police, lawyers or judges, probation officers, spiritualists, herbalists, natural therapists, and faith healers) is not included in this report.

Current Use

We asked respondents to identify the most recent time they had used any of the resources mentioned in the open-ended question or the checklist described above; we scored them as positive on *current* mental-health-

---

[2]The Vet Center utilization measure includes only services provided for mental health care, and does not include other services routinely provided by Vet Centers, including vocational, employment, benefits, or educational assistance, or legal counseling.

care use if they reported use within the past 12 months. If the respondent had received treatment for a mental health problem in a physical-health-care setting in the past six months, we also scored him or her as positive for current health-care use. The variables used in our analysis of current utilization were the following.

- Use of any VA mental-health-care services within past 12 months.
- Use of any (formal) mental-health-care services within the past 12 months, including VA and non-VA facilities.

PATTERNS OF MENTAL-HEALTH-CARE USE AMONG VIETNAM VETERANS

Differences Among Veterans and Civilians

Lifetime Use of Mental Health Services: VA and Any Formal Service Provider (see Exhibit IX-3). Lifetime use of "any" (VA or non-VA) mental health services was very similar for theater veterans as a group and their era veteran counterparts. Lifetime use of any mental health care service for theater veterans ranged from 27 percent (Black) to 35 percent (Hispanic), and era veteran rates were about 29 percent for all racial/ethnic subgroups.

However, a significantly greater proportion of male theater veterans than era veterans have ever used VA mental-health-care facilities (8 percent vs. 3 percent). Postmilitary use of VA mental-health-care services was significantly higher for White/other male theater veterans (7 percent) than era veterans (3 percent). Among Black and Hispanic theater veterans and their era veteran cohorts, differences in lifetime use of VA facilities were not significant.

All contrasts between theater veterans exposed to high war-zone stress and era veterans for lifetime use of VA mental-health-care services were statistically significant, with the exception of Black males (see Exhibit IX-3). Overall, 16 percent of theater veterans exposed to high war-zone stress have ever used VA mental health services, compared with 4 percent of era veterans.

Theater veterans exposed to high war-zone stress were significantly more likely to have used *any* (VA or non-VA) mental-health-care facility than era veterans (41 percent for theater veterans and 29 percent for era veterans). Among the racial/ethnic subgroups, White/other theater males exposed to high war-zone stress were much more likely than their era veteran counterparts to have used any mental health facility. Black male theater veterans were also significantly more likely to have ever used any mental health facility than other Black civilian cohorts.

EXHIBIT IX-3
Contrasts Among Major Study Groups for Mental Health Care

Major Study Group Contrasts	Ever Used			Used Last 12 Months	
	Any VA or non-VA	Any VA	Vet Center	Any VA or non-VA	Any VA
A. Males—Total					
1. Thr vs. Era	NS	Thr > Era**	NS	NS	NS
2. HWZ vs. Era	HWZ > Era**	HWZ > Era***	HWZ > Era**	NS	HWZ > Era*
3. LWZ vs. Era	NS	NS	NS	NS	NS
4. Thr vs. Civ	NS	NT	NT	NS	NT
5. HWZ vs. Civ	NS	NT	NT	NS	NT
B. Males—White/ Other					
1. Thr vs. Era	NS	Thr > Era**	NS	NS	NS
2. HWZ vs. Era	HWZ > Era*	HWZ > Era***	HWZ > Era*	NS	NS
3. LWZ vs. Era	NS	NS	NS	NS	NS
4. Thr vs. Civ	NS	NT	NT	NS	NT
5. HWZ vs. Civ	NS	NT	NT	NS	NT

C. *Males—Black*

1. Thr vs. Era	NS	NS	NS	NS	NS
2. HWZ vs. Era	NS	HWZ > Era**	NS	NS	NS
3. LWZ vs. Era	NS	NS	NS	NS	NS
4. Thr vs. Civ	NS	NT	NT	Thr > Civ***	NT
5. HWZ vs. Civ	HWZ > Civ*	NT	NT	HWZ > Civ***	NT

D. *Males—Hispanic*

1. Thr vs. Era	NS	NS	Thr > Era*	NS	Thr > Era*
2. HWZ vs. Era	NS	HWZ > Era***	HWZ > Era*	NS	HWZ > Era*
3. LWZ vs. Era	NS	NS	NS	NS	NS
4. Thr vs. Civ	NS	NT	NT	NS	NT
5. HWZ vs. Civ	NS	NT	NT	NS	NT

E. *Females—Total*

1. Thr vs. Era	NS	Thr > Era***	Thr > Era***	NS	Thr > Era***
2. HWZ vs. Era	NS	HWZ > Era***	HWZ > Era***	HWZ > Era*	HWZ > Era***
3. LWZ vs. Era	NS	NS	NS	NS	NS
4. Thr vs. Civ	NS	NT	NT	NT	NT
5. HWZ vs. Civ	NS	NT	NT	HWZ > Civ*	NT

Notes: 1. < = lower than; > = higher than.
2. *$p < 0.05$; **$p < 0.01$; ***$p < 0.001$; NS = not statistically significant; NT = not tested (0 cell).

Female theater veterans were significantly more likely to have received care from the VA than female era veterans (8 percent vs. 1 percent). Likewise, a higher percentage of female theater veterans exposed to high war-zone stress (16 percent) than era veterans (less than 1 percent) have ever used VA mental health resources.

As a group, 2 percent of male Vietnam theater veterans and 1 percent of male era veterans specifically sought mental health services from Vet Centers, a twofold difference that was not statistically significant. Within racial/ethnic subgroups, Hispanic theater veterans (5 percent) were significantly more likely than Hispanic era veterans (less than 1 percent) to have received mental health services from a Vet Center. In addition, nearly 5 percent of the total group of female theater veterans reported receiving mental health services from a Vet Center, in contrast to less than 0.5 percent of their era veteran counterparts, a difference that was statistically significant.

All contrasts between theater veterans with high war-zone stress and era veterans were statistically significant for mental health services received from Vet Centers, except for the contrasts involving Black males. Male theater veterans overall (including Whites/others and Hispanics) and female theater veterans exposed to high levels of war-zone stress were more likely than their era veteran counterparts to have received mental health services from a Vet Center.

Current Use of Mental-Health-Care Resources. Current VA use was not much higher for theater veterans as a group (3 percent) than for era veterans (2 percent), and the difference was not significant. Current use of any mental-health-care services was roughly 10 percent for both era and theater veterans.

Male Hispanic theater veterans (5 percent) were significantly more likely to have used VA mental-health-care services within the past 12 months than were their era veteran counterparts (less than 1 percent). For current use of "any" (VA or non-VA) mental health services, theater and era veterans did not differ significantly overall or within racial/ethnic subgroups. However, Black male theater veterans were much more likely to have sought mental health services from any provider (VA or non-VA) than their Black male civilian counterparts (11 percent vs. 2 percent).

Use of VA mental health services within the past 12 months was significantly greater for theater veterans who were exposed to high levels of war-zone stress (6 percent) than for era veterans (2 percent). Roughly 14 percent of male theater veterans exposed to high war-zone stress and 10 percent of era veterans reported recent use of any mental-health-care facility, a difference that was not statistically significant.

When we contrasted male racial/ethnic subgroups of era veterans and theater veterans with high war-zone stress, we found no significant differences in terms of recent use of "any" (non-VA or VA) mental health care. However, in terms of current VA use, Hispanic male theater veterans exposed to high war-zone stress were significantly more likely than era veterans (13 percent vs. less than 1 percent) to have received care within the past 12 months.

In the female study groups, current VA mental-health-care use was significantly higher for female theater veterans (4 percent) than for female era veterans (less than 1 percent). Female theater veterans with high war-zone stress (8 percent) were also significantly more likely to report current VA use than era veterans (less than 1 percent).

Although more female theater veterans (18 percent) than female era veterans (14 percent) reported recent use of any mental-health-care services (VA or non-VA), this difference was not significantly different. However, female theater veterans exposed to high war-zone stress were significantly more likely to have used any mental-health-care services than female era veterans in the recent past.

Differences Among Racial/Ethnic War Veterans

Race/Ethnicity and Mental-Health-Care Use. Exhibit IX-4 and Tables IX-2-1 and IX-2-2 in Volume II show that across racial/ethnic subgroups of Vietnam theater veterans, Black males were significantly more likely to have ever used VA mental health services than their White/other theater veteran counterparts (11 percent vs. 7 percent). In contrast, the 10 percent of Hispanic theater veterans who reported lifetime use of VA mental health services was not significantly different from the proportion of Black and White/other theater veterans who reported having ever sought these services from the VA.

Exposure to War-Zone Stress and Mental-Health-Care Use. When we contrasted the lifetime and current mental health service use patterns of theater veterans exposed to high war-zone stress with those exposed to low war-zone stress, striking differences emerged. Male theater veterans exposed to high levels of war-zone stress were significantly more likely than their lower-exposure counterparts to have ever sought mental health services from any mental-health-care facility (41 percent vs. 27 percent), the VA (6 percent vs. 5 percent), and Vet Centers (6 percent vs. 1 percent). In addition, theater veterans exposed to high war-zone stress were significantly more likely than their lower-exposure theater veteran counterparts to have received mental health treatment at a VA facility within the past 12 months.

EXHIBIT IX-4.
Contrasts Among Vietnam Theater Veteran Subgroups for Mental Health Care

Major Study Group Contrasts	Ever Used			Used Last 12 Months	
	Any VA or non-VA	Any VA	Vet Center	Any VA or non-VA	Any VA
A. *Race/Ethnicity*					
1. W/O vs. Blk	NS	Blk > W/O*	NS	NS	NS
2. W/O vs. Hisp	NS	NS	NS	NS	NS
3. Blk vs. Hisp	NS	NS	NS	NS	NS
B. *High vs. Low Warzone Stress*					
1. Males	HWZ > LWZ***	HWZ > LWZ***	HWZ > LWZ**	NS	HWZ > LWZ**
2. Females	NS	HWZ > LWZ***	HWZ > LWZ***	HWZ > LWZ**	HWZ > LWZ***
C. *PTSD vs. No PTSD*					
1. Males	PTSD > No PTSD***	PTSD > No PTSD***	NS	PTSD > No PTSD***	PTSD > No PTSD***
2. Females	PTSD > No PTSD***	PTSD > No PTSD***	PTSD > No PTSD***	PTSD > No PTSD***	PTSD > No PTSD***

D. *Service-Connected Physical Disability*

1. Males					
a. SCPD vs. None	SCPD > None***	SCPD > None***	SCPD > None*	SCPD > None**	SCPD > None*
b. High SCPD vs. None	High > None**	High > None**	NS	High > None**	High > None*
2. Females					
a. SCPD vs. None	NS	NS	NS	NS	NS
b. High SCPD vs. None	NS	NS	NS	NS	NS
E. *Substance Abuse vs. None*					
1. Males	SubAbuse > None***	SubAbuse > None***	SubAbuse > None*	SubAbuse > None**	SubAbuse > None*
2. Females	SubAbuse > None***	SubAbuse > None**	SubAbuse > None*	SubAbuse > None**	NS

Notes: 1. $<$ = lower than; $>$ = higher than.
2. $*p < 0.05$; $**p < 0.01$; $***p < 0.001$; NS = not statistically significant; NT = not tested (0 cell).

For female theater veterans, similar patterns were evident across levels of war-zone stress. Relative to female theater veterans who were exposed to low/moderate levels of war-zone stress, female veterans exposed to high levels were significantly more likely to report lifetime use of any mental health facility, the VA, or the Vet Center program. We also found dramatic differences when we contrasted the two groups' current use patterns. Twenty-four percent of female veterans exposed to high war-zone stress reported receiving treatment for mental health services at "any" facility within the past 12 months, while only 13 percent of their low/moderate-exposure cohorts received such treatment. This difference was statistically significant. Differences in rates of recent use of VA mental health services by level of war-zone stress were also statistically significant and in the expected direction (8 percent for high war-zone stress vs. less than 1 percent for low/moderate war-zone stress).

PTSD and Mental-Health-Care Utilization. Theater veterans with PTSD were significantly more likely to have used mental-health-care services than those without PTSD. Exhibit IX-4 shows that both men and women with PTSD were significantly more likely than their cohorts without the disorder to have ever used any mental-health-care service or VA facility. For example, the percentage of male and female theater veterans with PTSD who had ever used VA mental health facilities (20 percent male and 41 percent female) was significantly higher than the percentage among those without PTSD (5 percent, both male and female). Some 62 percent of male theater veterans with current PTSD had used any (VA or non-VA) mental-health-care services in their lifetime as compared with only 25 percent for those without PTSD. Among female theater veterans with current PTSD, 73 percent had used any mental-health-care services, as compared with 39 percent of those without PTSD. In addition, 31 percent of female theater veterans with PTSD have used the Vet Centers for help with mental health problems, compared with 2 percent of female theater veterans without PTSD. All these differences between those with and without PTSD were statistically significant for both men and women, except for Vet Center use among men.

Male theater veterans with PTSD reported significantly more current use of mental-health-care resources than theater veterans without PTSD. Among male theater veterans with PTSD, 22 percent reported that they had received care from VA or non-VA mental health services within the last 12 months, compared with 8 percent of veterans without PTSD. Even more striking were the contrasts for current use. Ten percent of theater veterans with PTSD reported recent use at any facility, versus 1 percent of theater veterans without PTSD. Regarding recent use of *VA* mental health facilities, female theater veterans with PTSD (28 percent) were more likely to have sought help than those without PTSD (1 percent). A significantly greater proportion of female veterans with PTSD also reported recent utilization of "any" mental-health-care services when compared with those without PTSD (55 vs. 14 percent).

SCPD and Mental-Health-Care Use. As shown in Exhibit IX-4, male theater veterans with SCPDs were significantly more likely to have ever used any mental-health-care services (46 percent) and VA facilities (17 percent) than those without SCPDs (29 percent and 6 percent, any and VA respectively). Similarly, male theater veterans with SCPDs were significantly more likely to have used Vet Centers for mental health needs than were theater veterans without SCPDs (6 percent vs. 2 percent). Males with SCPDs were significantly more likely than those without SCPDs to have used any mental health care services within the past 12 months (21 percent vs. 9 percent), as well as VA facilities (7 percent vs. 2 percent). Among female theater veterans, lifetime use of any mental health facility or VA service provider was not significantly different for those with and without SCPDs.

Lifetime Substance Abuse or Dependence and Mental-Health-Care Use. The contrasts (Exhibit IX-4) between theater veterans (both male and female) with substance abuse disorders and those without such disorders all indicated that theater veterans with a lifetime history of substance abuse or dependence were significantly more likely than theater veterans without substance abuse disorders to have ever used any mental health facility, VA mental health services, or Vet Centers. Similarly, male and female theater veterans with substance abuse disorders were significantly more likely than nonabusing veterans to have used any facilities and, for men, VA services, within the past 12 months.

BARRIERS TO MENTAL-HEALTH-CARE USE

In an effort to understand why veterans reporting mental health problems might not seek mental health care, we asked respondents if they ever had thought that they should have gone to a doctor or other mental health professional for a mental or emotional health problem but had not done so. Respondents reporting that they had not sought care in such situations were asked to indicate which of a list of potential reasons for not using care were the reasons they had not sought care (the reasons read to the respondent are shown in Exhibit IX-6). In addition, the respondent was asked which of the reasons was the most important. This series of questions about barriers to care was also asked of individuals who reported that there had been times in the past when professional mental health treatment *might* have benefited them but they had not sought it.

Exhibit IX-5 summarizes the responses of male Vietnam theater veterans who felt that they should have talked to a mental health professional at some time but did not or who felt they could have benefited from mental health treatment but had not sought it. (The data for women Vietnam theater veterans contained too few cases for a separate examination.) Male theater veterans who are likely PTSD cases (those with M-PTSD scores of 89 or higher) were almost four times as likely to report having mental health problems for which they did not seek care as those who are likely noncases (M-PTSD scores less than 89). However, those likely PTSD cases who had no prior experience with mental health care were less likely to report that they had mental health problems that might benefit from professional attention. Only about one-quarter of male theater

EXHIBIT IX-5
Proportion of Vietnam Theater Veterans Reporting
Recent Mental Health Problems for Which They Did Not Seek Help,
by PTSD Status and Use of Mental Health Services for Other Problems
(Standard errors in parentheses)

PTSD Status and Other Use of Mental Health Services	*Sample Size*	*Percent Reporting Problems for Which They Did Not Seek Care*
Likely PTSD Cases (M-PTSD ≥ 89)	315	40.2 (4.1)
Never used mental health services	146	26.1 (5.2)
Used mental health services only in the past	87	50.4 (7.4)
Used mental health services in past year	82	58.9 (8.1)
Likely noncases (M-PTSD < 89)	868	11.9 (1.5)

EXHIBIT IX-6

Percent of Male Vietnam Theater Veterans Perceiving Current Barriers to Mental Health Care Who Reported a Mental Health Problem for Which They Did Not Seek Care, By PTSD Status and Use of Mental Health Services

| Barriers to Care | Total* (N=245) | | Likely MPTSD Cases | | | | Likely Noncases (N=114) | |
| | | | Never Used Mental Health Services (N=46) | | Past Use Only of Mental Health Services (N=40) | | | |
	Perceived as a Barrier	Most Important Barrier	Perceived as a Barrier	Most Important Barrier	Perceived as a Barrier	Most Important Barrier	Perceived as a Barrier	Most Important Barrier
Want to solve problem on own	86	31	98	30	62	38	88	31
Would get better by itself	71	24	70	31	56	12	75	28
Think treatment probably would not help	54	8	52	5	55	14	54	7
Unsure where to go	43	4	37	6	54	4	37	4
Distrust mental health professionals	34	7	45	5	45	3	25	6
Afraid what they might find	27	4	41	1	49	4	11	5
Concerned about cost	36	11	27	9	42	17	32	10
Would take too much time	28	3	31	2	32	2	22	1
Concerned others might find out about problem	32	2	47	2	30	3	29	2
Concerned what others might think	31	3	49	4	25	2	29	2
Other reasons	12	5	18	5	6	1	8	3
Distance, transportation	6	0	0	0	6	0	4	0

*Includes 45 likely PTSD cases who reported receiving mental health care during the past 12 months.

veterans who were likely PTSD cases but who had never used mental health services acknowledged having a mental health problem for which they did not seek care. Even those with prior experience with professional mental-health-care services frequently did not seek care for their psychiatric problems: more than half of the likely PTSD cases who had also received mental health treatment at some time in their life reported not seeking needed care for a mental health problem. This group may include individuals who sought care for PTSD but either dropped out of treatment or had a recurrence of symptoms for which they did not seek care.

Exhibit IX-6 summarizes the barriers to mental health care reported by those male Vietnam theater veterans who reported not seeking mental health treatment for a problem that could have benefited from such treatment. It is important to note the small sample sizes for the subgroups of likely PTSD cases and to point out that only gross differences in proportions between these groups would be statistically significant. By far the most frequently reported reason for not seeking care was the hope or belief that the individual could solve the problem on his own. Interestingly, those individuals who had sought mental health treatment in the past were less likely to nurture this hope or belief. Individuals who had sought mental health treatment in the past were also less likely to agree with the second most frequently reported reason for not seeking care: the hope or belief that the problem would get better on its own. These two most frequently reported reasons were also those most frequently identified as the "most important reason" for not seeking care.

Other major reasons given for not seeking care were feeling as though treatment would not help, not knowing where to get help, distrust of mental health professionals, the respondent's fear of what he might learn from consulting a mental health professional, and the time and cost involved in seeking treatment. Not surprisingly, those with no past use of mental health services appear to be more concerned with others' finding out and others' opinions of them if they sought professional mental health treatment than those who had sought treatment previously.

SUMMARY

Vietnam theater veterans as a group (both men and women) were more likely to have used the VA for mental health services than their era veteran counterparts (7.5 percent vs. 3.3 percent for men, and 8.2 percent vs. 1.0 percent for women). Among women, theater veterans were also more likely than comparable era veterans to have ever sought assessment or treatment specifically for mental health problems at Vet Centers in particular (4.6 percent vs. 0.5 percent), while the rates of utilization of Vet Centers for such problems by Vietnam theater and era veteran men were quite similar (2.3 percent vs. 1.2 percent). Lifetime utilization of *any* mental health facility (that is, non-VA and VA combined) was essentially the same for theater and era veterans, among men and women. Comparisons of Vietnam era veterans with theater veterans most directly exposed to the adverse aspects of war were even more telling and consistent. Theater veteran men and women exposed to high levels of war-zone stress were significantly more likely than comparable era veterans to have ever received mental health services from a Vet Center, any VA mental health service (including VA Medical Centers and outpatient clinics), and (for men) any type of mental health facility (including private, state, and federal facilities). For example, male theater veterans who were exposed to high war-zone stress were more than four times (and women theater veterans more than 20 times) as likely as comparable era veterans to have ever sought treatment for mental health problems from an agency affiliated with the Veterans Administration (15.9 percent vs. 3.8 percent for men, and 15.8 percent vs. 0.7 percent for women). In addition, male theater veterans who were exposed to high levels of war-zone stress were more than three times as likely, and women eight times as likely, as comparable era veterans to have sought mental health services from the VA within the past 12 months (6.1 percent vs. 1.9 percent for men, and 8.1 percent vs. 0.1 percent for women).

The NSVG data thus suggest that Vietnam theater veterans — especially those exposed to high levels of war-zone stress — have made greater use of mental-health-care resources than their era veteran and civilian counterparts. In fact, there was not a single contrast on which theater veterans were significantly lower than comparable era veterans and civilians, and there were a great many on which they were more likely to have used services for mental health problems. Although further analyses are clearly needed to identify factors that explain the greater use of these services among Vietnam theater veterans, one plausible hypothesis is that this higher rate of use reflects their greater need for such services.

We also examined variations in mental-health-care use within White/ other, Black, and Hispanic subsamples of Vietnam theater veteran men. Overall, we found that the White/other and Hispanic subgroups used all mental health resources in much the same way as the total population of theater veterans. Among Blacks, however, the picture was somewhat different. For example, in contrast to the other two racial/ethnic subgroups, the proportions of Black theater and Black era veterans who had ever used VA mental health facilities did not differ significantly on any contrast. An examination of the lifetime VA usage rates for these groups revealed a similar propensity among both Black theater and Black era veterans to have used VA mental health services, thereby minimizing differences between these groups.

Another issue of considerable importance to both Congress and the VA is the use of mental health services by Vietnam veterans with PTSD. We found that both male and female theater veterans with PTSD were significantly more likely than theater veterans without this disorder to have ever used any type of formal mental health service. For example, male theater veterans with PTSD were nearly four times more likely than theater veterans without PTSD to have ever been treated for a mental health problem at a VA facility (20.0 percent vs. 5.2 percent), while the usage ratio for female theater veterans with and without PTSD was nearly 9 to 1 (41.4 percent vs. 4.7 percent). Similarly, we found that 62 percent of male and 73 percent of female theater veterans with current PTSD had made at least one visit to a mental-health-care provider for treatment of mental health problems at some point in their lives. Vietnam veterans with PTSD were also significantly more likely than their counterparts without this disorder to have used mental health services within the past 12 months. Some 22 percent of male and 55 percent of female theater veterans with a current diagnosis of PTSD had visited a health-care professional for treatment of a mental health problem within the past year, and approximately half of the facilities used for such treatment, in each case, were VA facilities.

These data on use of mental health services by Vietnam veterans with PTSD beget the age-old question, "Is the glass half empty or half full?". As is usually the case, the answer depends on one's perspective. Clearly, the NSVG data on utilization suggest that many veterans with PTSD are seeking and receiving mental health services through the auspices of federal, state, and private health-care providers. Yet, the findings also indicate that three-eighths of male and one-quarter of female Vietnam theater veterans with current PTSD have never seen a health professional about a mental health problem, and that roughly 78 percent of current PTSD cases among male theater veterans and 45 percent among female theater veterans have not done so within the past year. Since PTSD is a major and debilitating psychiatric disorder, a considerable unmet need for mental health services probably remains.

We also looked for significant variations in the use of mental health resources by level of SCPD and presence or absence of a lifetime diagnosis of substance abuse or dependence. Among male Vietnam theater veterans, those with SCPDs were significantly more likely than theater veterans without SCPDs to have reported seeking treatment for mental health problems at Vet Centers, any VA facility, and any mental health facility. Female veterans with SCPDs did not differ from their theater veteran counterparts on lifetime and current use of any mental health services. However, both male and female theater veterans with a lifetime diagnosis of substance abuse or dependance were more likely than their nonabusing and nonaddicted theater veteran counterparts to have used mental health services of all types, both since their separation from the military and within the past year.

CHAPTER X

PTSD Among Vietnam Veterans: A Family Perspective

COMMENTARY

What about the families of Vietnam veterans? Post-traumatic stress disorder not only affects the veteran, it also impacts on the lives of his or her loved ones. The effects of the disorder are myriad and far-reaching. Families of PTSD victims may have a father, mother, wife, or husband who wakes up in the middle of the night screaming, who is distant, unable to show emotion or affection, who becomes intensely angry over little things or becomes violent, who is nervous and restless, or who drinks heavily or uses drugs.

In the effort to gain a better understanding of the nature and extent of difficulties encountered by family members, we went directly to some of the veterans' husbands and wives (legal and common-law) for first-hand information. These men and women were asked to describe their own problems, as well as the problems of the veteran and the children living at home. Chapter X presents what we have learned thus far.

The family members of those with PTSD will probably not be surprised by many of our findings. In fact, they may recognize themselves in much of the material. Neither will the clinicians who treat PTSD sufferers be surprised. Whether we are being told about marital conflict, difficulties with children, family violence, or feelings of unhappiness and emotional disturbance among veterans' spouses, the information offered suggests that the toll of PTSD goes beyond that paid by the veteran—perhaps even into the next generation.

For those who are interested in reading more about the problems of Vietnam veterans' wives and families, *Vietnam Wives*, written by Aphrodite Matsakis (1988), may be helpful.

Our data, of course, cannot definitively address the issue of the extent to which PTSD symptoms bring about family problems, or, alternatively, whether PTSD victims attract equally troubled wives and husbands, resulting in very disturbed and unstable family environments. However, the similarities between spouses of veterans with and without PTSD suggest that the source of marital and family discord may well be PTSD and its associated problems.

In addition to determining the scope of issues connected with PTSD for the family, our survey had another purpose: verification. There are those who believe that some or all Vietnam veterans are "faking it" when they describe PTSD symptoms, that they only want sympathy or to obtain veterans' benefits. There are some who question the very existence of PTSD. Yet our study found a strong correlation between PTSD symptoms reported by the veterans themselves and reports of the veterans' symptoms from their spouses. Furthermore, there was no incentive in our survey to motivate respondents to claim to experience symptoms they did not experience. We believe that these factors provide strong indications that Vietnam veterans are not "making up" symptoms—a reality of which many husbands, wives, and children are already aware.

CHAPTER OVERVIEW

This chapter reports on analyses of the interviews conducted with the spouses or partners (that is, spouse or person with whom the veteran is living as though married) of Vietnam theater veterans. Data from these interviews indicate that there are more problems in the families of Vietnam veterans with PTSD than in the families in Vietnam veterans without PTSD. Among male veterans, the spouses/partners of those with PTSD appear to be less happy and satisfied, and to have more general distress, including feeling as though they might have a nervous breakdown, than the spouses/partners of those without PTSD. They also report more marital problems and more family violence than is found in families of those without PTSD. Due to the small number of spouses/partners of women veterans with PTSD, fewer statistically significant differences were found between the families of women veteran PTSD positives and PTSD negatives.

In many ways, the spouses/partners of those with PTSD resembled the spouses/partners of those without PTSD in their demographic characteristics, as well as the absence of significant alcohol or drug problems. Despite these similarities, it is impossible to determine accurately how many of the differences between families of PTSD positive or negatives are due to a direct effect of PTSD on the family and to what extent these problems result from a selection factor; i.e., people who become involved with a person troubled with PTSD may differ in important ways from those who do not.

Finally, the reports of the spouses/partners of those with PTSD were basically consistent with, and tended to support, the report of the veteran (detailed in other sections of this report) that the veteran with PTSD has had major problems in life functioning, in readjustment, and with symptoms of PTSD.

INTRODUCTION

Among other provisions, Public Law 98-160 called for the study of Vietnam veterans to include "an evaluation of the long-term effects of postwar psychological problems among Vietnam veterans on the families of such veterans (and on persons in other primary social relationships with such veterans)." To address this objective, for certain Vietnam theater veteran respondents, we conducted an interview with another person in the veteran's household subsequent to the NSVG interview with the veteran. This additional interview permitted an independent assessment of both the veteran's problems and the impact of such problems on the veteran's family. We selected as potential candidates for this follow-up interview all veteran respondents with a high probability of having PTSD, a large subset of those with a moderate probability of having PTSD, and a smaller subset of those with a low probability of PTSD. For the analyses presented in this chapter, the data were weighted to compensate for differences in the probabilities selection among the various groups.[1]

After the responses of theater veterans were screened to determine their eligibility and sampling rates, we drew a subsample for the Family Interview Subsample, and, for those chosen to participate, we then determined whether a spouse, or a person with whom the veteran was living as though

---

[1]The estimates and contrasts were computed using weights developed to weight the "spouse/partner" data up to that for the population of all theater veterans with a coresident spouse or partner. Age, sex, and (for males) race/ethnicity were used as the strata for the development of the weights, which were also adjusted for nonresponse.

married, was living in the household with the veteran respondent. This person, "the spouse/partner" (S/P), was asked to participate in the follow-up interview. The response rate for the Family Interview (FI) was 80 percent and included 466 men and women. A more detailed description of the Family Interview or "spouse/partner" sample is provided in Appendix A.

All of the data that are summarized in this chapter are found in Volume II, Tables X-1 to X-28. A summary of the contrasts presented in these tables is found in Exhibits X-1 and X-2. Based on data from the S/P report (except for some demographic information where noted), these tables

EXHIBIT X-1

Summary Results of the Statistical Contrasts for the Family Interview*

Background Characteristics of the Spouse/Partner (S/P) and the Couple, and the S/P's Assessment of the Veteran's Problems

	Male Veterans	Female Veterans
A. Background characteristics of S/P and couple		
Educational attainment of the S/P	NPTSD>PTSD*	PTSD>NPTSD***
Current marital status of couple[1]	PTSD more often married*	Not tested
Number of divorces among S/P's ever married	NS	NS
Length of S/P's relationship with veteran	NPTSD>PTSD***	NPTSD>PTSD***
Percent of years S/P worked during relationship[2]	NS	Not tested
Current work status of S/P[1]	NS	Not tested
Socioeconomic status of S/P's job	NS	NS
B. Spouse/partner's report of veteran's problems		
MPTSD score for veteran (S/P's report)	PTSD>NPTSD***	PTSD>NPTSD*
Whether S/P believes veteran has/had PTSD	PTSD>NPTSD***	Not tested
Readjustment problem index score for veteran	PTSD>NPTSD***	NS
Level of life functioning of veteran	NPTSD>PTSD***	NPTSD>PTSD*

*All results are based on the interview with the S/P except where noted.
NPTSD = not PTSD; *$p < 0.05$; **$p < 0.01$; ***$p < 0.001$; NS = not significant
[1]From the veteran respondent interview.
[2]Variable created using data from both veteran and S/P respondent.

EXHIBIT X-2

Summary Results of the Statistical Contrasts for the Family Interview*

Interaction Problems in the Veteran's Family,
and Self-Reported Problems of the Spouse/Partner (S/P)

	Male Veterans	Female Veterans
C. Interaction problems in veteran's family		
Marital problems index	PTSD>NPTSD***	NS
Family problems index score: all couples	NS	NS
Family problems index score: couples with children	NS	NS
Standard family violence index for veteran	PTSD>NPTSD***	NS
Alternate family violence index for veteran	PTSD>NPTSD***	NS
Standard family violence index for S/P	PTSD>NPTSD**	NS
Alternate family violence index for S/P	PTSD>NPTSD**	NS
Childhood behavior problems index	PTSD>NPTSD*	Not tested
Alternate childhood behavior problems index	PTSD>NPTSD* (clinical range)	Not tested
D. Self-reported problems of spouse/ partner		
Subjective well-being of the S/P	NPTSD>PTSD***	NPTSD>PTSD***
PERI demoralization score of the S/P	PTSD>NPTSD***	NS
Social isolation index score for the S/P	NS	NPTSD>PTSD***
Alcohol problems of the S/P	NS	NS
Drug problems of the S/P	Not tested	Not tested
Whether S/P ever felt like nervous breakdown	PTSD>NPTSD***	NS

*All results are based on the interview with the S/P.
NPTSD = not PTSD; *$p < 0.05$; **$p < 0.01$; ***$p < 0.001$; NS = not significant

permit an examination of both the differences in problems and characteristics of Vietnam theater veteran respondents with and without PTSD and the differences in the problems and characteristics of the families of these veterans. The classification of respondents into "PTSD positive" and "PTSD negative" in these tables was based on an adjusted 89+ cutoff score on M-PTSD. The adjustments were derived from the clinical subsample and were a way of compensating for the false-positive and false-negative rates on the M-PTSD by using information from the clinical subsample. A description of this adjustment procedure may be found in Volume II, Appendix D.

This chapter will look at differences between those with and without PTSD and their families for a variety of background characteristics and outcome measures. It will first provide a portrait of the spouses or partners of the veterans and the couples, including the age, race, educational attainment, work status, and the prestige of the occupation of the S/Ps. Next will follow a description of the S/P's perception of the adjustment and PTSD-related problems of the veteran. (Although the S/P may not have been aware of all the problems that the veteran had with adjustment and his or her PTSD symptomatology, it was important to obtain some confirmation of the veteran's self-report of adjustment and PTSD-related symptoms from a second source.) Third, this chapter will include a discussion of any interaction or relationship problems in the veteran's family that were reported by the S/P, including marital and family adjustment problems and family violence. Finally, the chapter will provide information on the S/P's self-reported emotional and behavioral problems, including subjective well-being, demoralization, and alcohol and drug problems. The chapter will conclude with a summary of the most important findings from the data described in the chapter.

Data from the Family Interview were analyzed separately for male and female theater veterans. All veterans respondents for whom a family interview was obtained were married to or living with a person of the opposite sex, except, possibly, for one person whose self-reported gender differed from the gender listed in the military record. Because the FI results for women theater veterans were based on only five female theater veterans with PTSD, extreme caution must be used in the interpretation of the estimates for the S/Ps of women theater veterans with PTSD and the contrasts between women theater veterans with and without PTSD and their S/Ps.

GENERAL FAMILY CHARACTERISTICS

Age, Race/Ethnicity, and Education

Information from these measures provided a profile of the Vietnam theater veteran's spouse/partner and of the couple.

THE MEASURES

Age of the spouse/partner was the age reported by the S/P in the FI.

Race/ethnicity of the spouse/partner was also taken from the FI. Categories are (1) White and other; (2) Black (not Hispanic); (3) Hispanic (includes Black and White Hispanics).

Educational attainment of spouse/partner was also self-reported on the FI. Educational attainment is coded as (1) less than high school; (2) high school graduate (includes "some college"); and (3) college degree. This last category was not defined for the respondent and so may include both associate degrees, bachelor degrees, graduate degrees, and professional degrees.

THE RESULTS. The majority of the S/Ps of male veterans were less than 40 years old, with a mean between 37 and 39 years. Most female veteran respondents were over 40 (mean between 44 and 46). The majority of the S/Ps of theater veterans were White. The S/Ps of male theater veterans with PTSD were somewhat more likely to be Black or Hispanic than were S/Ps of male theater veterans without PTSD ($p = 0.051$). Because of the elevated rates of PTSD in the male theater veteran Black and Hispanic subgroups, this is not surprising. Male veterans without PTSD tended to be more highly educated than those with PTSD, and the S/Ps of the male veterans without PTSD had significantly higher levels of education than those of the male veterans with PTSD.

Marital Status, Number of Divorces, and Length of Current Marriage/Relationship

THE MEASURES

Current Marital Status of the Couple. This is the same marital status variable that was used in the analysis of the data from the main (veteran) interview. The data were taken from the veteran respondent interview.

Number of Divorces of Spouse/Partner Among Those S/Ps Ever Married. This is the number of divorces among those spouse/partners who had ever been married as reported by the spouse/partner.

Length of the Spouse/Partner's Relationship with the Veteran (Time Was Married to or Lived with Veteran). This measure is based on the S/P's self-report of how long he or she had either lived with or had been married to the veteran respondent, although this report was also compared with the report of the veteran. In cases of major discrepancies between the two reports, other data, including the name of the S/P as reported by the veteran and the name of the S/P on the FI contact sheet, were examined. In all cases, it appeared that these were the same person.[2]

THE RESULTS. Since the FI was only conducted when the veteran was either married or living as though married, all couples in the FI had to meet one of these two criteria. Virtually all of the couples reported actually being married. For male theater veterans with PTSD, however, a larger proportion reported living as though married than did male theater veterans without PTSD. There was a marginal tendency ($p=0.086$) for more male theater veterans with PTSD than without PTSD to be living with or married to a woman who was divorced. In fact, 9 percent of male theater veterans with PTSD were living with or married to a woman who was divorced two or more times, as compared with 2 percent of male theater veterans without PTSD. The most striking relationship found among the marital/relationship variables was that between PTSD and the length of the marriage or live-in relationship. Both male and female veterans without PTSD tended to have been married to or living with their S/Ps significantly longer than their counterparts with PTSD. This translated into a five- to six-year difference between those with and without the disorder. Male theater veterans with PTSD had a mean length of relationship of ten years; for male theater veterans without PTSD, this mean was 16 years.

Employment Information

THE MEASURES

Percent of Years the Spouse/Partner Worked During the Relationship with the Veteran. This measure was computed by dividing the number of years spent working during the marriage/relationship by the length of the relationship in years. The number of years the S/P worked during the

---

[2]In addition to problems of recall, there are a number of legitimate reasons why such discrepancies in reports might exist; e.g., in the case of a couple living together for several years before marriage, a veteran respondent may report the length of the current marriage and the S/P may report the length of the total relationship, including time living together. Another reason for such discrepancies relates to couples living together as married. If the individuals lived separately for a period of time between periods of living together, it could well result in one respondent reporting the time they first started living together and the other reporting the last time they started living together.

marriage/relationship was only available in the veteran interview and so was extracted from there. The length of the relationship was taken from the FI.

Current Work Status of the Spouse/Partner. These data were taken from the FI interview. Currently not working includes ten cases in which the S/P was retired, a housewife, a student or disabled.

The Socioeconomic Status (SES) of the Spouse/Partner's Occupation. Information about the S/Ps occupation was taken from the veteran interview. Occupation was coded using the 1980 Census classification scheme developed by Stevens and Cho (1985). SES scores theoretically range from 0 to 100.

THE RESULTS. There were no significant differences between veterans with and without PTSD in the proportion of time that the S/P was employed while living with the veteran. The mean proportion of the relationship during which the spouse worked was 0.6 for S/Ps of male theater veterans and 0.85 for S/Ps of female theater veterans. There were no significant differences between male veterans with and without PTSD in the percent of S/Ps currently working. About 75 to 80 percent of the S/Ps of male theater veterans were currently working and 97 to 100 percent of the S/Ps of female theater veterans were currently working. In addition, although there was also some tendency for male theater veterans without PTSD to have an S/P with an occupation with higher prestige than that of S/Ps of veterans with PTSD, this did not reach statistical significance.

SPOUSE/PARTNER REPORT OF ADJUSTMENT AND PTSD PROBLEMS OF THE VETERAN

Reports of PTSD Problems Exhibited by the Veteran

In the following section, the S/P's assessment of the veteran's adjustment and PTSD-related problems is discussed. It is important to note that many of the symptoms of PTSD, including those about which we are asking, are private events, that is, thoughts and feelings that the veteran may not disclose to the S/P. For example, three of the four criterion B symptoms concern intrusive and distressing memories of traumatic events, of which the S/P may be unaware. Two problems associated with PTSD, avoidance and guilt, often inhibit the discussion of PTSD problems with others, including the S/P. Also, those with PTSD tend to have been in their relationships for shorter periods of time than other theater veterans. Thus, the S/P of a veteran with PTSD may not have been with the veteran long enough to detect some of these problems that the veteran chooses not to discuss. Consequently, one would expect that, in many cases, the S/P would not be able accurately to assess the extent of the veteran's PTSD symptoms or to say whether or not the veteran has PTSD. Nonetheless, we would expect to find a statistically significant relationship between the NVVRS diagnosis of PTSD and the S/P's rating of the veteran's PTSD problems. The absence of such a relationship would cast doubt on the accuracy of the veteran's self-report and the validity of the PTSD diagnosis, and/or imply a total lack of awareness of the veteran's problems by the S/P.

THE MEASURES

The M-PTSD Score of the Respondent as Reported by the Spouse/Partner. This measure used the same set of items that were used for the M-PTSD score for the veterans, except that the S/P answered the questions about the veteran's behaviors and problems, e.g., "She/He has nightmares of experiences in the military that really happened." Because some of these problems and experiences may not have been reported to the spouse or partner (e.g., "She/He is frightened by his/her urges"), there are more "don't know" responses reported by the spouses or partners of the veterans than by the veteran respondents themselves. To avoid artificially low scores when the spouse did not know some specific items were true of the veteran, the average score on the nonmissing items was used in place of the "don't know" responses in computing the total M-PTSD score, but only in cases in which less than half of the items on the M-PTSD scale were answered "don't know" or there were other missing data. In developing the composite diagnosis of PTSD used for the prevalence estimates, it was found that the best predictor of PTSD from the spouse's rating of the M-PTSD scale (for the veteran) was a cutoff of 85 on the M-PTSD. This measure correctly identified approximately 60 percent of the PTSD cases and misclassified approximately 10 percent of the negative cases. The 84 cutoff produced a kappa of approximately 0.50 with the composite diagnosis, with the SCID diagnosis, and with the veteran's M-PTSD score. The improved prediction of PTSD one gains by using the 84 instead of the 89 cutoff may result from the S/P's not being aware of the full extent of the veteran's problems with PTSD. Therefore, in the FI analysis, we used an 84 cutoff for M-PTSD, although we also examined the effects of using an 89 cutoff.

Spouse/Partner's Perception of Whether the Respondent Has/Had PTSD. The S/P was asked whether he or she knew what PTSD was. If so, the S/P was asked whether he or she believed that the veteran respondent had ever had PTSD, and if so, whether the S/P believed that the veteran respondent had PTSD now. Therefore, the response categories for this variable were "S/P doesn't know what PTSD is"; "S/P knows what PTSD is but doesn't believe veteran respondent ever had PTSD"; S/P knows what PTSD is and believes veteran respondent had PTSD in past but not currently"; "S/P knows what PTSD is and believes veteran respondent has PTSD *currently.*" It is important to point out, however, that this item undoubtedly had limited validity, and that among those S/Ps who reported that they knew what PTSD is, few would have been able accurately to "diagnose" the presence of PTSD or any other psychiatric disorder, except in the most extreme cases.

THE RESULTS. The S/Ps of veterans with PTSD were significantly more likely to rate those veterans as having a score of at least 84 on the M-PTSD scale than were S/Ps of veterans without PTSD. This was true for S/Ps of both male and female theater veterans.[3] S/Ps of male theater veterans with PTSD rated 60 percent of their partners as having an M-PTSD score of 84 or higher; S/Ps of veterans without PTSD rated only 8 percent of their partners as having an M-PTSD score of 84 or higher. For female theater veterans, 49 percent of the S/Ps rated veterans with PTSD as having an M-PTSD score of 84 or higher and only 1 percent of the veterans without PTSD as having a score this high. Using the 89 cutoff, the proportion of those S/Ps correctly identifying theater veterans with and without PTSD did not change for female theater veterans, but it did change somewhat for male theater veterans. S/Ps of male theater veterans rated 50 percent of those with PTSD as having an M-PTSD score of 89 or higher, and 4 percent of those without PTSD as having an M-PTSD score of 89 or higher. As discussed above, the fact that only 50 to 60 percent of the S/Ps of veterans with PTSD were sufficiently aware of the full extent of the veteran's symptomatology is not surprising for a disorder like PTSD, which involves many symptoms that are private events, such as intrusive thoughts and feelings of guilt. In fact, it would be surprising to find any instrument which, when administered to someone other than the individual with the disorder, could better predict the presence of any other specific psychiatric disorder.

---

[3]The correlation of the veteran's M-PTSD score with the S/P's M-PTSD score for the veteran was 0.61.

For male veterans, there was a statistically significant relationship between the S/P's perception of whether the veteran had or has PTSD and whether the veteran was classified as having PTSD.

Reports of Other Adjustment Problems of the Veteran

THE MEASURES

Veteran Respondent's Readjustment Index Score as Assessed by the Spouse/Partner. This Readjustment Index is a modified version of the one used for the veteran respondent. (Results based on the veteran respondent's responses were presented earlier as the Index of Readjustment Problems in Chapter VII.) Responses used in the FI analysis are based on the S/P's assessment of the readjustment problems of the veteran respondent. The FI (and NSVG) questionnaire on readjusting to civilian life had 12 items that were originally used in the Harris study, *Myths and Realities*, and the CBS poll on the tenth anniversary of the end of the Vietnam war. These questions asked about the following problems.

- trouble finding jobs
- trouble holding jobs
- trouble with the law
- drinking problems
- drug problems
- physical health problems
- mental health problems
- trouble with finishing school

Other problems included in the list were having enough money to live on, being discriminated against because of being a Vietnam veteran, finding meaning in life, and having problems with family. For purposes of these analysis, we used the following scale to code each of these items: 1 (never had the problem); 2 (past minor problem); 3 (past serious problem); and 4 (current serious problem). We computed a mean score across items by using all items for male veterans, but omitting three items for female veterans, because female veterans reported almost no problems of this type. (These three were drug problems, problems with the law, and problems with being discriminated against because of being a veteran.) If any of the items were coded as missing (but fewer than half), we substituted the mean of the nonmissing items as the score for the missing item(s).

S/P's Perception of the Level of Life Functioning of the Veteran. We used these measures to replicate previous research in this area. In an investigation of stress, work, and unemployment among Vietnam veterans and nonveterans (Vinokur, Caplan, & Williams, in press), a "significant other" (equivalent to spouse/partner in this study) was asked 14 questions measuring the life adjustment of a veteran respondent. To replicate that study, we also included these 14 items in the NVVRS Family Interview. In these items, the S/P was asked how well the veteran had done during the past week in the following areas: getting along with others; handling disagreements; avoiding arguments; staying "level-headed"; being calm; being pleasant; acting relaxed; showing affection; making decisions; accepting responsibilities; handling responsibilities; handling all things required of him or her in his or her personal life; giving people time and attention; working around the house. The veteran's success in each of these areas was assessed using a five-point scale, which ranged from 1 ("very poorly") to 5 ("exceptionally well"). A weighted correlation analysis was done to determine if all of the items were correlated. When we determined that they were (that is, that it was one general factor on which all the items loaded), an index was created as the mean of the individual items.

THE RESULTS. As reported by the spouse/partner, male theater veterans with PTSD both had more adjustment problems and are currently functioning less well than male theater veterans without PTSD. In fact, 80 percent of the male theater veterans were reported to be in the highest category on the Readjustment Problems Index as compared with only 20 percent of those without PTSD.[4] Similar percentage differences (69 percent as compared with 13 percent) were found for female theater veterans.

REPORTS OF RELATIONSHIP PROBLEMS

Marital and Family Problems

THE MEASURES

Marital Problems Index as Assessed by the Spouse/Partner. This also is an index for the veteran respondent, the results of which are presented in Chapter VI. Here, the index uses the S/P's responses on the series of items regarding how well the S/P and veteran respondent get along, how satisfied the S/P is with the relationship, how often the respondents argue, how often they show affection, etc. Index values are the mean scores across the items and range from 0 (no problems) to 5 (extreme degree of problems).

---

[4]The correlation between the Veteran's Readjustment Index Score and the S/P's Readjustment Index Score for the veteran was 0.58.

Family Adjustment Index for All Couples as Assessed by the Spouse/ Partner. This index measures both family adaptability and family cohesion for *all* couples. Again, the results for its use with the veteran respondent are found in Chapter VI, and a full description of the index can be found in that chapter. Briefly, family adjustment consists of balance in the areas of both cohesiveness and adaptability. That is, well-adjusted families are cohesive and reasonably close, but not pathologically tied together or alienated from each other. And they are adaptable rather than chaotic or extremely rigid. The Family Adjustment Index has three levels: balanced (on cohesion and adaptability); mid-range (out of balance on *either* cohesion or adaptability); extreme (out of balance on *both* cohesion and adaptability).

Family Adjustment Index for Couples with Children as Assessed by the Spouse/Partner. This is the same as the index just described except items where phrased to include both children and adults; for example, "Each family member has input in major family decisions" instead of "We each have input regarding major family decisions." Here, also, the index has three levels: balanced (on cohesion and adaptability); mid-range (out of balance on *either* cohesion or adaptability); and extreme (out of balance on *both* cohesion and adaptability).

Standard Family Violence Measures for the Spouse/Partner and for the Veteran; Alternate Family Violence Measures for the Spouse/Partner and for the Veteran. Four indices were created to assess family violence: two for the veteran respondent in the past year as reported by the spouse/partner, and the same two to assess the family violence of the spouse/partner in the past year, as self-reported. One of these indices, *the standard family violence measure*, is the family violence index developed by Straus (1979). The second index, *the alternate family violence measure*, uses the same items, plus one additional item, but scores the items differently. These four indices, then, are based on the S/P's reports, that is, the indices assessing the S/P's family violence were based on the S/P's self-reported behavior, and the indices assessing the veteran respondent's family violence were based on the S/P's report of the behavior of the veteran respondent. (Chapter VII contains analyses for an index of *all* types of violent acts reported by the veteran respondent.)

Scoring of the Family Violence Indices. Eight types of violent acts are included in the standard family violence measure: throwing something at someone; pushing/grabbing someone; slapping someone; kicking/biting/ hitting someone (unarmed); hitting someone with an object; beating up someone; threatening someone with a knife or gun; and actually using a knife or gun on someone. Each item was scored 0 (never in the past year); 1 (once in the past year); 2 (twice in the past year); 3 (three to five times/past year); 4 (six to ten times/past year); 5 (11 to 20 times/past year); 6 (more than 20 times in the past year). The mean of the nonmissing items was substituted for the missing items when less than half the items were missing. The score on the Standard Index is the total score across all items. The alternate family violence measure is the total number of violent acts committed in the past year. To compute the alternate index, for each item in the standard index, the values 0–6 are replaced with the mean number of occasions the value represents, that is, the values 0–2 remain unchanged, but the value 3 becomes 4 (the mean of three to five times that the original value of 3 represented). Similarly, the value 4 on the standard index becomes 8 in the alternate index (the mean of six to ten times). In addition, the alternate index includes one additional item, "threatened to hit or throw something," since threats may also be perceived as a form of abuse. The score on the alternate index is the total score across all nine recoded items.

THE RESULTS. For male theater veterans, those with PTSD reported more marital problems than those without PTSD. The distributions and mean differences are similar but more extreme for female theater veterans.[5] (For example, 51 percent of the S/Ps of female veterans with PTSD were in the most severe category on marital problems, as compared with 10 percent of the S/Ps of female theater veterans with PTSD.)

For male theater veterans (both those with children and all couples), those without PTSD tended to have better family adjustment than those with PTSD; but this difference did not reach statistical significance ($p = .088$ for families with children; $p = 0.192$ for all families).[6]

For male theater veterans, family violence, both violence by the veteran and violence by the significant other, was more prevalent among those families in which the veteran had PTSD than in families in which the veteran did not have PTSD. The mean number of violent acts committed in the past year (including threats) by male theater veterans with PTSD was three; for those male theater veterans without PTSD it was one. Interestingly, the mean number of violent acts committed by the S/Ps of male theater veterans with PTSD in the past year was five, while for the S/Ps of those without PTSD it was one. This relatively high mean for the

---

[5]The correlation of the veteran's Marital Problem Index with that of the S/P's was 0.53.
[6]The correlation of the S/P's family adjustment Indices with those of the veteran respondent were 0.08 and 0.05. This lack of congruence is in line with research in this field, which suggests that such incongruence may reflect marital and family problems (e.g., Bernard, 1972).

S/Ps of male veterans with PTSD appears to result, in part, from the fact that 9 percent of these S/Ps committed 13 or more acts of family violence in the past year, thereby raising the mean. However, on both indices, a higher proportion of male veterans with PTSD committed at least some acts of family violence in the past year than their (female) S/Ps.

For female theater veterans, those with PTSD and their S/Ps tended to exhibit more family violence than those without PTSD and their S/Ps; but these differences did not reach statistical significance.

Behavior Problems of Children

THE MEASURES

Childhood Behavior Problems Score and Alternate Childhood Behavior Problems Score. To assess the problems of the children of Vietnam veterans, we used the Childhood Behavior Checklist (CBCL) (Achenbach, 1978). The reliability and validity of the profile developed from the CBCL have been demonstrated in a variety of studies (Achenbach & Edelbrock, 1983). A separate checklist was completed by the S/Ps for each child between six and 16 years of age living in the home of the veteran and S/P. Each item in the CBCL is scored (0) not true; (1) somewhat or sometimes true; and (3) very true or often true. These items are then summed to create a raw score, the "total behavior problems score." (The CBCL has a variety of subscales, but the total behavior problems score has been found to be that most highly related to clinical status.) This total raw score is then normed to T scores developed by Achenbach using data from a random community sample of 1,442 parents. These T scores are computed separately by sex and by age of child (six to 11 and 12 to 16) to account for age and sex differences.

All known previous research with the CBCL used the child as the unit of analysis. For the analysis of the FI interview, we were concerned with differences in problems across all of the children in the family of the veteran. To examine this, we created two variables, the *childhood behavior problem score*, which was the T score for the child aged six to 16 with the *highest* number of problems. The *alternate childhood behavior problem score* is the *mean* T score across all children aged six to 16. One cut point used for the categorical versions of both of the problem score variables is the raw score (for each age-gender category) that Achenbach uses as the normal/clinical range cutpoint. This is the 90 percentile for the standardization group. Within the normal range, the "no/few problems" group has a T score of less than 50, which indicates that the probability that their score came from a clinical sample is approximately 10 percent or less. The cut point used to divide the clinical range was computed by using the T score that created two approximately equal size groups (ignoring PTSD status and sex of veteran) among those scoring in the clinical range. The cut point used was between the T scores of 67 and 68.

THE RESULTS. In the family sample, only two of the female veterans with PTSD had children. Therefore, the data for females are not presented.

Overall, children of male theater veterans with PTSD had more behavioral problems than did children of male theater veterans without PTSD. When examining the data for the children with the most behavioral problems, we find that male veterans with PTSD were more likely to have at least one child with behavioral problems than male veterans without PTSD. Although the overall test across the PTSD/non-PTSD groups was significant for scores on the behavioral checklist (using four levels), when we examined the tests produced for each level of scores, we found that the most important difference was the proportion of those who have had at least one child with some behavioral problems.

When examining the data for the mean behavioral problem score across children, we found that the major difference was in the proportion of veterans whose children's "average" score was in the clinical range. When comparing the PTSD/non-PTSD groups on the mean score measure, we found that the children of those with PTSD were more likely to have a problem in the clinical range than the children of those without PTSD, and that the overall test for finer distinctions (that is, the four-level variable) was not significant. The average score across children for those with PTSD was in the clinical range of 35 percent for those with PTSD, compared with only 14 percent for those without PTSD. When further examining the tests for differences between the PTSD/non-PTSD groups for all four levels of the measure, we found that the major difference was in the "clinical range, mild" level, indicating that the biggest differences between the groups were that the average scores of the children of those with PTSD were more likely to be in the low clinical range than those of veterans without PTSD.

SELF-REPORTED PROBLEMS OF THE SPOUSE

Sense of Well-being and Nonspecific Distress

THE MEASURES

Subjective Well-Being of the Spouse/Partner. The S/P questionnaire contained items that asked about both the S/P's perceived happiness and life satisfaction. The first item was taken from Gurin et al. (1960) and asked whether "taking things all together," the respondent was very happy, pretty happy, or not too happy "these days." The second item was a measure of life satisfaction taken from the 1976 *Americans View Their Mental Health Study* (Veroff et al., 1981). This question asked, "In general, how satisfying do you find the way you're spending your time these days?" Answer choices were "completely satisfying," "pretty satisfying," and "not at all satisfying." These two items were combined into one variable and scored the same for the S/P as it was for the veteran respondent: categories ranged from "very unhappy and not very satisfied" to "very happy and completely satisfied."

PERI Demoralization Score (Self-Reported Nonspecific Distress) of the Spouse/Partner. We also used the demoralization measure from the Psychiatric Epidemiology Research Interview (PERI) (Dohrenwend, 1982; Dohrenwend, Levav, & Strout, 1986) as described in Chapter VII in the FI. We combined a subset of eight of the PERI scales into one scale, and used the short version of this scale for both the veteran respondent and the S/P respondent. We refer to this measure as "nonspecific distress" because it taps distress symptoms that are associated with a variety of psychiatric disorders. The scoring of the PERI is the same as described in Chapter VII: the score is the mean of all nonmissing items if less than half the items were missing. The range is from low (0–0.49) to high (1.5 or greater).

THE RESULTS. Among both male and female theater veterans, the S/Ps of theater veterans with PTSD had a strong tendency to be less happy and satisfied than the S/Ps of theater veterans without PTSD. More than half of the S/Ps of veterans (male and female) without PTSD scored in the two highest categories on the Subjective Well-Being Index (Happiness and Satisfaction Index), while only 11–15 percent of the S/Ps of veterans (male and female) with PTSD scored in the two highest categories.

S/Ps of male theater veterans with PTSD and higher PERI demoralization scores than those of male theater veterans without PTSD. Forty-three percent of S/Ps of male theater veterans with PTSD were in the highest category on demoralization, as compared with 15 percent of the S/Ps of those without PTSD. There was also some tendency for the S/Ps of female theater veterans with PTSD to have higher demoralization scores than S/Ps of those without PTSD.

Social Isolation, Alcohol Problems, and Drug Problems

THE MEASURES

Social Isolation Index Score of the Spouse/Partner. The S/P's questionnaire contained only four of the 22 questions related to social isolation that had been asked of the veteran respondent. Two of these four items asked about the number of close friends/relatives the respondent had. The third asked whether the S/P had friends or relatives (excluding the veteran respondent) that he or she (that is, the S/P) could "tell just about anything to, someone you can count on for understanding and advice." The last item asked whether the S/P respondent had problems he or she could not discuss with friends or relatives. An index was created that gave one point for each of the following responses: zero close friends; zero relatives the S/P feels close to and can talk with; "No" to whether the S/P has friends or relatives (excluding the veteran respondent) that he or she could "tell just about anything to"; and "Yes" to whether the S/P respondent had problems he or she could not discuss with friends or relatives. The total score, then, ranges from 0 to 4.

Alcohol Problems of the Spouse/Partner. We used the Brief Michigan Alcoholism Screening Test (Brief MAST) to assess the alcohol problems of the spouse/partner. The Brief MAST was developed by Pokorny and colleagues (Pokorny, Miller, & Kaplan, 1972) and is a short version of the 25-item MAST (Michigan Alcoholism Screening Test) developed by Selzer (1971). For those indicating that they drink alcohol, the Brief MAST contains ten items that ask whether the respondent feels he or she is a normal drinker; whether the respondent's friends or relatives feel the respondent is a normal drinker; whether the respondent has ever attended an Alcoholics Anonymous meeting; whether the respondent has had a wide variety of different problems associated with drinking, including getting into fights, having work problems, being in a hospital or getting arrested, having relationship problems, having health problems, neglecting responsibilities; and whether the respondent had ever sought help from someone for a drinking problem. This screening test is scored by counting two points for each item above (coded in the direction of indicating an alcohol problem), except for three items that are considered to be more highly related to alcoholism. These three items (attending AA; seeking help for drinking; and being hospitalized for drinking) each receive five points toward the total score. Using this method of scoring, and a cutoff of six or more, Pokorny found that none of the known alcoholics were below the cut point and only seven of the 62 known nonalcoholics were above the cut point. The values on the Brief Mast variable were "Doesn't drink alcohol"; "Drinks alcohol but few or no alcohol problems"; and "Probable alcoholic."

Drug Problems of the Spouse/Partner as Self-Assessed. The ten items from the Brief Mast were also reworded to ask about drug problems instead of alcohol problems. These items asked whether the respondent feels drugs are a problem for him or her; whether the respondent's friends or relatives feel that drugs are a problem for the respondent; whether the respondent has ever had treatment or counseling for drugs; whether or not the respondent has had a wide variety of different problems associated with drugs, including getting into fights, having work problems, being in a hospital or getting arrested, having relationship problems, having health problems, neglecting responsibilities; and whether the respondent had ever sought help from someone for a drug problem. Because so few respondents reported having drug problems, response categories were necessarily: "Doesn't use drugs"; "Uses drugs but no problems"; "Uses drugs and has some problems."

THE RESULTS. Among the S/Ps of male theater veterans, there was no significant difference in levels of social isolation between those with and without PTSD. Among the S/Ps of female theater veterans, the S/Ps of veterans with PTSD tended to have *lower* isolation scores than S/Ps of veterans without PTSD.

S/Ps of those with PTSD were also no more likely than S/Ps of those without PTSD to report major alcohol problems. However, among S/Ps of male veterans with PTSD, the mean is not only higher than that for S/Ps of those without PTSD, but also the standard error for the mean was rather large, which suggests that a subset of these S/Ps may have significant alcohol problems. The amount of reported drug use among S/Ps was so small as to preclude statistical testing of such differences.

Other Psychological Problems

THE MEASURE

Whether Spouse/Partner Reported Ever Having Felt as Though He or She Were Having a Nervous Breakdown. The S/P's analysis includes the item, "When problems come up, have you ever felt as though you were going to have, or were close to having, a nervous breakdown?" A similar item was used in both the 1957 and 1976 *Americans View Their Mental Health Studies* (Gurin, Veroff, & Feld, 1960; Veroff, Douvan, & Kulka, 1981).

THE RESULTS. More of the S/Ps of veterans with PTSD reported having felt as though they were going to have a nervous breakdown at some point in their lives than did S/Ps of veterans without PTSD. This tendency was significant for male veterans. In fact, 55 percent of the S/Ps of male theater veterans reported feeling this way as compared with 30 percent of the S/Ps of male theater veterans with PTSD.

SUMMARY

Overall, the interview with the spouse/partner of Vietnam theater veterans (that is, spouse or person living with as though married) indicated that the families of Vietnam veterans with PTSD have more problems than the families of Vietnam veterans without PTSD. We cannot accurately determine how many of these problems are caused directly by PTSD's effect on the family and how many of these problems result from selection factors (that is, persons who become involved with an individual with PTSD may differ in important ways from those who do not). However, in many ways, the S/Ps of those with PTSD resembled the S/Ps of those without PTSD. Both the S/Ps of those with and without PTSD were predominantly in their late 30s to mid-40s and White. In addition, S/Ps from both groups were currently working and had worked for the majority of the time they had maintained their relationship with the veteran. S/Ps of male veterans had about 13 years of education and the S/Ps of female veterans had an average of 16 years of education. Overall, the prestige of the S/P's occupation did not differ significantly for the two comparison groups (those with and without PTSD). As a group, the S/Ps of those with PTSD did not appear to have more alcohol or drug problems or to be more socially isolated than the S/Ps of those without PTSD. And while there was a somewhat increased tendency for the S/Ps of those with PTSD to report having been divorced, this tendency did not reach statistical significance, and most individuals in both comparison groups had never been divorced.

Despite these similarities, among male veterans, the S/Ps of those with PTSD appeared to be less happy and satisfied and to have more general distress (including feeling that they might have a nervous breakdown) than the S/Ps of those without PTSD. The S/Ps of veterans with PTSD reported more marital problems and more family violence than did the families of those without PTSD. Although families of male veterans with PTSD tended to have poorer family adjustment than families of male veterans without PTSD, this relationship did not rech statistically significicance. Children of male veterans with PTSD had more behavioral problems, including more behavioral problems severe enough to be of clinical significance, than did the children of male veterans without PTSD.

Because of the problem of sample size for women with PTSD, any results should be taken cautiously. Among women theater veterans, the strongest differences between PTSD positives and negatives were that the S/Ps of the positives were much less happy and satisfied than the S/Ps of those without PTSD. In addition, the couples in which the veteran had PTSD had been together for a shorter time than couples in which the veteran did not have PTSD.

Finally, the reports of the S/Ps of those with PTSD were basically consistent with, and tended to support, the veterans' reports (detailed in other chapters) that the veterans had major problems with readjustment, life functioning, and symptoms of PTSD.

CHAPTER XI

Recommendations for Future Study

COMMENTARY

What should we do with all of this information? Is there more to be learned from the data that have been collected than appears in this report? Where do we go from here? These are good questions, because in spite of the huge amount of information provided in this volume, not every question of potential concern to veterans and their families, or to scientists, health-care providers, and public policy planners has been addressed or answered fully. As you have seen in the preceding chapters, we have focused our analyses on answering the specific questions that Congress asked concerning Vietnam veterans. We hope we have been able to do this successfully. However, we also recognize that there are many important questions that were beyond the scope of the Congressional mandate and for which the analyses conducted in this report provide few or limited answers. Fortunately, the NVVRS database was designed with the goal of providing a valuable resource for answering other key questions.

In this chapter, we suggest that further examination of NVVRS data can help to clarify our understanding of a wide range of critical issues, such as the aftermath of exposure to extreme war events; the nature of the syndrome of PTSD; racial and ethnic differences in postwar adjustment; the broader impact of PTSD on individuals and families; paths that veterans take to seek and use mental health services; and ways to improve the assessment of PTSD. We hope that our suggestions for future analysis of the NVVRS data will spark continued interest in examining this rich repository of information on the men and women of the Vietnam generation.

CHAPTER OVERVIEW

We prepared this report to address the specific issues raised in the Congressional mandate. Therefore, it is primarily a descriptive report. As such, it serves the useful purpose of describing the levels of postwar psychological problems among Vietnam veterans, and it provides the kinds of information needed by federal policy makers to formulate mental health service program plans.

However, the report leaves unanswered many questions about Vietnam service and its sequelae. Many such questions refer to the more fine-grained details that can be examined owing to the depth and breadth of the Readjustment Study database, but some are more fundamental. For example, a more complete understanding of the full spectrum of readjustment problems among Vietnam veterans will require extensive multivariate analyses that were beyond the scope of this report.

Therefore, although publication of this report represents an important milestone and end point in the life of the Readjustment Study, it is not a "final" report. Rather, it represents the first in what is hoped will be a series of reports that reveal the details of the study's findings. The database that has been created through conduct of the NVVRS is an extremely rich resource for use in addressing issues of scientific interest as well as of policy import.

In recognition of these facts, the research team felt it important to recognize explicitly the descriptive nature of this report, and to record some of our thoughts about the directions in which subsequent analyses of the Readjustment Study database might profitably be aimed. This chapter provides an outline of our thoughts about some initial directions that such further analyses should take.

The outline is intended as an illustrative, rather than exhaustive, listing of the potential uses of the database. Recommendations were made for analyses in the following major areas.

1. aftermath of trauma
2. PTSD
3. factors of race and ethnicity
4. broader impact of PTSD
5. paths to seeking help
6. improving ways of detecting PTSD
7. scientific and methodological issues

Additional studies of this type would provide a more detailed and complete understanding of the problems of readjustment to civilian life among Vietnam veterans revealed in the previous chapters of this report.

AFTERMATH OF TRAUMA

One of the major strengths of the Readjustment Study database is the richness of detail that it provides about exposure to trauma and the occurrence of stress-reaction symptoms. Among the many important questions that can be addressed are:

- What is the relationship between specific aspects of trauma and the subsequent development of stress-reaction symptoms, controlling for differences in background characteristics?
- Why do some people exposed to a given level of trauma develop PTSD and others do not?
- What is the role of early childhood trauma in subsequent exposure to trauma and in the development of PTSD?
- What is the role of social support, and other forms of coping, both before and after exposure to trauma, in the development of PTSD?
- What characteristics distinguish people with PTSD who seek mental health treatment from those who do not?
- What characteristics predict those whose PTSD will become chronic and those whose PTSD is more time-limited?

PTSD

The Readjustment Study collected more data on more people with PTSD than any study in history. These data can make a tremendous contribution to the major revision of the *Diagnostic and Statistical Manual of Mental Disorders* that is now being organized (to result in the publication in 1992 of DSM-IV). Important information concerning the accuracy and completeness of the current criteria, natural history and course of illness, and co-occurrence with other disorders can be developed through more thorough analysis.

Some of the specific questions that can be addressed with the data include the following.

- What are the essential elements of PTSD as it occurs in a community (non-treatment-seeking) population?
- What is the relationship between PTSD and dysfunctions in other (nonpsychological) aspects of peoples lives?
- Are the risk factors for PTSD the same for men and women, and what is the role of occupational factors in the development of

PTSD in female Vietnam veterans (many of whom were nurses and encountered their trauma while carrying out their nursing duties)?
- What are the typical natural history and course of PTSD?
- What is the role of dissociation in the etiology and course of PTSD?
- Are there identifiable subtypes of PTSD based on the regular co-occurrence of particular subsets of symptoms?
- Are the other psychiatric disorders that regularly co-occur with PTSD true comorbid syndromes, or are they better understood as epiphenomena of PTSD, or risk factors for PTSD, etc.?
- Should the patterning and numbers of symptoms required to meet criteria for the diagnosis be revised to adjust the threshold for PTSD "caseness" (that is, are the current rules too lenient or too strict)?

FACTORS OF RACE AND ETHNICITY

One consistent finding throughout this report is that there are differences among the racial and ethnic subgroups in the prevalence of a wide variety of readjustment problems. Although the multivariate analyses described in Chapter V provide some insights, much more work is required to gain a more complete understanding of the determinants of these differences. Some of the important questions include:

- Are there fundamental and systematic differences in the symptomatic expression of PTSD in minority group members?
- What characteristics account for the apparently greater vulnerability to PTSD among Hispanic theater veterans?
- Are there other identifiable subgroups with increased vulnerability to the development of PTSD?
- Would a detailed, multidimensional examination of the Vietnam experience reveal differences that are related to the current prevalence of PTSD?
- What are the differences among racial/ethnic subgroups in the relationships among PTSD, other psychiatric disorders, and risk factors?

BROADER IMPACT OF PTSD

In this report, we have for the most part focused on the impact of PTSD on the mental health status of the individual who has it. In doing so, we have found that it is often a debilitating, chronic disorder. We have also provided data suggesting that PTSD is related to a number of other problems in life functioning. These findings suggest that the role of PTSD in the broader spectrum of life adjustment should be examined. Although the findings described in this report are consistent with the hypothesis that PTSD plays a central role in the pervasive life maladjustment of trauma victims, much additional analysis remains to be done before that hypothesis is firmly established.

Whereas analyses of the relationship of PTSD to nonpsychological aspects of life functioning are one way in which the broader impact of PTSD can be assessed, another is to examine the secondary impact of PTSD: the impact on others in the lives of people who have PTSD. Chapter X of this report provided a first look at this issue. However, there are a variety of other questions that can be examined.

- What are the specific patterns of disruptions of adjustment in children of those with PTSD and how are these different from problems in adjustment of the children of parents with other psychiatric illnesses?
- What are the perceptions about communication patterns on the part of the spouse with PTSD as compared with the spouse married to someone with PTSD, and in what ways might this influence treatment decisions (for example, couples therapy)?
- What is the role of racial/ethnic factors in family structure and family functioning that produce different types of adjustment problems for those with PTSD and their loved ones?

PATHS TO SEEKING HELP

An essential policy step, once the scope of a problem is defined and the magnitude of the service need assessed, is the development of a realistic plan for provision of services and implementation of treatment programs. Chapter IX of this report has presented some of the information required to inform treatment planning policy. There are, nonetheless, additional issues regarding utilization of both health and mental health services that could profitably be explored using the NVVRS data.

- What are the regional differences in patterns of utilization, adjusted for the level of need?
- What is the influence of racial/ethnic factors in health-care utilization, both in the general health and the specialty mental-health-care sectors?
- What are the "unmet" needs in terms of mental health services as well as medical services, based on descriptions of physical health problems?

- What factors appear to facilitate or inhibit utilization of services, such that a new model for the provision of services might be developed?
- What is the influence of psychiatric disorders on the utilization of health and mental health services, and what impact might clear specification of co-occurring disorders have on the design of treatment provisions?

IMPROVING WAYS OF DETECTING PTSD

One of the major features of the Readjustment Study is the use of multiple measures in formulating the PTSD diagnosis. As a result, we gained a great deal of experience with a variety of measures, using different methods, sources of information, etc. Systematic examination of those data would result in improved methods of assessment for PTSD for both clinical and community research uses. Among the important uses of the data in this regard are:

- What is the optimum instrument or set of instruments for use in identifying PTSD cases in a community setting?
- What is the optimum instrument or method for assessing the severity of specific traumatic events and their salience to PTSD?
- How can structured clinical interviewing be modified to increase the sensitivity to PTSD?
- What brief screening scales can be used in clinical situations to help improve identification of PTSD in the clinic?

SCIENTIFIC AND METHODOLOGICAL ISSUES

Finally, the Readjustment Study database is useful for examining a vast array of scientific and methodological issues. Many aspects of the Readjustment Study design represent methodological innovations whose full implications should be examined in detail. Some examples of such aspects include the theater and era veteran sample designs, the two-stage approach to the clinical subsample, the methods used in creating warzone stress indices, and the methods used in making the PTSD diagnosis. The Readjustment Study database is fertile ground for investigating many methodological issues. Among those that are of immediate interest are:

- What is the correspondence between survey- and clinically based diagnoses for disorders other than PTSD?
- What is the correspondence between self-reported and collateral-reported psychiatric symptom information?

- What is the impact of alternative conceptualizations of war-zone-stress exposure?
- Does a past history of mental health treatment significantly affect people's survey interview report of psychiatric symptoms?
- Do the conclusions about psychiatric disorder prevalence and mental health service use based on information collected in a survey interview differ from those based on information collected by a mental health clinician?

SUMMARY

To summarize, the breadth of the Readjustment Study's Congressional mandate required collection of a substantial amount of data. While this report presents a massive amount of information, the findings presented represent only the tip of the proverbial iceberg. We have presented descriptive findings concerning a wide variety of aspects of life adjustment, because the mandate indicated a needs assessment focus: How many veterans have what kinds of readjustment problems? It is important to realize, however, that to meet fully the study's multiple objectives, much more data had to be collected than have been presented in this report. The Readjustment Study database contains data that have not yet been summarized, and many of the findings that have been presented should ultimately be more fully analyzed. The most obvious first step in such analysis is to examine the many readjustment outcomes in a multivariate framework that would permit enhanced understanding of the phenomena. We intend to pursue such analysis, and hope that others will join in that pursuit.

CHAPTER XII

Overview

The complexity of issues addressed in a study of this magnitude are by now self-evident. The level of detail in findings and interpretation at once clarify and overwhelm. The following overview is offered to provide access to a more general, thematic perspective of the study.

OVERVIEW OF FINDINGS KEYED TO
SPECIFIC ISSUES OF PUBLIC LAW 98-160

The Congressional mandate for the National Vietnam Veterans Readjustment Study required that certain specific issues be addressed. In this chapter, we present findings keyed to the specific issues raised.

The Prevalence of Post-Traumatic Stress Disorder Among Vietnam Veterans

One of the major scientific challenges of conducting the NVVRS was the development of a reliable and valid method for identifying cases of PTSD. To address this problem, and ultimately to increase the accuracy of the NVVRS estimates of PTSD prevalence, we included *multiple* PTSD measures in the study. We took this approach in acknowledgment of the fact that no *single* PTSD assessment is completely error-free. Therefore, instead of relying on a single PTSD diagnostic indicator, current PTSD diagnoses in the NVVRS were made on the basis of information from multiple indicators. The PTSD diagnosis based on information from multiple indicators is called the *composite* diagnosis. It is the *convergence* of information across PTSD indicators, and the cross-measure confirmation of the diagnosis that results from a multimeasure "triangulation" approach, that provides the foundation for the credibility of the NVVRS PTSD prevalence estimates. This "multimeasure triangulation approach" did *not* specify a positive diagnosis if only one of the measures suggested the presence of PTSD, a strategy sometimes employed when multiple measures are used. Rather, under the procedure employed by the NVVRS, a conflict among multiple measures might lead to either a "negative" or a "positive" diagnosis, depending on the preponderance of evidence.

To address the "service needs assessment" aspect of the Congressional mandate, we have presented prevalence estimates for two "types" of PTSD: the full PTSD syndrome and "partial" PTSD. Estimates of the prevalence of "partial" PTSD are estimates of the percent whose stress-reaction symptoms are of either insufficient intensity or breadth to qualify as the full PTSD syndrome and yet still may warrant professional attention. People with partial PTSD today may have had a full syndrome in the past that is currently in partial remission, or they may have never met the full criteria for the disorder. Nevertheless, they do have clinically significant stress-reaction symptoms that could benefit from treatment. Thus, they represent an additional component of the total spectrum of potential "need for treatment."

Additionally, we have presented prevalence rates with respect to two specific reference periods: *current* prevalence and *lifetime* prevalence. Current PTSD prevalence is the percent of those who have the disorder *today*, whereas the lifetime prevalence rate is the percent who have met the diagnostic criteria for the PTSD diagnosis at some time during their lives (including those who currently have the disorder). Taken together, lifetime and current prevalence of full and partial PTSD provide a relatively complete picture of the stress-reaction sequelae of exposure to trauma.

NVVRS findings indicate that 15.2 percent of all male Vietnam theater veterans are current cases of PTSD. This represents about 479,000 of the estimated 3.14 million men who served in the Vietnam theater. Among Vietnam theater veteran women, current prevalence is estimated to be 8.5 percent of the approximately 7,200 women who served, or about 610 current cases.

For both males and females, current PTSD prevalence rates for theater veterans are consistently higher than rates for comparable era veterans (2.5 percent male, 1.1 percent female) or civilian counterparts (1.2 percent male, 0.3 percent female). These differences are even more striking when Vietnam era veterans and civilians are compared with the subgroup of Vietnam theater veterans exposed to high levels of war-zone stress. Rates of PTSD among the latter are dramatically higher than those observed among theater veterans exposed to low or moderate levels of war-zone stress.

Among male theater veterans, differences in current PTSD prevalence rates were also found among the racial/ethnic subgroups. The current PTSD prevalence rate is 27.9 percent among Hispanics, 20.6 percent among Blacks, and 13.7 percent among Whites/others.

Additionally, NVVRS findings indicate that the *current* prevalence of *partial* PTSD is 11.1 percent among male theater veterans and 7.8 percent among female theater veterans. Together, this represents about 350,000 veterans—in addition to the 480,000 with the full PTSD syndrome today—who have trauma-related symptoms that may benefit from professional treatment.

NVVRS findings indicate that the *lifetime* prevalence of PTSD is 30.9 percent among male theater veterans and 26.9 percent among females. The *lifetime* prevalence of *partial* PTSD among male theater veterans is 22.5 percent, and among female theater veterans is 21.2 percent. These findings mean that over the course of their lives, more than half of male theater veterans and nearly half of female theater veterans have experienced clinically significant stress reaction symptoms. This represents about 1.7 million veterans of the Vietnam war.

A comparison of the current and lifetime PTSD prevalence rates shows that about one-half of the male theater veterans and one-third of the female theater veterans who have *ever* had PTSD *still* have it today. Also, of those theater veterans who have ever had significant stress-reaction symptoms (full or partial PTSD), about half of males and one-third of females are experiencing some degree of clinically significant stress-reaction symptoms today. These findings are consistent with the conceptualization of PTSD as a chronic, rather than acute, disorder.

Thus, Vietnam theater veterans as a group are much more "at risk" for having PTSD than are era veterans or civilian counterparts. This leads to an important question: What is it about the characteristics or experiences of Vietnam veterans that puts them at risk? The contrasts of PTSD prevalence rates between theater veterans and the era veteran and civilian counterpart comparison groups provide some information in this regard. However, those comparisons are not completely satisfying, because whether or not an individual served in the military and/or was sent to Vietnam was not a random event. On the contrary, many powerful social forces operated to determine who served in the military, and, within the military, who served in Vietnam. Because of this nonrandom assignment, differences that we observe today in current PTSD prevalence among the study groups *may* be attributable to differences in the experiences of the groups (for example, service in Vietnam), but they may also result from differences in some characteristics or experiences that theater veterans *brought with them* to their military service.

We conducted a series of multivariate statistical analyses to assess the role of a large group of potential predisposing factors in current PTSD prevalence. In addition, we extended the analyses to assess the contribution of exposure to war-zone stress to current PTSD prevalence among theater veterans after the effect of predisposing factors had been taken into account.

Results of these multivariate analyses indicated that theater veterans differed from era veterans and civilian counterparts on some background characteristics that might have rendered theater veterans more vulnerable to the development of PTSD. Nevertheless, the current PTSD prevalence rate is much higher among theater veterans even after these differences in potential predisposing factors are taken into account. Additionally, the analyses showed clearly that exposure to war-zone stress in Vietnam plays a significant role in determining who among theater veterans has PTSD today, even after a broad array of potential predisposing factors have been taken into account.

Taken together, these results are consistent with a model of PTSD that posits a role for individual vulnerability (potentially including biological, psychological, and sociodemographic predisposing factors) *and* a role for exposure to environmental factors (specifically, war-zone stressors) in determining who among theater veterans gets PTSD. However, it is clear that exposure to war-zone stress makes a substantial contribution to the development of PTSD in war veterans that is independent of a broad range of potential predisposing factors.

The Prevalence of Other Postwar Psychological Problems Among Vietnam Veterans

While the primary focus of the Readjustment Study was to establish the prevalence of PTSD among Vietnam veterans, Public Law 98–160 also clearly expressed a parallel focus on the prevalence of other problems in readjusting to civilian life. These were referred to as other "postwar psychological problems." Although the range of such problems that might have been examined is extremely broad, the Readjustment Study sought to establish the prevalence of other postwar psychological problems in two basic classes: (1) other forms of psychiatric disorder (in addition to PTSD) as defined in DSM-III; and (2) more general forms of personal or psychological problems, ranging from general psychological distress to malfunctions in marital or family roles to violent or criminal behavior.

The prevalence of psychiatric disorders other than PTSD was assessed in the National Survey of the Vietnam Generation by the Diagnostic Interview Schedule (DIS), from which *lifetime* (*ever* had the disorder) and *current* (within the past six months) prevalence rates were assessed among Vietnam veterans and their peers for nine specific disorders. (These disorders are described in Chapter VI.) NSVG prevalence rate estimates for these psychiatric disorders among male Vietnam theater veterans are as follows:

	Ever Had the Disorder	*Had the Disorder In the Past Six Months*
Affective disorders		
Major depressive episode	5.1	2.8
Manic episode	0.8	0.7
Dysthymia	4.2	—
Anxiety disorders		
Panic disorder	1.8	0.9
Obsessive compulsive disorder	1.8	1.5
Generalized anxiety disorder	14.1	4.5
Substance-abuse disorders		
Alcohol abuse or dependence	39.2	11.2
Drug abuse or dependence	5.7	1.8
Antisocial personality disorder	9.5	2.0

Alcohol abuse or dependence and generalized anxiety disorder were by far the most prevalent disorders, both currently and in the past, among men who served in the Vietnam theater. Overall, almost half (49.1 percent) of Vietnam theater veterans met the criteria for at least one of these disorders at some point in their lives, and over one in six (17.1 percent) had at least one disorder currently (within the past six months). Since alcohol abuse or dependence accounted for a substantial proportion of these "any disorder" rates, overall rates excluding alcohol disorders were also examined. When alcohol disorders are excluded, over one-fourth (26.5 percent) of Vietnam theater veteran men have had at least one of the other disorders at some time in their lives, and just under one in 11 (8.6 percent) currently have at least one such disorder.

In general, however, such rates were *not* substantially higher than those observed among Vietnam era veterans (45.8 percent lifetime and 13.3 percent current for "any disorder"; 24.3 percent lifetime and 5.2 percent current for "any disorder," excluding alcohol disorders), except for a current major depressive episode and current obsessive compulsive disorder. In contrast, there were several disorders for which rates of lifetime or current disorder among Vietnam theater veteran men were significantly higher than for their civilian counterparts, including lifetime rates of major depression, dysthymia, obsessive compulsive disorder, alcohol abuse or dependence, and antisocial personality disorder, as well as current rates of major depressive episode and antisocial personality disorder.

Moreover, among those most heavily involved in the war—those exposed to high levels of war-zone stress—rates of psychiatric disorder other than PTSD were substantially higher: almost two-thirds (63.3 percent) had experienced one of these nine disorders at some time in their lives, and almost half of these (29.8 percent) currently had at least one such disorder. Even when alcohol disorders are excluded, these rates are still 43.1 and 18.0 percent respectively. Looking across all types of disorder, with few exceptions, Vietnam theater veteran men exposed to high levels of war-zone stress exhibited significantly higher rates of psychiatric disorder than either Vietnam era veterans or the civilian counterparts.

Based on these results, it appears that having served in Vietnam per se (as compared with serving elsewhere in the military during the Vietnam era) did not greatly increase one's risk of psychiatric disorder other than PTSD. However, the number of psychiatric disorders for which theater veteran rates were significantly higher than civilians (though not era veterans) suggests that serving in the military during that time period may well have been a risk factor (or at least a correlate) in its own right for certain types of psychiatric disorder. By far the most important risk factor for virtually all of these disorders, however, was direct and intensive participation in the war and the resulting high exposure to combat and other dimensions of war-zone stress. By comparison with either their era veteran and civilian peers or with fellow veterans serving in the Vietnam theater who were exposed to low or moderate levels of war stress, Vietnam theater veteran men with high levels of exposure to war-zone stress have clearly been subject to higher rates of psychiatric disorder in their lives even when PTSD (per se) is not considered.

Among the more general forms of personal or psychological functioning examined were nonspecific psychological distress and general problems of readjusting to civilian life. Almost 17 percent of Vietnam theater veterans reported very high current levels of general psychological distress. A substantial minority (44.5 percent) of men who served in Vietnam also reported having had at least one serious postwar readjustment problem, and approximately 60 percent of those who have ever had such problems (26.0 percent) reported that they have continued to experience at least one such problem. Overall, then, approximately one in four Vietnam theater veterans currently has at least one serious readjustment problem, and approximately 6 percent have four or more. However, Vietnam theater veterans were not significantly higher than their era veteran counterparts on *either* of these measures of postwar psychological problems. In contrast, those exposed to high levels of combat and other war stress reported significantly higher levels of nonspecific distress and readjustment problems than Vietnam era veterans or other Vietnam theater veterans exposed to lower levels of war-zone stress. One-third (32.2 percent) of the men serving in Vietnam and exposed to high war stress scored at the highest level on nonspecific distress. Over two-thirds reported having had at least one serious readjustment problem, and almost one-fourth reported having had four or more. Also, over four in ten (42.1 percent) currently have at least one such problem.

Similarly, 40 percent of Vietnam theater veteran men have been divorced at least once (10 percent had two or more divorces), 14.1 percent report high levels of marital problems, and 23.1 percent have high levels of parental problems. One in 12 reports being very unhappy or dissatisfied with life, one in eight is extremely isolated from other people, and one in ten has been homeless or vagrant at some time during life. Over one Vietnam veteran in four scored high on active expression of hostility, and 46.8 percent had committed at least one violent act during the past year (9.4 percent having committed 13 or more). In each case, however, the prevalence rates of these problems or behaviors for Vietnam theater veterans were not very different from the rates for veterans who served elsewhere during the Vietnam era. Also, in each case, however, Vietnam veterans exposed to high levels of war stress had significantly higher rates of these problems than era veterans, civilians, and Vietnam theater veterans with low to moderate levels of war stress exposure. For example, Vietnam veterans exposed to high war-zone stress were twice as likely as those exposed to lower levels of war stress to be very unhappy or unsatisfied with their lives (12.5 versus 6.2 percent), to be highly isolated from others (21.7 versus 9.7 percent), and to have committed 13 or more violent acts during the past year (14.4 versus 7.6 percent). Thus the subset of Vietnam veterans who most literally and directly fought the war were also at high risk for the development of a broad array of other postwar psychological or readjustment problems.

The Relationship Between PTSD and Other Postwar Psychological Problems

In addition to establishing the prevalence of PTSD and of other "postwar psychological problems" among Vietnam veterans, the Congressional mandate also specified that information be collected on the relationship between PTSD and these other types of problems. A more basic way of asking this question is: What does it *mean* to be a Vietnam veteran with PTSD? What types of other problems do such men have, and what is the overall quality of their lives?

Other than the obviously debilitating nature of PTSD symptoms in and of themselves, NVVRS findings indicate that Vietnam veterans with PTSD lead profoundly disrupted lives. Whether this indicates a profound impact of PTSD on the development of other adjustment problems, that those with prior adjustment problems are more prone to PTSD, or that PTSD and other adjustment problems share common risk factors—all of which are undoubtedly true to some degree—has not as yet been thoroughly explored with these data. Nevertheless, the evidence presented in this report serves to underline the nagging suspicion derived from previous research on more limited samples that having PTSD is associated with other problems in virtually every domain of these veterans' lives.

Men who served in the Vietnam theater and who currently suffer from PTSD were significantly less well adjusted than those who do not currently meet criteria for this disorder on almost every indicator of postwar psychological adjustment included in the NSVG. It is important to note that included among the latter are some men who suffered from the full-blown disorder at some time previously in their lives, some who currently (still) have significant PTSD symptomatology (i.e., partial PTSD), and others who suffer from psychiatric disorders other than PTSD. Nevertheless, differences between these two groups are striking, and they are remarkably consistent. For example, well over half (55.8 percent) of the men with PTSD score at the highest levels of nonspecific psychological distress, compared with less than 10 percent (9.5) of those without PTSD. Similarly, virtually all veterans with PTSD suffered from at least one other psychiatric disorder at some time during their lives (three-fourths even if one excludes alcohol disorders) and *half* (40.6 percent if alcohol disorders are excluded) currently suffer from at least one other disorder (comparable figures for those without PTSD were 40.6 and 11.5 respectively). Vietnam veteran men with PTSD had significantly higher rates of both lifetime and current disorder for every specific psychiatric diagnostic assessed in the NSVG.

In turn, this pattern of disorder appears to have penetrated virtually every other area of these veterans' lives. Overall, 97 percent reported having at least one serious readjustment problem since leaving the military, and over one-third (35.6 percent) reported four or more. Seven of ten (69.7 percent) have at least one such problem currently, and over one in five (22.1 percent) have four or more. Veterans with PTSD are five times more likely than those without to be unemployed, and one in five has a history of extreme postmilitary occupational instability. Almost one-fourth are currently separated or living with someone as though they were married, 70 percent have been divorced (35 percent two or more times), 49 percent have high levels of marital or relationship problems, 55 percent have high levels of problems with parenting, and half report poor levels of overall family functioning. One in four is very unhappy or dissatisfied with his life, almost half (47.3 percent) report extreme levels of isolation from other people, and 34.8 percent have been homeless or vagrant at one time or another. Four in ten also report high levels of actively expressed hostility, and 36.8 percent had committed six or more acts of violence during the past year (19.8 percent had committed 13 or more). Almost half had been arrested or in jail at least once—34.2 percent more than once—and 11.5 percent had been convicted of a felony. In every instance, these rates for Vietnam veterans with PTSD are at least *twice* the rate of men not currently suffering from the disorder, and often the ratio is considerably higher.

The Relationship Between Service-Connected Disabilities and Postwar Psychological Problems

An estimated 11 percent of Vietnam theater veterans have a current service-connected disability (SCPD). Thus, approximately 346,000 Vietnam theater veterans have been officially certified by the Veterans Administration as having one or more service-connected physical disabilities.

Vietnam theater veterans with SCPDs were significantly more likely than those without to have current PTSD. Specifically, an estimated 21.4 percent of Vietnam theater veterans with SCPDs met criteria for a current diagnosis of PTSD compared with 14.5 percent of theater veterans without SCPDs. Yet theater veterans with SCPDs were no more likely than those without SCPDs to suffer a variety of other major psychological disorders, including affective disorders (major depressive episode, manic episode, and dysthymia), several anxiety disorders (panic disorder and obsessive-compulsive disorder), substance abuse or dependence, and antisocial personality disorder. One important exception, however, is that theater veterans with an SCPD were more likely to have suffered from generalized anxiety disorder than their counterparts without SCPDs. Theater veterans with SCPDs were also more likely currently to suffer from nonspecific psychological distress than their counterparts without SCPDs. In addition, theater veterans with SCPDs were more likely than theater veterans without SCPDs to be unemployed, to report higher levels of occupational instability, to have never been married, and to report that they were unhappy or dissatisfied with their lives.

In sum, findings from the NSVG indicate that Vietnam theater veterans with service-connected disabilities are almost 50 percent more likely than those without SCPDs to have PTSD today. In addition, those with SCPDs are more likely to have a positive history of generalized anxiety disorder, to have symptoms of nonspecific psychological distress, and to be dissatisfied with their current life circumstances. This findings clearly suggest that Vietnam theater veterans with service-connected physical disabilities are at elevated risk for a variety of readjustment problems.

The Relationship Between Alcohol and Drug Abuse and Postwar Psychological Problems

As described earlier, the estimated lifetime prevalence of alcohol abuse or dependence among male theater veterans is 39.2 percent, and the estimate for current alcohol abuse or dependence is 11.2 percent. The corresponding estimates for lifetime and current drug abuse or dependence are 5.7 percent and 1.8 percent respectively.

Male theater veterans with current PTSD are two to six times as likely to abuse alcohol or drugs as those without the disorder (22.2 percent versus 9.2 percent for current alcohol abuse dependence and 6.1 percent versus 1.0 percent for current drug abuse). These figures corroborate the clinical impression of high comorbidity of PTSD with alcohol and drug abuse and underscore the need for coordinated treatment programs.

A strong association is also found between having had a substance abuse disorder (that is, either an alcohol or drug disorder) and the presence of other postwar psychological problems. Male theater veterans with lifetime substance abuse are four to five times more likely to have a lifetime or current major depressive episode or lifetime dysthymia than those without these substance abuse disorders. Much higher rates are also seen for both lifetime and current manic episode, panic disorder, and generalized anxiety disorder. These results are consistent with the hypothesis that individuals with psychiatric disorders such as these self-medicate in an attempt to ameliorate their symptoms. Male theater veterans with lifetime substance abuse are also four to six times more likely to meet criteria for antisocial personality disorder (ASP), a finding that parallels other results in studies of nonveteran populations of a high co-occurrence of substance abuse in those with ASP.

With regard to general indexes of adjustment, male theater veterans who meet the criteria for lifetime substance abuse have greater numbers of serious postmilitary and current readjustment problems, are less likely to have completed either high school or college, are more likely to be currently not working, and to have higher levels of occupational instability. They are also less likely to be currently married and more likely to have had multiple divorces, and they report greater difficulties in marital and parental role functioning. They also report being more socially isolated, exhibiting more violence, and having overall lower levels of subjective well-being.

In conclusion, it appears that veterans who, at some time in their lives, have met the criteria for an alcohol abuse or dependence disorder or a drug abuse or dependence disorder show significantly more impairment on almost every measure of postwar adjustment and psychological well-being than those who never became heavily involved with psychoactive substances.

CHAPTER XIII

Epilogue: "A Self-Guide for Vietnam Veterans"

by David A. Grady

Historically the epilogue is a dramatic device used in theater. It is a commentary upon a play, which is delivered following the production. An epilogue allows the author to speak to the audience outside the body of the actual work. The purpose is usually to present further dialogue to make the work more meaningful. Following this tradition, Chapter XIII is meant to serve as a kind of epilogue—to provide commentary that goes beyond the study it follows with the expressed goal of making that work more valuable to you, the audience.

This chapter is written specifically for veterans and those who care about their readjustment. It avoids, as much as possible, the use of jargon and data in making its points. In addition to further clarification of topics already presented, the chapter contains new material that expands upon that found in the study. A summary of the study's major findings is provided, as is a more detailed explanation of post-traumatic stress disorder and a historical context for understanding the psychological readjustment of Vietnam veterans. Finally, solutions for those who need help for their readjustment problems, particularly PTSD, are offered.

DAVID A. GRADY, PSY. D., is a twice-wounded, disabled Vietnam combat veteran who served as a rifleman with the Fifth Marine Regiment in 1968. He has done extensive professional work with the Vietnam veteran population concerning readjustment problems—including post-traumatic stress disorder—and other issues. In addition to vast experience in research, consultation, and education in the area of readjustment, Dr. Grady is an active lobbyist on behalf of veterans, working toward more effective programs to meet their needs.

THE IMPORTANCE OF THE NVVRS

The National Vietnam Veterans Readjustment Study (NVVRS) stands as arguably the finest mental health epidemiologic study ever completed. It represents a significant advance compared with previous large-scale studies of Vietnam veterans' psychological readjustment (i.e., Centers for Disease Control Vietnam Experience Study, 1988; Egendorf, Kadushin, Laufer, Rothbart, & Sloan, 1981). The value of this study comes from the quality of its sample and the ambitious and rigorous manner in which it conceptualized and measured psychological readjustment and postwar psychological problems including post-traumatic stress disorder (PTSD). The study sample is clearly the most representative group of Vietnam veterans yet employed by researchers, and as such it allows for a high degree of confidence in its findings. It can be assumed that the readjustment of the veterans documented in this study is likely quite comparable to that of all other living Vietnam veterans. In addition, the study utilized the best existing measures of war-zone stress, PTSD, and other postwar psychological problems. When necessary it developed more accurate measures of these variables. It also utilized multiple measures for important variables, the most important of which being PTSD, in order to be sensitive to their presence. The NVVRS has through its creative approach both extended earlier research and set the standard for future studies.

Major Findings

Although very complex, the NVVRS can be distilled into some simple truths about the readjustment of Vietnam veterans today. Though such an endeavor does not do justice to the study as a whole, it allows us, freed from many details, to focus on the larger picture. Following are six significant findings that are central to understanding Vietnam veterans' current readjustment.

Most Vietnam Veterans Have Successfully Readjusted

The NVVRS's most important finding is that today the majority of veterans who served in Southeast Asia have, through whatever pain and suffering they experienced, successfully readjusted and become contributing members of society. They currently experience few symptoms of PTSD or other readjustment problems. This has to be gratifying to all who care about Vietnam veterans' mental health.

A Significant Minority Continue to Suffer as a Result of Vietnam

In a similar sense, the realization that a significant minority currently have PTSD, significant stress-reaction symptoms, or other postwar psychological problems must command the attention of all who are concerned about the welfare of America's veterans. The realization that at some point in their lives almost a third of male and over a quarter of female Vietnam veterans had diagnosable PTSD, and that today almost half of these men and a third of these women still suffer from it, is sobering. The finding that these veterans lead profoundly disrupted lives is cause for great alarm.

Those Who Fought the War Continue to Suffer the Most

Those men and women who endured the most trauma during the war are today the most likely to be experiencing psychological problems as a result. This is true with respect to stress symptoms, PTSD, other psychiatric conditions, physical health problems, and the other postwar readjustment problems assessed. This group is also the most likely to have used physical and mental health services.

Not All Are at Equal Risk for Experiencing PTSD

Overall, Black and Hispanic veterans have experienced more mental health and life adjustment problems following service in Vietnam than have White veterans. Substantial differences in PTSD prevalence rates exist among the various minority groups. In particular, Hispanic male veterans are more likely to currently have PTSD. In general, the rates for male Vietnam veterans are higher than for females on all measures of psychological problems.

Those Involved With Troubled Veterans Have Themselves
Become Casualties

A particularly tragic finding was that those who are close to a veteran with PTSD also become casualties of the disorder. Spouses and partners report more general psychological distress and less happiness and satisfaction with their lives. Children tend to have more behavior problems. The suffering of these families is only now being recognized.

Most Affected Veterans Are Not Currently Receiving Treatment

Today the most affected group of veterans, both male and female, are those who were exposed to high levels of war-zone stress, those who developed PTSD, and those with a substance abuse disorder during their lifetime. The majority of these veterans are not currently receiving treatment for these problems. Undoubtedly this contributes to the high current prevalence rates for stress-reaction symptoms and PTSD.

It is appropriate here to remind the reader that a great deal of analysis of the data collected for this study remains to be completed. This initial report was intended solely to meet the statuatory obligations of the research team. Many of the perhaps most promising analyses remain to be completed on the currently existing database. Chapter XI presented some of the intriguing questions that remain to be answered.

At this point you may be feeling a need for more information about PTSD. You may want to know why such a problem exists and if it is a new condition. You may be thinking about your own difficulties, or those of a loved one, readjusting following the war. You may be thinking, "What do I do now?" or "Where do I go for help?" Answers to these questions and others follow.

POST-TRAUMATIC STRESS DISORDERS IN VIETNAM VETERANS

> Sacrificing a portion of your
>   consciousness so you won't have
>   to deal with
>   Being there
>   and
>   building mental blocks
>   so you won't have to deal with
>   having been there.

(Al Hubbard as cited in Haley, 1974)

Post-traumatic stress disorder (PTSD) is the most severe form of reaction to a traumatic life event. It is officially recognized (APA, 1987) as the development of a characteristic symptom pattern in an individual following the experience of a psychologically traumatic life event. Such an event is also known as a traumatic stressor. The traumatic stressor is considered to be the *cause* of, that is, it provides both the necessary and sufficient conditions for, the subsequent development of PTSD. Post-traumatic stress disorder is *not* considered a mental illness but a natural reaction to an overwhelmingly stressful, even catastrophic, event. PTSD develops some time after the danger or horror is over.

Traumatic stressors are events that are outside the range of usual human experience. A traumatic stressor would be expected to be markedly distressing to almost anyone experiencing it. Such experiences often involve overwhelming fear, devastating loss, and exposure to the grotesqueness possible in human existence. One professional has defined traumatization as the experience of becoming an object. Examples of traumatic stressors that sometimes cause PTSD include: a serious threat to one's life or physical integrity; a serious threat or harm to one's children, spouse, or other close relatives and friends; sudden destruction of one's home or community; and seeing another person who has recently been, or is being, seriously injured or killed as the result of an accident or physical violence. In the case of Vietnam veterans, the traumatic events occurred while in the Southeast Asian war zone, usually in combat, but also in other life-threatening or shocking situations. Many Vietnam veterans experienced multiple traumatic experiences, as well as enduring the cumulative effects of war-zone stress in general.

The PTSD syndrome (i.e., pattern of related symptoms) of Vietnam veterans has also been labeled post-Vietnam syndrome or delayed stress reaction by some. It is important to realize that anyone can develop PTSD following any type of traumatic experience. Vietnam veterans represent only one group of individuals who are currently experiencing this problem.

Not everyone who is traumatized develops PTSD. We know that following traumatization there is a necessary recovery period in which the event is psychologically processed, or "digested," so that a personal meaning for the experience is developed. This meaning allows the survivor to integrate the experience into an understanding of who he or she is and what the world is. When this occurs the recovery is complete and the individual can move on in life. When this process is blocked or breaks down, psychological problems, including PTSD, can develop. Whether individuals complete or fail to complete recovery following traumatization appears to be a function of who they are, the nature of the trauma, and the nature of their recovery environment. Some individuals have more coping resources than others and are therefore better able to manage the impact of a traumatic experience. Some types of trauma are routinely more destructive to those who survive them. The routinized traumatization inherently found in war zones has always challenged veterans' capacity to recover. Finally, the nature of a recovery environment, supportive or nonsupportive of recovery, impacts on survivors as they attempt to put the pieces together following their traumatization. Many feel that the nonsupportive society to which Vietnam veterans returned following their service was in part responsible for the psychological problems they later encountered.

Post-traumatic stress disorder is the most severe though by no means the only psychological difficulty possible, following traumatization. To be diagnosed as *currently* experiencing PTSD you must have experienced each of the following three symptoms for more than a month.

Symptoms

The first symptom is a persistent, unwanted reexperiencing of Vietnam-related material or intense psychological distress when exposed to reminders of Vietnam. The reexperiencing can include thoughts, ideas, images, feelings, dreams or fantasies that focus on or touch upon some aspect of your traumatic experiences in Vietnam. Any reminder of Vietnam experiences can produce extreme distress: thoughts or pictures of Vietnam unexpectedly entering your mind; sights (e.g., treelines), sounds (e.g., whoosh of helicopter blades), or smells (e.g., odor of diesel fuel). Anything you associate with Vietnam might trigger a painful reexperiencing of some events or feelings you had there. You might experience flashbacks during which you feel and/or act as if you were actually back in Vietnam (for example, you might react inappropriately with survival tactics in a stressful situation). The lack of control over when and how intensely your Vietnam-related material is reexperienced and the inability to prevent significant distress when so reminded are crucial aspects of this symptom.

The second symptom is a persistent avoidance of stimuli associated with Vietnam or a more general numbing of responsiveness to the external world. This symptom often results in social isolation and feelings of alienation from society. This sense of estrangement from others would not have been present (at least to the same degree) before service in Vietnam. This symptom has been labeled "psychic numbing" or "emotional anesthesia" by some, and examples include: efforts to avoid thoughts or feelings associated with the trauma; efforts to avoid activities or situations that arouse recollections of the trauma; an inability to recall an important aspect of the trauma (also known as psychogenic amnesia); a markedly diminished interest in significant life activities (such as family, work, or hobbies); a feeling of detachment or estrangement from others; an inability to feel emotions of any type, especially those feelings associated with intimacy; and a sense of a foreshortened future. An inability to feel comfortable with people even when desired is a crucial aspect of this symptom.

The third symptom is really a collection of cognitive, emotional, and behavioral conditions related to increased arousal that occur in PTSD. At least *two* of the following conditions (which would not have been present to the same degree before service in Vietnam) *must* be present: (1) difficulty falling or staying asleep; (2) irritability or outbursts of anger; (3) difficulty concentrating; (4) hypervigilance (extreme alertness and watchfulness); (5) an exaggerated startle response (extreme reaction to sudden and unexpected stimuli); (6) physiological reactivity (such as increased heart or breathing rates) when exposed to events that resemble or symbolize a salient aspect of traumatic Vietnam experiences.

To summarize, if you are currently experiencing post-traumatic stress disorder, you will have experienced a traumatic experience while in Southeast Asia, that is, combat or other life-threatening or horrific situations. As a result, for more than a month you will have: (A) suffered from recurrent, involuntary reexperiencing of Vietnam-related material or significant distress when reminded of Vietnam; (B) been persistent in your avoidance of Vietnam reminders or experienced a more general numbing or responsiveness to your environment and the people in it, and (C) had an increased level of arousal as indicated by at least *two* of the six problems listed above. It is important to note that PTSD can develop after a long, seemingly problem free period, even many years following your service in Southeast Asia.

However, it is possible to have only "partial PTSD." Others have called this "sub-clinical PTSD." In the NVVRS, partial PTSD meant that three to five PTSD symptoms were present that could potentially benefit from professional help. Such conditions can be as painful and as disruptive as the full PTSD syndrome. Partial PTSD may represent a formerly full PTSD in partial remission or the early stages of the development of a full PTSD. It may also be a limited form of stress reaction that will not evolve into something more.

It is important to remember that PTSD is not the only painful legacy of service in Southeast Asia. There are many other unresolved emotional issues still haunting many veterans. One common problem related to war-zone PTSD is what is known as "survivor's guilt." This involves feelings of guilt about the fact that you survived when others did not or about something you did, or didn't do, in order to survive. Though survivor's guilt is no longer considered a necessary part of PTSD, it afflicts veterans with and without PTSD. It can be quite painful and disruptive and may require professional help for resolution to take place.

The intensity of PTSD symptoms can vary greatly over time. The level of impairment in functioning caused by PTSD can be mild or it can completely disrupt every aspect of one's existence. Over time symptoms can fluctuate, stay the same, or become progressively more disruptive. As the NVVRS has shown, for many Vietnam veterans PTSD has become a chronic condition. Many veterans may not be sure that their current problems are directly related to their Vietnam experiences. Powerful psychological defenses, such as denial, may keep awareness of the true conflicts from occurring. Many veterans do not make this connection until they have had treatment. PTSD symptoms are often exacerbated by current life stresses. Your family, friends, and co-workers may in turn be severely affected by, and confused about, your problems and feelings.

There is, as the NVVRS has documented, a very high degree of co-occurrence of other psychiatric conditions and nonspecific distress. Substance abuse, particularly the abuse of alcohol, is commonly found in veterans who have been exposed to high levels of war-zone stress and those with PTSD. Many mental health professionals believe that the alcohol, or other substance, is used by the veteran with PTSD, or other painful symptoms, in an attempt to self-medicate or diminish the stress symptoms and feelings. This coping strategy is doomed to failure, and in the long run, it produces a significant number of problems of it's own independent of the enduring stress symptoms.

In the media many psychological and social problems experienced by Vietnam veterans have been mistakenly attributed to PTSD when in fact these conditions are not formally considered a part of the disorder. Such simplistic labeling confuses the real cause of these problems and has furthered the negative stereotyping of Vietnam veterans commonly found in this culture. Only the symptoms noted above constitute PTSD. However, many of the symptoms of PTSD can indirectly contribute to other problems (such as divorce or unemployment) in a veteran's life following military service. The experience of other life difficulties may relate indirectly to some aspect of Vietnam experiences or to experiences that the veteran may have had since returning home that have come to symbolize what it means to be a Vietnam veteran in our society. They may also be indicative of other problems related to who the veteran is or how he or she copes with problems.

SOME HEAVY BUSINESS

I sometimes find myself wondering, in a sudden panic, whether I'm not in the way of developing great numb patches in my sensibility of which I shall never be cured—even if I do come through this war. Delicacy of feeling. What a wonderful expression! Shall I ever again know what delicacy of feeling is? I may be nervous, irritable, exasperated by trifles, but shall I ever recover that sensitiveness which is the mark of the civilized man? I sometimes see myself in the future transformed into a sort of invalid who has suffered an amputation of all his delicate sentiments, like a man who has lost all his fingers and can only feel things with a couple of stumps. And there will be millions of us like that.

(Romains, 1940)

Combat as the prime occasion of deliberate risks to life and limb imposed severe stress, involving the deepest anxieties and the most primitive threats to personal integrity.

(Stouffer et al., 1949)

It has long been recognized that battle can wound the mind and soul as surely as the limbs. These invisible wounds can be as devastating as any gunshot or explosion. Throughout the ages many have documented both the immediate and the chronic psychological effects of war-zone service. In other times, labels such as shell shock, combat fatigue, and neurosis have been used. These conditions were essentially the same as what we today call PTSD. One of the earliest, yet remarkably contemporary, accounts of the psychological consequences of battle is provided by a non-veteran. In his play "Henry IV, Part I" written in 1597, William Shakespeare recounts, through a concerned wife's soliloquy, the residues of battle past that have afflicted her husband, the warrior Hotspur. Shakespeare's description of his suffering is almost an exact representation of the current conceptualization of post-traumatic stress disorder. (See Exhibit XIII-1.)

The psychological casualties of war have had a tremendous impact on modern psychiatry. The movement to develop today's system of specific diagnostic criteria for all mental disorders was in large part due to the limitations of existing diagnostic systems for adequately diagnosing the war-stress reactions of World War II (APA, 1952). The first edition of such a system, *The Diagnostic and Statistical Manual of Mental Disorders*, or DSM-I (APA, 1952), included the diagnostic category of "gross stress reaction," which was appropriate for war-stress reactions. However, this diagnosis was eliminated in DSM-II (APA, 1968), ironically at the height of the Vietnam war, with no clearly comparable category being substituted. In the DSM-III (APA, 1980), the diagnosis of PTSD was introduced and it

EXHIBIT XIII-1

A trauma survivor's significant others can often recount in exquisite detail their loved one's traumatic residues. Here the warrior Hotspur's legacies of battles past are described by his wife, the Lady Percy.

O, my good lord, why are you thus alone?
For what offence have I this fortnight been
C A banish'd woman from my Harry's bed?
Tell me, sweet lord, what is't that takes from thee
Thy stomach, pleasure
and thy golden sleep?
Why dost thou bend thine eyes upon the earth, **D**
And start so often when thou sit'st alone?
Why hast thou lost the fresh blood in thy cheeks;
C And given my treasures and my rights of thee
To thick-eyed musing and cursed melancholy?
In thy faint slumbers I by thee have watch'd,
And heard thee murmur tales of iron wars;
Speak terms of manage to thy bounding steed;
Cry 'Courage! to the field!' And thou hast talk'd
Of sallies and retires, or trenches, tents,
Of pallisadoes, frontiers, parapets,
Of basilisks, of cannon, culverin,
Of prisoners' ransom and of soldiers slain,
B And all the currents of a heady fight,
Thy spirit within thee hath been so at war
And thus hath so bestirr'd thee in thy sleep,
That beads of sweat have stood upon thy brow,
Like bubbles in a late-disturbed stream;
And in thy face strange motions have appear'd,
Such as we see when men restrain their breath
On some great sudden hest. O, what portents are these?
Some heavy business hath my lord in hand,
And I must know it, else he loves me not.

Act II, Scene III
Henry IV, Part I
William Shakespeare (1597)

B = Intrusive reexperiencing
C = Numbing of responsiveness/reduced involvement with external world
D = Increased arousal

was revised in DSM-III-R (APA, 1987). Research and clinical reports from around the world have confirmed the presence of PTSD in veterans of all cultures and countries.

In addition to providing an impetus for accurate diagnosis, the demands for treatment of large numbers of traumatized veterans spurred the development of effective treatments both for reactions that occurred on the battlefield, as well as those that occurred outside the war zone. Particularly following WW I and WW II great gains were made in diagnosing and treating stress reactions. Sad to say, many of these lessons were forgotten and had to be relearned with Vietnam veterans.

HELP FOR PTSD

The only report that should not be accepted at face value, although one may chose not to challenge it initially, is the patient's report that combat in Vietnam had no effect on him.

(Haley, 1974)

Treatment

Though some veterans have not experienced significant problems related to their Vietnam experiences, others have been able to resolve their problems by themselves or through a supportive family or church. Still others need professional help to finally "come home from the war." Seeking help for whatever problems you continue to have as a result of your service in Southeast Asia is a critical step. At this point, there is effective treatment available for those experiencing stress reactions, including PTSD, and associated conditions. Many veterans have been able to find significant relief after being treated specifically for PTSD.

It is important to note that only a mental health professional can accurately determine if you have PTSD. Caution should be exercised in seeking treatment. Treatment for PTSD is most effective when attempted with a mental health professional who is experienced and knowledgeable about PTSD in general and about war-related PTSD in particular. Finding an individual who is also familiar with the Vietnam war may also facilitate treatment. However, many mental health professionals do not accept the validity of the PTSD diagnosis. Some may be confused about the presence of PTSD because other conditions or issues are present. Still others are not knowledgeable about how to treat PTSD once it is recognized.

The treatment of choice for stress reactions, including PTSD, is psychotherapy (Committee on Veterans Affairs, United States Senate, 1988; Friedman, 1988). This may be provided in an individual or group format. Psychotherapy provides the opportunity to psychologically work through, that is, identify and resolve the conflicts resulting from traumatic war-zone experiences. What is called for is the confronting of memories and emotions from Vietnam that remain undigested. These residuals are responsible for current suffering. The experiences and their meanings can, once worked through, be more fully integrated into the veteran's current psychological makeup. This type of psychotherapy can itself be very painful and disruptive. Often veterans will feel worse before they feel better. However, the long-term payoff is well worth the short-term suffering. This type of psychotherapy can be accomplished in a number of ways.

An important part of effective treatment for PTSD is being able to talk with other veterans who share your experiences both over there and since returning home. This can be done as a formal part of treatment in rap groups or group therapy, or it can be accomplished informally through joining veterans organizations or finding other Vietnam veterans with whom to talk.

For some veterans, medication is a useful adjunct to the psychotherapy. It can provide relief from distressing symptoms of anxiety and depression and thereby facilitate treatment for those veterans who could not tolerate the psychotherapy without it. Medication alone, however, is never sufficient to alleviate the suffering found in war-related PTSD.

Treatment Resources

The Department of Veterans Affairs is the acknowledged expert in diagnosing and treating war-related PTSD and associated conditions. The Chief Medical Director of the DVA has stated before Congress that the organization remains, ". . . committed to ongoing excellence in treating the psychological as well as the physical trauma of war . . . that all relevant staff should be skilled at performing a thorough assessment and evaluation of veterans with PTSD . . ." (Committee on Veterans Affairs, U.S. Senate, 1988). The DVA offers a full range of treatment options for PTSD and associated psychological conditions. Although there are competent mental health professionals outside of the DVA who can provide appropriate treatment, the DVA remains a good starting point for seeking such services.

The DVA offers a variety of outpatient and inpatient (in hospital) treatment options where various levels of care are available. Outpatient care allows the veteran to continue his or her lifestyle with minimal disruption due to treatment. Outpatient options include: vet centers, outpatient clinics, mental hygiene clinics and partial hospitalization programs (day hospitals and day treatment centers). Inpatient treatment requires admission to a DVA medical center, which causes disruption in work and family life. In general, inpatient treatment is necessary only for the most severe cases of PTSD or associated psychological problems. At present, most inpatient treatment is provided on general psychiatry units. In addition, there are currently 15 specialized inpatient PTSD Units around the country where only veterans with PTSD are treated. Recently PTSD clinical treatment teams have been established at 23 DVA medical centers around the country. At the end of the chapter a current listing of these various resources is provided. Following are descriptions of these treatment options.

Vet Centers

There are 194 Vet Centers located throughout the United States, Puerto Rico, and the U.S. Virgin Islands. Any Vietnam era veteran who is experiencing readjustment difficulties is entitled to readjustment counseling services at these centers. Family members can also be included in the treatment process when necessary. Most of the staff either served in Vietnam themselves (60%) or during the Vietnam era (25%). The centers are easy to reach and are more informal than other DVA treatment facilities. Each center has at least one mental health professional and a number of trained counselors available to treat readjustment problems including PTSD. Vet Center services include individual, group, and family counseling and psychotherapy, evaluation and referral of cases appropriate for care at other DVA facilities, and provision of aftercare or follow-up for veterans being discharged from inpatient treatment. For veterans who live a distance from DVA facilities, the Vet Centers can authorize treatment of readjustment problems through contracts with local non-DVA professionals at no cost to you closer to your hometown. In addition, Vet Centers can provide assistance with other related problems such as employment or other DVA benefit programs.

Outpatient Clinics, Mental Hygiene Clinics, Day Hospitals, and Day Treatment Centers

These facilities provide a full range of traditional outpatient mental health services including individual psychotherapy and medication. Many facilities provide group psychotherapy and/or family therapy. These programs are staffed by mental health professionals who can treat all forms of psychological problems including substance abuse. They are located at DVA Medical Centers or function at different sites as independent facilities. Currently there are outpatient PTSD programs operating at the DVA medical centers in Albuquerque, N.M., and in Minneapolis. Day hospitals and day treatment centers provide a full day of treatment while allowing the veteran to return home at night and over weekends and holidays. There are PTSD day programs at the DVA medical centers in Boston and in Pittsburgh.

General Psychiatry Units

Most inpatient treatment for PTSD is provided on general psychiatry units within DVA Medical Centers. These units exist at all DVA medical centers. Veterans with PTSD are treated along with veterans experiencing other psychological problems. There may be little or no specialized treatment for PTSD available.

Specialized Inpatient PTSD Units

These units are staffed by professionals who are expert in diagnosing and treating war-related PTSD. Special PTSD treatment approaches are utilized and treatment is generally for a more extended period of time. An evaluation is necessary for admission to these units. Treatment may be provided in steps or phases. An important feature of these units is being able to complete treatment with a group of veterans experiencing similar problems and facing similar issues. Follow-up care is usually required to maintain gains made. There are currently four PTSD/substance use disorder pilot projects where veterans who suffer from both PTSD and a substance abuse disorder can be treated *concurrently* for both conditions. All other DVA facilities treat these conditions independently, usually consecutively. These pilot programs are located at the DVA medical centers in Lyons, N.J.; Milwaukee; Little Rock; and Palo Alto.

PTSD Clinical Treatment Teams

These teams are composed of four mental health professionals (e.g., psychiatrists, psychologists, social workers, nurses, or allied health professionals) who are expert in the diagnosis and treatment of war-related PTSD. They offer PTSD treatment to veterans as well as provide consultation and education to other medical and mental health professionals at DVA facilities in their geographic area.

Compensation and Rehabilitation for PTSD

A great American truth . . . bloomed in the years after the Revolution and the War of 1812: People who fight wars, be they volunteers or conscripts, expect to be paid, pensioned and nurtured for their sacrifices. But people who do not fight wars—even wars they approve of and perhaps even encouraged—tend to believe that those who do should perform deeds of combat as an act of patriotism. Noncombatants, it would seem, feel that soldiers should not trivialize their patriotism in a sea of complaints about old wounds suffered in battles long forgotten.

(Severo & Milford, 1989)

There is one great fear in the heart of every serviceman and it is not that he will be killed or maimed, but that when he is finally allowed to go home and piece together what he can of life, that he will be made to feel that he has been a sucker for the sacrifices he has made.

(Anonymous WW II soldier cited in Stouffer et al., 1949)

It seems clear from the above quotes that soldiers need to know that their society and government will acknowledge their sacrifices on the battlefield and care for them if they return wounded or demoralized. It also seems clear that following the war, combatants and non-combatants view such sacrifices differently. Vietnam veterans were not the first group to be confused by their homecoming and angered by their treatment following the battle. The government provides a full range of rehabilitative and compensation services to those veterans who are disabled, physically or mentally, as a result of their military service. This commitment is as old as American government although it has often suffered in its execution.

It has been almost ten years since PTSD was accepted as a formal diagnostic category, thereby making its sufferers eligible, if the condition is determined to be related to military service, for benefits from the Department of Veterans Affairs. This study has found that of the approximately 3.2 million Vietnam veterans, 480,000 currently meet the full diagnostic criteria for PTSD. The majority of these veterans have not asked their government for compensation. As of March 29, 1989, only 20,549 Vietnam veterans have received disability compensation for PTSD related to their military service. The current figure represents only 4.3 percent of the potentially eligible veterans! PTSD cases account for only 6 percent of all the current psychoneurotic disability compensation cases.

If you believe you have war-related PTSD or you know of a veteran who does, you should consider applying for disability compensation. This can be done at any DVA facility or with the assistance of a veterans' service organization. If you wish to apply for such benefits, all you need to do to begin the application process is to call or write your local DVA facility (e.g., Vet Center, Regional Office). If you are determined by the DVA to have war-related PTSD, you become entitled to a number of benefits for as long as you are disabled. You become eligible for a monthly compensation check, the amount of which is commensurate with your level of disability. You also become eligible for priority care for your disability at DVA treatment facilities. You may also become eligible for educational or job training benefits. Your dependents may become eligible for benefits also.

Many veterans are not interested in disability compensation. However, this program represents an attempt by a grateful government to honor its commitment to its veterans who have sacrificed so much for their country. If you have been disabled because of PTSD, the benefits noted above can help you regain some of what you have lost in the years since your service.

VA FACILITIES—WHERE TO GO FOR HELP

VA installations are listed below by state. Information on VA benefits may be obtained from the following installations: Regional Offices (RO); other offices (O); Regional Office and Insurance Centers in Philadelphia and St. Paul, and United States Veterans Assistance Centers (USVAC). Abbreviations of other installations are as follows: MC—Medical Center (Hospital); D—Domiciliary Care; NHC—Nursing Home Care; OPC—Outpatient Clinic (independent); OCH—Outpatient Clinic (physically separated from hospital); OCS—Outpatient Clinic Satellite

Alabama

Birmingham (MC) 35233
700 S. 19th St.
(205) 933-8101

Mobile (OCS) 36617
2451 Fillingim St.
(205) 690-2875

Montgomery (MC) 36109
215 Perry Hill Rd.
(205) 272-4670

Montgomery (RO) 36104
474 S. Court St.

If you reside in the local
  telephone area of:
Birmingham—322-2492
Huntsville—539-7742
Mobile—432-8645
Montgomery—262-7781

All other Alabama areas—
  (800) 392-8054

Tuscaloosa (MC&NHC) 35404
Loop Rd.
(205) 553-3760

Tuskegee (MC&NHC) 36083
(205) 727-0550

Alaska

Anchorage (RO&OC)
99501
235 E. 8th Avenue

If you live in the local
  telephone area of:
Anchorage 279-6116

All other Alaska communities—
  (800) 478-2500

Arizona

Phoenix (MC&NHC) 85012
7th St. & Indian School Rd.
(602) 277-5551

Phoenix (RO) 85012
3225 N. Central Ave.

If you live in the local
  telephone area of:
Phoenix—263-5411

All other Arizona areas—
  (800) 352-0451

Prescott (MC&D) 86313
(602) 445-4860

Tucson (MC&NHC) 85723
3601 S. 6th Ave.
(602) 792-1450

Arkansas

Fayetteville (MC) 72701
1100 N. College Ave.
(501) 443-4301

Little Rock (RO) 72214
Building 65, Ft. Roots
North Little Rock, AR
Mailing: P.O. Box 1280
North Little Rock, 72215
370-3800

If you live in the local
  telephone area of:
Little Rock—370-3800

All other Arkansas areas—
  (800) 482-5434

Little Rock (MC, D&HC)
4300 West Seventh St. 72205
(501) 661-1201
(501) 372-8361

California

East Los Angeles
(USVAC) 90022
VA Ambulatory Care Facility
5400 E. Olympic Blvd.
Commerce
(213) 266-6898

Fresno (MC&NHC) 93703
2615 E. Clinton Ave.
(209) 225-6100

Livermore (MC&NHC) 94550
(415) 447-2560

Loma Linda (MC&NHC)
92357
11201 Benton St.
(714) 825-7084

Long Beach (MC&NHC)
90822
5901 E. 7th St.
(213) 498-1313

Los Angeles (RO) 90024
Federal Building
11000 Wilshire Blvd.
West Los Angeles

Counties of Inyo, Kern, Los
Angeles, Orange, San
Bernardino, San Luis Obispo,
Santa Barbara and Ventura:

If you live in the local
telephone area of:
Central LA — 879-1303
Inglewood — 645-5420
La Crescenta — 248-0450
Malibu/Santa Monica —
451-0672
San Fernando/Van Nuys —
997-6401
San Pedro/Long Beach —
833-5241
Sierra Madre — 355-3305
West Los Angeles — 479-4011
Whittier — 945-3841
Outside LA:
Anaheim — 821-1020
Bakersfield — 834-3142
Huntington Beach — 848-1500
Ontario — 983-9784
Oxnard — 487-3977
San Bernardino — 884-4874
Santa Ana — 543-8403
Santa Barbara — 963-0643

All other areas of the above
counties — (800) 352-6592

Counties of Alpine, Lassen,
Modoc and Mono served by:
Reno, NV (RO) 89520
245 E. Liberty

If you live in the above
California counties —
(800) 648-5406

West Los Angeles
(MC,NHC,&D)
90073
11301 Wilshire Blvd.
(213) 478-3711

Los Angeles (OC) 90013
425 S. Hill St.
(213) 688-2000

Martinez (MC) 94553
150 Muir Rd.
(415) 228-6800

Oakland (OCS) 94612
1515 Clay St.
(415) 273-7125

Palo Alto (MC,D&HC) 94304
3801 Miranda Ave.
(415) 493-5000

Sacramento (OCS) 95820
4600 Broadway
(916) 440-2625

San Diego (RO) 92108
2022 Camino Del Rio North
Counties of Imperial,
Riverside, and San Diego:

If you live in the local
telephone area of:
Riverside — 686-1132
San Diego — 297-8220

All other areas of the above
counties — (800) 532-3811

San Diego (MC&NHC) 92161
3350 LaJolla Village Dr.
(714) 453-7500

San Diego (OCH) 82108
Palomar Building
2022 Camino Del Rio North

San Francisco (RO) 94105
211 Main St.

If you live in the local
telephone area of:
Freemont — 796-9212
Fresno — (800) 652-1296
Modesto — 521-9260
Monterey — 649-3550
Oakland — 893-0405
Palo Alto — 321-5615
Sacramento — 929-5883
San Francisco — 495-8900
San Jose — 998-7373
Santa Rosa — 544-3520
Stockton — 948-8860
Vallejo — 552-1556

All other areas of Northern
California —
(800) 652-1240

San Francisco (MC) 94121
4150 Clement St.
(415) 221-4810

Santa Barbara (OCS) 93110
4440 Calle Real
(805) 683-1491

Sepulveda (MC&NHC) 91343
16111 Plummer St.
(210) 894-0271

Colorado

Denver (RO) 80225
44 Union Blvd.
P.O. Box 25126

If you live in the local
telephone area of:
Colorado Springs — 475-9911
Denver — 980-1300
Pueblo — 545-1764

All other Colorado areas —
(800) 332-6742

Colorado Springs (OCS)
875 Moreno Drive 80905
(303) 633-2901

Denver (MC&NHC) 80220
1055 Clermont St.
(303) 399-8020

Fort Lyon (MC&NHC) 81038
(303) 456-1260

Grand Junction (MC&NHC)
81501
2121 North Ave.
(303) 242-0731

Connecticut

Hartford (RO) 06103
450 Main St.

If you live in the local
telephone area of:
Bridgeport — 384-9861
Danbury — 743-2791

Hartford — 278-3230
New Haven — 562-2113
New London — 447-0377
Norwalk — 853-8141
Stamford — 325-4039
Waterbury — 757-0347

All other Connecticut areas —
(800) 842-4315

Newington (MC) 06111
555 Willard Ave.
(203) 666-4361

West Haven (MC&NHC)
06516
W. Spring St.
(203) 932-5711

Delaware

Wilmington (RO) 19805
1601 Kirkwood Highway

If you live in the local
telephone area of:
Wilmington — 998-0191

All other Delaware areas —
(800) 292-7855

Wilmington (MC&NHC) 19805
1601 Kirkwood Highway
(302) 994-2511

District of Columbia

Washington, D.C. (RO) 20421
941 N. Capitol St., N.E.
(202) 872-1151

Washington, D.C. (MC&NHC)
20422
50 Irving St., N.W.
(202) 745-8000

Florida

Bay Pines (MC,D,NHC,&
OCH) 33504
1000 Bay Pines Blvd., N
(813) 398-6661

Daytona Beach (OCS) 32017
(904) 253-7765

Fort Myers (OCS) 33901
2070 Carrell Road
(813) 939-3939

Gainesville (MC,NHC) 32602
Archer Rd.
(904) 376-1611

Jacksonville (O) 32202
Post Office & Courthouse
Bldg.
311 W. Monroe St.
356-1581

Jacksonville (OCS) 32206
1833 Boulevard
(904) 791-2751

Lake City (MC&NHC) 32055
801 S. Marion St.
(904) 755-3016

Miami (MC&NHC) 33125
1201 N.W. 16th St.
(305) 324-4455

Miami (O) 33130
Federal Building, Rm. 103A
51 S.W. 1st Ave.
(305) 358-0669

Oakland Park (OCS) 33334
5599 N. Dixie Highway
(305) 771-2101

Orlando (OCS) 32806
83 W. Columbia St.
(305) 425-7521

Pensacola (OCS) 32501
(904) 476-1100

Port Richey (OCS) 33568
(813) 869-3203

Riviera Beach (OCS) 33404
Exec. Plaza, 301 Broadway
(305) 845-2800

St. Petersburg (RO) 33731
144 1st Ave. S.

If you live in the local
telephone area of:
Cocoa/Cocoa Beach
783-8930
Daytona Beach — 255-8351
Ft. Lauderdale/Hollywood —
522-4725
Ft. Myers — 334-0900
Gainesville — 376-5266
Jacksonville — 356-1581
Lakeland/Winter Haven —
688-7499
Melbourne — 724-5600
Miami — 358-0669
Orlando — 425-2626
Pensacola — 434-3537
Sarasota — 366-2939
Tallahassee — 224-6872
Tampa — 299-0451
West Palm Beach — 833-5734
St. Petersburg/Clearwater —
898-2121

All other Florida areas —
(800) 282-8821

Tampa (MC&NHC) 33612
13000 N. 30th St.
(813) 972-2000

Georgia

Atlanta (RO) 30365
730 Peachtree St. N.E.

If you live in the local
telephone area of:
Albany — 439-2331
Atlanta — 881-1776

Augusta — 738-5403
Columbus — 324-6646
Macon — 745-6517
Savannah — 232-3365

All other Georgia areas —
(800) 282-0232

Augusta (MC&NHC) 30910
2460 Wrightsboro Road
(404) 724-5116

Decatur (MC,NHC) 30033
1670 Clairmont Rd.,
(404) 321-6111

Dublin (MC,D&NHC) 31021
(912) 272-1210

Guam

VA Office
U.S. Naval
Regional Medical Center
P.O. Box 7613
FPO San Francisco, 96630
(671) 344-9200
(671) 344-5260

Hawaii

Honolulu (RO) 96813
PJKK Federal Bldg.
300 Ala Moana Blvd.
Mailing:
P.O. Box 50188
Honolulu 96850

If you live in the local
telephone area of:
Is. of Oahu — 541-1000
Is. of Hawaii — 961-3661
Is. of Kauai, Lanai, Maui &
Molokai — (800) 232-2535

Honolulu (OPC) 96850
P.O. Box 50188
300 Ala Moana Blvd.
(808) 541-1600

Idaho

Boise (RO) 83724
Federal Bldg. and
U.S. Courthouse
550 W. Fort St., Box 044

If you live in the local
telephone area of:
Boise — 334-1010

All other Idaho areas —
1-800 632-2003

Boise (MC&NHC) 83702
500 West Fort
(208) 336-5100

Illinois

Chicago (MC) 60611
333 E. Huron St. (Lakeside)
(312) 943-6600

Chicago (MC) 60680
(West Side)
820 S. Damen Ave.
(312) 666-6500

Chicago (RO) 60680
536 S. Clark St.

If you live in the local
telephone area of:
Bloomington/Normal—
829-4374
Carbondale—457-8161
Champaign-Urbana—
344-7505
Chicago—663-5510
Decatur—429-9445
E. St. Louis—274-5444
Peoria—674-0901
Rockford—968-0538
Springfield—789-1246

All other Illinois areas—
(800) 972-5327

Danville (MC&NHC) 61832
1900 E. Main St.
(217) 442-8000

Hines (MC&NHC) 60141
Roosevelt Rd. & 5th Ave.
(312) 343-7200

Marion (MC) 62959
Main St.
(618) 997-5311

North Chicago (MC,D&NHC)
60064
Buckley Rd., Rt. 137
(312) 688-1900

Peoria (OCS) 61605
411 Dr. Martin Luther King Dr.
(309) 671-7350

Indiana

Evansville (OCS) 47708
214 S.E., 6th St.
(812) 465-6202

Fort Wayne (MC&NHC) 46805
1600 Randalia Dr.
(219) 426-5431

Indianapolis (RO) 46204
575 N. Pennsylvania St.

If you live in the local
telephone area of:
Anderson/Muncie—289-9377
Evansville—426-1403

Ft. Wayne—422-9189
Gary/Hammond/E. Chicago—
886-9184
Indianapolis—269-5566
Lafayette/W. Lafayette—
742-0084
South Bend—232-3011
Terre Haute—232-1030

All other Indiana areas—
(800) 382-4540

Indianapolis (MC&NHC)
46202
1481 W. 10th St.
(317) 635-7401

Marion (MC&NHC)
46952 E. 38th St.
(317) 674-3321

Iowa

Des Moines (RO) 50309
210 Walnut St.
284-0219

All other Iowa areas—
(800) 362-2222

Des Moines (MC) 50310
30th & Euclid Ave.
(515) 255-2173

Iowa City (MC) 52240
Hwy. 6 West
(319) 338-0581

Knoxville (MC&NHC) 50138
1515 W. Pleasant St.
(515) 842-3101

Kansas

Leavenworth (MC,NHC,&D)
66048
4201 S. 4th St., Trafficway
(913) 682-2000

Topeka (MC&NHC) 66622
2200 Gage Blvd.
(913) 272-3111

Wichita (RO) 67211
Blvd. Office Park
901 George Washington Blvd.

If you live in the local
telephone area of:
Kansas City—432-1650
Topeka—357-5301
Wichita—264-9123

All other Kansas areas—
(800) 362-2444

Wichita (MC&NHC) 67218
5500 E. Kellogg
(316) 685-2221

Kentucky

Lexington (MC&NHC) 40507
Leestown Rd.
(606) 233-4511

Louisville (RO) 40202
600 Federal Place

If you live in the local
telephone area of:
Lexington—253-0566
Louisville—584-2231

All other areas—
(800) 292-4562

Louisville (MC) 40202
800 Zom Ave.
(502) 895-3401

Louisiana

Alexandria (MC&NHC) 71301
Shreveport Hwy.
(318) 473-0010

New Orleans (RO) 70113
701 Loyola Ave.

If you live in the local
telephone area of:
Baton Rouge—343-5539
New Orleans—561-0121
Shreveport—424-8442

All other Louisiana areas—
(800) 462-9510

New Orleans (MC) 70146
1601 Perdido St.
(504) 568-0811

Shreveport (MC&O) 71130
510 E. Stoner Ave.
(318) 424-8442 (Office)
(318) 221-8411 (Hospital)

Maine

Portland (O) 04101
175 Lancaster St.
775-6391

Togus (MC&RO Center)
04330

If you live in the local
telephone area of:
Portland—775-6391
Togus—623-8000

All other Maine areas—
(800) 452-1935

Togus (MC&NHC) 04330
Route 17 East
(207) 623-8411

Maryland

Counties of Montgomery and
Prince Georges:
Washington, DC (RO) 20421
941 N. Capitol St. N.E.

If you live in the above
Maryland counties — 872–1151

All other Maryland Counties:
Baltimore (RO) 21201
31 Hopkins Plaza
Federal Building

If you live in the local
telephone area of:
Baltimore — 685–5454

All other Maryland areas —
(800) 492–9503

Baltimore (OCH) 21201
31 Hopkins Plaza
Federal Building
(301) 962–4610

Baltimore (MC) 21218
3900 Loch Raven Blvd.
(301) 467–9932

Baltimore (Prosthetics Research
and Development Center)
21201
103 S. Gay St.
(301) 962–3934

Fort Howard (MC&NHC) 21052
Old N., Point Rd.
(301) 477–1800

Perry Point (MC&NHC) 21902
(301) 642–2411

Massachusetts

Bedford (MC&NHC) 01730
200 Spring Rd.
(617) 275–7500

Boston (MC) 02130
150 S. Huntington Ave.
(617) 232–9500

Towns of Fall River and New
Bedford and counties of
Barnstable, Dukes,
Nantucket, part of
Plymouth, and Bristol are
served by:
Providence, R.I. (RO) 02903
380 Westminster Mall
(800) 556–3893

Remaining Massachusetts
counties served by:
Boston (RO) 02203
John Fitzgerald Kennedy
Federal Bldg.
Government Center

If you live in the local
telephone area of:
Boston — 227–4600
Brockton — 588–0764
Fitchburg/Leominster —
342–8927
Lawrence — 687–3332
Lowell — 454–5463
Springfield — 785–5343
Worcester — 791–3595

All other Massachusetts areas —
(800) 392–6015

Boston (OC) 02108
17 Court St.
(617) 223–2020

Brockton (MC&NHC) 02401
940 Belmont St.
(617) 563–4500

Lowell (OCS) 01852
Old Post Office Bldg.
50 Kearney Square
(617) 453–1746

New Bedford (OCS) 02740
53 N. Sixth St.
(617) 997–0721

Northampton (MC&NHC)
01060
N. Main St.
(413) 584–4040

Springfield (OCS) 01103
1550 Main St.
(413) 785–0301

West Roxbury (MC) 02132
1400 VFW Parkway
(617) 323–7700

Worcester (OCS) 01608
595 Main St.
(617) 793–0200

Michigan

Allen Park (MC&NHC) 48101
Southfield & Outer Drive
(313) 562–6000

Ann Arbor (MC&NHC) 48105
2215 Fuller Rd.
(313) 769–7100

Battle Creek (MC&NHC)
49016
5500 Armstrong Rd.
(616) 966–5600

Detroit (RO) 48226
Patrick V McNamara
Federal Bldg.
477 Michigan Ave.

Gaylord (OCS) 49735
850 N. Otsego
(517) 732–5725

If you live in the local
telephone area of:
Ann Arbor — 662–2506
Battle Creek — 962–7568
Detroit — 964–5110
Flint — 234–8646
Grand Rapids — 456–8511
Kalamazoo — 344–0156
Lansing/E. Lansing —
484–7713
Muskegon — 726–4895
Saginaw — 754–7475

All other Michigan areas —
(800) 482–0740

Grand Rapids (OCS) 49503
260 Jefferson St., S.E.
(616) 459–2200

Iron Mountain (MC&NHC)
49801
H Street
(906) 774–3300

Saginaw (MC&NHC) 48602
1500 Weiss St.
(517) 793–2340

Minnesota

Minneapolis (MC) 55417
54th St. & 48th Ave., South
(612) 725–6767

St. Cloud (MC&NHC) 56301
8th St. No. 44th Ave.
(612) 252–1670

St. Paul (RO & Insurance
Center) 55111
Federal Bldg., Fort Snelling

If you live in the local
telephone area of:
Duluth — 722–4467
Minneapolis — 726–1454
Rochester — 288–5888
St. Cloud — 253–9300
St. Paul — 726–1454

Counties of Becker, Beltrami,
Clay, Clearwater, Kittson,
Lake of the Woods,
Mahnomen, Marshall,
Norman, Otter Tail,
Pennington, Polk, Red
Lake, Roseau, and Wilkin
are served by:
Fargo, ND (RO)
(800) 437–4668

All other Minnesota areas —
(800) 692–2121

St. Paul (OCH) 55111
Fort Snelling
(612) 725–6767

Mississippi

Biloxi (MC,D&NHC) 39531
Pass Rd.
(601) 388-5541

Jackson (MC&NHC) 39216
1500 E. Woodrow Wilson Dr.
(601) 362-4471

Jackson (RO) 39269
100 W. Capitol St.

If you live in the local
  telephone area of:
Biloxi/Gulfport — 432-5996
Jackson — 965-4873
Meridian — 693-6166

All other Mississippi areas —
  (800) 682-5270

Missouri

Columbia (MC&NHC) 65201
800 Hospital Dr.
(314) 443-2511

Kansas City (MC) 64128
4801 Linwood Blvd.
(816) 861-4700

Kansas City (O) 64106
Federal Office Bldg.
601 E. 12th St.
(800) 392-3761

Poplar Bluff (MC&NHC) 63901
Hwy. 67 North
(314) 686-4151

St. Louis (RO) 63103
Federal Bldg.
1520 Market St.
St. Louis — 342-1171

All other Missouri areas —
  (800) 392-3761

St. Louis (H&NHC) 63106
915 N. Grand Blvd.
(314) 652-4100

Montana

Fort Harrison (RO) 59636

If you live in the local
  telephone area of:
Fort Harrison/Helena
  442-6839
Great Falls — 761-3215

All other Montana areas —
  (800) 332-6125

Billings (OCH) 59101
1127 Alderson Ave.
(406) 657-6786

Fort Harrison (MC) 59636
Wm. St. Hwy. 12 W.
(406) 442-6410

Miles City (MC&NHC) 59301
210 S. Winchester
(406) 232-3060

Nebraska

Grand Island (MC&NHC)
  68801
2201 N. Broad Well
(308) 382-3660

Lincoln (RO) 68508
Federal Bldg.
100 Centennial Mall North

If you live in the local
  telephone area of:
Lincoln — 471-5001
Omaha — 341-1024

All other Nebraska areas —
  (800) 742-7554

Lincoln (MC) 68510
600 S. 70th St.
(402) 489-3802

Omaha (MC) 68105
4101 Woolworth Ave.
(402) 346-8800

Nevada

Las Vegas (OCS) 89102
1703 W. Charleston
(702) 385-3700

Reno (MC&NHC) 89520
1000 Locust St.
(702) 786-7200

Reno (RO) 89520
1201 Terminal Way

If you live in the local
  telephone area of:
Las Vegas — 368-2921
Reno — 329-9244

All other Nevada areas —
  (800) 992-5740

New Hampshire

Manchester (RO) — 03101
Norris Cotton Federal Bldg.
275 Chestnut St.

If you live in the local
  telephone area of:
Manchester — 666-7785

All other New Hampshire
  areas — (800) 562-5260

Manchester (MC&NHC)
  03104
718 Smyth Rd.
(603) 624-4366

New Jersey

East Orange (MC&NHC)
  07019
Tremont Ave. & S. Center
(201) 676-1000

Lyons (MC,D,&NHC) 07939
Valley & Knollcroft Rd.
(201) 647-0180

Newark (RO) 07102
20 Washington Place

If you live in the local
  telephone area of:
Atlantic City — 348-8550
Camden — 541-8650
Clifton/Paterson/Passaic —
  472-9632
Long Branch/Asbury Park —
  870-2550
New Brunswick/Sayreville —
  828-5600
Newark — 645-2150
Perth Amboy — 442-5300
Trenton — 989-8116

All other New Jersey areas —
  (800) 242-5867

Newark (OCH) 07102
20 Washington Place
(201) 645-3491

New Mexico

Albuquerque (RO) 87102
Dennis Chavez Federal Bldg.
U.S. Courthouse
500 Gold Ave., S.W.

If you live in the local
  telephone area of:
Albuquerque — 766-3361

All other New Mexico areas —
  (800) 432-6853

Albuquerque (MC&NHC)
  87108
2100 Ridgecrest Dr., S.E.
(505) 265-1711

New York

Albany (MC&NHC) 12208
113 Holland Ave.
(518) 462-3311

Albany (O) 12207
Leo W. O'Brien Federal Bldg.
Clinton Ave. & N. Pearl St.
(800) 442-5882

Batavia (MC&NHC) 14020
Redfield Pkwy.
(716) 343-7500

Bath (MC,D,&NHC) 14810
Argonne Ave.
(607) 776-2111

Bronx (MC&NHC) 10468
130 W. Kingsbridge Rd.
(212) 584-9000

Brooklyn (MC,D,& NHC)
11209
800 Poly Place
(212) 836-6600

Brooklyn (OC) 11205
35 Ryerson St.
(212) 330-7785

Buffalo (RO) 14202
Federal Bldg.
111 W. Huron St.

If you live in the local
telephone area of:
Binghamton—772-0856
Buffalo—846-5191
Rochester—232-5290
Syracuse—476-5544
Utica—735-6431

All other areas of Western
New York State—
(800) 462-1130

Buffalo (MC&NHC) 14215
3495 Bailey Ave.
(716) 834-9200

Canandaigua (MC&NHC)
14424
Ft. Hill Ave
(716) 394-2000

Castle Point (MC,D,&NHC)
12511
(914) 831-2000

Montrose (MC,D&NHC)
10548
Old Albany Post Rd.
(914) 737-4400

New York City (MC) 10010
1st Ave. at E. 24th St.
(212) 686-7500

New York City (RO) 10001
252 Seventh Ave. at 24th St.

Counties of Albany, Bronx,
Clinton, Columbia,
Delaware, Dutchess, Essex,
Franklin, Fulton, Greene,
Hamilton, Kings,
Montgomery, Nassau, New
York, Orange, Otsego,

Putnam, Queens,
Rensselaer, Richmond,
Rockland, Saratoga,
Schenectady, Schoharie,
Suffolk, Sullivan, Ulster,
Warren, Washington,
Westchester:

If you live in the local
telephone area of:
Nassau—483-6188
New York—620-6901
Poughkeepsie—452-5330
Westchester—723-7476

All other areas in the above
counties—(800) 442-5882

New York City (OCH) 10001
252 7th Ave. at 24th St.
(212) 620-6636

Northport (MC) 11768
Long Island—Middleville Rd.
(516) 261-4400

Rochester (O&OCS) 14614
Federal Office Bldg. and
Courthouse
100 State St.
232-5290 (O)
(716) 263-5734 (OCS)

Syracuse (O) 13260
U.S. Courthouse and
Federal Building
100 S. Clinton St.
476-5544

Syracuse (MC&NHC) 13210
Irving Ave. & University Pl.
(315) 476-7461

North Carolina

Asheville (MC&NHC) 28805
(704) 298-7911

Durham (MC) 27705
508 Fulton St.
(919) 286-0411

Fayetteville (MC&NHC) 28301
2300 Ramsey St.
(919) 488-2120

Salisbury (MC&NHC) 28144
1601 Brenner Ave.
(704) 636-2351

Winston-Salem (OCH) 27102
Federal Bldg.
251 N. Main St.
(919) 761-3562

Winston-Salem (RO) 27155
Federal Bldg.
251 N. Main St.

If you live in the local
telephone area of:
Asheville—253-6861
Charlotte—375-9351
Durham—683-1367
Fayetteville—323-1242
Greensboro—274-1994
High Point—887-1202
Raleigh—821-1166
Winston-Salem—748-1800

All other North Carolina
areas—(800) 642-0841

North Dakota

Fargo (RO) 58102
655 First Ave., North

If you live in the local
telephone area of:
Fargo—293-3656

All other North Dakota areas—
(800) 342-4790

Fargo (MC&NHC) 58102
Elm & 21st Ave., North
(701) 232-3241

Ohio

Brecksville (MC,D,&NHC)
44141
10000 Brecksville Rd.
(216) 526-3030

Chillicothe (MC&NHC) 45601
17273 State Route 104
(614) 773-1141

Cincinnati (MC&NHC) 45220
3200 Vine St.
(513) 861-3100

Cincinnati (O) 45202
Rm. 1020, Federal Off. Bldg.
550 Main St.
579-0505

Cleveland (MC) 44106
10701 E. Boulevard
(216) 791-3800

Cleveland (RO) 44199
Anthony J. Celebrezze
Federal Bldg.
1240 E. 9th St.

If you live in the local
telephone area of:
Akron—535-3327
Canton—453-8113
Cincinnati—579-0505
Cleveland—621-5050
Columbus—224-8872
Dayton—223-1394
Springfield—322-4907

Toledo—241-6223
Warren—399-9985
Youngstown—744-4383

All other Ohio areas—
(800) 362-9024

Columbus (O) 43215
Rm. 390 Fed. Bldg.
200 N. High St.
224-8872

Columbus (OC) 43221
2090 Kenny Rd.
(614) 469-5665

Dayton (MC,D&NHC) 45428
4100 W. 3rd St.
(513) 268-6511

Toledo (OCS) 43614
3333 Glendale Ave.
(419) 259-2000

Oklahoma

Muskogee (MC) 74401
Memorial Station
Honor Heights Dr.
(918) 683-3261

Muskogee (RO) 74401
Federal Bldg.
125 S. Main St.

If you live in the local
   telephone area of:
Lawton—357-2400
Muskogee—687-2500
Oklahoma City—235-2641
Stillwater—377-1770
Tulsa—583-5891

All other Oklahoma areas—
(800) 482-2800

Oklahoma City (O) 73102
200 N.W. 5th St.
(405) 235-2641

Oklahoma City (MC) 73104
921 N.E. 13th St.
(405) 272-9876

Tulsa (OCS) 74101
635 W. 11th St.
(918) 581-7152

Oregon

Portland (MC,D,&NHC)
97207
3710 SW
U.S. Veterans Hospital Rd.
(503) 222-9221

Portland (RO) 97204
Federal Bldg.
1220 SW. 3rd Avenue

If you live in the local
   telephone area of:
Portland—221-2431

All other Oregon areas—
(800) 452-7276

Portland (OCH) 97207
P.O. Box 1036
8909 SW Barbur Blvd.
244-9222

Roseburg (MC&NHC) 97470
New Garden Valley Blvd.
(503) 672-4411

White City (D) 97501
Hwy. 62
(503) 826-2111

Pennsylvania

Allentown (OCS) 18104
2937 Hamilton Blvd.
(215) 776-4304

Altoona (MC&NHC) 16603
Pleasant Valley Blvd.
(814) 943-8164

Butler (MC,D,&NHC) 16001
New Castle Rd.
(412) 287-4781

Coatesville (MC,D,&NHC)
19320
Black Horse Rd.
(215) 384-7711

Erie (MC&NHC) 16501
135 E. 38th St.
(814) 868-8661

Harrisburg (OCS) 17108
Federal Bldg.
228 Walnut St.
(717) 782-4590

Lebanon (MC&NHC) 17042
South Lincoln Ave.
(717) 272-6621

Philadelphia (MC) 19104
University & Woodland Aves.
(215) 382-2400

Philadelphia (OCH) 19102
1421 Cherry St.
(215) 382-2400

Philadelphia (RO & Insurance
   Center) 19101
P.O. Box 8079
5000 Wissahickon Ave.

Counties of Adams, Berks,
   Bradford, Bucks, Cameron,
   Carbon, Centre, Chester,
   Clinton, Columbia,
   Cumberland, Dauphin,

Delaware, Franklin, Juniata,
   Lackawanna, Lancaster,
   Lebanon, Lehigh, Luzerne,
   Lycoming, Mifflin, Monroe,
   Montgomery, Montour,
   Northampton,
   Northumberland, Perry,
   Philadelphia, Pike, Potter,
   Schuylkill, Snyder, Sullivan,
   Susquehanna, Tioga, Union,
   Wayne, Wyoming, and York:

If you live in the local
   telephone area of:
Allentown/Bethlehem/
   Easton—821-6823
Harrisburg—232-6677
Lancaster—394-0596
Philadelphia—438-5225
Reading—376-6548
Scranton—961-3883
Wilkes-Barre—824-4636
Williamsport—322-4649
York—846-6311

All other areas in the above
   counties—(800) 822-3920

Pittsburgh (RO) 15222
1000 Liberty Ave.

If you live in the local
   telephone area of:
Pittsburgh—281-4233

All other areas in Western
   Pennsylvania—
   (800) 242-0233

Pittsburgh (OCH) 15222
1000 Liberty Ave.
(412) 644-6750

Pittsburgh (MC&NHC) 15240
University Drive C
(412) 683-3000

Pittsburgh (MC) 15206
Highland Drive
(412) 363-4900

Sayre (OCS) 18840
Guthrie Square
(717) 888-8062

Wilkes-Barre (O) 18701
19-27 N. Main St.
824-4636

Wilkes-Barre (MC&NHC)
18711
1111 E. End Blvd.
(717) 824-3521

Philippines

Manila (RO&OC) 96528
1131 Roxas Blvd. (Manila)
APO San Francisco (Air Mail)

Puerto Rico

Mayaguez (OCS) 00708
Road Number 2
(809) 833-4600
Ask for Ext. 204

San Juan (MC) 00921
Barrio Monacillos
Rio Piedras GPS Box 4867
(809) 764-4545

San Juan (RO) 00918
U.S. Courthouse & Fed. Bldg.
Carlos E. Chardon St.
Hato Rey
(800) 753-4141

Rhode Island

Providence (RO) 02903
380 Westminster Mall

If you live in the local
  telephone area of:
Providence—273-4910

All other Rhode Island areas—
  (800) 322-0230

Providence (MC) 02908
Davis Park
(401) 273-7100

South Carolina

Charleston (MC) 29403
109 Bee St.
(803) 577-5011

Columbia (RO) 29201
1801 Assembly St.

If you live in the local
  telephone area of:
Charleston—723-5581
Columbia—765-5861
Greenville—232-2457

All other South Carolina
  areas—(800) 922-1000

Columbia (MC&NHC) 29201
Gamers Ferry Rd.
(803) 677-4000

Greenville (OCS) 29601
120 Mallard St.
(803) 232-7303

South Dakota

Fort Meade (MC) 57741
I 90/Hwy. 34
(605) 347-2511

Hot Springs (MC&D) 57747
Off 5th St.
(605) 745-4101

Sioux Falls (MC&NHC) 57101
2501 W. 22nd St.
(605) 336-3230

Sioux Falls (RO) 57117
P.O. Box 5046
2510 W. 22nd St.

If you live in the local
  telephone area of:
Sioux Falls—336-3496

All other South Dakota
  areas—(800) 952-3550

Tennessee

Chattanooga (OCS) 37411
Bldg. 6300 East Gate Center
(615) 899-4650

Knoxville (OCS) 37919
9047 Executive Park Dr.
Suite 100
(615) 558-1319

Memphis (MC&NHC) 38104
1030 Jefferson Ave.
(901) 523-8990

Mountain Home (MC,D&NHC)
Lamont St. 37684
(615) 926-1171
Johnson City
(615) 926-1171

Murfreesboro (MC&NHC)
37130
Lebanon Hwy.
(615) 893-1360

Nashville (RO) 37203
110 9th Ave., S.

If you live in the local
  telephone area of:
Chattanooga—267-6587
Knoxville—546-5700
Memphis—527-4583
Nashville—736-5251

All other Tennessee areas—
  (800) 342-8330

Nashville (MC) 37203
1310 24th Ave., S.
(615) 327-4751

Texas

Amarillo (MC) 79106
6010 Amarillo Blvd., W.
(806) 355-9703

Beaumont (OCS) 77701
3385 Fannin St.
(713) 838-0271

Big Spring (MC&NHC) 79720
2400 S. Gregg St.
(915) 263-7361

Bonham (MC,D&NHC) 75418
Ninth & Lipscomb
(214) 583-2111

Corpus Christi (OCS) 78404
1502 S. Brownlee Blvd.
(512) 888-3251

Dallas (O) 75216
U.S. Courthouse and
  Fed. Office Bldg.
1100 Commerce St.
824-5440

Dallas (MC&NHC) 75210
4500 S. Lancaster Rd.
(214) 376-5451

El Paso (OC) 79925
5919 Brook Hollow Dr.
(915) 541-7890

Fort Worth (O) 76102
819 Taylor St.
336-1641

Houston (RO) 77054
2515 Murworth Dr.

Counties of Angelina,
  Aransas, Atacosa, Austin,
  Bandra, Bee, Bexar,
  Bianco, Brazoria, Brewster,
  Brooks, Caldwell, Calhoun,
  Cameron, Chambers,
  Colorado, Comal, Crockett,
  DeWitt, Dimmitt, Duval,
  Edwards, Fort Bend, Frio,
  Galveston, Gillispie, Goliad,
  Gonzales, Grimes,
  Guadalupe, Hardin, Harris,
  Hays, Hidalgo, Houston,
  Jackson, Jasper, Jefferson,
  Jim Hogg, Jim Wells,
  Karnes, Kendall, Kenedy,
  Kerr, Kimble, Kinney,
  Kleberg, LaSalle, Lavaca,
  Liberty, Live Oak,
  McCulloch, McMullen,
  Mason, Matagorda,
  Maverick, Medina, Menard,
  Montgomery, Nacogdoches,
  Newton, Nueces, Orange,
  Pecos, Polk, Real, Refugio,
  Sabine, San Augustine, San
  Jacinto, San Patrico,
  Schleicher, Shelby, Starr,
  Sutton, Terrell, Trinity, Tyler,
  Uvalde, Val Verde, Victoria,
  Walker, Waller, Washington,
  Webb, Wharton, Willacy,
  Wilson, Zapata, Zavala:

If you live in the local
  telephone area of:
Beaumont—838-6222
Corpus Christi—884-1994
Edinburg/McAllen/Pharr—
  383-8168

Houston—664-4664
San Antonio—226-7661
Texas City/Galveston—
948-3011

All other areas in the above
counties—(800) 392-2200

Houston (MC&NHC) 77211
2002 Holcombe Blvd.
(713) 795-4411

Kerrville (MC&NHC) 78028
Memorial Blvd.
(512) 896-2020

Lubbock (O&OC) 79401
Federal Building
1205 Texas Ave.
(806) 743-7219 (OC)
(800) 792-3271 (Waco RO)
747-5256

Marlin (MC) 76661
1016 Ward St.
(817) 883-3511

McAllen (OCS) 78501
3711 North 10th St.
(512) 682-4581

San Antonio (MC) 78284
7400 Merton Minter Blvd.
(512) 696-9660

San Antonio (O) 78285
307 Dwyer Ave.
226-7661

San Antonio (OC) 78285
307 Dwyer Ave.
(512) 225-5511

Temple (MC,D,&NHC)
76501
1901 S. First
(817) 778-4811

Waco (RO) 76799
1400 N. Valley Mills Dr.

If you live in the local
telephone area of:
Amarillo—376-7202
Austin—477-5831
Dallas—824-5440
El Paso—545-2500
Ft. Worth—336-1641
Killeen—699-2351
Lubbock—747-5256
Waco—772-3060
*Bowie County served by
Little Rock, AR (RO) 72114
Bldg. 65 Ft. Roots North,
Little Rock, AR
(800) 643-5688

All other counties served by
Waco—(800) 792-3271

Waco (MC&NHC) 76711
4800 Memorial Drive
(817) 752-6581

Utah

Salt Lake City (RO) 84147
P.O. Box 11500
Federal Bldg.
125 S. State St.

If you live in the local
telephone area of:
Ogden—399-4433
Provo/Orem—375-2902
Salt Lake City—524-5960

All other Utah areas—
(800) 662-9163

Salt Lake City (MC&NHC)
84148
500 Foothill Blvd.
(801) 582-1565

Vermont

White River Junction (RO)
05001

If you live in the local
telephone area of:
White River Junction—
295-2582

All other Vermont areas—
(800) 622-4134

White River Junction
(MC&NHC)
N. Hartland Rd. 05001
(802) 295-9363

Virginia

Hampton (MC,D&NHC)
23667
Emancipation Dr.
(804) 722-9961

Richmond (MC&NHC) 23249
1201 Broad Rock Rd.
(804) 230-0001

Northern Virginia
Counties of Arlington and
Fairfax and the cities of
Alexandria, Fairfax, and
Falls Church:

Washington, DC (RO) 20421
941 N. Capitol St., N.E.

If you live in the above
Virginia counties or cities—
872-1151

Roanoke (RO) 24011
210 Franklin Rd., SW.

If you live in the local
telephone area of:
Hampton—722-7477
Norfolk—627-0441
Richmond—648-1621
Roanoke—982-6440

All other Virginia areas—
(800) 542-5826

Salem (MC&NHC) 24153
1970 Roanoke Blvd.
(703) 982-2463

Washington

Seattle (RO) 98174
Federal Bldg.
915 2nd Ave.

If you live in the local
telephone area of:
Seattle—624-7200
Tacoma—383-3851

All other Washington areas—
(800) 552-7480

Portland (MC,D&NHC)
3710 SW., U.S. Veterans
Hospital Rd.
(503) 222-9221

Seattle (MC&NHC) 98108
1660 S. Columbian Way
(206) 762-1010

Spokane (MC) 99208
N. 4815 Assembly St.
(509) 328-4521

Tacoma (MC,D,&NHC)
98493
American Lake
(206) 582-8440

Vancouver (MC,D,&NHC)
98661
3710 S.W. U.S. Veterans Rd.
(503) 222-9221

Walla Walla (MC) 99362
77 Wainwright Dr.
(509) 525-5200

West Virginia

Beckley (MC&NHC) 25801
200 Veterans Ave.
(304) 255-2121

Clarksburg (MC) 26301
Milford/Chestnut Sts.
(304) 923-3411

Counties of Brooke, Hancock,
Marshall and Ohio
Pittsburgh, PA (RO) 15222
1000 Liberty Ave.

If you live in the local
telephone area of:
Wheeling—232-1431
Other: (800) 642-3520
(Huntington, WV RO)

Remaining counties in
West Virginia served by:

Huntington, (RO) 25701
640 Fourth Avenue

If you live in the local
telephone area of:
Huntington—529-5720
Parkersburg—485-9790

All other areas in West
Virginia—(800) 642-3520

Huntington (MC) 25704
1540 Spring Valley Dr.
(304) 420-6741

Martinsburg (MC,D,&NHC)
25401
Route 9
(304) 263-0811

Wisconsin

Madison (MC) 53705
2500 Overlook Terrace
(608) 256-1901

Milwaukee (RO) 53295
5000 W. National Ave., Bldg. 6

If you live in the local
telephone area of:
Madison—257-5467
Milwaukee—383-8680
Racine—637-6743

All other Wisconsin areas—
(800) 242-9025

Tomah (MC&NHC) 54660
County Trunk E.
(608) 372-3971

Milwaukee (MC,D&NHC)
53295
5000 W. National Ave.
(414) 384-2000

Wyoming

Cheyenne (RO) 82001
2360 E. Pershing Blvd.

If you live in the local
telephone area of:
Cheyenne—778-7396

All other Wyoming areas—
(800) 442-2761

Cheyenne (MC&NHC) 82001
2360 E. Pershing Blvd.
(307) 778-7550

Sheridan (MC) 82801
Fort Rd.
(307) 672-3473

SPECIALIZED INPATIENT PTSD UNITS

Northampton, MA 01060	(413) 584-4040
Togus, ME 04330	(207) 623-8411
Buffalo, NY 14215	(716) 834-9200
Montrose, NY 10548	(914) 737-4400
Coatesville, PA 19320	(215) 384-7711
Lyons, NJ 07939	(201) 647-0180
Augusta, GA 30910	(404) 724-5116
Bay Pines, FL 33504	(813) 398-6661
Tomah, WI 54660	(608) 372-3971
North Chicago, IL 60611	(312) 943-6600
Little Rock, AR 72205	(501) 661-1201
Topeka, KS 66622	(913) 272-3111
Phoenix, AZ 85012	(602) 277-5551
Tacoma, WA 98493	(206) 582-8440
Palo Alto, CA 94304	(415) 493-5000

PTSD CLINICAL TEAMS

Boston, MA	Minneapolis, MN
Canandaigua, NY	New Orleans, LA
San Juan, Puerto Rico	Dallas, TX
Philadelphia, PA	San Antonio, TX
Baltimore, MD	Kansas City, KS
Mountain Home, TN	Denver, CO
Charleston, SC	Albuquerque, NM
Jackson, MS	Los Angeles (Outpatient Clinic), CA
Gainesville, FL	San Francisco, CA
Battle Creek, MI	Boise, ID
Chicago (West Side), IL	Seattle, WA
Hines, IL	

VETERANS ADMINISTRATION READJUSTMENT COUNSELING SERVICE

Vet Center Program Directory

Alabama

VVRC
1425 S. 21st Street
Suite 108
Birmingham, AL 35205
(205) 933-0500
(205) 939-2050

VET CENTER
110 Marine Street
Mobile, AL 36604
(205) 694-4194

Alaska

VVRC
4201 Tudor Centre Drive
Anchorage, AK 99508
(907) 563-6966

VET CENTER
712 10th Avenue
Fairbanks, AK 99705
(907) 456-4208
(907) 456-4238

VET CENTER SATELLITE
P.O. Box 1883
Kenai, AK 99611
(907) 283-5205

VET CENTER SATELLITE
1075 Check Street
Suite 111
Wasilla, AK 99687
(907) 376-4318

Arizona

VET CENTER
141 E. Palm Lane
Suite 100
Phoenix, AZ 85004
(602) 261-4769

VET CENTER
637 Hillside Avenue
Suite A
Prescott, AZ 86301
(602) 778-3469

VET CENTER
727 North Swan
Tucson, AZ 85711
(602) 323-3271

Arkansas

VET CENTER
Riverview Center North
201 W. Broadway—Suite A
North Little Rock, AR 72114
(501) 378-6395

California

VET CENTER
859 South Harbor Blvd.
Anaheim, CA 92805
(714) 776-0161
(213) 596-3101

VET CENTER
1899 Clayton Road
Suite 140
Concord, CA 94520
(415) 680-4526

VET CENTER
157 East Valley Parkway
Suite 1C
Escondido, CA 92025
(619) 747-7305

VET CENTER
305 "V" Street
Eureka, CA 95501
(707) 444-8271

VET CENTER
1340 Van Ness Avenue
Fresno, CA 93721
(209) 487-5660

VVRC
251 West 85th Place
Los Angeles, CA 90003
(213) 215-2380

VET CENTER
2000 Westwood Blvd.
Los Angeles, CA 90025
(213) 475-9509

VET CENTER SATELLITE
515 North Gate Boulevard
Terre Linda, CA 94903
(415) 492-8364
(415) 492-8365

VET CENTER
455 Reservation Road
Suite E
Marina, CA 93933
(408) 384-1660

VET CENTER
VA East L.A. Clinic
5400 E. Olympic Blvd., #126
Commerce, CA 90022
(213) 728-9966

VET CENTER
287—17th Street
Oakland, CA 94612
(415) 763-3904

VET CENTER
4954 Arlington Avenue
Suite A
Riverside, CA 92504
(714) 359-8967

VET CENTER
1111 Howe Avenue
Suite 390
Sacramento, CA 95825
(916) 978-5477

VET CENTER
2900 6th Avenue
San Diego, CA 92103
(619) 294-2040

VET CENTER
25 Van Ness Avenue
San Francisco, CA 94102
(415) 431-6021

VET CENTER
967 West Hedding
San Jose, CA 95126
(408) 249-1643

VET CENTER
32 West 25th Avenue
Room #202
San Mateo, CA 94403
(415) 570-5918

VET CENTER
1300 Santa Barbara Street
Santa Barbara, CA 93101
(805) 564-2345

VET CENTER
16126 Lassen Street
Sepulveda, CA 91343
(818) 892-9227

VET CENTER
313 N. Mountain Avenue
Upland, CA 91786
(714) 982-0416
(800) 826-6993

Colorado

VET CENTER
207 Canyon Blvd.
Suite 201A
Boulder, CO 80302
(303) 440-7306

VET CENTER
411 So. Tejon
Suite G
Colorado Springs, CO 80903
(719) 471-9992

VET CENTER
1820 Gilpin Street
Denver, CO 80218
(303) 861-9281

Connecticut

VET CENTER
370 Market Street
Hartford, CT 06120
(203) 240-3543
(203) 240-3544

VET CENTER
562 Whalley Avenue
New Haven, CT 06511
(203) 773-2232
(203) 773-2236

VET CENTER SATELLITE
16 Franklin Street
Room 109
Norwich, CT 06360
(203) 887-1755

Delaware

VET CENTER
VA Medical Center, Building 2
1601 Kirkwood Highway
Wilmington, DE 19805
(302) 994-2878

District of Columbia

VET CENTER
737½ 8th Street, S.E.
Washington, DC 20003
(202) 745-8400
(202) 745-8402

Florida

VET CENTER
400 East Prospect Road
Ft. Lauderdale, FL 33334
(305) 563-2992

VET CENTER
255 Liberty Street
Jacksonville, FL 32202
(904) 791-3621

VET CENTER
412 N.E. 39th Street
Miami, FL 33137
(305) 573-8830

VET CENTER
5001 S. Orange Avenue
Suite A
Orlando, FL 32809
(407) 648-6151

VET CENTER
Spectrum Centre
2311 10th Avenue, N. #13
Lake Worth, FL 33461
(407) 585-0441

VET CENTER
15 W. Strong Street
Suite 100 C
Pensacola, FL 32501
(904) 479-6665

VET CENTER
1800 Siesta Drive
Sarasota, FL 33579
(813) 952-9406

VET CENTER
235 31st Street, North
St. Petersburg, FL 33713
(813) 327-3355

VET CENTER
249 E. 6th Avenue
Tallahassee, FL 32303
(904) 681-7172

VET CENTER
1507 W. Sligh Avenue
Tampa, FL 33604
(813) 228-2621

Georgia

VET CENTER
922 W. Peachtree Street
Atlanta, GA 30309
(404) 347-7264

VET CENTER
8110 White Bluff Road
Savannah, GA 31406
(912) 927-7360

Hawaii

VET CENTER
Hilo Shopping Center
1261 Kilauea Ave., Suite 260
Hilo, HI 96720
(808) 969-3833

VET CENTER
1370 Kapiolani Blvd.
Suite 201
Honolulu, HI 96814
(808) 541-1764

VET CENTER
3367 Kuhio Highway
Suite 101
Lihue, HI 96733
(808) 246-1163

VET CENTER
Pottery Terrace, Fern Building
75-5995 Kuakini Hwy.
Suite 415
Kailua-Kona, HI 96740
(808) 329-0574
(808) 329-0575

VET CENTER
Ting Building
35 Lunalilo, Room 101
Wailuku, HI 96793
(808) 242-8557

Idaho

VET CENTER
210 West State Street
Boise, ID 83702
(208) 342-3612

VET CENTER
1975 South 5th Street
Pocatello, ID 83201
(208) 232-0316

Illinois

VVRC
5505 South Harper
Chicago, IL 60637
(312) 684-5500

VET CENTER
1607 W. Howard Street
Room #200
Chicago, IL 60626
(312) 764-6595

VET CENTER
1600 Halsted Street
Chicago Heights, IL 60411
(312) 754-0340

VET CENTER
1269 N. 89th Street
East St. Louis, IL 62203
(618) 397-6602

VET CENTER
1529 46th Avenue
Room #6
Moline, IL 61265
(309) 762-6954

VET CENTER
155 South Oak Park Avenue
Oak Park, IL 60302
(312) 383-3225
(312) 383-3226

VET CENTER
605 N.E. Monroe
Peoria, IL 61603
(309) 671-7300

VET CENTER
624 South 4th Street
Springfield, IL 62702
(217) 492-4955

Indiana

VET CENTER
101 N. Kentucky Avenue
Evansville, IN 47711
(812) 425-0311

VET CENTER
528 West Berry Street
Fort Wayne, IN 46802
(219) 423-9456

VET CENTER
2236 West Ridge Road
Gary, IN 46408
(219) 887-0048

VET CENTER
3833 Meridian
Indianapolis, IN 46208
(317) 927-6440

Iowa

VET CENTER
2600 Harding Road
Des Moines, IA 50310
(515) 284-4929

VET CENTER
706 Jackson
Sioux City, IA 51101
(712) 233-3200

Kansas

VET CENTER
413 S. Pattie
Wichita, KS 67211
(316) 265-3260

Kentucky

VET CENTER
1117 Limestone Road
Lexington, KY 40503
(606) 276-5269

VET CENTER
736 South First Street
Louisville, KY 40202
(502) 589-1981

Louisiana

VET CENTER
2103 Old Minden Road
Bossier City, LA 71112
(318) 742-2733

VVRC
1529 N. Claiborne Avenue
New Orleans, LA 70116
(504) 943-8386

Maine

VET CENTER
352 Harlow Street
Bangor, ME 04401
(207) 947-3391
(207) 947-3392

VET CENTER
63 Treble Street
Portland, ME 04101
(207) 780-3584
(207) 780-3585

Maryland

VET CENTER
777 Washington Blvd.
Baltimore, MD 21230
(301) 539-5511

VET CENTER
7 Elkton Commercial Plaza
South Bridge Street
Elkton, MD 21921
(301) 398-0171
(301) 398-0172

VET CENTER
1015 Spring Street
Suite 101
Silver Spring, MD 20910
(301) 745-8441
(301) 745-8397

Massachusetts

VET CENTER
800 North Main Street
Avon, MA 02322
(508) 580-2730
(508) 580-2731

VET CENTER
480 Tremont Street
Boston, MA 02116
(617) 451-0171
(617) 451-0172

VET CENTER
71 Washington Street
Brighton, MA 02135
(617) 782-1032
(617) 782-1013

VET CENTER SATELLITE
73 East Merrimack Street
Lowell, MA 01852
(617) 453-1151
(617) 452-9528

VET CENTER
330 Union Street
New Bedford, MA 02740
(508) 999-6920

VET CENTER
1985 Main Street
Northgate Plaza
Springfield, MA 01103
(413) 737-5167
(413) 737-5168

VET CENTER
8 Worcester Street
West Boylston, MA 01583
(508) 835-2709

Michigan

VET CENTER
1940 Eastern Avenue, S.E.
Grand Rapids, MI 49507
(616) 243-0385

VET CENTER
1766 Fort Street
Lincoln Park, MI 48146
(313) 381-1370

VET CENTER
20820 Greenfield Road
Oakpark, MI 48237
(313) 967-0040
(313) 967-0041

Minnesota

VET CENTER
405 E. Superior Street
Duluth, MN 55802
(218) 722-8654

VVRC
2480 University Avenue
St. Paul, MN 55114
(612) 644-4022

Mississippi

VET CENTER SATELLITE
767 W. Jackson Street
Biloxi, MS 39530
(601) 435-5414

VET CENTER
158 E. Pascagoula Street
Jackson, MS 39201
(601) 965-5727

Missouri

VET CENTER
3931 Main Street
Kansas City, MO 64111
(816) 753-1866
(816) 753-1974

VET CENTER
2345 Pine Street
St. Louis, MO 63103
(314) 231-1260

Montana

VET CENTER
1127 Alderson
Billings, MT 59102
(406) 657-6710

VET CENTER
929 S.W. Higgins Street
Missoula, MT 59803
(406) 721-4918
(406) 721-4919

Nebraska

VET CENTER
920 L Street
Lincoln, NE 68508
(402) 476-9736

VET CENTER
5123 Leavenworth Street
Omaha, NE 68106
(402) 553-2068

Nevada

VET CENTER
704 South 6th Street
Las Vegas, NV 89101
(702) 388-6368

VET CENTER
1155 W. 4th Street
Suite 101
Reno, NV 89503
(702) 323-1294

New Hampshire

VET CENTER
103 Liberty Street
Manchester, NH 03104
(603) 668-7060
(603) 668-7061

New Jersey

VET CENTER
626 Newark Avenue
Jersey City, NJ 07306
(201) 656-6986

VET CENTER
327 Central Avenue
Linwood, NJ 08221
(609) 927-8387

VET CENTER
75 Halsey Street
Newark, NJ 07102
(201) 622-6940

VET CENTER
318 East State Street
Trenton, NJ 08608
(609) 989-2260
(609) 989-2261

New Mexico

VET CENTER
4603 4th Street, N.W.
Albuquerque, NM 87107
(505) 345-8366
(505) 345-8876

VET CENTER SATELLITE
4251 E. Main
Farmington, NM 87401
(505) 327-9684
(505) 327-9685

VET CENTER SATELLITE
1996 St. Michael's Drive
Warner Plaza, Suite 5
Santa Fe, NM 87501
(505) 988-6562

New York

VET CENTER
875 Central Avenue
Albany, NY 12206
(518) 438-2508

VET CENTER
116 West Main Street
Babylon, NY 11702
(516) 661-3930

VET CENTER
226 East Fordham Road
Rooms #216-#217
Bronx, NY 10458
(212) 367-3500
(212) 367-3501

VVRC
165 Cadman Plaza, East
Brooklyn, NY 11201
(718) 330-2825
(718) 330-2826

VET CENTER
351 Linwood Avenue
Buffalo, NY 14209
(716) 882-0505
(716) 882-0508

VET CENTER
45—20 83rd Street
Elmhurst, NY 11373
(718) 446-8233
(718) 446-8234

VET CENTER
166 West 75th Street
New York, NY 10023
(212) 944-2917
(212) 944-2930

VET CENTER
294 South Plymouth Avenue
Rochester, NY 14608
(716) 263-5710

VET CENTER
210 North Townsend Street
Syracuse, NY 13203
(315) 423-5690
(315) 423-5691

VET CENTER
200 Hamilton Avenue
White Plains Mall
White Plains, NY 10601
(914) 684-0570

North Carolina

VET CENTER
223 S. Brevard Street
Suite 103
Charlotte, NC 28202
(704) 333-6107

VET CENTER
4 Market Square
Fayetteville, NC 28301
(919) 323-4908

VET CENTER
2009 Elm-Eugene Street
Greensboro, NC 27406
(919) 333-5366

VET CENTER
150 Arlington Boulevard
Suite B
Greenville, NC 27834
(919) 355-7920

North Dakota

VET CENTER
1322 Gateway Drive
Fargo, ND 58103
(701) 237-0942

VET CENTER
108 East Burdick Expressway
Minot, ND 58701
(701) 852-0177

Ohio

VET CENTER
30 East Hollister Street
Cincinnati, OH 45219
(513) 569-7140

VET CENTER
11511 Lorain Avenue
Cleveland, OH 44111
(216) 671-8530

VET CENTER
2134 Lee Road
Cleveland Heights, OH 44118
(216) 932-8471

VET CENTER
1054 East Broad Street
Columbus, OH 43205
(614) 253-3500

VET CENTER
6 So. Patterson Boulevard
Dayton, OH 45402
(513) 461–9150
(513) 461–9151

Oklahoma

VET CENTER
3033 N. Walnut
Suite 101W
Oklahoma City, OK 73105
(405) 270–5184

VET CENTER
1855 East 15th Street
Tulsa, OK 74104
(918) 581–7105

Oregon

VET CENTER
1966 Garden Avenue
Eugene, OR 97403
(503) 687–6918

VET CENTER SATELLITE
615 North West 5th Street
Grants Pass, OR 95726
(503) 479–6912

VET CENTER
2450 S.E. Belmont
Portland, OR 97214
(503) 273–5370

VET CENTER
318 Church, N.E.
Salem, OR 97301
(503) 362–9911

Pennsylvania

VET CENTER
G. Daniel Baldwin Bldg.
Rm. 1&2
1000 State Street
Erie, PA 16501
(814) 453–7955

VET CENTER
1007 North Front Street
Harrisburg, PA 17102
(717) 782–3954

VVRC
5000 Walnut Street
McKeesport, PA 15132
(412) 678–7704

VET CENTER
1026 Arch Street
Philadelphia, PA 19107
(215) 627–0238

VET CENTER
5601 North Broad Street
Room #204
Philadelphia, PA 19141
(215) 924–4670

VET CENTER
954 Penn Avenue
Pittsburgh, PA 15222
(412) 765–1193

VET CENTER
959 Wyoming Avenue
Scranton, PA 18509
(717) 344–2676

Puerto Rico

VET CENTER SATELLITE
52 Gonzalo Marin Street
Arecibo, PR 00612
(809) 879–4510
(809) 879–4581

VET CENTER SATELLITE
35 Mayor Street
Ponce, PR 00731
(809) 848–4078
(809) 848–4039

VVRC
Condomino Medical Center
   Plaza
Suite LC8A & LC9, La Riviera
Rio Piedras, PR 00921
(809) 783–8794

Rhode Island

VET CENTER
789 Park Avenue
Cranston, RI 02920
(401) 467–2046
(401) 467–2056

South Carolina

VET CENTER SATELLITE
1313 Elmwood Avenue
Columbia, SC 29201
(803) 765–9944

VET CENTER
904 Pendelton Street
Greenville, SC 29601
(803) 271–2711

VET CENTER
3366 Rivers Avenue
No. Charleston, SC 29405
(803) 747–8387

South Dakota

VET CENTER
610 Kansas City Street
Rapid City, SD 57701
(605) 348–0077
(605) 348–1752

VET CENTER
115 North Dakota Street
Sioux Falls, SD 57102
(605) 332–0856

Tennessee

VET CENTER
2 Northgate Park
Suite 108
Chattanooga, TN 37415
(615) 752–5234

VET CENTER
703 South Roan Street
Johnson City, TN 37601
(615) 928–8387

VET CENTER
2817 East Magnolia Avenue
Knoxville, TN 37917
(615) 971–5866

VET CENTER
One North Third Street
Memphis, TN 38103
(901) 521–3506

Texas

VET CENTER
2900 West 10th Street
Amarillo, TX 79106
(806) 376–2127

VET CENTER
3401 Manor Road
Suite 102
Austin, TX 78723
(512) 476–0607
(512) 476–0608

VET CENTER
3134 Reid Drive
Corpus Christi, TX 78404
(512) 888–3101

VET CENTER
5415 Maple Avenue
Suite 114
Dallas, TX 75235
(214) 634–7024

VET CENTER
2121 Wyoming Street
El Paso, TX 79903
(915) 542–2851
(915) 542–2852

VET CENTER
1305 W. Magnolia
Suite B
Forth Worth, TX 76104
(817) 921-3733

VET CENTER
4905A San Jacinto
Houston, TX 77004
(713) 522-5354
(713) 522-5376

VVRC
8100 Washington Avenue
Suite 120
Houston, TX 77007
(713) 880-8387

VET CENTER
717 Corpus Christi
Laredo, TX 78040
(512) 723-4680

VET CENTER
3208 34th Street
Lubbock, TX 79410
(806) 743-7551

VET CENTER
1317 E. Hackberry Street
Suite G
McAllen, TX 78501
(512) 631-2147

VET CENTER
3404 West Illinois
Suite 1
Midland, TX 79703
(915) 697-8222

VET CENTER
107 Lexington Avenue
San Antonio, TX 78205
(512) 229-4025

VET CENTER
1916 Fredericksburg Road
San Antonio, TX 78201
(512) 229-4120

Utah

VET CENTER SATELLITE
750 North 200 West
Suite 105
Provo, UT 84601
(801) 377-1117

VET CENTER
1354 East 3300, South
Salt Lake City, UT 84106
(801) 584-1294

Vermont

VET CENTER
359 Dorset Street
South Burlington, VT 05401
(802) 862-1806

VET CENTER
Gilman Office Center, Bldg. #2
Holiday Inn Drive
White River Junction, VT 05001
(802) 295-2908

Virgin Islands

VET CENTER SATELLITE
United Shopping Plaza
Suite 4 — Christiansted
St. Croix, VI 00820
(809) 778-5553
(809) 778-5755

VET CENTER SATELLITE
Havensight Mall
St. Thomas, VI 00801
(809) 774-6674

Virginia

VET CENTER
7450½ Tidewater Drive
Norfolk, VA 23505
(804) 587-1338

VET CENTER
1030 W. Franklin Street
Box 83
Richmond, VA 23220
(804) 353-8958

VET CENTER
320 Mountain Avenue, S.W.
Roanoke, VA 24014
(703) 342-9726

VET CENTER
7024 Spring Garden Drive
Brookfield Plaza
Springfield, VA 22150
(703) 866-0924

Washington

VET CENTER
1322 East Pike Street
Seattle, WA 98122
(206) 442-2706

VET CENTER
26 West Mission Street
Spokane, WA 99201
(509) 327-0274

VET CENTER
4801 Pacific Avenue
Tacoma, WA 98408
(206) 473-0731

West Virginia

VET CENTER
314 Neville Street
Beckley, WV 25801
(304) 252-8220
(304) 252-8229

VET CENTER
1591 Washington Street East
Charleston, WV 25301
(304) 343-3825

VET CENTER
1191 Pineview Drive
Morgantown, WV 26505
(304) 291-4001
(304) 291-4002

VET CENTER
701 Mercer Street
Princeton, WV 24740
(304) 425-5653
(304) 425-5661

VET CENTER
Social Ministries Building
#7 13th Street
Wheeling, WV 26003
(304) 233-0880 Ext. 271

VET CENTER SATELLITE
1014 6th Avenue
Huntington, WV 25701
(304) 523-8387

VET CENTER
138 West King Street
Martinsburg, WV 25401
(304) 263-6776
(304) 263-6778

Wisconsin

VET CENTER
147 South Butler Street
Madison, WI 53703
(608) 264-5343

VET CENTER
3400 Wisconsin
Milwaukee, WI 53208
(414) 344-5504

Wyoming

VET CENTER SATELLITE
111 S. Jefferson
Casper, WY 82601
(307) 235-8010

VET CENTER
3130 Henderson Drive
Cheyenne, WY 82001
(307) 778-7370

SUGGESTED READINGS

The following books can provide more information on Vietnam veterans' readjustment as well as PTSD. This list is a starting place for your search. It is neither exhaustive nor exclusionary.

Brende, J. O., & Parson, E. R. (1985). *Vietnam veterans: The road to recovery.* New York: Plenum Press.

Egendorf, A. (1985). *Healing from the war. Trauma & transformation after Vietnam.* Boston: Houghton Mifflin Company.

Freedman, D., & Rhoads, J. (1987). *Nurses in Vietnam. The forgotten veterans.* Austin, TX: Texas Monthly Press, Inc.

Goldman, P., & Fuller, T. (1983). *Charlie company. What Vietnam did to us.* New York: William Morrow and Company, Inc.

Hendin, H., & Pollinger Haas, A. (1984). *Wounds of war: The psychological aftermath of combat in Vietnam.* New York: Basic Books, Inc.

MacPherson, M. (1984). *Long time passing: Vietnam and the haunted generation.* Garden City, NY: Doubleday.

Matsakis, A. (1988). *Vietnam wives. Women and children surviving life with veterans suffering post traumatic stress disorder.* Kensington, MD: Woodbine House.

Scruggs, J. C., & Swerdlow, J. L. (1985). *To heal a nation: The Vietnam Veterans Memorial.* New York: Harper & Row.

Severo, R., & Milford, L. (1989). *The wages of war. When America's soldiers came home—from Valley Forge to Vietnam.* New York: Simon and Schuster.

Terry, W. (1984). *Bloods: An oral history of the Vietnam war by black veterans.* New York: Random House.

Van Devanter, L. M. (1983). *Home before morning: The story of an Army nurse in Vietnam.* New York: Beaufort Books.

Walker, K. *A piece of my heart. The stories of twenty-six American women who served in Vietnam.* Novato, CA: Presidio Press.

References

Achenbach, T. M. (1978). The child behavior profile: I. Boys aged 6–11. *Journal of Consulting and Clinical Psychology, 46*(3), 478–488.

Achenbach, T. M., & Edelbrock, C. (1983). *Manual for the child behavior checklist and revised child behavior profile.* Burlington, VT: University of Vermont.

American Psychiatric Association. (1952). *Diagnostic and statistical manual of mental disorders* (1st ed.). Washington, DC: Author.

American Psychiatric Association. (1980). *Diagnostic and statistical manual of mental disorders* (3rd ed.). Washington, DC: Author.

American Psychiatric Association. (1987). *Diagnostic and statistical manual of mental disorders* (3rd ed. rev.). Washington, DC: Author.

Andrews, F. M., & Withey, S. B. (1976). *Social indicators of well-being.* New York: Plenum Press.

Anthony J. (1985). Comparison of the lay DIS and standardized psychiatric diagnosis. *Archives of General Psychiatry, 42,* 667–675.

Bassuk, E. (1984). The homeless problem. *Scientific American, 251,* 40–45.

Bernard, J. (1972). *The future of marriage.* New York: World Publishing Co.

Blazer, D., George, L. K., Landerman, R., Pennybacker, M. L., Melville, M. L., Woodbury, M., Manton, K. G., Jordan, K., & Locke, B. Psychiatric disorders: A rural/urban comparison. *Archives of General Psychiatry, 42,* 651–656.

Boulanger, G., & Kadushin, C. (1985). *The Vietnam veteran redefined.* Hillsdale, NJ: Lawrence Erlbaum.

Buchbinder, J. T. (1979). Self-report assessment of the post-Vietnam syndrome. *Dissertation Abstracts International, 40,* 1880B.

Burke, J. (1986). Diagnostic categorization by the Diagnostic Interview Schedule (DIS): A comparison with other measures of assessment. In J. E. Barrett & R. M. Rose (Eds.), *Mental disorder in the community: Progress and challenge.* New York: Guilford Press.

Burke, J., & Regier, D. A. (1985). Assessing performance of the Diagnostic Interview Schedule. In J. Barrett (Ed.), *Mental disorder in the community: Progress and challenge.* New York: Guilford Press.

Burnam, M. A., Karno, M., Hough, R. L., Escobar, J. I., & Forsythe, A. B. (1983). The Spanish Diagnostic Interview Schedule: Reliability and comparison with clinical diagnoses. *Archives of General Psychiatry, 40,* 1189–1196.

Campbell, A., Converse, P. E., & Rodgers, W. L. (1976). *The quality of American life.* New York: Russell Sage Foundation.

Canino, G., Bird, H. R., & Shrout, P. E. (1987). The Spanish Diagnostic Interview Schedule. *Archives of General Psychiatry, 44,* 720–726.

Card, J. (1983). Lives After Vietnam: The personal impact of military service. Lexington, MA: Lexington Books.

Cattell, R. B., & Vogelman, S. (1977). A comprehensive trial of the scree and KG criteria for determining the number of factors. Multivariate Behavioral Research, 12, 289–325.

Centers for Disease Control. (1988a). Health status of Vietnam veterans I. Psychosocial characteristics. Journal of the American Medical Association, 259(18), 2701–2707.

Centers for Disease Control. (1988b). Vietnam experience study, Volume IV: Psychological and neuropsychological evaluation. Atlanta, GA: Author.

Centers for Disease Control (1988c). Health status of Vietnam veterans: II. Physical health. Journal of the American Medical Association, 259(18), 2708–2714.

Chromy, J. R. (1979). Sequential sample selection methods. In American Statistical Association, Proceedings of the Survey Research Methods Section.

Cohen, S., Mermelstein, R., Kamarck, T., & Hoberman, H. (1985). Measuring the functional components of social support. In I. G. Sarason & B. Sarason (Eds.), Social support: Theory, research and applications (pp. 73–94). The Hague, The Netherlands: Martinus Nijhoff.

Committee on Veterans Affairs, United States Senate. (1988). Prepared statement of John Gronvall, M.D., Chief Medical Director of the Veterans Administration. Oversight on posttraumatic stress disorder (S. Hrg. 100–900). Washington, DC: U.S. Government Printing Office.

Defense Manpower Data Center. (September 1984). Official guard and reserve manpower strengths and statistic. Arlington, VA: Department of Defense.

Defense Manpower Data Center. (Undated). Distribution of active duty forces by service, rank, sex, and ethnic group, DMDC-3035. Arlington, VA: Department of Defense.

Dohrenwend, B. P. (1982). Psychiatric Epidemiology Research Interview (PERI). New York: Columbia University, Social Psychiatry Research Unit.

Dohrenwend, B. P., Levav, I., & Shrout, P. (1986). Screening scales from the Psychiatric Epidemiology Research Interview. In M. M. Weissman, J. K. Meyers, & C. E. Ross (Eds.), Community surveys of psychiatric disorder. New Brunswick, NJ: Rutgers University Press.

Dohrenwend, B. D., & Shrout, P. B. (1981). Toward the development of a two-stage procedure for case identification and classification in psychiatry epidemiology. Research in Community and Mental Health, 2, 295–323.

Donald, C. A., & Ware, J. E., Jr. (1984). The measurement of social support. Research in Community and Mental Health, 4, 325–370.

Duncan, O. D. (1961). A socioeconomic index for all occupations. In A. J. Reiss Jr. (Ed.), Occupations and social status. New York: Free Press.

Eaton, W. W., & Kessler, L. G. (Eds.). (1985). Epidemiologic field methods in psychiatry: The NIMH Epidemiologic Catchment Area Program. New York: Academic Press.

Egendorf, A. (1982). The postwar healing of Vietnam veterans: Recent research. Hospital and Community Psychiatry, 33(11), 901–908.

Egendorf, A., Kadushin, C., Laufer, R. S., Rothbart, G., & Sloan, L. (1981). Legacies of Vietnam: Comparative adjustment of veterans and their peers. Washington, DC: U.S. Government Printing Office.

Fischer, V., Boyle, J. M., Bucuvalas, M., & Schulman, M. A. (1980). Myths and realities: A study of attitudes toward Vietnam era veterans. Washington, DC: U.S. Government Printing Office.

Folsom, R. E. (December 1984). National Vietnam Veteran Readjustment Study: Sample size and power considerations (Working paper no. 1, contract no. V101 (93) P-400). Research Triangle Park, NC: Research Triangle Institute.

Foy, D. W., & Card, J. J. (1987). Combat-related post-traumatic stress disorder etiology: Replicated findings in a national sample of Vietnam-era men. Journal of Clinical Psychology, 43, 28–31.

Foy, D. W., Carroll, E. M., & Donahoe, C. P. (1987). Etiological factors in the development of PTSD in clinical samples of Vietnam combat veterans. Journal of Clinical Psychology, 43, 17–27.

Foy, D. W., Sipprelle, R. C., Rueger, D. B., & Carroll, E. M. (1984). Etiology of posttraumatic stress disorder in Vietnam veterans: Analysis of premilitary, military and combat exposure influences. *Journal of Consulting and Clinical Psychology, 52,* 72–87.

Frank, J. D. (1973). *Persuasion and healing.* Baltimore: Johns Hopkins.

Friedman, M. J. (1988). Toward rational pharmacotherapy for posttraumatic stress disorder: An interim report. *The American Journal of Psychiatry, 145*(3), 281–285.

Frye, J. S., & Stockton, R. A. (1982). Discriminant analysis of posttraumatic stress disorder among a group of Vietnam veterans. *American Journal of Psychiatry, 139,* 52–56.

Gallers, J., Foy, D. W., & Donahoe, C. P. (1985). *Combat-related posttraumatic stress disorder: An empirical investigation of traumatic violence exposure.* Paper presented at the annual convention of the American Psychology Association, Los Angeles.

Green, M. A., & Berlin, M. A. (1987). Five psychosocial variables related to the existence of post-traumatic stress disorder symptoms. *Journal of Clinical Psychology, 43*(6), 643–649.

Griffin, M., Weiss, R., Mirin, S., Wilson, H., & Bouchard-Voelk, B. (1987). The use of the Diagnostic Interview Schedule in drug-dependent patients. *American Journal of Drug and Alcohol Abuse, 13,* 281–291.

Gurin, G., Veroff, J., & Feld, S. C. (1960). *Americans view their mental health.* New York: Basic Books.

Haley, S. (1974). When the patient reports atrocities. Specific treatment considerations of the Vietnam veteran. *Archives of General Psychiatry, 30,* 191–196.

Hammond, R. (1980). *1979 national survey of veterans* (Research Monograph no. 14). Washington, DC: Veterans Administration, Office of Controller, Reports and Statistics Service.

Helzer, J. E., Robins, L. N., & McEvoy, M. A. (1988). Post-traumatic stress disorder in the general population, Findings of the epidemiologic catchment area survey. *The New England Journal of Medicine, 317,* 1630–1634.

Helzer, J., Robins, L., McEvoy, L., Spitznagel, E., Stolzman, R., Farmer, R., & Brockington, I. (1985). A comparison of clinical and Diagnostic Interview Schedule diagnoses. *Archives of General Psychiatry, 42,* 657–666.

Hendricks, L., Bayton, J., Collins, J., Mathura, C., McMillan, S., & Montgomery, T. (1983). The NIMH Diagnostic Interview Schedule: A test of its validity in a population of Black adults. *Journal of the National Medical Association, 75,* 667–671.

Hesselbrock, V., Stabenau, J., Hessellbrock, M., Mirkin, P., & Meyer, R. (1982). A comparison of two interview schedules. *Archives of General Psychiatry, 39,* 674–677.

Horowitz, M. J., Wilner, N., & Alvarez, W. (1979). Impact of event scale: A measure of subjective stress. *Psychometric Medicine, 41,* 209–218.

Keane, T. M., Caddell, J. M., & Taylor, K. L. (1988). Mississippi scale for combat-related posttraumatic stress disorder: Three studies in reliability and validity. *Journal of Consulting and Clinical Psychology, 56*(1), 85–90.

Keane, T. M., Malloy, P. F., & Fairbank, J. A. (1984). Empirical development of an MMPI subscale for the assessment of combat-related posttraumatic stress disorder. *Journal of Consulting and Clinical Psychology, 52,* 888–891.

Keane, T. M., Scott, W. O., Chavoya, G. A., Lamparski, D. M., & Fairbank, J. A. (1985). Social support in Vietnam veterans with post-traumatic stress disorder: A comparative analysis. *Journal of Consulting and Clinical Psychology, 53*(1), 95–102.

Koch, G. G., Freeman, D. H., Jr., & Freeman, J. L. (1975). Strategies in the multivariate analysis of data from complex surveys. *International Statistical Review, 43,* 59–78.

Laufer, R. S., Gallops, M. S., & Frey-Wouters, E. (1984). War stress and trauma: The Vietnam veteran experience. *Journal of Health and Social Behavior, 25,* 68–85.

Laufer, R. S., Yager, T., Frey-Wouters, E., & Donnellan, J. (1981). Postwar trauma: Social and psychological problems of Vietnam veterans in the aftermath of the Vietnam war. In A. Egendorf, C. Kadushin, R. S. Laufer, G. Rothbart, & L. Sloan (Eds.), *Legacies of Vietnam: Comparative adjustment of veterans and their peers.* New York: Center for Policy Research.

Mantell, D. M., & Pilisuk, M. (Eds.). (1975). Soldiers in and after Vietnam. *Journal of Social Issues, 31.*

Myers, J. K., Weissman, M. M., Tischler, G. L., Holzer, C. E., Leaf, P. J., Orvaschel, H., Anthony, U. C., Boyd, J. H., Burke, J. D., Kramer, M., & Stoltzman, R. (1984). Six-month prevalence of psychiatric disorders in three communities. *Archives of General Psychiatry, 41*, 959–967.

Nace, E. P., O'Brien, C. P., Mintz, J., Ream, N., & Meyers, A. L. (1978). Adjustment among Vietnam veteran drug users two years post-service. In C. R. Figley (Ed.), *Stress disorders among Vietnam veterans: Theory, research, and treatment.* New York: Brunner/Mazel.

Norquist, G. S., Hough, R. L., Golding, J. M., & Escobar, J. I. (1988). *Psychiatric disorder in male veterans and nonveterans.* Manuscript submitted for publication.

Olson, D. H., Bell, R., & Portner, J. (1978). *Family adaptability and cohesion evaluation scales.* Unpublished manuscript. Minneapolis: University of Minnesota, Family Social Science Department.

Olson, D. H., McCubbin, H. I., Barnes, H. L., Larsen, A. S., Muxen, M. J., & Wilson, M. A. (1983). *Families: What makes them work.* Beverly Hills, CA: Sage Publications.

Penk, W. E., Robinowitz, R., Roberts, W. R., Patterson, E. T., Dolan, M. P., & Atkins, H. G. (1981). Adjustment differences among male substance abusers varying in degree of combat experience in Vietnam. *Journal of Consulting and Clinical Psychology, 49*, 426–437.

Pentland, B., & Dwyer, J. (1985). Incarcerated Vietnam veterans. In S. M. Sonnenberg, A. S. Blank Jr., & J. A. Talbott (Eds.), *The trauma of war: Stress and recovery in Viet Nam veterans* (pp. 403–416). Washington, DC: American Psychiatric Press.

Petrick, N., Rosenberg, A. M., & Watson, C. G. (1983). Combat experience and youth: Influences on reported violence against women. *Professional Psychology: Research and Practice, 14*(6), 895–899.

Pokorny, A. D., Miller, B. A., & Kaplan, H. (1972). The brief MAST: A shortened version of the Michigan Alcoholism Screening Test. *American Journal of Psychiatry, 129*(3), 342–345.

Rademacher, D. C. (Undated). *Megarecords management.* Unpublished manuscript, National Personnel Records Center.

Regier, D. A., Myers, J. K., Kramer, M., Robins, L. N., Blazer, D. G., Hough, R. L., Eaton, W. W., & Locke, B. Z. (1984). The NIMH Epidemiologic Catchment Area Program: Historical context, major objectives, and study population characteristics. *Archives of General Psychiatry, 41*, 934–941.

Robins, L. N. (1985). Epidemiology: Reflections on testing the validity of psychiatric interviews. *Archives of General Psychiatry, 42*, 918–924.

Robins, L. N., Helzer, J. E., Croughan J., & Ratcliff, K. S. (1981). National Institute of Mental Health Diagnostic Interview Schedule: Its history, characteristics, and validity. *Archives of General Psychiatry, 38*, 318–389.

Robins, L. N., Helzer, J. E., Ratcliff, K. S., & Seyfried, W. (1982). Validity of the Diagnostic Interview Schedule, version II: DSM-III diagnoses. *Psychological Medicine, 12*, 855–870.

Robins, L. N., Helzer, J. E., Weissman, M. M., Orvaschel, H., Gruenberg, E., Burke, J. D., & Regier, D. A. (1984). Lifetime prevalence of specific psychiatric disorders in three sites. *Archives of General Psychiatry, 41*, 949–958.

Romains, J. (1940). *Men of good will, Vol. VIII: Verdun.* New York: Knopf.

Rothbart, G. S., Fine, M., & Sudman, S. (1982). On finding and interviewing the needles in the haystack: The uses of multiplicity sampling. *Public Opinion Quarterly, 46*, 408–421.

Schindler, F. E. (1980). Treatment by systematic desensitization of a recurring nightmare of a real life trauma. *Journal of Behavior Therapy and Experimental Psychiatry, 2*, 53–54.

Selzer, M. L. (1971). The Michigan alcoholism screening test: The quest for a new diagnostic instrument. *American Journal of Psychiatry, 127*, 1653–1658.

Severo, R., & Milford, L. (1989). *The wages of war. When America's soldiers came home — from Valley Forge to Vietnam.* New York: Simon and Schuster.

Shaw, D. M., Churchill, C. M., Noyes, R., Jr., & Loeffelholz, P. L. (1987). Criminal behavior and post-traumatic stress disorder in Vietnam veterans. *Comprehensive Psychiatry, 28*(5), 403–411.

Smith, J. R. (1985). Individual psychotherapy with Viet Nam veterans. In S. M. Sonnenberg, A. S. Blank Jr., & J. A. Talbott (Eds.), *The trauma of war: Stress and recovery in Viet Nam veterans* (pp. 124–163). Washington, DC: American Psychiatric Press.

Spanier, G. B. (1976). Measuring dyadic adjustment: New scales for assessing the quality of marriage and similar dyads. *Journal of Marriage and the Family, 38,* 115–128.

Stevens, G., & Cho, J. H. (1985). Socioeconomic indexes and the new 1980 Census Occupational Classification Scheme. *Social Sciences Research, 14,* 142–168.

Stouffer, S. A., Lumsdaine, R., Williams, R., Smith, M., Janis, I., Star, S., & Cottrell, L. (1949). *The American soldier: Combat and its aftermath* (Vol. II). Princeton, NJ: Princeton University Press.

Straus, M. (1979). Measuring intrafamily conflict and violence: The Conflict Tactics Scales. *Journal of Marriage and the Family, 41,* 75–88.

Straus, M. A., Gelles, R. J., & Steinmetz, S. K. (1980). *Behind closed doors: Violence in the American Family.* New York: Anchor Books.

Strayer, R., & Ellenhorn, L. (1975). Vietnam veterans: A study exploring adjustment patterns and attitudes. *Journal of Social Issues, 31,* 81–93.

U.S. Bureau of the Census. (1982). *Statistical abstract of the United States: 1982–83* (103rd ed.). Washington, DC: U.S. Government Printing Office.

U.S. Bureau of the Census. (1987). *Statistical abstract of the United States: 1988* (108th ed.). Washington, DC: U.S. Government Printing Office.

Veroff, J., Douvan, E., & Kulka, R. A. (1981). *The inner American: A self-portrait from 1957 to 1976.* New York: Basic Books.

Veterans Administration, Office of Information Management and Statistics. (November 1984). *Veteran population: September 30, 1984* (VA Publication No. RCS 70-0561). Washington, DC: U.S. Government Printing Office.

Vinokur, A., Caplan, R. D., & Williams, C. C. (in press). Effects of recent and past stresses on mental health: Coping with unemployment among Vietnam veterans and non-veterans. *Journal of Applied Social Psychology.*

Walker, J. I. (1981). The psychological problems of Vietnam veterans. *Journal of the American Medical Association, 246*(6), 781–782.

Walker, J. I., & Cavenar, J. O. (1982). Vietnam veterans: Their problems continue. *Journal of Nervous and Mental Disease, 170,* 174–180.

Wilson, J. P. (1978). *Identity, ideology and crisis: The Vietnam veteran in transition* (Vol. 2). Washington, DC: Disabled American Veterans.

Wilson, J. P. (1980). *Forgotten warriors: America's Vietnam era veterans.* Washington, DC: Disabled American Veterans Association.

Wittchen, H., Semler, G., & von Zerssen, D. (1985). A comparison of two diagnostic methods. Clinical ICD diagnoses vs. DSM-III and research diagnostic criteria using the Diagnostic Interview Schedule (Version 2). *Archives of General Psychiatry, 42,* 677–684.

Worthington, E. R. (1977). Post-service adjustment and Vietnam era veterans. *Military Medicine, 142,* 865–866.

Yager, T., Laufer, R., & Gallops, M. (1984). Some problems associated with war experience in men of the Vietnam generation. *Archives of General Psychiatry, 41,* 327–333.

Index

314

Contributing Authors

Richard A. Kulka, Ph.D.
National Opinion Research Center, University of Chicago, Chicago, IL

William E. Schlenger, Ph.D.
Research Triangle Institute, Research Triangle Park, NC

John A. Fairbank, Ph.D.
Research Triangle Institute, Research Triangle Park, NC

Richard L. Hough, Ph.D.
San Diego State University, San Diego, CA

B. Kathleen Jordan, Ph.D.
Research Triangle Institute, Research Triangle Park, NC

Charles R. Marmar, M.D.
*Langley Porter Psychiatric Institute, University of
California, San Francisco, CA*

Daniel S. Weiss, Ph.D.
*Langley Porter Psychiatric Institute, University of
California, San Francisco, CA*

David A. Grady, Psy.D.
Friends Hospital, Philadelphia, PA

Printed in Great Britain
by Amazon

85209432R00201